Implementing Enterprise Cybersecurity With AI

Shahnaz Fatima
Amity University, Lucknow, India

Susanta Das
https://orcid.org/0000-0002-9314-3988
Ajeenkya D.Y. Patil University, India

Rajiv Pandey
https://orcid.org/0000-0003-3348-9888
Amity University, Lucknow, India

IGI Global
Scientific Publishing
Publishing Tomorrow's Research Today

Vice President of Editorial Melissa Wagner
Director of Acquisitions Mikaela Felty
Director of Book Development Jocelynn Hessler
Production Manager Mike Brehm
Cover Design Jose Rosado

Published in the United States of America by
IGI Global Scientific Publishing
701 East Chocolate Avenue
Hershey, PA, 17033, USA
Tel: 717-533-8845 | Fax: 717-533-7115
Website: https://www.igi-global.com E-mail: cust@igi-global.com

Library of Congress Cataloging-in-Publication Data

Names: Fatima, Shahnaz, 1973- editor | Das, Susanta, 1975- editor | Pandey, Rajiv, 1966- editor
Title: Implementing enterprise cybersecurity with AI / edited by: Shahnaz Fatima, Susanta Das, Rajiv Pandey.
Description: Hershey PA : Information Science Reference, [2026] | Includes bibliographical references. | Summary: "Implementing Enterprise Cybersecurity with AI distinguishes itself from competitor books by offering a practical, comprehensive guide specifically tailored for enterprise environments. Unlike other titles that focus purely on theory or generic AI applications, this book provides actionable, step-by-step strategies for integrating AI into existing cybersecurity frameworks. It addresses the specific challenges faced by large organizations, covering areas such as automated threat detection, endpoint security, predictive intelligence, and compliance with AI. The emphasis on practical implementation ensures that readers can immediately apply the concepts to their own enterprise systems"-- Provided by publisher.
Identifiers: LCCN 2025005813 (print) | LCCN 2025005814 (ebook) | ISBN 9798337322520 hardcover | ISBN 9798337322537 paperback | ISBN 9798337322544 ebook
Subjects: LCSH: Computer security | Artificial intelligence--Industrial applications
Classification: LCC QA76.9.A25 I47 2026 (print) | LCC QA76.9.A25 (ebook)
LC record available at https://lccn.loc.gov/2025005813
LC ebook record available at https://lccn.loc.gov/2025005814

British Cataloguing in Publication Data
A Cataloguing in Publication record for this book is available from the British Library.

Table of Contents

Preface xii

Acknowledgment xvi

Chapter 1
Machine Learning vs. AI: Key Concepts 1
Binastya Anggara Sekti, Universitas Esa Unggul, Indonesia

Chapter 2
Artificial Intelligence (AI) in Cybersecurity: Foundations, Applications, and Research Trends 29
Aditya Shrivastav, Ajeenkya D.Y. Patil University, India
Kashvi Chaturvedi, Ajeenkya D.Y. Patil University, India
Sunil Sankathala, Ajeenkya D.Y. Patil University, India
Krutika Patre, Ajeenkya D.Y. Patil University, India
Atharva Haresh Saraf, Ajeenkya D.Y. Patil University, India
Susanta Das, Ajeenkya D.Y. Patil University, India

Chapter 3
AI-Driven Threat Detection and Prevention: Enhancing Cybersecurity with Machine Learning and Predictive Intelligence 57
Tarun Kumar Vashishth, IIMT University, Meerut, India
Vikas Sharma, SRM Institute of Science and Technology, India
Sangeeta Sharma, IAMR College, Meerut, India
Mukesh Kumar Sharma, Chaudhary Charan Singh University, Meerut, India
Rajeev Sharma, IIMT Engineering College, Meerut, India
Sachin Chaudhary, IIMT University, Meerut, India
Aarushi Vashishth, Ajay Kumar Garg Engineering College, India

Chapter 4
Anomaly Detection With Machine Learning 85
T. K. Shaik Shavali, Lords Institute of Engineering and Technology, India
Sunita Vinod Mahale, Independent Researcher, India
S. Manikandan, Kongunadu College of Engineering and Technology, India
Sachin Vasant Chaudhari, Sanjivani College of Engineering, Ahmednagar, India
Fateh Bahadur Kunwar, Rajasthan Technical University, India
C. S. Sandeep, Jawaharlal College of Engineering and Technology, India
V. Bhoopathy, Sree Rama Engineering College, India

Chapter 5
Comprehensive AI-Driven Approach to Cybersecurity in Fifth-Generation Networks 111
Ashok P., Symbiosis Institute of Digital and Telecom Management, India
Sandeep Prabhu, Symbiosis Institute of Digital and Telecom Management, India
Srushtee Bhalerao, Symbiosis Institute of Digital and Telecom Management, India
Prathamesh Prabhu, George Washington University, USA

Chapter 6
Leveraging Artificial Intelligence for Advanced Threat Detection and Autonomous Response in Cybersecurity 135
Venkata Ramana Kaneti, VNR Vignana Jyothi Institute of Engineering and Technology, India
D. Jayasutha, Kathir College of Engineering, India
B. Yamini, SRM Institute of Science and Technology, India
M. G. Dinesh, Easa College of Engineering and Technology, India
L. A. Anto Gracious, R.M.K. College of Engineering and Technology, India
P. Girija, Panimalar Engineering College, India

Chapter 7
Utilization of Packet Tracer for Strengthening Network Security: Methods, Implementation, and Assessment... 161
Krishanu Kundu, G.L. Bajaj Institute of Technology and Management, Greater Noida, India

Chapter 8
Machine Learning in Cyber Security: A Literature Review 181
Pooja Dehankar, Ajeenkya D.Y. Patil School of Engineering, India
Sudipta Banerjee, Symbiosis Institute of Technology, Symbiosis International University, Pune, India
Susanta Das, Ajeenkya D.Y. Patil University, India

Chapter 9
Next Generation Firewall: A Comprehensive Analysis and Practical Applications 201
Brindha Subburaj, Vellore Institute of Technology, Chennai, India
T. Subbulakshmi, Vellore Institute of Technology, Chennai, India
M. Sidharth, Vellore Institute of Technology, Chennai, India

Chapter 10
The Phishing Epidemic: Threats, Techniques, and Countermeasures 229
Shalomo Agarwarkar, Gujarat University, India
Kiranbhai R. Dodiya, Gujarat University, India
Kapil Kumar, Gujarat University, India

Compilation of References 257

About the Contributors 291

Index 303

Detailed Table of Contents

Preface xii

Acknowledgment xvi

Chapter 1
Machine Learning vs. AI: Key Concepts 1
Binastya Anggara Sekti, Universitas Esa Unggul, Indonesia

Artificial Intelligence (AI) and Machine Learning (ML) are transformative technologies reshaping industries, particularly in enterprise cybersecurity. AI refers to the broader concept of machines or systems simulating human intelligence, enabling decision-making, problem-solving, and task automation. ML, a subset of AI, focuses on algorithms and models that enable systems to learn from data and improve performance over time. These technologies have become essential in addressing modern cybersecurity challenges by enhancing detection, response, and predictive capabilities in the face of increasingly sophisticated threats. It explores practical applications, including the use of ML for anomaly detection and AI for automating threat response and prediction. The discussion also highlights how these technologies can work together synergistically to enhance cybersecurity defenses. Through case studies and examples, readers gain insights into their real-world implementation, challenges, and emerging trends, along with ethical considerations for their use in enterprise security strategies.

Chapter 2
Artificial Intelligence (AI) in Cybersecurity: Foundations, Applications, and Research Trends 29
Aditya Shrivastav, Ajeenkya D.Y. Patil University, India
Kashvi Chaturvedi, Ajeenkya D.Y. Patil University, India
Sunil Sankathala, Ajeenkya D.Y. Patil University, India
Krutika Patre, Ajeenkya D.Y. Patil University, India
Atharva Haresh Saraf, Ajeenkya D.Y. Patil University, India
Susanta Das, Ajeenkya D.Y. Patil University, India

AI has been a disruptive technology in the sphere of cybersecurity, followed by an ever-growing more complex threat environment, featuring advanced persistent threats (APTs), ransomware, and zero-day exploits that would usually overcome conventional cybersecurity defenses. AI is the architecture of intelligent systems, capable of simulating human cognition either through ML, DL, NLP and expert systems in small-scale (as narrow AI) or large-scale (as general AI and superintelligence) versions. The CIA of confidentiality, integrity, and availability can also be reinforced in the case of cybersecurity because AI can be employed in order to make predictions and countermeasures to newly developed threats, such as malware, phishing, and intrusion. This chapter discusses applications of AI in cybersecurity together with its concepts, threat environments, & applications such as threat detection, intrusion prevention, & predictive analytics. It includes case studies in the industries, bibliometric research patterns, and future perspective of new technologies, ethical and regulatory matters.

Chapter 3
AI-Driven Threat Detection and Prevention: Enhancing Cybersecurity with Machine Learning and Predictive Intelligence 57

Tarun Kumar Vashishth, IIMT University, Meerut, India
Vikas Sharma, SRM Institute of Science and Technology, India
Sangeeta Sharma, IAMR College, Meerut, India
Mukesh Kumar Sharma, Chaudhary Charan Singh University, Meerut, India
Rajeev Sharma, IIMT Engineering College, Meerut, India
Sachin Chaudhary, IIMT University, Meerut, India
Aarushi Vashishth, Ajay Kumar Garg Engineering College, India

The rapid changes in the cyber threat landscape in the digital age have changed the design of security mechanisms to support proactive and adaptive security capabilities that can detect, predict, and respond to attacks in real time. This chapter discusses the potential of integrating Artificial Intelligence (AI), Machine Learning (ML), and Predictive Intelligence for cybersecurity through proactive threat detection and prevention. The chapter covers how AI-based predictive models can analyze vast and complex (and rich) data and identify hidden/novel attack patters, detect anomalies for faster incident response, and features supervised, unsupervised, and deep learning models for intrusion detection, malware analysis, and phishing prevention as well as predictive intelligence to help prevent zero-day attacks and other new avenues of security threats. Examples of real-world applications and case studies show how AI-powered solutions can dramatically cut down false-positives, leap-frog situational awareness, and increase resiliency and preparedness for an organization.

Chapter 4
Anomaly Detection With Machine Learning 85
T. K. Shaik Shavali, Lords Institute of Engineering and Technology, India
Sunita Vinod Mahale, Independent Researcher, India
S. Manikandan, Kongunadu College of Engineering and Technology, India
Sachin Vasant Chaudhari, Sanjivani College of Engineering, Ahmednagar, India
Fateh Bahadur Kunwar, Rajasthan Technical University, India
C. S. Sandeep, Jawaharlal College of Engineering and Technology, India
V. Bhoopathy, Sree Rama Engineering College, India

The structures know how to observe activity utilizing actual data thanks for cutting intelligence procedures. In order for systems to demonstrate action that is derived from previous interactions, procedures that are founded on those interactions can be developed. In order to identify out-of-the-ordinary occurrences in certain networks, predictive methods are employed. The encryption techniques can detect net abuse and are able to develop with various types of inputs. Machinery supervision and recognizing fraud are two applications of this concept. Whenever tackling multifaceted, extremely complicated, nonlinear information dividends, traditional techniques for statistics can be ineffective. Advancements in recognizing anomalies have been substantial via the introduction of ML, especially DL and unstructured learning methods. In order to provide light on the present modern facilities and upcoming study areas, this part delves through the core ideas, methods, methods, and practical uses of finding anomalies via artificial intelligence.

Chapter 5
Comprehensive AI-Driven Approach to Cybersecurity in Fifth-Generation Networks 111
Ashok P., Symbiosis Institute of Digital and Telecom Management, India
Sandeep Prabhu, Symbiosis Institute of Digital and Telecom Management, India
Srushtee Bhalerao, Symbiosis Institute of Digital and Telecom Management, India
Prathamesh Prabhu, George Washington University, USA

The AI-enabled risk management framework for 5G networks represents a significant advance in telecommunications security, in particular addressing the challenges posed by next-generation 5G networks. The key aspect of this article is to integrate established risk management principles with state-of-the-art artificial intelligence (AI). This new integration facilitates a dynamic approach to 5G security, allowing the system to evolve as new threats emerge. Unlike static security systems, AI-enabled risk management systems use adaptive controls, using AI to analyze real-time threat intelligence and adjust its security accordingly. Integrating AI enables the system to intelligently address complex security challenges specific to 5G, combats multiple vulnerabilities. In doing so, risk AI-enabled planning for 5G networks not only protects against current threats but unexpected security. The approach, marks a significant step forward in the effort to secure the next generation of mobile networks mark, highlighting the critical role AI plays in shaping the future of network security.

Chapter 6
Leveraging Artificial Intelligence for Advanced Threat Detection and Autonomous Response in Cybersecurity 135
Venkata Ramana Kaneti, VNR Vignana Jyothi Institute of Engineering and Technology, India
D. Jayasutha, Kathir College of Engineering, India
B. Yamini, SRM Institute of Science and Technology, India
M. G. Dinesh, Easa College of Engineering and Technology, India
L. A. Anto Gracious, R.M.K. College of Engineering and Technology, India
P. Girija, Panimalar Engineering College, India

The increasing complexity and volume of cyber threats demand advanced solutions beyond traditional methods. This chapter explores the integration of emerging Artificial Intelligence (AI) technologies in cybersecurity, highlighting their transformative role in threat detection, prevention, and response. Key AI techniques such as machine learning, deep learning, natural language processing, and reinforcement learning are explored for their applications in malware detection, phishing prevention, network security, and autonomous defense systems. The chapter also discusses challenges like data privacy, model bias, and resource requirements, alongside future directions involving IoT, 5G, cloud integration, and quantum computing. In summary, AI holds significant potential to drive the development of intelligent, adaptive, and proactive cybersecurity systems that can safeguard digital infrastructure in a continuously evolving threat landscape.

Chapter 7
Utilization of Packet Tracer for Strengthening Network Security: Methods, Implementation, and Assessment.. 161
Krishanu Kundu, G.L. Bajaj Institute of Technology and Management, Greater Noida, India

DHCP servers play a crucial role in dynamically allocating IP addresses and optimizing resource utilization. When a user types a domain name into their web browser, DNS servers translate it into IP addresses and point users to the relevant server. A web server's main job is to store, process, and provide users requested websites or information. In modern network security practices, tools like Cisco Packet Tracer have been implemented to enhance system security. This work discusses the integration of DHCP, DNS, and web servers to fortify network infrastructure. Enforcing strong password policies is essential for preventing unauthorized access and data breaches. Requiring complex passwords strengthens security measures and minimizes vulnerabilities associated with password use. The study also looks at how DNS servers resolve IPv4 addresses and URLs, providing a thorough grasp of internet communication procedures.

Chapter 8
Machine Learning in Cyber Security: A Literature Review 181
Pooja Dehankar, Ajeenkya D.Y. Patil School of Engineering, India
Sudipta Banerjee, Symbiosis Institute of Technology, Symbiosis International University, Pune, India
Susanta Das, Ajeenkya D.Y. Patil University, India

Rise in cyber-attacks has prompted organizations to change to a smarter & more proactive approach to cyber security. ML is a component of a larger AI ecosystem, & has really disrupted our thinking around cyber security. This chapter will examine the application of ML in the domain of cyber security to describe its strengths & its weaknesses. We will investigate how ML algorithms can sift through substantial datasets to find patterns, & irregular behavior, and detect threats that could point to advanced persistent threats (APT). It will explain how to achieve this by utilizing traditional isolation- & detection-based cyber security frameworks & understanding their limitations which we can then move to ML approaches. We will see that the approach of ML to cyber security could greatly transform the field because it has the potential to provide automated incident response, enables detection of threats in real time, & is capable of improving security visibility significantly. However, it is important to note that ML success will depend on having sufficient and quality training data.

Chapter 9
Next Generation Firewall: A Comprehensive Analysis and Practical Applications 201
Brindha Subburaj, Vellore Institute of Technology, Chennai, India
T. Subbulakshmi, Vellore Institute of Technology, Chennai, India
M. Sidharth, Vellore Institute of Technology, Chennai, India

This chapter provides an extensive discussion on Next Generation Firewalls (NGFWs) and its significance in the recent security infrastructure. Tradition firewalls filters traffic using packet metadata, whereas NGFWs are bundled with security features like application and user awareness, Deep Packet Inspection, Intrusion Prevention

System, Virtual Private Network, etc. which enables intelligent threat detection. The evolution of firewalls, the security profiles and configuring these security features are presented in this chapter. An experimentation using machine learning algorithm is carried out to filter traffic and make intelligent decision on whether to allow or deny a traffic. A log record dataset consisting of history of traffic logs is used to train the machine learning model namely XGBoost classifier. The classifier attains AUC Score of 0.998, which shows the significance of integrating machine learning capabilities with next generation firewalls for intelligent threat detection.

Chapter 10
The Phishing Epidemic: Threats, Techniques, and Countermeasures 229
Shalomo Agarwarkar, Gujarat University, India
Kiranbhai R. Dodiya, Gujarat University, India
Kapil Kumar, Gujarat University, India

Phishing scams, often seen as simple tricks, actually use complex tactics causing major financial, digital, and personal losses globally. Exploiting human behavior and urgency, attackers deceive victims through fake websites, messages, calls, and more. As technology evolves, phishing grows more advanced, using tools like scripts and malicious payloads. This chapter explores the causes, techniques, psychological impact, and countermeasures of phishing. It also analyzes two major phishing case studies to show the scale of harm. Lastly, it highlights effective prevention methods, combining technical defenses with awareness to help individuals and organizations stay protected.

Compilation of References 257

About the Contributors 291

Index 303

Preface

In today's hyper-connected digital landscape, enterprise cybersecurity has evolved into a critical and complex domain, demanding innovative solutions that go beyond traditional defensive measures. The rapid growth of cyber threats—ranging from sophisticated malware and ransomware attacks to advanced persistent threats and zero-day exploits—poses unprecedented challenges to organizations worldwide. To counteract these evolving dangers, artificial intelligence (AI) and its subset, machine learning (ML), have emerged as transformative forces in reshaping the cybersecurity paradigm.

Implementing Enterprise Cybersecurity With AI is designed to provide readers—security professionals, researchers, and technology leaders alike—with a comprehensive exploration of how AI-driven technologies can be harnessed to enhance cybersecurity defenses at scale. The book delves into the foundational concepts of AI and ML, highlighting their distinct roles and symbiotic relationship in modern security architectures. It further examines the advantages and limitations of AI integration, ethical considerations, and the practical realities of deploying these advanced systems in enterprise environments.

Through a series of in-depth chapters, the book covers cutting-edge applications such as anomaly detection, threat prediction, autonomous response, and AI-powered risk management—particularly within emerging technologies like 5G networks and next-generation firewalls. By blending theoretical insights with real-world case studies and experimental research, this work illuminates the pathways toward building adaptive, resilient, and proactive cybersecurity frameworks.

As organizations continue to face increasingly dynamic threat landscapes, the intelligent application of AI offers not only enhanced detection and mitigation capabilities but also the promise of automated, scalable security solutions. This book aims to equip its readers with the knowledge, tools, and critical perspectives necessary to navigate and lead this transformative shift.

I hope that this volume serves as both a practical guide and an inspiration for advancing enterprise cybersecurity through the power of artificial intelligence.

ORGANIZATION OF THE BOOK

Implementing Enterprise Cybersecurity With AI is thoughtfully structured to provide readers with a comprehensive understanding of how Artificial Intelligence (AI) and Machine Learning (ML) are revolutionizing cybersecurity in enterprise environments. The book progresses from foundational concepts to advanced applications, research insights, and practical case studies. The book is organized into twelve chapters. A brief description of each of the chapters follows:

Chapter 1. Machine Learning vs AI: Key Concepts

Establishes the foundational definitions and differences between AI and ML, emphasizing their transformative impact on cybersecurity. The chapter explores practical applications such as anomaly detection and automated threat response, as well as ethical considerations surrounding their implementation.

Chapter 2. Artificial Intelligence (AI) in Cybersecurity: Foundations, Applications, and Research Trends

Explores AI architectures from narrow to general AI, highlighting their use in reinforcing cybersecurity principles like confidentiality, integrity, and availability. The chapter includes discussions on emerging threats, industrial applications, bibliometric trends, and regulatory issues.

Chapter 3. AI-Driven Threat Detection and Prevention: Enhancing Cybersecurity with Machine Learning and Predictive Intelligence

Focuses on leveraging AI, ML, and predictive models to proactively detect, predict, and prevent cyberattacks in real time. It covers various learning models and demonstrates how AI reduces false positives and strengthens incident response through real-world case studies.

Chapter 4. Anomaly Detection with Machine Learning

Delves into advanced ML techniques, including deep and unstructured learning, for identifying unusual network behaviors and detecting fraud or abuse. The chapter emphasizes how ML overcomes limitations of traditional statistical methods in handling complex, nonlinear data.

Chapter 5. Comprehensive AI-Driven Approach to Cybersecurity in Fifth-Generation Networks

Highlights the integration of AI with risk management frameworks tailored for 5G networks. It demonstrates how adaptive, AI-enabled controls enhance security by analyzing real-time threat intelligence and addressing complex vulnerabilities unique to next-generation mobile infrastructure.

Chapter 6. Leveraging Artificial Intelligence for Advanced Threat Detection and Autonomous Response in Cybersecurity

Examines cutting-edge AI techniques such as reinforcement learning and natural language processing applied to malware detection, phishing prevention, and autonomous defense. The chapter also discusses challenges like data privacy and model bias, while exploring future technologies like IoT and quantum computing.

Chapter 7. Utilization of Packet Tracer for Strengthening Network Security: Methods, Implementation, and Assessment

Focuses on network security enhancements through simulation tools like Cisco Packet Tracer, discussing DHCP, DNS, and web server integration, alongside password policy enforcement to prevent unauthorized access and data breaches.

Chapter 8. Machine Learning in Cybersecurity: A Literature Review

Reviews current research on ML in cybersecurity, highlighting how ML algorithms detect advanced persistent threats (APTs) by analyzing large datasets. The chapter critiques traditional cybersecurity frameworks and illustrates the transformative potential of ML-based detection and response systems.

Chapter 9. Next Generation Firewall: A Comprehensive Analysis and Practical Applications

Explores the evolution of firewalls to Next Generation Firewalls (NGFWs) that incorporate intelligent security features like Deep Packet Inspection and user awareness. It presents a machine learning experiment using XGBoost to improve traffic filtering and threat detection efficacy.

Chapter 10. The Phishing Epidemic: Threats, Techniques, and Countermeasures

Provides an in-depth look at phishing tactics exploiting human behavior and urgency, the evolution of phishing technologies, and their global impacts. It includes case studies and practical prevention strategies combining technical defenses and user education.

Acknowledgment

We are grateful to all the contributors and reviewers for their valuable input. We also extend our sincere thanks to our family members, friends, and colleagues for their constant support throughout the development and submission of this project.

Shahnaz Fatima
Amity University, India

Susanta Das
Ajeenkya D Y Patil University, India

Rajiv Pandey
Amity University, India

Chapter 1
Machine Learning vs. AI: Key Concepts

Binastya Anggara Sekti
https://orcid.org/0000-0001-5489-4888
Universitas Esa Unggul, Indonesia

ABSTRACT

Artificial Intelligence (AI) and Machine Learning (ML) are transformative technologies reshaping industries, particularly in enterprise cybersecurity. AI refers to the broader concept of machines or systems simulating human intelligence, enabling decision-making, problem-solving, and task automation. ML, a subset of AI, focuses on algorithms and models that enable systems to learn from data and improve performance over time. These technologies have become essential in addressing modern cybersecurity challenges by enhancing detection, response, and predictive capabilities in the face of increasingly sophisticated threats. It explores practical applications, including the use of ML for anomaly detection and AI for automating threat response and prediction. The discussion also highlights how these technologies can work together synergistically to enhance cybersecurity defenses. Through case studies and examples, readers gain insights into their real-world implementation, challenges, and emerging trends, along with ethical considerations for their use in enterprise security strategies.

1. INTRODUCTION

In the digital era, understanding the basic concepts of Machine Learning (ML) and Artificial Intelligence (AI) is very important in designing and implementing AI-based cybersecurity strategies. Although some of its applications have similar application scopes, AI and ML actually have fundamental differences in terms of

DOI: 10.4018/979-8-3373-2252-0.ch001

approaches, application environments, and capabilities. The scope of AI applications is vast, especially as intelligent systems that can replace humans, such as in natural language processing, pattern recognition, and decision-making support applications. On the other hand, ML has evolved into real-world applications that are able to learn from large data sets and gradually improve their capabilities without the need for specific programming. ML algorithms have been well used to detect mechanical faults in manufacturing equipment based on previous data and experience. The integration of ML and AI in manufacturing has been able to create a smarter, more efficient, and adaptable production system (Sekti, 2025a).

Based on the different objectives of ML and AI, in the field of cybersecurity, it can be distinguished the specific role of AI and ML in detecting, responding, and preventing cyber threats. AI is primarily used to develop defense strategies that can be flexible against different types of cyber threats, while ML focuses more on recognizing various patterns of cyber attacks and analyzing data anomalies based on prior knowledge. Further discussion will explain the concepts of AI and ML and how they can synergize to build intelligent and sustainable cybersecurity systems in the context of business organizations. The role of AI in preventing cyberattacks is very broad, namely being able to carry out threat detection, incident response, vulnerability assessment, mitigation strategy, and predictive analysis. When industrial systems integrate ML for cybersecurity, so does the evolving threat of adversarial machine learning (AML) attacks. AML techniques can be in the form of model extraction, exploiting vulnerabilities in the ML model to manipulate security defenses that can lead to system failures (Sekti, 2025b).

1.1 Machine Learning Concepts

The concept of machine learning has actually been around for a long time, since around the 1950s, but the term "machine learning" itself was first introduced by Arthur Samuel as an American Computer Scientist working at IBM in 1959. At that time, Arthur Samuel developed a chess game program on the computer, and the chess game could be played by a computer. This can happen after previously building a model from training data used for future predictions without an explicit programming creator (Çetinkaya et al., 2024). Currently, the application of machine learning continues to grow in the real world, helping with tasks that require calculations based on previous data to perform various analyses and predictions. Machine learning continues to evolve and is used in various fields, such as disease diagnosis in the health sector, weather prediction in meteorology, and solving problems that require highly complex data calculations, such as data science. ML can assist in weather forecasting, climate modeling, and data assimilation with greater accuracy (Affendi et al., 2025). In the cybersecurity field, machine learning techniques have been applied to prevent cyberattacks on Internet of Things (IoT) devices using specific algorithms (Ortiz-Ruiz et al., 2024).

Based on how it works, ML is part of AI because it makes computers "smart" after acquiring enough knowledge to complete the tasks assigned to them. Machine learning also has specific algorithms for analyzing data, recognizing patterns, making predictions, or processing data into information that is important for a decision support system. The development of Machine Learning has gone through several lengthy stages, and at present, its applications have expanded significantly, providing immense benefits. Advances in computing technology, the variety of datasets, and developments in machine learning algorithms are three fundamental factors driving progress in modern machine learning. (Sevilla et al., 2022). Below is the history of machine learning development:

- 1950s: The initial concept of machine learning began to be developed to create a simple artificial neural network called a perceptron. This perceptron is still very simple because it uses binary classification to separate the data into 2 classes.
- 1960s: Research on Machine Learning continued to be developed, but progress was very slow due to limited computing and data facilities.
- 1980s: Machine learning began to gain attention again after the development of several learning algorithms such as algorithms such as neural networks and decision trees.
- 1990s: Machine Learning became more recognized after being applied to several practical applications, such as pattern recognition, fingerprint recognition, and speech recognition.
- 2000s-present: Machine Learning booms after big data science and the birth of computers with greater data processing speeds.

1.2 The Need for Cybersecurity

Today's technological advancements have made more and more activities using computers and working and storing data in internet-connected data storage places. The rapid development of technology has also encouraged the industrial revolution, until there is the term Industry 4.0. The term Industry 4.0 is a representation of the 4th Industrial Revolution, which is the occurrence of digital transformation in the manufacturing industry and other sectors. Industry 4.0 involves the integration of several latest technologies such as the Internet of Things (IoT), Artificial Intelligence (AI), Big Data, and Robotics to improve efficiency, productivity, and product quality. This Industry 4.0 paradigm is constantly encouraging the use of various sensor devices and computers to make smart factories, which continuously collect data related to production (Sekti, 2025a).

For organizations that have implemented Industry 4.0, they have succeeded in achieving significant operational efficiencies, improving the quality of goods and services, and reducing costs. This is because it takes advantage of digital transformation that builds an intelligent interconnection of people, processes, data, and things connected to the virtual world. As a result, the interconnectivity between enterprise information technology (IT) and industrial control system (ICS) environments has given rise to new attacks, namely cyber attacks on critical infrastructure operators (Malatji et al. 2022). Cybersecurity is a set of practices, technologies, and policies designed to protect computer systems, networks, devices, and data from various cyber threats like hacking, data theft, malware attacks, and other cyberattacks.

In general, the aspects of cybersecurity are:

- Network Security, which is protecting the network infrastructure from unauthorized access and cyberattacks.
- Application Security, which guarantees that software and applications do not have vulnerabilities that can be exploited by attackers.
- Data Security, which is protecting sensitive data with encryption and data protection policies.
- Cloud security, which is securing cloud-based systems from attacks and data leaks.
- Operational Security, which is managing and monitoring user activities and system access policies.

Cybersecurity focuses on preventing, detecting, and responding to cyber threats to ensure the integrity, confidentiality, and availability of information is maintained. If cyberattacks are ignored or not handled properly, a variety of harmful impacts can occur, including financial losses, data theft, and operational disruptions that harm businesses and individuals. Some of the consequences that can occur without cybersecurity are:

- Theft of Personal Data and Sensitive Information in the form of personal data, such as identity numbers, financial information, and login credentials.
- Ransomware and Loss of Access to the System, where the data is encrypted and there are other parties who demand a ransom.
- Operational Disruption and Loss of Productivity due to Distributed Denial-of-Service (DDoS) attacks that can cripple websites and online services.
- Reputational Damage and Loss of Customer Trust due to customer data leakage.

- Threats to Critical Infrastructure, i.e. attacks on power grids, healthcare services, or government systems, can cause major chaos.

1.3 The need to prevent Cyberattacks

Artificial Intelligence is a branch of computer science that focuses on developing expert systems that can think similarly to human intelligence. AI is designed to perform tasks that require thought that humans normally do, such as decision-making, problem-solving, learning, as well as pattern recognition, image processing, and language recognition. In practice, AI can work independently or as a support for other systems in improving the efficiency and effectiveness of its work. Currently, AI has had a wide impact on society, where AI can make business processes more efficient, improving the quality of decisions, and improving existing products and services (Davenport & Mittal, 2023).

Below are examples of AI-based systems:

- Rules-Based System, which is a system with logical rules in making decisions.
- Expert System, that is, a system that is built to be able to try to resemble human knowledge in completing a task.
- Natural Language Processing, that is, a system that is designed to be able to understand human language so that it can interact with humans.
- Computer Vision, which is the analysis of images and videos to detect objects or patterns.

Until now, AI technology has been widely applied in large industries to improve operational efficiency, reduce human error, and speed up decision-making. In support of cybersecurity, AI is also used to detect cyber threats, automate security systems, and safeguard the entire organization's digital assets (Chatterjee et al., 2021). In the cybersecurity environment, AI has proven its capabilities and can proactively detect various cyber threats quickly and accurately. The following are the benefits of implementing artificial intelligence in the industry:

- AI can help detect and prevent cyber threats and attacks.
- AI can strengthen security features in identity authentication with facial recognition, voice, fingerprint, etc.
- To prevent phishing attacks and social manipulation, AI can recognize fake domains.

ML is one of the branches of computer science that continues to grow rapidly, and was originally a part of AI. ML is an AI-based system that can learn from previous or given data and can automatically continue to improve its performance without the need to create an explicit program. ML has algorithms that can recognize patterns, make the necessary predictions, and continuously improve its capabilities over time. Troubleshooting with high-dimensional data can be done with ML quickly and accurately (Shiwangi et al., 2023). When viewed from the type of learning, ML is classified as:

- Supervised Learning is a learning model that utilizes labeled data, such as the classification of spam or non-spam emails.
- Unsupervised Learning, which is a model that looks for patterns in unlabeled data, such as the detection of anomalies in financial transactions.
- Reinforcement Learning, which is a learning model through interaction with the environment and receiving feedback based on decisions made.

Machine Learning (ML) provides significant benefits in various fields of work in the cybersecurity area. ML can perform big data analysis and predict cyber threats by recognizing attack patterns. Below are examples of the functions of machine learning:

- In data traffic, ML is able to identify unusual and suspicious patterns, and perform blocks before a breach occurs. These systems are called Intrusion Prevention Systems (IPS) and Intrusion Detection Systems (IDS)
- In keeping the network secure, ML can recognize new variants of malware based on characteristics similar to known malware.
- In sectors engaged in the financial sector, ML can recognize abnormal transactions. For example, in e-commerce and the banking sector.
- ML can recognize different types of attacks with its knowledge from historical data. In this case, ML is acting as threat intelligence.

Machine Learning (ML) and Artificial Intelligence (AI) basically have different functions, but when combined, they will be able to synergize and produce a very sophisticated system in cybersecurity. AI can function to be able to mimic human cognitive abilities in solving problems, reasoning, and learning. AI itself has various branches of concentration, such as expert systems, NLP systems, robotics, and computer vision. The main goal of AI is to create machines that can adapt and continuously improve their capabilities over time in automation and decision-making. In today's development of AI, AI is the key supporter in the development of Industry 4.0 (Hansen & Bøgh, 2021).

As a branch of AI, the main role of ML have main focus is to develop algorithms that can learn from the data provided and can adapt. Generally, a system is explicitly programmed for every issue, but ML systems evolve based on data and can adapt to new situations. ML is not like traditional AI systems that follow pre-set rules, but ML models use pattern recognition and statistical analysis to improve their performance over time. This ability to adapt makes ML indispensable for case resolution, such as fraud detection, predictive analytics, and real-time detection of cybersecurity threats. In recent years, machine learning has become increasingly used in various manufacturing industries due to its ability to identify complex nonlinear relationships and improve computing efficiency (Cakir et al., 2021).

Some of the growing science based on AI are:

- Symbolic AI is a rule-based decision-making system that is commonly used in expert systems.
- Machine Learning is a data-driven model that can perform dynamic learning and decision-making.
- Deep Learning is a branch of ML that uses neural network architecture to interpret complex patterns and unstructured data.

Based on the cybersecurity context, there is a fundamental difference between AI and ML, namely that ML-based models can improve the quality of AI-powered solutions can always be able to improve threat detection and response capabilities. The previous study outlines the differences between AI and ML by studying applications in several industries and examining how these technologies can revolutionize cybersecurity frameworks.

Machine Learning and Artificial Intelligence are often thought of as the same technology, but upon closer inspection, they have different ways of working and different goals. AI is a field of computer science that broadly creates systems capable of acting like humans in problem-solving, decision-making, predictions, and various other tasks that require experience. Other fields based on AI include computer vision, natural language processing, robotics technology, and expert systems. AI-powered applications can enable computers to mimic human-like intelligence, allowing them to adapt and improve their capabilities over time. By understanding the benefits and how AI and ML work correctly, they can provide numerous advantages and ease in solving complex problems, handling large amounts of data, and mitigating harmful effects if incorrect actions or decisions are made.

Machine Learning (ML), is a part of AI, which uses statistical algorithms and various computational models that make the system learn from existing data and at the same time improve its performance over time. When compared to traditional AI systems, where traditional AI models work on pre-given rules, but ML models can recognize patterns in big data and can make predictions in decision-making. This flexible nature of ML makes ML permanent or indispensable for many applications because ML can adapt in multiple languages and can be scaled, such as for cybersecurity, fraud detection, and predictive analytics.

Based on its nature, AI can be divided into several technological approaches:

- Symbolic AI: Utilizes predefined rules and logical frameworks for decision-making, such as in expert systems.
- Machine Learning: Leverages statistical models and techniques based on data to facilitate learning.
- Deep Learning: As a subset of advanced ML that leverages multi-layered neural network algorithms in interpreting complex data patterns.

Grasping the distinctions and interplay between artificial intelligence and machine learning is essential for cybersecurity systems. A cybersecurity system that combines AI and ML technologies aims to be able to handle large data sets, be able to detect anomalies that arise, and provide answers quickly. Today, all organizations have started building AI-based frameworks to create system resilience from various cyber threats. In the next discussion, the concept of the framework and the scope of its application in improving the capabilities of the cybersecurity system will be presented.

2. UNDERSTANDING OF ARTIFICIAL INTELLIGENCE

2.1 Definition and Scope

Artificial Intelligence is a branch of computer science that develops intelligent systems to be able to perform tasks that are usually done by humans. Some jobs that are usually done by humans and applied to AI, for example:

- Can learn from data and experience
- Can make logical and rules-based decisions
- Can recognize patterns
- Able to recognize, understand, and produce human language

AI is a broad field that aims to create machines capable of simulating human thinking. These systems can handle large data sets, recognize patterns, and make decisions with little human input (Dwivedi et al., 2021). Based on the level of the problem, AI has three categories of solutions:

- Narrow AI: Developed for specific functions, such as filtering spam emails, recognizing faces, and detecting cybersecurity threats.
- General AI: A theoretical AI system that possesses human-like cognitive abilities across multiple domains.
- Super AI: An ambition that AI can surpass human intelligence in various aspects, such as decision-making abilities.

2.2 AI Scope of Implementation

The advent of AI technology has transformed various business organizations, where companies can leverage AI to increase productivity, innovate, and improve the quality of decision-making more quickly and accurately. Below is a description of the benefits of AI that have been felt in various types of organizations.

Healthcare

Healthcare is a very important domain because health is essential for everyone. With the use of AI, several healthcare technologies have developed rapidly. Deep learning, a type of AI model, has been widely used in radiology to read and understand the meaning of radiological images in order to improve the accuracy of early detection systems for various types of diseases, such as tuberculosis, cancer, and cardiovascular conditions (Benjamens et al., 2020).

The use of natural language processing has helped humans understand patient clinical records that are in various formats for use in clinical decision-making and as data for medical research. NLP in the form of chatbots has developed significantly and can help healthcare providers filter through numerous patient questions, remind patients of their healthcare schedules, and answer patient questions in the form of interactive dialogues. An example of its application is the Da Vinci robot, known as an advanced AI-based robotic surgical system that can enhance precision in high-stakes surgical procedures performed by surgeons. Additionally, AI-based personalized healthcare systems can provide tailored services for each individual, customized according to their healthcare plans based on their lifestyle and genetic profiles.

Finance

In the financial sector, AI can also be used to improve the security of financial transactions, and streamline financial bureaucratic procedures that are generally ineffective. The use of AI-powered fraud detection systems can help analyze the number of incoming financial transactions in real-time, AI can identify suspicious activity when it finds irregularities in financial behavior (Chatterjee et al., 2021). Another benefit, in the credit scoring model, by adopting AI, can be used for more accurate and faster risk assessment, so that it can improve the loan approval process. AI-based trading algorithms can help financial institutions optimize investment portfolios and execute trades at optimal times to maximize returns. In an improvement in customer service, AI chatbots will handle account-based queries, payment processing, and investment advice, reducing response times and certainly improving service quality. Risk management platforms also use AI to model and predict market fluctuations.

Manufacturing

AI has transformed manufacturing through predictive maintenance, quality control, and process automation. Predictive maintenance systems that use AI to help analyze sensor data, identify early signs of equipment wear and tear as well as maintenance failures can minimize unplanned downtime (Javaid et al., 2022). Advanced robotics powered by machine learning enhance assembly line efficiency and flexibility, adapting to variations in production requirements. AI-driven quality control systems leverage computer vision to detect minute product defects that are invisible to the human eye, ensuring consistent quality. The use of AI in the field of supply chain management has helped in logistics planning, predicting future demand, and optimizing stock levels, which will certainly have an impact on reducing operational costs and improving shipping efficiency.

Retail and E-commerce

AI can drive everyone's shopping experience and can improve operational efficiency in the retail sector. An AI-based recommendation engine powered by deep learning and collaborative filtering can recommend needed products based on browsing behavior and previous purchase records, so E-commerce can significantly increase sales conversions (Dubey et al., 2020). With AI support, a dynamic pricing system can make price adjustments or discounts based on the number of demands, competition from similar products, and inventory levels. NLP is used to support chatbots so that they can provide 24/7 customer service support, as well as improve the user experience. Inventory management systems using AI can also detect stock levels in real-time and provide recommendations for reorders, so that product stock availability will be in line with optimal conditions. Sentiment analysis features can help retailers know the customer feedback information and thus be able to create the right marketing strategy. Figure 1 shows the domain of Artificial Intelligence.

Figure 1. Domain of Artificial Intelligence

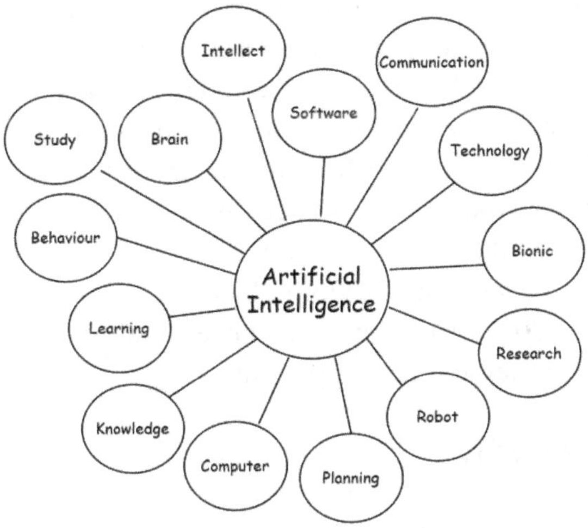

Cybersecurity

AI plays a crucial role in strengthening a company's cybersecurity by quickly finding, mitigating, and responding to threats. The AI-powered Security Information and Event Management (SIEM) platform analyzes network traffic, user behavior, and system logs to detect possible security incidents. (Adriko & Nurse, 2024; Mishra et al., 2022; Ortiz-Ruiz et al., 2024; Vessels et al., 2019; Yoo & Jo, 2023). Anomaly detection systems can detect suspicious activity that may be a threat from insiders or outside threats. Tools for real-time malware analysis leverage AI to be able to identify new malware strains based on their behavior patterns, even if they rely solely on signature-based detection. AI-based incident response systems can assist organizations in dealing with attacks by enabling cyber threat containment procedures, such as isolating endpoints that have been compromised by a threat. In addition, AI is also used for vulnerability management by scanning systems for weaknesses and recommending mitigation strategies.

Autonomous Vehicles

AI is the main technology used in autonomous vehicles. With the help of AI, it can accommodate perception, quick decision-making, and real-time navigation. Deep learning models are used for sensor data analysis from autonomous vehicle cameras, and ultrasonic sensors to identify and classify objects in front of them such as pedestrians, vehicles, or traffic signs. Deep learning algorithms are used to improve decision-making in complex traffic environments, the goal of which is to enable vehicles to safely navigate dynamic environments. AI-powered route planning systems can optimize routes based on traffic situations, road closures, so that fuel efficiency can be achieved, among other things. Human-machine interfaces (HMIs) in autonomous vehicles can establish communication and control with humans, which can improve user experience and safety. Autonomous vehicle technology has become popular, where this technology requires accurate positioning in the face of uncertainties such as pedestrians, random objects, road types, and traffic control systems (Parekh et al., 2022). Continuous advances in AI algorithms will bring fully autonomous vehicles faster and closer to reality.

2.3 AI in Cybersecurity

Fast AI data processing and the ability to detect anomalies have made it an indispensable tool for every organization in building its modern cybersecurity framework. The rapid development of technology today has created a global need for efforts to combat various cyber threats (Sadik et al., 2020). Below will be some of the main areas of artificial intelligence's role in cybersecurity strategy.

1. AI-Enhanced Security Information and Event Management (SIEM) is an AI-powered solution to analyze large amounts of security data in real time, identify threats, and provide critical insights to address them. SIEM works automatically to connect multiple events to be able to uncover potential attacks.
2. Automated Malware Analysis, which is an AI system that uses behavioral analysis to detect zero-day malware attacks as well as polymorphic threat types that evade traditional signature-based defenses.
3. The automated incident response system is an AI-based incident response system that can recognize unusual activity and perform automatic isolation actions such as blocking certain IP addresses, isolating devices suspected of being infected with malware, and changing passwords.
4. User Behavior Analysis (UBA) is a machine learning model that can detect and analyze user behavior and subsequently identify anomalies that indicate threats from insiders.
5. Threat Intelligence Integration is a system that combines global threat intelligence data with internal threat detection systems to provide risk-based action recommendations.

To obtain a sustainable cybersecurity system, AI can help cybersecurity professionals and practitioners detect and understand various unusual activities that could pose strategic threats and prepare appropriate incident responses. AI's ability to process large amounts of data quickly makes it an important tool for various business organizations. Companies that incorporate AI into their cybersecurity frameworks will be far more prepared and proactive in identifying and preventing various cyber threats, mitigating or reducing risks, and adapting to new types of emerging threats before incidents occur.

3. UNDERSTANDING OF MACHINE LEARNING

3.1 Definition and Key Characteristics

Machine learning is a development of artificial intelligence technology that uses certain learning algorithms to learn from a set of data and draw conclusions based on processed data. Unlike traditional learning systems that always use certain rules, ML models can conduct learning and continue to improve their abilities. This kind of flexibility is particularly appropriate in an ever-changing environment, such as in cybersecurity, where new threats and behaviors are constantly evolving.

The properties of machine learning in general are:

1. Data-Driven Learning: ML models require historical and real-time data for training and validation in improving their capabilities. The more data and diversity there are, the higher the predictability and classification of ML. That jam ML has continuous learning capabilities that traditional learning systems do not possess.
2. Pattern Recognition: One of the abilities of is to recognize patterns and know the complex relationships of a set of data that may be too much or even impossible for humans to do. For example, to look for abnormal activity in data traffic in computer network systems that may be indicative of a cybersecurity breach.
3. Adaptability and Scalability: The ability to adapt when new data becomes available without the need for manual reprogramming. Thus ML can automatically evolve in line with changes in the environment, such as adapting to new types of malware or new types of phishing. ML models can also be developed to manage large and varied amounts of data, which suits the needs of business organizations.
4. Supervised, Semi-Supervised and Unsupervised Learning: Based on the type of learning, ML can be divided into three types of learning, namely supervised learning (models trained using labeled data), unsupervised learning (models trained to uncover hidden patterns in unlabeled data), and semi-supervised learning (combined models). Examples of supervised learning are spam detec-

tion or user authentication controls, while unsupervised learning methods are used for the detection of anomalies that occur on devices.

5. Automation: Complex and repetitive tasks can be done by machine learning, so humans don't have to do repetitive tasks but can concentrate on other tasks that are more important or needed. In cybersecurity systems, ML can independently identify, classify, and respond to new threats automatically with minimal human intervention or even no intervention required.
6. Model Generalization: ML can work well with invisible data, as well as ensure accuracy not only on training datasets but also on new data. In the cyber security system, this is very necessary because new cyber attack methods will continue to emerge.

Based on the properties of ML above, it is necessary to sort out again what are the properties used in improving the cybersecurity system. The ML capabilities that can be chosen are its ability to handle large data sets, detect anomalies quickly, and continue to develop its capabilities by learning so that it can build a strong cybersecurity system in dealing with various cyber threats in real-time.

3.2 The Type of Machine Learning

There are several types of learning in machine learning that are currently known. Table 1 shows the three types of machine learning.

Table 1. Types of Machine Learning

Type	Description	Example
Supervised Learning	Learns from labeled datasets to make predictions	Phishing email classification, fraud detection
Unsupervised Learning	To identify unknown patterns in unlabeled data	Anomaly detection in network clustering, traffic
Reinforcement Learning	Learns by interacting with an environment and receiving rewards	AI-driven penetration testing, automated firewall tuning

3.3 ML in Cybersecurity

ML is crucial in cybersecurity by:

- Identifying and mitigating threats through predictive analytics.
- Detecting anomalies and malicious activities in real-time.
- Automating threat intelligence and risk assessment processes.

Example: ML in Anomaly Detection

The important role of machine learning in cybersecurity systems is its ability to detect anomalies in a system early on, before damage occurs as a result of those anomalies. Traditional security systems that use predefined rules often escape new types of threats that come along. Instead, with a machine learning model, the system can analyze the datasets that pass through the network and user behavior to detect unusual patterns in real-time. For example, unsupervised learning techniques such as clustering algorithms to detect zero-day attacks by knowing deviations from normal behavior. This concept can be seen in an illustration that explains the role of machine learning in cybersecurity. Figure 2 shows an ML Model for Anomaly Detection in Cybersecurity.

Figure 2. ML Model for Anomaly Detection in Cybersecurity

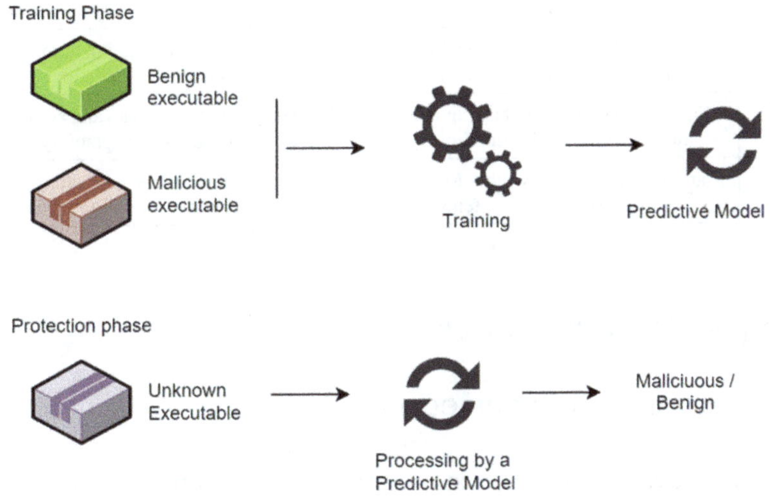

AI and ML have transformed enterprise cybersecurity systems to provide advanced capabilities for detection, prevention, and response to various threats. Understanding their differences, synergies, and ethical implications is essential for leveraging these technologies effectively. As AI and ML continue to evolve, organizations must adopt strategic frameworks to integrate them seamlessly into cybersecurity operations while addressing associated challenges.

4. KEY DIFFERENCES BETWEEN AI AND ML

If you look at how it works, the activities in the ML concept are actually ML is part of the AI concept, namely learning to decision-making. But when it comes to their impact on applications, ML and AI have differences. These differences are outlined in Table 2.

Table 2. Differences Between AI and ML

Feature	Artificial Intelligence	Machine Learning
Definition	AI is a very broad field of computer science that aims to resemble human intelligence.	ML is a part of AI that aims to make machines able to learn from the data provided and make predictions.
Scope	Encompasses various fields, including ML, robotics, expert systems, NLP, and more.	Focuses on statistical learning models to analyze and interpret data.
Decision-Making	Uses predefined rules, logic-based reasoning, or ML-based models.	Relies on training data and pattern recognition to improve predictions.
Flexibility	Can incorporate different techniques, including ML and symbolic AI.	Primarily depends on data and computational models for adaptability.
Human Intervention	Can function with or without ML; may rely on rule-based systems.	Requires human-labeled training data for supervised learning models.

4.1 Example: AI vs. ML in Cybersecurity

Artificial Intelligence in Cybersecurity

AI is used in cybersecurity for automated threat detection and response. For instance, AI-driven security systems, such as IBM Watson for Cybersecurity, use NLP and knowledge graphs to analyze security threats in real time. AI-powered SIEM platforms can correlate security incidents across multiple sources to provide a comprehensive view of potential threats.

Machine Learning in Cybersecurity

Machine learning models, with their ability to detect unusual activity, detect fraud, and recognize malware, are now widely used to combat various cyber threats. For example, an intrusion detection system (IDS) is an ML-based system that can analyze data traffic activity within a network to identify suspicious activity. IDS can use supervised or unsupervised learning techniques (Ortiz-Ruiz et al., 2024).

4.2 Visual Representation of AI and ML

The conceptual difference between ML and AI in cybersecurity systems is that their objectives are different, but they can complement each other in a modern cybersecurity framework. AI technology has a very broad concept that encompasses various human functions, such as pattern recognition, decision-making, and reasoning about a problem. Meanwhile, ML technology has developed in a more specific direction, namely the ability to learn from data that has been provided in order to recognize patterns, detect anomalies, and perform other predictive capabilities. Although AI-based security solutions can automatically respond to threats in real time and make decisions like humans, ML technology also plays a crucial role in enhancing threat detection accuracy by analyzing large datasets and adapting to various new types of attacks. When combined, these two technologies can complement each other within the context of a comprehensive cybersecurity framework. This synergy will provide a more dynamic, efficient, and proactive cybersecurity strategy capable of addressing evolving cyber threats in real time. Figure 3 shows the conceptual differences between AI and ML in cybersecurity.

Figure 3. Difference between AI and ML

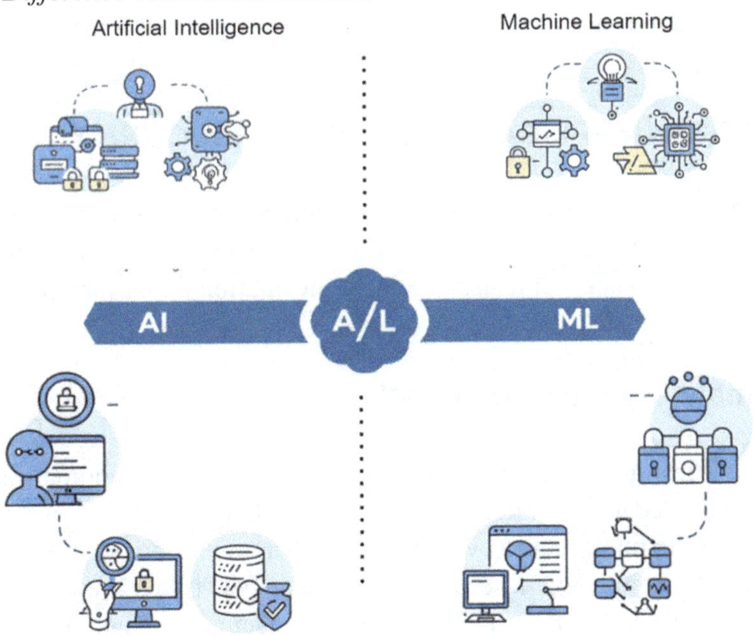

4.3 Challenges in AI and ML Implementation

Despite their advantages, both AI and ML present several challenges. Table 3 outlines the Challenges in AI and ML Implementation.

Table 3. Challenges in ML and AI Implementation

Challenge	Artificial Intelligence	Machine Learning
Data Dependency	May work with rule-based systems, requiring less data.	Heavily relies on high-quality training datasets.
Complexity	Can be highly complex due to multiple AI subfields.	Complexity depends on the ML model, such as deep learning requiring large datasets.
Transparency	May lack explainability, particularly in deep learning.	Some ML models, particularly black-box ones, are challenging to interpret.

AI and ML in this regard have transformed the company's cybersecurity systems, namely in advanced capabilities for threat detection, prevention, and response. Understanding the differences, synergies, and ethical implications is essential to make effective use of these technologies. As AI and ML continue to evolve, organizations need to adopt a strategic framework for seamlessly integrating them into cybersecurity operations while addressing the challenges that arise.

5. PRACTICAL APPLICATIONS IN CYBERSECURITY

AI and ML contribute to the creation of enterprise cybersecurity systems. This technology improves threat detection, automates security processes, and reduces response times to cyber incidents. Below is information about the applications of AI and ML in cybersecurity:

5.1 Anomaly Detection Using ML

Machine learning models are widely used in detecting data anomalies and user behavior. ML-based anomaly detection systems can help reveal any unusual activity that may be able to make them a cyber threat, such as unauthorized intrusion or data theft. For example, in network security systems, an ML-based Intrusion Detection System (IDS) will check data traffic activity to detect any deviations from normal conditions. Techniques such as this clustering, which uses unsupervised learning, are highly effective in detecting the likelihood of a zero-day attack.

5.2 AI for Automated Threat Response

AI-based security systems aim to be able to automatically respond to incoming cyber threats by analyzing attack activity patterns and taking predetermined precautions. The system uses a deep learning model to detect malicious activity and trigger automated actions, such as blocking the IP address where the malicious activity comes from or isolating a system that is compromised by foreign objects, etc. For example, the AI-based Security Orchestration, Automation, and Response (SOAR) Platform has integrated AI models in performing early security alert analysis tasks and automating incident response workflows, thereby reducing the acceleration of action takes that needs to be done.

5.3 Predictive Threat Intelligence

Predictive analytics, AI, and ML systems can detect every potential security threat that comes. By examining the attack history, AI-based threat intelligence systems can predict emerging threats and provide recommendations to address those threats. An example is IBM Watson for Cybersecurity, which uses natural language processing and machine learning techniques to sift through large amounts of threat intelligence data and identify new attack patterns in real time. This allows security teams to be able to take precautions from any cyber threat that will certainly be detrimental if not addressed.

5.4 AI-Driven Phishing Detection

AI models are effective in finding anomalies and preventing phishing attacks by evaluating email content, senders' suspicious actions, and embedded links. Supervised learning models that have been trained with phishing datasets can accurately distinguish between legitimate and malicious emails.

Example: Google's AI-based Gmail security system blocks more than 100 million phishing attempts every day using a deep learning model by analyzing email metadata and detecting suspicious patterns.

5.5 AI in Endpoint Security

With AI support, an Endpoint Security system can significantly improve endpoint security by previously being able to identify and counter malware, ransomware, and other endpoint threats with the help of AI. In addition, with AI support, the Endpoint Detection and Response (EDR) System will continuously observe all endpoint activities, detect malicious behavior, and thwart various cyberattack actions.

An example is AI-based EDR solutions, such as Microsoft Defender, which using machine learning models can detect various advanced cyber threats that come and automatically remediate threats.

5.6 AI in Identity and Access Management (IAM)

IAM solutions that have used AI technology provide enhanced authentication and access control functions by leveraging pre-existing biometric data and behavioral analytics. IAM models like this will be able to detect various unauthorized access attempts and maintain authentication adaptively to improve transaction security. For example, AI-powered authentication systems, such as Okta's Adaptive MFA, have also used machine learning technology to study user behavior and implement risk-based authentication.

5.7 AI in Malware Analysis

Deep learning models are used by AI-based malware analysis systems to detect newly discovered types of malware. Once malware is detected, the system analyzes file signatures, behavior, and structure to try to find malicious software before it causes serious damage. An example of this is Cylance, a deep learning-based malware detection system that uses AI-based data classification algorithms to identify and stop malware attacks.

The combination of AI and ML has transformed the face of business organizations' cybersecurity models by enabling intelligence capabilities to detect, prevent, and respond to various cyber threats. Understanding their differences, synergies, and ethical implications is essential to effectively leveraging this technology. As AI and ML continue to evolve, every organization will be able to have the tools to build a strategic cybersecurity framework.

6. ETHICAL CONSIDERATIONS IN AI AND ML FOR CYBER SECURITY

In addition to the many benefits of AI and ML for organizations, the application of ML and AI to cybersecurity systems can also raise ethical issues that need to be considered, namely compliance, decision transparency, and accountability. Concerns about ethical issues are a natural implication of this technology when incorporated into a cybersecurity system framework.

6.1 Bias in AI Models

One ethical issue that plagues security systems with the adoption of AI and ML is algorithmic bias. Algorithmic bias can lead to errors if the training data is not sufficiently balanced or lacks sufficient diversity, which ultimately results in less accurate predictions due to a tendency toward certain data groups. For example, an AI-based fraud detection system trained on financial institutions may perform poorly in identifying fraud patterns when applied to non-financial institutions, potentially leading to incorrect decision-making (Barredo Arrieta et al., 2020).

Strategies to avoid these problems include:

- Ensuring that the training data set is sufficiently diverse and representative of the problem.
- Regularly checking AI models to ensure fairness and absence of bias.
- Always using XAI to improve the transparency of the AI model used.

6.2 Privacy Implications

AI-based cybersecurity solutions typically require large data sets, which can contain sensitive user information. The collection, storage, and processing of personal data can pose dangerous privacy concerns, i.e. if AI models are used for surveillance, behavioral tracking, or threat detection.

Mitigation Strategies:

- The application of AI techniques to maintain data confidentiality such as differential privacy and federated learning.
- Compliance with global data protection regulations, such as GDPR and CCPA, to ensure secure data handling.
- Provide users with transparency and control over their personal data.

6.3 Transparency and Explainability

AI and ML models can function like “black boxes”, which means that these model's decision-making processes cannot be easily interpreted by humans. The lack of transparency in this black box model can lead to ethical issues, namely when an AI model is needed and used for high-risk decision-making.

Mitigation Strategies:

- Using explainable AI (XAI) techniques to provide an explanation of something that a human can interpret into a decision model.

- AI vendors and cybersecurity companies must disclose how their AI models work and what data they use.
- Asking regulatory bodies to issue transparency standards in AI-based cybersecurity applications.

6.4 Accountability and Governance

AI-based security systems will be able to operate autonomously, but will raise questions about accountability if they turn out to be errors, breaches or misclassifications. If an AI system that goes wrong in recognizing legitimate users is going to be a security threat, who should be responsible—is it the developer, the organization, or the AI itself?

Mitigation Strategies:

- Establishing clear legal and ethical guidelines for AI accountability.
- Implementing human-in-the-loop (HITL) systems where AI decisions are reviewed by cybersecurity professionals before execution.
- Ensuring AI governance frameworks align with industry best practices and legal standards.

6.5 Weaponization of AI in Cybersecurity

AI has been proven to be used defensively as well as offensively in addressing cybersecurity. What is happening today is that malicious actors are using AI to carry out more sophisticated cyberattacks, such as AI-based phishing, automated hacking, and ML techniques that are not aligned.

Mitigation Strategies:

- Developing AI-driven defense mechanisms that can detect and neutralize AI-based threats.
- Conducting continuous research on adversarial AI to anticipate and counteract potential attacks.
- Collaborating with policymakers and international organizations to regulate the misuse of AI in cybersecurity.

7. CONCLUSION

Machine Learning (ML) and Artificial Intelligence (AI) have transformed cybersecurity technology by detecting and responding to threats faster and more accurately than ever before. With these two technologies it has transformed cybersecurity to be proactive from reactive, which can enable organizations to perform anomaly detection, respond automation, and adapt from various evolving threats in real-time. If ML and AI capabilities are combined, a system can be designed to process large amounts of complex data with minimal human intervention, but still provide recommendations or solutions for us in dealing with increasingly sophisticated cyber attacks.

The rapid advancement of technology today has created a new challenge. AI-based decisions are essential for every organization, but they must be made correctly. Algorithm bias can arise in machine learning, data confidentiality, and transparency in the decision-making process must be taken into consideration because they must be handled correctly. Ethical considerations such as bias in ML algorithms, data privacy issues, and transparency in decision-making processes must be addressed to ensure the proper implementation of AI. Criminal actors also exploit AI to commit cybercrimes, so high vigilance is required in the use of ML and AI in various business activities.

Every organization needs to put in place a thorough ethical framework and responsible AI governance procedures to use ML and AI to support cybersecurity systems. This involves utilizing explainable AI (XAI) to guarantee decision-making accuracy, enhance operational transparency, and adhere to privacy laws like the CCPA and GDPR. Building trust and resilience in AI-based cybersecurity solutions requires the use of ongoing audits, user supervision, and workforce skill development. Every firm may take advantage of AI and ML's positive potential to support a strong cybersecurity strategy in the face of upcoming problems by striking a balance between innovation and ethical responsibility.

REFERENCES

Adriko, R., & Nurse, J. R. C. (2024). Does Cyber Insurance Promote Cyber Security Best Practice? An Analysis Based on Insurance Application Forms. *Digital Threats : Research and Practice*, *5*(3), 1–39. Advance online publication. DOI: 10.1145/3676283

Affendi, M. R. N., Hussin, M., & Hasan, D. (2025). A Study of the High-Performance Computing Parallelism in Solving Complexity of Meteorology Data and Calculations. *Journal of Advanced Research in Applied Sciences and Engineering Technology*, *54*(1), 16–26. DOI: 10.37934/araset.54.1.1626

Barredo Arrieta, A., Díaz-Rodríguez, N., Del Ser, J., Bennetot, A., Tabik, S., Barbado, A., Garcia, S., Gil-Lopez, S., Molina, D., Benjamins, R., Chatila, R., & Herrera, F. (2020). Explainable Artificial Intelligence (XAI): Concepts, taxonomies, opportunities and challenges toward responsible AI. *Information Fusion*, *58*, 82–115. DOI: 10.1016/j.inffus.2019.12.012

Benjamens, S., Dhunnoo, P., & Meskó, B. (2020). The state of artificial intelligence-based FDA-approved medical devices and algorithms: An online database. *NPJ Digital Medicine*, *3*(1), 1–8. DOI: 10.1038/s41746-020-00324-0 PMID: 32984550

Cakir, M., Guvenc, M. A., & Mistikoglu, S. (2021). The experimental application of popular machine learning algorithms on predictive maintenance and the design of IIoT based condition monitoring system. *Computers & Industrial Engineering*, *151*, 106948. Advance online publication. DOI: 10.1016/j.cie.2020.106948

Çetinkaya, H. F., & Yenidünya, A. F. çetinkaya, S., & Tüzün, B. (2024). Deep learning and machine learning and their application on computational chemistry. In *Emerging Engineering Technologies and Industrial Applications* (pp. 21–35). DOI: 10.4018/979-8-3693-1335-0.ch002

Chatterjee, S., Rana, N. P., Dwivedi, Y. K., & Baabdullah, A. M. (2021). Understanding AI adoption in manufacturing and production firms using an integrated TAM-TOE model. *Technological Forecasting and Social Change*, *170*, 120880. Advance online publication. DOI: 10.1016/j.techfore.2021.120880

Davenport, T. H., & Mittal, N. (2023). How companies can prepare for the coming "AI-first" world. *Strategy and Leadership*, *51*(1), 26–30. DOI: 10.1108/SL-11-2022-0107

Dubey, R., Gunasekaran, A., Childe, S. J., Bryde, D. J., Giannakis, M., Foropon, C., Roubaud, D., & Hazen, B. T. (2020). Big data analytics and artificial intelligence pathway to operational performance under the effects of entrepreneurial orientation and environmental dynamism: A study of manufacturing organisations. *International Journal of Production Economics, 226*, 107599. Advance online publication. DOI: 10.1016/j.ijpe.2019.107599

Dwivedi, Y. K., Hughes, L., Ismagilova, E., Aarts, G., Coombs, C., Crick, T., Duan, Y., Dwivedi, R., Edwards, J., Eirug, A., Galanos, V., Ilavarasan, P. V., Janssen, M., Jones, P., Kar, A. K., Kizgin, H., Kronemann, B., Lal, B., Lucini, B., & Williams, M. D. (2021). Artificial Intelligence (AI): Multidisciplinary perspectives on emerging challenges, opportunities, and agenda for research, practice and policy. *International Journal of Information Management, 57*, 101994. Advance online publication. DOI: 10.1016/j.ijinfomgt.2019.08.002

Hansen, E. B., & Bøgh, S. (2021). Artificial intelligence and internet of things in small and medium-sized enterprises: A survey. *Journal of Manufacturing Systems, 58*, 362–372. DOI: 10.1016/j.jmsy.2020.08.009

Javaid, M., Haleem, A., Singh, R. P., Suman, R., & Gonzalez, E. S. (2022). Understanding the adoption of Industry 4.0 technologies in improving environmental sustainability. *Sustainable Operations and Computers, 3*, 203–217. DOI: 10.1016/j.susoc.2022.01.008

Malatji, M., Marnewick, A. L., & Von Solms, S. (2022). Cybersecurity capabilities for critical infrastructure resilience. *Information and Computer Security, 30*(2), 255–279. DOI: 10.1108/ICS-06-2021-0091

Mishra, A., Alzoubi, Y. I., Gill, A. Q., & Anwar, M. J. (2022). Cybersecurity Enterprises Policies: A Comparative Study. *Sensors (Basel), 22*(2), 1–35. DOI: 10.3390/s22020538 PMID: 35062504

Ortiz-Ruiz, E., Bermejo, J. R., Sicilia, J. A., & Bermejo, J. (2024). Machine Learning Techniques for Cyberattack Prevention in IoT Systems: A Comparative Perspective of Cybersecurity and Cyberdefense in Colombia. *Electronics (Basel), 13*(5), 824. Advance online publication. DOI: 10.3390/electronics13050824

Parekh, D., Poddar, N., Rajpurkar, A., Chahal, M., Kumar, N., Joshi, G. P., & Cho, W. (2022). A Review on Autonomous Vehicles: Progress, Methods and Challenges. *Electronics (Basel), 11*(14), 1–18. DOI: 10.3390/electronics11142162

Sadik, S., Ahmed, M., Sikos, L. F., & Najmul Islam, A. K. M. (2020). Toward a sustainable cybersecurity ecosystem. *Computers, 9*(3), 1–17. DOI: 10.3390/computers9030074

Sekti, B. A. (2025a). Machine learning and artificial intelligence (AI) in manufacturing. In *Integrating Digital Innovation and Integrated Frameworks in Manufacturing* (pp. 255–292). DOI: 10.4018/979-8-3373-1082-4.ch011

Sekti, B. A. (2025b). Adversarial Machine Learning in Industrial Cybersecurity: Challenges and Solutions. In *AI-Enhanced Cybersecurity for Industrial Automation* (pp. 363–386). IGI Global Scientific Publishing. DOI: 10.4018/979-8-3373-3241-3.ch018

Sevilla, J., Heim, L., Ho, A., Besiroglu, T., Hobbhahn, M., & Villalobos, P. (2022). Compute Trends Across Three Eras of Machine Learning. In *Proceedings of the International Joint Conference on Neural Networks* (Vol. 2022-July). DOI: 10.1109/IJCNN55064.2022.9891914

Shiwangi, K. M., Sandhu, J. K., & Sahu, R. (2023). Effective Heart-Disease Prediction by Using Hybrid Machine Learning Technique. *Proceedings of the International Conference on Circuit Power and Computing Technologies, ICCPCT 2023*, 1670–1675. DOI: 10.1109/ICCPCT58313.2023.10245785

Vessels, L., Heffner, K., & Johnson, D. (2019). *Cybersecurity Risk Assessment for Space Systems. In 2019 IEEE Space Computing Conference*. SCC., DOI: 10.1109/SpaceComp.2019.00006

Yoo, J., & Jo, Y. (2023). Formulating Cybersecurity Requirements for Autonomous Ships Using the SQUARE Methodology. *Sensors (Basel)*, *23*(11), 5033. Advance online publication. DOI: 10.3390/s23115033 PMID: 37299766

KEY TERMS AND DEFINITIONS

Artificial Intelligence (AI): As a branch of computer science, AI is designed to match human intelligence in terms of understanding things, doing things, and providing considerations for decision making.

Black-Box Model: is a model of AI that is made to perform the decision-making process that is difficult for humans to understand or explain.

Deep Learning (DL): DL is a branch of ML that uses artificial neural networks with many layers (deep neural networks) to analyze complex and unstructured types of data, such as text, images, or sounds.

Explainable AI: or XAI is an effort to translate the results of AI so that they can be understood and interpreted by humans

Internet of Things (IoT): The Internet of Things (IoT) is a concept in which a system consists of physical devices equipped with sensors, software, and network connectivity that can be connected through the Internet so that data can be exchanged in real-time.

Machine Learning (ML): ML is a part of AI where with certain ML algorithms can create a machine to continuously learning from data in order to increase their abilities without having to use explicit programming.

Natural Language Processing: or NLP is a model as a branch of AI that allows a computer system to understand, interpret, and generate human language.

Neural Networks: are a computational model inspired by the workings of the human brain and can be used by DL to recognize complex types of patterns.

Supervised Learning: Supervised Learning is a type of ML in which models are trained using labeled datasets to be able to predict the output of certain input data.

Unsupervised Learning: is a type of machine learning model that uses certain algorithms to find patterns or structures in data in the absence of data labels.

Chapter 2

Artificial Intelligence (AI) in Cybersecurity: Foundations, Applications, and Research Trends

Aditya Shrivastav
https://orcid.org/0009-0000-8461-8171
Ajeenkya D.Y. Patil University, India

Krutika Patre
https://orcid.org/0009-0001-7969-4409
Ajeenkya D.Y. Patil University, India

Kashvi Chaturvedi
https://orcid.org/0009-0005-3192-3400
Ajeenkya D.Y. Patil University, India

Atharva Haresh Saraf
https://orcid.org/0009-0006-3842-5508
Ajeenkya D.Y. Patil University, India

Sunil Sankathala
https://orcid.org/0009-0004-7809-7647
Ajeenkya D.Y. Patil University, India

Susanta Das
https://orcid.org/0000-0002-9314-3988
Ajeenkya D.Y. Patil University, India

ABSTRACT

AI has been a disruptive technology in the sphere of cybersecurity, followed by an ever-growing more complex threat environment, featuring advanced persistent threats (APTs), ransomware, and zero-day exploits that would usually overcome conventional cybersecurity defenses. AI is the architecture of intelligent systems, capable of simulating human cognition either through ML, DL, NLP and expert systems in small-scale (as narrow AI) or large-scale (as general AI and superintelligence) versions. The CIA of confidentiality, integrity, and availability can also be reinforced in the case of cybersecurity because AI can be employed in order to make predictions and countermeasures to newly developed threats, such as malware, phishing, and intrusion. This chapter discusses applications of AI in cybersecurity together with its concepts, threat environments, & applications such as threat detection, intru-

DOI: 10.4018/979-8-3373-2252-0.ch002

sion prevention, & predictive analytics. It includes case studies in the industries, bibliometric research patterns, and future perspective of new technologies, ethical and regulatory matters.

1. INTRODUCTION

Artificial intelligence (AI) is one of the most accelerated changes in the sphere of cybersecurity in the context of increasing complexity and sophistication of present-day cyber threats (Ofusori et al., 2024). Digital infrastructures are becoming more prolific and more critical, and that is why exposure to cyberattacks is also becoming more serious and renders the traditional rule-based security strategies ineffective. In this case, AI integration can provide security systems with a chance to transcend reactive strategies, with predictive analytics, machine learning, and autonomous decision-making identifying, neutralizing, and anticipating dynamic threats (Mohamed, 2025). This is the capability of AI to manage very large volumes of non-homogeneous data, discover subtle trends, and be flexible to the changing strategies of adversaries that forms the basis of cybersecurity resilience in a digital first world (Mohamed, 2025; Ofusori et al., 2024; Achuthan et al., 2024).

The recent risk of more sophisticated cyberattacks caused by the presence of advanced persistent threats (APTs), ransomware, and zero-day attacks emphasizes the need to have sophisticated defense measures (Achuthan et al., 2024). Needless to say, AI based solutions have proven to be highly developed in terms of threat detection, malware classification, intrusion detection and incident response that are capable of providing real time analysis and automation which is better than the signature based solutions. Deep learning, federated, and explainable AI also assist in the development of robust and explainable security systems which are especially significant in high-stakes sectors like finance, healthcare, and critical infrastructure (Mohamed, 2025). Even the dual-use character of AI, though, amplifies the scope of threat as malicious individuals apply AI tools to carry out specific and sophisticated attacks. The given duality is one of the reasons to make resilient, trustful, and transparent AI systems, and it is one of the aspects of interest in the current cybersecurity research (Mohamed, 2025; Achuthan et al., 2024; Vulpe et al., 2024).

New advancements in AI in cybersecurity have demonstrated considerable progress in real-time threat detection, behavioral analytics, adversarial machine learning defense, and automatic compliance with security (Mohamed, 2025). It is possible to expand the possibilities of cyber defense by applying AI and the new technologies of blockchain, the Internet of Things (IoT), and privacy saving computation (Folorunso et al., 2024). The current research also states explainability and ethical issues and has resulted in the creation of AI algorithms that are transparent in decision-making, along with algorithms resistant to adversarial exploitation. As cyber threats continue to be a dynamic and intelligent threat, the flexibility and versatility of AI-enabled defensive solutions is the only thing that defines organizational and individual resiliency (Mohamed, 2025; Achuthan et al., 2024; Folorunso et al., 2024). In this chapter, the author discusses AI in the field of cybersecurity, its key applications, advances, and ethics and points out that it is a significant aspect in combating threats and internet resilience.

2. WHAT IS ARTIFICIAL INTELLIGENCE (AI)?

The scientific and engineering discipline of creating intelligent machines, capable of performing tasks that have traditionally been performed by human intellect, is generally termed as AI, and the processes considered crucial to the field are learning, reasoning, problem-solving, perception, and language understanding, and they are assisted by the computational systems that simulate cognitive processes (Ang et al., 2023). The very idea of AI is a set of algorithms and data enabling the machine to perceive, interpret, and respond to the complex environment, and the systems are developed to develop, think, and rectify its mistakes, and therefore become more accurate and more versatile in the long run. To illustrate it, AI systems have been shown to be capable of applying these cognitive principles to handle complex information to facilitate the diagnosis in medical imaging (Ang et al., 2023). The competencies of AI lie along the narrow spectrum of artificial intelligence (ANI) that handles a single, narrow task, like voice recognition, image recognition, and recommendation system, or medical diagnostics, to the hypothetical artificial general intelligence (AGI) and artificial superintelligence (ASI). Whereas ANI is applied in systems such as Siri, Alexa, and domain-specific applications, AGI is also viewed as the self-educating system that is general enough to solve intellectual problems at the human level, and ASI is a hypothetical threshold at which AI becomes wiser than humans in the imagination, judgment, and decision-making. Both AGI and ASI remain rather hypothetical models that have much to do in terms of ethical and technical aspects (Ang et al., 2023).

The achievement of AI is also highlighted by the development of the key approaches that drive the contemporary uses. Machine learning as a subfield of AI is concerned with creating algorithms, according to which systems learn on the basis of data and can be improved, without a particular reprogramming, where supervised learning (with labeled data) and unsupervised learning (finding trends in unlabeled information) are the methodological foundations of an array of applications (Rashid & Kausik, 2024). Deep learning builds on the principle of multilayered artificial neural networks, which enable the discovery of multidimensional and more complex patterns, to achieve the breakthrough in computer vision, speech recognition, and autonomous navigation (Rashid & Kausik, 2024). In order to augment these advances, natural language processing (NLP) enables computational systems to input, understand and generate human language, and has been used in virtual assistants, sentiment analysis, automated translators, and advanced conversational agents. Large language models, such as GPT-3, are an instance of the integration of deep learning with NLP and are able to show an unparalleled level of fluency and knowledge in any language situation (Rashid and Kausik, 2024). At the same time, the expert systems use decision-making knowledge architecture founded on rules to simulate decision-making of a human expert in activities such as diagnosis, troubleshooting, and knowledge management in disciplines such as medicine, finance, and engineering (Rashid & Kausik, 2024). All these theoretical foundations, categories, and technical successes create the picture of the multidimensionality of AI that forms a nexus within the frames of which its deployment into the field of cybersecurity can be analyzed critically.

3. WHAT IS CYBERSECURITY?

Cybersecurity is generally interpreted to mean the organization and combination of resources, processes, and structures aimed at securing cyberspace and the systems that can be realized by means of cyberspace against occurrences that run amok with property rights and endanger the information safety of both technical and human aspects. This idea has been characterized to make cybersecurity an interdisciplinary sphere by nature, drawing on technology, law, management and psychology and is a wide spectrum of technical defenses, risk management approaches, policy frameworks, and human based defenses, all of which are focused upon maintaining confidentiality, integrity and availability of digital resources (Craigen et al., 2014). The development of cybersecurity has been tightly tied to the progress in the domain of information technologies and the development of the threat. Efforts may be traced to the emergence of networked computing, like ARPANET, and international frameworks and norms started to form after 1997 when the international community started to realize the growing dangers of a hyperconnected world (Madnick et al., 2023). Since, the discipline has grown tremendously with greater norm construction and alternating in activity- and law-centered views, since which a three stage developmental model has been proposed, with activities and cases taking off during 2016-17 before leveling in scale and orientation. This development is both the technological change and the increased necessity of resilient and team-based and globally coordinated digital security (Madnick et al., 2023).

At the core of cybersecurity is the CIA Triad Confidentiality, Integrity, and Availability that forms a framework of control upon which policy and technical controls should be designed (Abidde et al., 2023). Confidentiality guarantees that sensitive information is available only to the people who are supposed to know, which may be as a result of encryption and access control. Integrity ensures that information is accurate and consistent by ensuring that it is not modified or destroyed by someone who is not authorized to access the information, involving techniques like hashing, checksums and validation. Availability ensures that information and essential services are constant and available to authorized users by use of redundancy, failover as well as disaster recovery planning. Collectively, these two principles form a long-term socio-technical basis of competent risk management in cybersecurity (Abidde et al., 2023).

Regardless of these frameworks, the threat landscape has been changing over time, and the defining challenges include malware, phishing, and advanced persistent threats (APTs). Malware, which is premeditated to intrude, disrupt, or cause damage to computer systems, manifests itself in various forms such as viruses, worms, ransomware, and spywares, which are both systems-vulnerable and human-trustworthy. Even though machine learning-powered methods of detection have become more prevalent in the modern world, malware remains a constantly changing and dangerous threat that adversaries are constantly evolving to avoid (Azeem et al., 2023). Phishing as one of the most common types of cybercrime is used to influence people to disclose sensitive data by using tricks in their message delivery such as fraudulent email messages, websites, or other online platforms. Phishing has developed since the 1990s to use different communication solutions and psychological advantages to cause significant financial, reputational, and operational damage in any sector, and human vulnerability and the development of attack vectors continue to impede proper mitigation (Alkhalil et al., 2021). Also of great importance are the APTs, which are very advanced targeted cyberattacks that are usually planned by well-resourceful opponents who want to maintain a long-term unauthorized access. Using multi-stage tactics like the social engineering and zero-day exploits, APTs travel within the network laterally, hide themselves, and utilize systemic vulnerabilities over period of time. Their tenacity, flexibility, and strategic focus leave organizations with a continuous challenge of identifying, containing and managing such threats (Mat et al., 2024).

4. IMPLEMENTING AI IN CYBERSECURITY

AI has proved to be the game changer in the world of cybersecurity offering more advanced features to the different defense systems and highly surpassing the old signature based systems. It has been applied particularly effectively in the context of threat detection and prevention, and technologies based on machine learning (ML) and deep learning (DL) can be used to analyze patterns, anomalies, and new attack vectors in real-time and in perplexing data streams (Rahman et al., 2025). The algorithms, such as Random Forest, Support Vector Machines (SVM), and deep neural networks, provide dynamic protection measures that enhance accuracy of detection and reduce response period and adopt dynamic mitigation measures in a variety of settings (Kumar et al., 2025; Rahman et al., 2025). Another area of application of AI in network security is in intrusion detection systems (NIDS) that utilize hybrid AI-ML models, and reportedly it can detect anomalies and zero-day exploits with a high level of detection (almost 96.2) and low false positive rate. Explainable AI (XAI) is further integrated to enhance even further on the aspect of interpretability, which allows security analysts to understand and validate findings of detection that are of paramount importance in cloud infrastructures, industrial networks, and the Internet of Things (IoT) (Rabiu et al., 2025; Arnob et al., 2025; Sowmya & Anita, 2023).

The same advancement has been reported in malware and phishing detection with AI algorithms that utilize behavioral analysis, file features extraction algorithms, and natural language processing (NLP) algorithms, including transformers-based models, to identify malicious behavior more accurately than ever. AI-based phishing defense systems recognize advanced social engineering methods and react timely by modifying their detection algorithms to a new threat at a faster and more efficient rate than conventional detection systems (Ansari et al., 2022; Sankaramma, 2025). In addition to reactive defense, AI is utilized to assist in predictive security and proactive risk evaluation based on the historic data to foresee the potential of the attack and precondition the proactive mitigation. More popular are time-series forecasting algorithms such as long short-term memory (LSTM) networks which are used to detect the ransomware campaigns and phishing waves days or weeks prior to the actual attack so that the organization can allocate their resources more effectively, predict the attack, and go into a reactive and proactive security posture (Aljohani, 2025; Dwivedi et al., 2019).

Regardless of such advancements, AI-based cybersecurity has been met with significant challenges that restrict its use in real life. Training data biases may result in a false positive or false negative, reducing model robustness and limiting their capacity to be applied to novel threats (Roshanaei et al., 2024). The inexplicability of complex models continues to be a challenge to credibility among analysts, and this argument justifies the applicability of explainability as a sustainable AI-use pillar (Bhandari, 2025). In addition, the data poisoning and model evasion adversarial attacks are introduced as vulnerabilities in learning systems that are a threat to reliability and create new opportunities to attack other vulnerabilities (Admass et al., 2023). This is further complicated by the operational challenges of high computing costs, privacy concerns, and the problem of scalability that prevents the implementation of AI to real world security architecture (Muneer et al., 2024). The only way to overcome these limitations is to possess powerful frameworks involving adversarial training, dynamic security, and ethical AI, and consequently ensure the plausible and sound application of AI in cybersecurity.

5. CASE STUDIES AND REAL-WORLD APPLICATIONS

AI has strengthened enterprise cybersecurity as it can be automated, perform intrusion detection and behavioral traffic analytics. The accuracy of machine learning algorithms in detecting anomalies with precision when used in AI-driven tools in enterprises is improved, and thereby detecting more developed threats, such as zero-day exploits and insider attacks (Rabiu et al., 2025). Real-time data integration with behavioral analytics will aid these systems to identify 150,000 or more threats per minute and roughly eight out of 10 attacks will not lead to successful compromise. Such AI-based threat intelligence is applicable in signatureless detection techniques that can never be outsmarted by the conventional techniques in detecting phishing and malware attacks due to finding the anomalies in network traffic and user behaviors. Despite these advantages, companies continue to grapple with the issue of data quality limitations, privacy, and algorithmic bias, transparency, and complexities of integration that can only be solved through continued review and elaboration of ethical governance frameworks that enable the implementation of AI (Rabiu et al., 2025; Kwentoa, 2025). At the national security level, AI is changing the cyber defense strategies by establishing advanced anticipatory analytics and automated threat detection and enhancing coordination of reaction to the incident. In real-time threat detection and optimization of defensive workflows, AI is becoming more significant in business-critical infrastructure such as power grids, communication networks, and transportation networks (Mansur, 2025). Using AI-enabled national cybersecurity frameworks, the emphasis on the collaboration between the government and businesses and the centralized leadership and dynamic regulation could be seen in the attempt to build the resilient defense ecosystems. It is confirmed that AI-based practices not only increase the ability to eliminate and reduce risks, but also alter the governance structure of the situation with national security, and this fact makes the creation of new global standards and the collaboration of the states a key to handling advanced cyber-attacks. Issues based on ethical, legal, and workforce development become an essential aspect at this tier that can influence the realization of AI-based cybersecurity systems in the long term (Mansur, 2025; G, 2025).

Another instance of the shift in AI in terms of cybersecurity is specific industry applications. The financial industry has been one of the most common areas of use of AI to enhance the degree of protection against fraud, phishing, and targeted attacks of sensitive financial data. Recognizing the abnormality of general transactions, anticipating emerging threats, and robotization of response, AI enhances fraud detection and prevention, confidential data protection, and retention of customers. The real-life result of the study suggests that the models of artificial intelligence built on the historical and real-time data demonstrate superior performance over the traditional signature-based methods and the existence of such analytics as real-time analytics, anomaly detection, and predictive insights will enable the financial institutions to become more proactive in dealing with the evolving threat in the online finance landscapes (Kumar et al., 2023). AI is also being implemented in the healthcare sector to ensure that electronic health records and other medical systems are not compromised by cyber threat which is increasingly becoming worse. Adherence to such approaches as machine learning and natural language processing ensures that the task of identifying anomalies, malware, and zero-day exploits threatening to attack healthcare databases is performed even quicker. The latest trends also presupposed the introduction of the concept of generative AI to facilitate the creation of digital healthcare facilities to guarantee the active minimization of risks and, simultaneously, adhere to the rigorous provisions of data privacy laws. It is also possible that the AI-based solutions will overcome the most critical challenges of healthcare cybersecurity by making sure that patient information is safe and reducing vulnerabilities (Qurashi et al., 2025; Virk et al., 2025; Khan et al., 2024). Similarly, AI application in smart cities cybersecurity is concerned with the security of Cloud-IoT infrastructures that support the foundation of the basic services related to transport, utilities, and governmental administration. Predictive analytics, real-time threats, and adaptive response measures are included in the citywide cybersecurity systems and contribute to the possibility to withstand breaches, disruption, and intrusion into privacy. Those virtual replicas of the city infrastructure (digital twins) have been becoming connected to AI so as to simulate the scenario of an attack, determine the vulnerability of it, and trial out mitigation measures beforehand. As the IoT devices in the smart cities are very interconnected, the communication between them should always be observed and processed by artificial intelligence to prevent a system breakdown that results in the failure of other systems (Vempati, 2024; G, 2025).

The distinctive cybersecurity issues of the heterogeneity of devices, constrained computational resources, and dynamical patterns of interaction are processed with the help of AI in the broader context of the IoT. AI and machine learning based dependency-based risk assessments allow quantification of cascading risks of compromised nodes, and defense against defensive responses prioritization in real-time. The use of explainable AI solutions has been incorporated to promote transparency and trust to AI-driven decisions and this would improve the efficacy of the activities of cybersecurity professionals. In addition, risk transference, i.e., cyber insurance, can be performed using AI because it provides an opportunity to develop effective and sound risk models. The successful process of detecting and avoiding risks in the AI-based methods in diverse areas, including medical services, smart cities, and industrial IoT networks, is also confirmed with the assistance of empirical datasets of IoT networks (Radanliev et al., 2024; Ighofiomoni et al., 2025).

6. BIBLIOMETRIC ANALYSIS OF AI IN CYBERSECURITY RESEARCH

The bibliometric analysis on the studies concerning AI as cybersecurity, which is carried out on the foundation of the information about the publications retrieved in Lens.org, provides the comprehensive list of the studies on the topic, the influential researchers and a theoretical framework of the field. The curve (Figure 1) obtained by calculating the annual publications trend of AI research in the field of cybersecurity using the Lens.org accessed information, indicates the shifting pattern of the subject of the decade 2000-2025. The level of publications was not that high during the early years of the 2000-2015 period as it was a period when the idea to apply AI to cybersecurity was young and had no permanent attention of researchers. Around 2016, output was slowly rising, with machine learning and deep learning becoming common in industries and this made them used in intrusion detection, anomaly detection, and threat analysis. The volume of scholarly production in that area grows exponentially and almost 7,000 articles occurred in 2021, which could be explained by the fact that the necessity to combat more advanced cyberattacks grows with the proliferation of big data, cloud computing, and IoT environments. In 2022-2023, the most active was publication activity where close to 8,000 contributions were made after which there was a deviation. This apparent deceleration might be a stagnation of general researchers and a move to more niche areas, such as explainable AI, adversarial AI, and risk management with AI involved. The decline to approximately 6,000 publications in 2025 may mean either uncompleted collection of publications of the most current year or a real contraction of research output which is a good move in the right direction that the field is maturing slowly. In whole, this trend demonstrates that the sphere of AI in cybersecurity has already left its niche as a research field and has gotten an established status as a field of study, which is at the heart of addressing the multi-layered nature of the modern digital threats.

Figure 1. Year-wise publication trend on AI in cybersecurity (Source: Lens Database) (Lens, 2025).

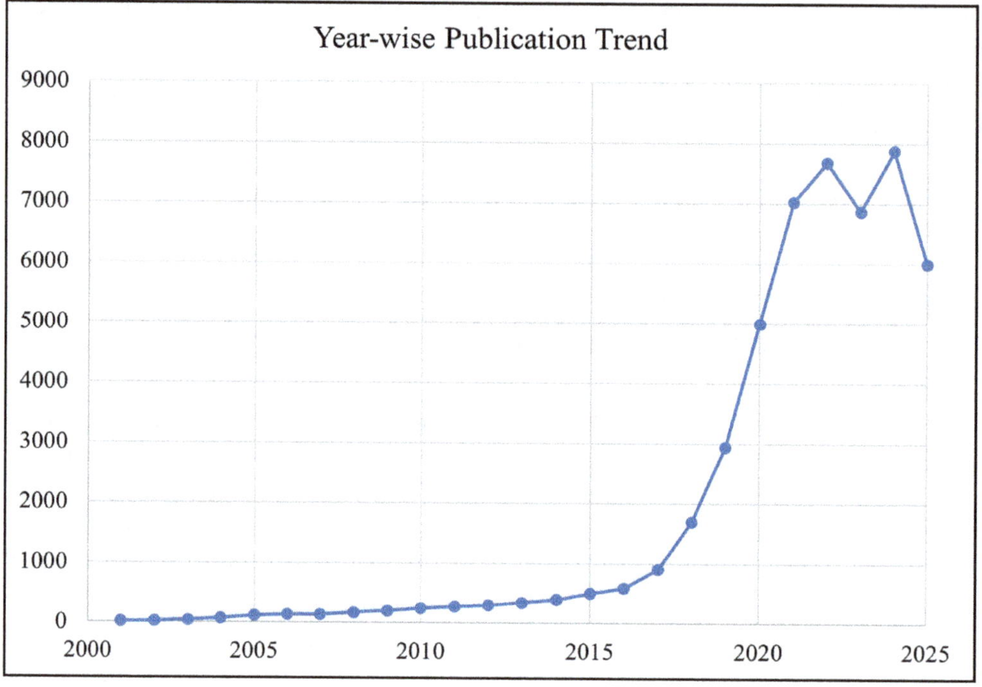

The spread of the academic publications in the world reveals that this is very varied within the country, publishers, authors, and in the institutions as presented in Tables 1 to 4. It is possible to observe the preponderance of national contribution by United States (Table 1) and the significant gap between the United States and the other countries due to the 5,192 publications that show its strong system of research and highly developed industry-academia contacts and specific investments in AI-based security systems. The European nations lead the pack with the Netherlands (3,502) and Germany (3,074) becoming the hubs in the field of secure networks, data privacy, and AI-assisted intrusion detection. The key ones include Switzerland (2,885) and the United Kingdom (2,813) as well and this proves the point that Europe is one of the hotspots of the modern-day cybersecurity research. Comparatively, the Asian and Middle East countries such as Egypt (494), China (342), India (212), South Korea (184), and Saudi Arabia (131) have also had less publications, however, remain the signs of the rapid development and the efforts to orient to the world leaders. The fact that these regions are among the top ten ones indicates that the research space continues to be diversified, and new economies invest more in AI-based cybersecurity.

Table 1. Top 10 contributing countries in AI and cybersecurity publications (Source: Lens Database) (Lens, 2025).

Country	Count
United States	5192
Netherlands	3502
Germany	3074
Switzerland	2885
United Kingdom	2813
Egypt	494
China	342
India	212
South Korea	184
Saudi Arabia	131

This can also be noted in the publishing industry where few large outlets determine the industry (Table 2). The number of publications owned by springer science and business media LLC is 8,815 and it demonstrates its hegemonic status in disseminating the state of the art research in the field. IEEE is historic leader in the area of computing and engineering scholarship (5,971) and MDPI AG (3,199) underlines the emergence of open-access platforms. Elsevier BV (1,880) and Wiley (1,618) are the two other contributors of the research in the field of AI and cybersecurity, which ensures the wide international availability of the studies. The presence of sub-brands at Springer and MDPI signifies how diversifying portfolios of the two publishers make them more prominent, whilst ACM (856) and IGI global (693) have a niche but a substantial position, particularly in the computer science-oriented publishers. All these tendencies are aimed at the concentration of distribution in the internationally accepted publishing houses, which results in the attainment of the academic impact and availability.

Table 2. Top 10 publishers of AI and cybersecurity research (Source: Lens Database) (Lens, 2025).

Publisher	Count
Springer Science and Business Media LLC	8815
IEEE	5971
MDPI AG	3199
Institute of Electrical and Electronics Engineers (IEEE)	2921
Elsevier BV	1880
Wiley	1618
Multidisciplinary Digital Publishing Institute (MDPI)	1295
ACM	856
Springer International Publishing	750
IGI Global	693

The impacts of leading writers are high at the personal level (Table 3). Kim-Kwang Raymond Choo is the 247-publication author who is regarded as a world leader in the field of digital forensics, cybercrime, and threat intelligence based on artificial intelligence. Wei Wang (211) and Yang Liu (202) also do not lag much behind them and contribute greatly to the topic of network security, machine learning-based anomaly identification and classification models. Brij B. Gupta (157) has established himself in the sphere of the research on cloud and social media security, and Lei Wang (139) has given the background information on the threat modeling with the help of AI. Productivity of the field has been ensured by the work of other scholars such as Mark Stamp (118), Lei Zhang, Mohsen Guizani, Jian Wang and Yu Wang as these reveal narrow areas of the discipline such as cryptographic security to wireless networks and hence the coverage of the individual scholarship in the field.

Table 3. Top 10 most prolific authors in AI and cybersecurity research (Source: Lens Database) (Lens, 2025).

Author's Name	Count
Kim-Kwang Raymond Choo	247
Wei Wang	211
Yang Liu	202
Brij B Gupta	157
Lei Wang	139
Mark Stamp	118

continued on following page

Table 3. Continued

Author's Name	Count
Lei Zhang	111
Mohsen Guizani	108
Jian Wang	99
Yu Wang	98

The institutions are also another major player in shaping the research scenario (Table 4). China is having a massive state-funded investment in AI and cybersecurity and it is observed in the Chinese Academy of Sciences, the highest number of publications of 1,835 in the globe. This is further supported by the University of Chinese Academy of Sciences (885) which is based on a well-established national research infrastructure. The increasing contribution of Middle East is King Saud University (674), but the institutional concentration in China is proved by a cluster of Chinese universities including Beijing University of Posts and Telecommunications (589), University of Electronic Science and Technology of China (588), Wuhan University (587), Xi an Jiaotong University (542), Northwestern Polytechnical University (499), Shanghai Jiao Tong University (498) and Tsinghua University (495). This institutional climate is indicative of the fact that AI-oriented cybersecurity has been an agenda in the program of certain nations, particularly in Asia but Western leadership has continued to be prolific in terms of scope and breadth.

Table 4. Top 10 contributing institutions in AI and cybersecurity research (Source: Lens Database) (Lens, 2025).

Institution Name	Count
Chinese Academy of Sciences	1835
University of Chinese Academy of Sciences	885
King Saud University	674
Beijing University of Posts and Telecommunications	589
University of Electronic Science and Technology of China	588
Wuhan University	587
Xi'an Jiaotong University	542
Northwestern Polytechnical University	499
Shanghai Jiao Tong University	498
Tsinghua University	495

Bibliometric mapping is also used in illuminating intellectual mapping of the field. The keywords co-occurrence network (Figure 2) gives an idea of the multidisciplinary research setting, which is subdivided into particular topics. The most important group is concentrated around AI in healthcare security, and the keywords are artificial intelligence, humans, health care, prognosis and diagnosis, and extends to the areas of telemedicine and COVID-19 since the safety of sensitive medical information during the pandemic is an issue that needs to be addressed with the assistance of AI. The other dominating cluster includes machine learning, deep learning, intrusion detection, malware classification, and encryption that highlight the importance of AI in the security of network infrastructures. The third group is associated with cybersecurity and emerging technologies and privacy that include blockchain, IoT, industry 4.0, and smart cities, which reflect the introduction of AI into the socio-technical field. Another group, which is less critical but equally significant, is concerned with cryptography, steganography, and image processing, dedicating in turn a special interest to secure communication and data hiding, and another one group relates AI applications to the industrial security, smart manufacturing, and SCADA systems, as the issue of securing critical infrastructure starts to gain more attention.

Figure 2. Bibliometric keyword co-occurrence network of AI in cybersecurity research generated using VOSviewer (Source: Lens Database; created using VOSviewer) (Lens, 2025; Van Eck & Waltman, 2022).

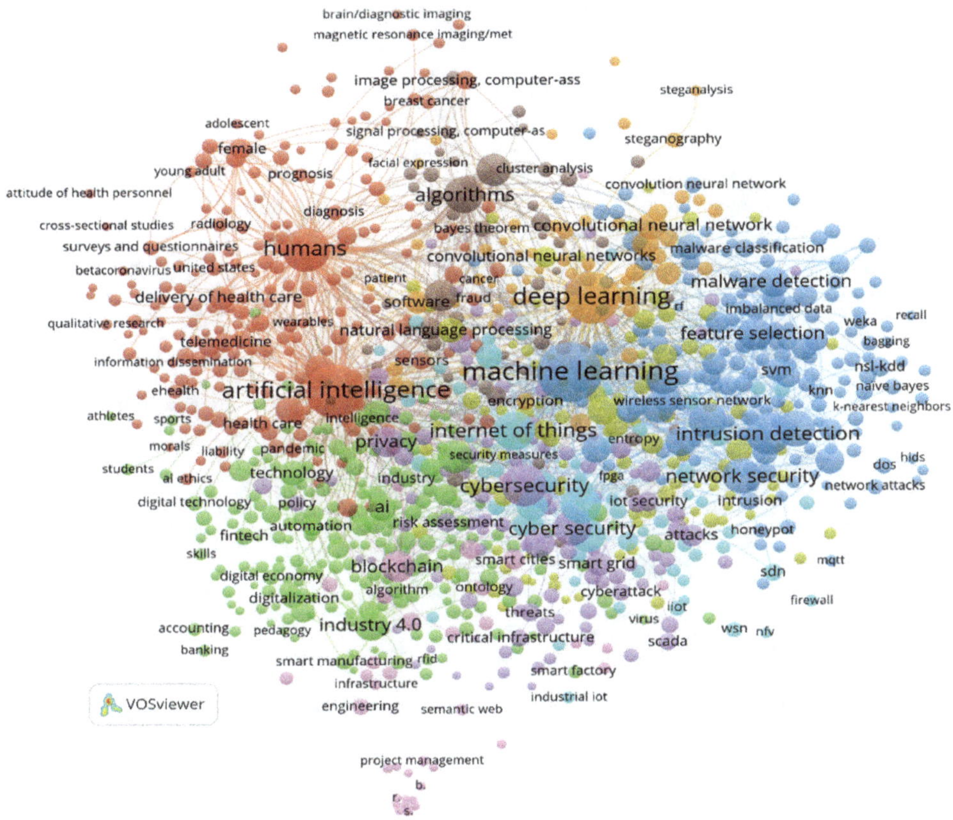

The visualization of the temporal overlay of the study and the emergence of the themes of the research during the years 2019-2023 is represented in Figure 3. The first work in 2019-2020 (blue nodes) was conducted on the basic security concerns, such as intrusion detection, malware classification, and encryption. It became more interdisciplinary (including such themes as blockchain, privacy, IoT security, and smart cities) in 2020-2021 (green nodes) and focused on integrating AI-based security products into the broader digital ecosystem. In the most recent area (2022-2023, yellow nodes), research has extended to healthcare and human-centered security and some areas of focus are beginning to appear, such as telemedicine, wearables, prognosis, image processing, and natural language processing. This shift, of course, is not provided by the technological progress only but also by the response to the demands of the society, i.e. in the COVID-19 years to the digital health security.

Figure 3. Overlay bibliometric keyword co-occurrence map of AI in cybersecurity research (2019–2023) generated using VOSviewer (Source: Lens Database; created using VOSviewer) (Lens, 2025; Van Eck & Waltman, 2022).

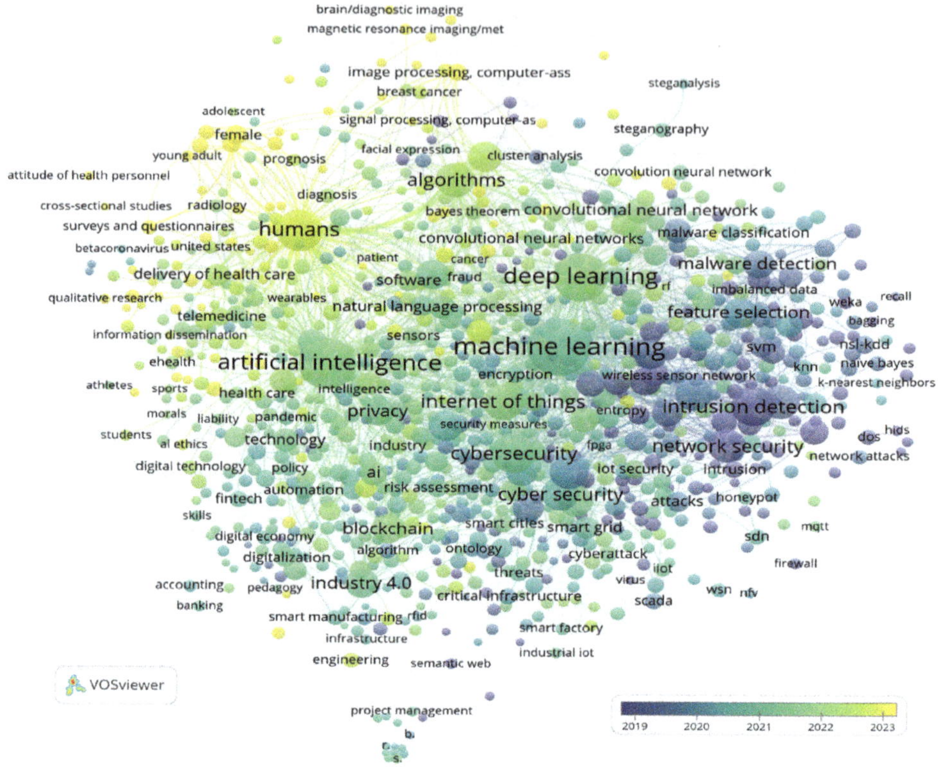

Besides these findings, the density visualization (Figure 4) also identifies the strength of the research in terms of themes. Their core revolves around machine learning, artificial intelligence, deep learning, intrusion detection, and network security and makes them the center of the AI-based cybersecurity. The most popular are the IoT, blockchain, big data analytics, industry 4.0 and cyber-physical systems, but the new ethical frontiers are explainable AI, digital twins, emotion recognition, and metaverse security. Such duality is an area of research that is cemented at its core and at the same time it extends towards new inter-disciplinary frontiers.

Figure 4. Density bibliometric map of keyword co-occurrence in AI and cybersecurity research generated using VOSviewer (Source: Lens Database; created using VOSviewer) (Lens, 2025; Van Eck & Waltman, 2022).

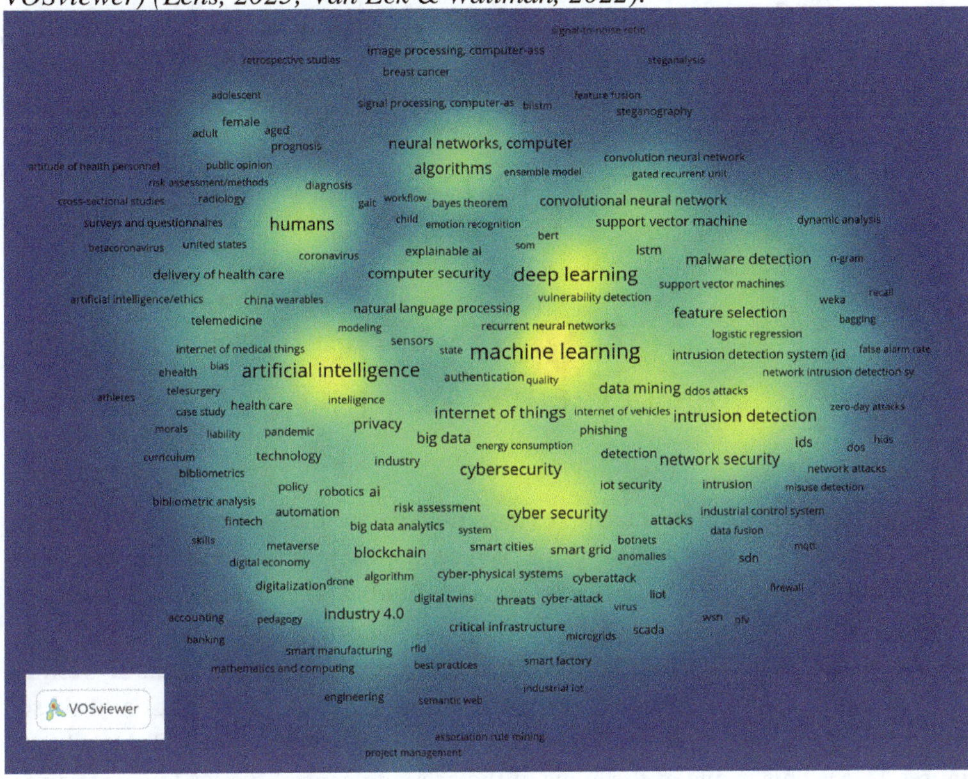

Finally, a visualization that is also a complementary one is the word cloud visualization (Figure 5), which identifies frequency-based salience of important words. Some of the most common terms in the size include machine learning, security, detection, artificial intelligence, intrusion, and classification, as they are the raw words in the discipline. The added keywords that encompass blockchain, IoT, privacy, neural networks, and big data will highlight how AI applications will be expanded to the broader cybersecurity environments. Meanwhile, the words that are no larger than phishing, adversarial attacks, digital forensics, smart grid, and Industry 4.0 suggest the future challenges and spheres of use, which denotes the dynamism and flexibility of the field.

Figure 5. Word cloud visualization of frequently occurring keywords in AI and cybersecurity research (Source: Lens Database) (Lens, 2025).

Collectively, these bibliometric reviews underscore the fact that AI in the area of cybersecurity has changed in terms of research periphery, to an area of global significance, and an interdisciplinary research field. The convergence of the conventional area of intrusion detection and network security and the expansion of the research to the healthcare, blockchain, IoT, and industrial systems can be seen in the quantitative data as the trends of publications, the global distribution of these, productivity of authors and institutions, and bibliometric mapping (Tables 1 - 4; Figures 1 - 5). This is one of the signs of the growing centrality of AI in reaction to the current cyber threats, and this is also the genesis of a new set of specialties that will herald the next wave of research in the field of critical study.

7. FUTURE DIRECTIONS AND RESEARCH GAPS

An artificial intelligence (AI) directive paired with quantum computing is bringing about a cybersecurity paradigm shift by offering an unprecedented amount of computer processing power to cryptanalysis and high-level cryptography protocol design (Devadas & T, 2025). Quantum machine learning allows analyzing a high dimensional data and training models with high speed with the help of quantum algorithms such as Quantum Support Vector Machines and Quantum Neural Networks that demonstrate better performance in the realm of real life threats. Nevertheless, the intersection of these efficient technologies leads to severe issues particularly in regards to the resilience of AI schemes to quantum-enabled adversarial assaults and urgent necessity of post-quantum cryptographic conventions, hence, exposing significant gaps in the research (Mohamed, 2025; Pineda et al., 2025). Concurrently with these tendencies, decentralized infrastructures of security, resistant to tampering, and based on AI and blockchain, are also in the process of integration. The cryptographic registry of blockchain and the application of AI-enhanced anomaly detection make the cyberspace security procedures more intense, transparent, and accessible in massive digital ecosystems (Saleh, 2024). However, there are still issues with such aspects as interoperability, scalability, and energy efficiency, which require interdisciplinary research on sustainable, secure models of next-generation cyber-physical systems (Saleh, 2024; Sinha et al., 2024).

Besides the technical horizon, there are also ethical and policy implications of AI use to the sphere of cybersecurity. The key problems are algorithmic bias, the data privacy, the absence of transparency in the decision-making process, and the uncertainties about the liabilities in case of the automated misjudgment (Radanliev, 2025). The aggravating nature of these concerns is reinforced by the black box nature of advanced artificial intelligence, such as deep neural networks, which diminishes explainability, trust and auditing the interventions in high stakes security contexts (Oloyede, 2024). Despite the fact that, new frameworks which can enable fairness, transparency, and inclusiveness in the adoption of AI are providing helpful insights, the harmonization of global regulation is still in its early stages. Thus, viable, responsible, and explainable AI, along with collaboration in global policy, is an urgent requirement in the responsible application (Camilleri, 2023; Radanliev, 2025; Kaur et al., 2023).

In the meantime, a rapidly evolving threat landscape provides sufficient opportunities of innovation and new research prospects. Explainable AI Federated learning helps in the decentralized and privacy-aware threat intelligence that is critical in addressing the regulatory compliance and data sovereignty issues (Jada & Mayayise, 2023). One of the research directions which have gained a central spot of interest is adversarial machine learning that examines offensive and defensive application of AI in digital ecosystems. AI-based security orchestration, automation, and response (SOAR) platforms also simplify adaptive defense but once again, it has new challenges of false positives, accountability and operational transparency (Jada & Mayayise, 2023; Camilleri, 2023). The new directions of quantum-enhanced cryptanalysis and blockchain-based digital identity management will probably alter the cybersecurity paradigms but are subjected to the existing constraints in the model verification and verification under adversarial conditions. Furthermore, the exploration of the sustainable and resource efficient AI models according to the demands of the environmental and social governance (ESG) proves to be a more noteworthy part of the studies. A way out of these compound problems should be interdisciplinary, socio-technical in the sense that it allows full implementation of the transformational capabilities of AI in cybersecurity (Pineda et al., 2025; Mohamed, 2025; Devadas and T, 2025).

8. CONCLUSION

AI application to cybersecurity is a paradigm shift of reactive, unintelligent defense measures to proactive, smart systems that can predict and counteract advanced offenses in an ever-more connected digital environment. This chapter has clarified the underlying principles of AI- the cognitive simulation of AI by ML, DL, NLP, and expert systems, and the integration with the main tenets of cybersecurity as represented by the CIA triad. Going beyond the constraints of signature-based practices, AI facilitates real-time anomaly detection, behavioral analytics and automated response mechanisms as demonstrated by high-accuracy uses in intrusion detection (e.g. 96.2% via hybrid models), malware classification, phishing mitigation, and predictive forecasting with LSTM networks. These breakthroughs do not only improve the effectiveness of detection, but also make scalable solutions applicable to a wide range of areas, such as enterprise threat intelligence (150,000 threats per minute) to national security systems that can protect critical infrastructure such as power grids and transportation systems.

The practical practice of case studies also supports the transformative power of AI: in finance, AI supports fraud detection with anomaly detection in transaction activity; in healthcare, ML and generative AI ensure the security of electronic records without violating privacy laws; in smart cities and IoT, digital twins and explainable AI simulate vulnerability to avert cascading failures; and in high-level ecosystems, dependency-based risk measurements reduce the heterogeneity of devices. Nevertheless, these advantages are marred by recurrent issues, such as algorithm bias (false positive) caused by black box implementations, loss of trust in the black box through adversarial attacks (data poisoning), and operational costs, such as high learning rates and degradation of privacy. The evolution of AI should be informed by ethical requirements, such as fairness, transparency, accountability, and inclusivity, especially since it has a dual-use character that gives defenders and attackers equal power.

In the future, it is necessary to fill such gaps in research: to develop quantum-AI hybrids to support post-quantum cryptography, blockchain-AI fusions to support decentralized integrity, federated learning to support privacy-preserving intelligence, address adversarial robustness by improving verification, and have global policies on ethical AI governance in line with ESG principles. With the development of cyber threats by intelligent adversaries, an interdisciplinary approach with technologists, policymakers, ethicists, and domain specialists will be vital in order to use

AI agility to build resilient and fair digital societies. Finally, judicious use of AI in cybersecurity is not only strengthening defenses, but also transforming trust in the hyperconnected world in which it guarantees sustainability in innovation amid the growing risks. Researchers should focus on these frontiers in future studies in order to achieve the full potential of AI as a protector of digital sovereignty.

REFERENCES

Abidde, W. N., Eyidia, N., & Eme, E. S. J. (2023). CIA Triad: A review of the confidentiality, integrity and availability of data in a system of connected networks. *International Research Journal of Modernization in Engineering Technology and Science*, *7*(3), 12824–12828. https://www.irjmets.com/uploadedfiles/paper/issue_3_march_2025/68704/final/fin_irjmets1744339796.pdf

Achuthan, K., Ramanathan, S., Srinivas, S., & Raman, R. (2024). Advancing cyber-security and privacy with artificial intelligence: Current trends and future research directions. *Frontiers in Big Data*, *7*, 1497535. Advance online publication. DOI: 10.3389/fdata.2024.1497535 PMID: 39703783

Admass, W. S., Munaye, Y. Y., & Diro, A. A. (2023). Cyber security: State of the art, challenges and future directions. *Cyber Security and Applications*, *2*, 100031. DOI: 10.1016/j.csa.2023.100031

Aljohani, A. A. (2025). *Integrating AI-Driven predictive models for enhanced cyber threat detection and mitigation*. https://spast.org/ojspath/article/view/5347

Alkhalil, Z., Hewage, C., Nawaf, L., & Khan, I. (2021). Phishing Attacks: A recent comprehensive study and a new anatomy. *Frontiers of Computer Science*, *3*, 563060. Advance online publication. DOI: 10.3389/fcomp.2021.563060

Ang, T. L., Choolani, M., See, K. C., & Poh, K. K. (2023). The rise of artificial intelligence: Addressing the impact of large language models such as ChatGPT on scientific publications. *Singapore Medical Journal*, *64*(4), 219–221. DOI: 10.4103/singaporemedj.SMJ-2023-055 PMID: 37006087

Ansari, M. F., Sharma, P. K., & Dash, B. (2022). Prevention of phishing attacks using AI-Based cybersecurity awareness training. *International Journal of Smart Sensor and Adhoc Network*, 61–72. https://doi.org/DOI: 10.47893/IJSSAN.2022.1221

Arnob, A. K. B., Chowdhury, N. R. R., Chaiti, N. N. A., Saha, N. S., & Roy, N. A. (2025). A comprehensive systematic review of intrusiondetection systems: emerging techniques,challenges, and future research directions. *Journal of Edge Computing*. https://doi.org/DOI: 10.55056/jec.885

Azeem, M., Khan, D., Iftikhar, S., Bawazeer, S., & Alzahrani, M. (2023). Analyzing and comparing the effectiveness of malware detection: A study of machine learning approaches. *Heliyon*, *10*(1), e23574. DOI: 10.1016/j.heliyon.2023.e23574 PMID: 38187275

Bhandari, R. (2025). AI and Cybersecurity: Opportunities, challenges, and governance. *EDPACS*, 1–9. https://doi.org/DOI: 10.1080/07366981.2025.2544363

Camilleri, M. A. (2023). Artificial intelligence governance: Ethical considerations and implications for social responsibility. *Expert Systems: International Journal of Knowledge Engineering and Neural Networks*, *41*(7), e13406. Advance online publication. DOI: 10.1111/exsy.13406

Craigen, D., Diakun-Thibault, N., & Purse, R. (2014). Defining cybersecurity. *Technology Innovation Management Review*, *4*(10), 13–21. DOI: 10.22215/timreview/835

Devadas, R. M., & T, S. (2025). Quantum Machine Learning: A Comprehensive Review of Integrating AI with Quantum Computing for Computational Advancements. *MethodsX*, *14*, 103318. DOI: 10.1016/j.mex.2025.103318 PMID: 40331033

Dwivedi, Y. K., Hughes, L., Ismagilova, E., Aarts, G., Coombs, C., Crick, T., Duan, Y., Dwivedi, R., Edwards, J., Eirug, A., Galanos, V., Ilavarasan, P. V., Janssen, M., Jones, P., Kar, A. K., Kizgin, H., Kronemann, B., Lal, B., Lucini, B., & Williams, M. D. (2019). Artificial Intelligence (AI): Multidisciplinary perspectives on emerging challenges, opportunities, and agenda for research, practice and policy. *International Journal of Information Management*, *57*, 101994. DOI: 10.1016/j.ijinfomgt.2019.08.002

Folorunso, N. A., Adewumi, N. T., Adewa, N. A., Okonkwo, N. R., & Olawumi, N. T. N. (2024). Impact of AI on cybersecurity and security compliance. *Global Journal of Engineering and Technology Advances*, *21*(1), 167–184. DOI: 10.30574/gjeta.2024.21.1.0193

G, R. K. C. (2025). The Strategic role of AI in enhancing national cybersecurity frameworks. *Asian Journal of Research in Computer Science, 18*(6), 378–389. https://doi.org/DOI: 10.9734/ajrcos/2025/v18i6708

Ighofiomoni, M. O., Ojerinde, J. S., Iqmat, O., Issah, P. P., Similoluwa, A. O., Oluwaseun, O., David, E. T., Idowu, A., Emmanuel, I. M., & Chinonyerem, C. A. (2025). Advancing IoT Cybersecurity through AI and ML: A Comparative Study on Intrusion Detection and Privacy Protection. *Asian Journal of Advanced Research and Reports*, *19*(8), 159–174. DOI: 10.9734/ajarr/2025/v19i81122

Jada, I., & Mayayise, T. O. (2023). The impact of artificial intelligence on organisational cyber security: An outcome of a systematic literature review. *Data and Information Management*, *8*(2), 100063. DOI: 10.1016/j.dim.2023.100063

Kaur, R., Gabrijelčič, D., & Klobučar, T. (2023). Artificial intelligence for cybersecurity: Literature review and future research directions. *Information Fusion*, *97*, 101804. DOI: 10.1016/j.inffus.2023.101804

Khan, M. M., Shah, N., Shaikh, N., Thabet, A., Alrabayah, T., & Belkhair, S. (2024). Towards secure and trusted AI in healthcare: A systematic review of emerging innovations and ethical challenges. *International Journal of Medical Informatics*, *195*, 105780. DOI: 10.1016/j.ijmedinf.2024.105780 PMID: 39753062

Kumar, N. B. H., Nuka, N. S. T., Malempati, N. M., Sriram, N. H. K., Mashetty, N. S., & Kannan, N. S. (2025). Big Data in Cybersecurity: Enhancing Threat Detection with AI and ML. *Metallurgical and Materials Engineering*, *31*(3), 12–20. DOI: 10.63278/1315

Kumar, R., Grover, N., Singh, R., Kathuria, S., Kumar, A., & Bansal, A. (2023). Imperative role of artificial intelligence and big data in finance and banking sector. *2022 International Conference on Sustainable Computing and Data Communication Systems (ICSCDS)*, 523–527. https://doi.org/DOI: 10.1109/ICSCDS56580.2023.10105062

Kwentoa, I. K. (2025). AI-Driven Threat Intelligence for Enterprise Cybersecurity. *Journal of Next-Generation Research 5.0*. https://doi.org/DOI: 10.70792/jngr5.0.v1i4.125

Lens, (2025). *Search results for "Artificial Intelligence (AI) in Cybersecurity"*. The Lens. Retrieved September 22, 2025, from https://www.lens.org/lens/search/scholar/list?q=(%22Artificial%20Intelligence%22%20OR%20%22AI%22%20OR%20%22Machine%20Learning%22%20OR%20%22Deep%20Learning%22%20OR%20%22Neural%20Networks%22)%20AND%20(%22Cybersecurity%22%20OR%20%22Cyber%20Security%22%20OR%20%22Information%20Security%22%20OR%20%22Network%20Security%22%20OR%20%22Intrusion%20Detection%22%20OR%20%22Malware%20Detection%22)&p=0&n=10&s=_score&d=%2B&f=false&e=false&l=en&authorField=author&dateFilterField=publishedYear&orderBy=%2B_score&presentation=false&preview=true&stemmed=true&useAuthorId=false

Madnick, B., Huang, K., & Madnick, S. (2023). The evolution of global cybersecurity norms in the digital age: A longitudinal study of the cybersecurity norm development process. *Information Security Journal a Global Perspective*, *33*(3), 204–225. DOI: 10.1080/19393555.2023.2201482

Mansur, M. A. (2025). National security and cyber defense in the rise of artificial super intelligence. *European Scientific Journal*, *21*(10), 116. DOI: 10.19044/esj.2025.v21n10p116

Mat, N. I. C., Jamil, N., Yusoff, Y., & Kiah, L. M. (2024). A systematic literature review on advanced persistent threat behaviors and its detection strategy. *Journal of Cybersecurity*, *10*(1), tyad023. Advance online publication. DOI: 10.1093/cybsec/tyad023

Mohamed, N. (2025). Cutting-edge advances in AI and ML for cybersecurity: A comprehensive review of emerging trends and future directions. *Cogent Business & Management*, *12*(1), 2518496. Advance online publication. DOI: 10.1080/23311975.2025.2518496

Muneer, S., Farooq, U., Athar, A., Raza, M. A., Ghazal, T. M., & Sakib, S. (2024). A Critical Review of Artificial intelligence based Approaches in Intrusion Detection: A Comprehensive analysis. *Journal of Engineering*, *2024*(1), 1–16. DOI: 10.1155/2024/3909173

Ofusori, L., Bokaba, T., & Mhlongo, S. (2024). Artificial intelligence in cybersecurity: A comprehensive review and future direction. *Applied Artificial Intelligence*, *38*(1), 2439609. Advance online publication. DOI: 10.1080/08839514.2024.2439609

Oloyede, J. (2024). Ethical Reflections on AI for Cybersecurity: Building trust. SSRN *Electronic Journal*. https://doi.org/DOI: 10.2139/ssrn.4733563

Pineda, V. G., Valencia-Arias, A., Giraldo, F. E. L., & Zapata-Ochoa, E. A. (2025). Integrating artificial intelligence and quantum computing: A systematic literature review of features and applications. *International Journal of Cognitive Computing in Engineering*. https://doi.org/DOI: 10.1016/j.ijcce.2025.08.002

Qurashi, S. N., Sobia, F., Hetany, W. A., & Sultan, H. (2025). *Enhancing cybersecurity defenses in healthcare using AI: A pivotal role in fortifying digital health infrastructure*. Deleted Journal., DOI: 10.47852/bonviewMEDIN52024121

Rabiu, S. M., Aminu, B. K., & Zubairu, D. A. (2025). AI-Driven Network Intrusion Detection Systems: A systematic review of hybrid models, Zero-Day attack mitigation, and emerging challenges in cybersecurity. *International Journal of Computer Applications*, *187*(8), 27–33. DOI: 10.5120/ijca2025925016

Radanliev, P. (2025). AI Ethics: Integrating transparency, fairness, and privacy in AI development. *Applied Artificial Intelligence*, *39*(1), 2463722. Advance online publication. DOI: 10.1080/08839514.2025.2463722

Radanliev, P., De Roure, D., Maple, C., Nurse, J. R. C., Nicolescu, R., & Ani, U. (2024). AI security and cyber risk in IoT systems. *Frontiers in Big Data*, *7*, 1402745. Advance online publication. DOI: 10.3389/fdata.2024.1402745 PMID: 39449740

Rahman, M. M., Dhakal, K., Gony, N. M. D., Sd, M. K. S., & Rahman, M. M. D. (2025). AI integration in cybersecurity software: Threat detection and response. *International Journal of Innovative Research and Scientific Studies*, *8*(3), 3907–3921. DOI: 10.53894/ijirss.v8i3.7403

Rashid, A. B., & Kausik, M. K. (2024). AI Revolutionizing Industries Worldwide: A comprehensive overview of its diverse applications. *Hybrid Advances*, *7*, 100277. DOI: 10.1016/j.hybadv.2024.100277

Roshanaei, M., Khan, M. R., & Sylvester, N. N. (2024). Navigating AI cybersecurity: Evolving landscape and challenges. *Journal of Intelligent Learning Systems and Applications*, *16*(03), 155–174. DOI: 10.4236/jilsa.2024.163010

Saleh, A. M. S. (2024). Blockchain for secure and decentralized artificial intelligence in cybersecurity: A comprehensive review. *Blockchain Research and Applications*, *5*(3), 100193. DOI: 10.1016/j.bcra.2024.100193

Sankaramma, T. S. (2025). AI-Driven Phishing Detection: Advanced machine learning strategies for identifying malicious websites. *International Journal of Science Engineering and Technology*, *13*(2), 1–5. DOI: 10.61463/ijset.vol.13.issue2.267

Sinha, S. K., Modak, S. K. S., Tyagi, P. K., & Azad, C. (2024). Enhancing Cybersecurity with Blockchain: A Decentralized Approach to Securing Digital Infrastructure. *ACM*, 1–6. https://doi.org/DOI: 10.1145/3745812.3745846

Sowmya, T., & Anita, E. M. (2023). A comprehensive review of AI based intrusion detection system. *Measurement. Sensors*, *28*, 100827. DOI: 10.1016/j.measen.2023.100827

Van Eck, N. J., & Waltman, L. (2022). *VOSviewer* manual (Version 1.6.18). Leiden University, CWTS. Retrieved from https://www.vosviewer.com/documentation/Manual_VOSviewer_1.6.18.pdf

Vempati, N. S. (2024). Securing Smart Cities: A Cybersecurity perspective on integrating IoT, AI, and machine learning for digital twin creation. *Deleted Journal*, *20*(5s), 2817–2827. DOI: 10.52783/jes.3052

Virk, A., Alasmari, S., Patel, D., & Allison, K. (2025). Digital Health Policy and Cybersecurity Regulations regarding artificial intelligence (AI) implementation in healthcare. *Cureus*. Advance online publication. DOI: 10.7759/cureus.80676 PMID: 40236368

Vulpe, S., Rughini , R., urcanu, D., & Rosner, D. (2024). AI and cybersecurity: A risk society perspective. *Frontiers of Computer Science*, *6*, 1462250. Advance online publication. DOI: 10.3389/fcomp.2024.1462250

ADDITIONAL READINGS

Ansari, M. F., Dash, B., Sharma, P., & Yathiraju, N. (2022). The Impact and Limitations of Artificial intelligence in Cybersecurity: A literature review. *International Journal of Advanced Research in Computer and Communication Engineering, 11*(9). Advance online publication. DOI: 10.17148/IJARCCE.2022.11912

Capuano, N., Fenza, G., Loia, V., & Stanzione, C. (2022). Explainable Artificial Intelligence in CyberSecurity: A survey. *IEEE Access : Practical Innovations, Open Solutions, 10*, 93575–93600. DOI: 10.1109/ACCESS.2022.3204171

Jawhar, S., Miller, J., & Bitar, Z. (2024). AI-Based Cybersecurity Policies and Procedures. *2024 IEEE 3rd International Conference on AI in Cybersecurity (ICAIC)*, 1–5. https://doi.org/DOI: 10.1109/ICAIC60265.2024.10433845

Li, J. (2018). Cyber security meets artificial intelligence: A survey. *Frontiers of Information Technology & Electronic Engineering, 19*(12), 1462–1474. DOI: 10.1631/FITEE.1800573

Lier, S. K., Eppers, T. M., Gerlach, J., Müller, P., & Breitner, M. H. (2025). An iterative five-phase process model to successfully implement AI for cybersecurity in a corporate environment. *Electronic Markets, 35*(1), 56. Advance online publication. DOI: 10.1007/s12525-025-00802-x

Rana, M. (2025). Impact of Blockchain and Big data on Global Economy. *Journal of Computer Science and Technology Studies*. https://doi.org/DOI: 10.32996/jcsts

Salem, A. H., Azzam, S. M., Emam, O. E., & Abohany, A. A. (2024). Advancing cybersecurity: A comprehensive review of AI-driven detection techniques. *Journal of Big Data, 11*(1), 105. Advance online publication. DOI: 10.1186/s40537-024-00957-y

KEY TERMS AND DEFINITIONS

Artificial Intelligence (AI): The simulation of human intelligence processes by machines to perform tasks like reasoning, learning, and decision-making.

Blockchain: A decentralized and secure digital ledger that records transactions in a transparent and tamper-proof manner.

Cybersecurity: The practice of protecting computer systems, networks, and data from digital attacks, unauthorized access, or damage.

Internet of Things (IoT): A network of interconnected physical devices that collect, share, and act on data over the Internet.

Intrusion Detection: The process of monitoring systems or networks to identify unauthorized access or malicious activities.

Machine Learning (ML): A subset of AI that enables systems to automatically learn and improve from data without explicit programming.

Threat Detection: The identification and analysis of potential security risks or malicious behaviors within digital environments.

Chapter 3
AI-Driven Threat Detection and Prevention: Enhancing Cybersecurity with Machine Learning and Predictive Intelligence

Tarun Kumar Vashishth
https://orcid.org/0000-0001-9916-9575
IIMT University, Meerut, India

Vikas Sharma
https://orcid.org/0000-0001-8173-4548
SRM Institute of Science and Technology, India

Sangeeta Sharma
IAMR College, Meerut, India

Mukesh Kumar Sharma
https://orcid.org/0000-0003-3071-5931
Chaudhary Charan Singh University, Meerut, India

Rajeev Sharma
https://orcid.org/0000-0002-3354-558X
IIMT Engineering College, Meerut, India

Sachin Chaudhary
https://orcid.org/0000-0002-8415-0043
IIMT University, Meerut, India

Aarushi Vashishth
https://orcid.org/0009-0006-0895-1208
Ajay Kumar Garg Engineering College, India

ABSTRACT

The rapid changes in the cyber threat landscape in the digital age have changed the design of security mechanisms to support proactive and adaptive security capabilities that can detect, predict, and respond to attacks in real time. This chapter discusses the potential of integrating Artificial Intelligence (AI), Machine Learning (ML), and Predictive Intelligence for cybersecurity through proactive threat detection and

DOI: 10.4018/979-8-3373-2252-0.ch003

prevention. The chapter covers how AI-based predictive models can analyze vast and complex (and rich) data and identify hidden/novel attack patters, detect anomalies for faster incident response, and features supervised, unsupervised, and deep learning models for intrusion detection, malware analysis, and phishing prevention as well as predictive intelligence to help prevent zero-day attacks and other new avenues of security threats. Examples of real-world applications and case studies show how AI-powered solutions can dramatically cut down false-positives, leap-frog situational awareness, and increase resiliency and preparedness for an organization.

1. INTRODUCTION

The emergence of digital transformation, cloud adoption, and hyper-connected ecosystems has created an exponentially expanding threat landscape and cybersecurity has only advanced to become the most alarming challenge for society today. Limited traditional security mechanisms, which are contingent on static rules and signatures detection, and reactive defense safeguards, are no longer adequate to combat the sophistication of modern cyberattacks such as repossession mitigated by advanced persistent threats (APTs), ransomware, and AI-driven attacks. AI (Artificial Intelligence) and ML (Machine Learning) are trending technologies that offer transformational value. They have the ability today to transform threat detection and prevention altogether (Samuel, 2024). AI-based applications on the other hand are able to interpret all earthly standardised or unstandardised data in their path and readout where patterns exist, deviations of standard model and model inputs may signify possible and predicted attack vectors, as well as automate real time responses which are simply not feasible or practicable with human thinking power on a base level. Shifting discussion of defensive cybersecurity capabilities from reactive to proactive and predictive defense and cybersecurity measures can lead to increased accuracy, lower false-positive rates, better response times, and ultimately better protection of the digital infrastructures. This chapter is to provide a context for how AI and predictive intelligence are redefining the foundations of cybersecurity, illustrate examples of operationalization in major industries, and discuss some keys to the future of cybersecurity technology and changes (Mahmud et al., 2025).

1.1 Background of Cybersecurity Challenges in the Digital Era

Though organizational capacity in terms of infrastructure, capability, development, and resources for cybersecurity have and will all evolve with the digital era providing ontological and epistemic connectivity to the unknown corners of the digital world in both large- and small-way. The emergence of mobile, cloud computing and IoT technologies - connected to 5G technology - all increase the attack area. Cybercriminals and hacktivists have an increasing number of attack vectors to exploit digital infrastructures through IoT devices, mobile devices and would-be victims utilizing less trusted digital connections. Outdated perimeter-based security measures alone are insufficient, as modern threats can often penetrate traditional firewall and signature-based systems. Through various advanced attack vectors, such as advanced persistent threats (APTs), ransomware campaigns, distributed denial-of-service (DDoS) attacks, and phishing efforts, today's modern threats are simply becoming harder to identify and manage. Also, the dimension of seeing what measure of the quantity of data, which is created in our digital ecosystems effectively, rendered proper ruling identified rule framework, almost impossible. Organizations have got to represent the other cyber area issues to clear themselves against in an effective manner, i.e., enemies in insider threats, possibly not enemies, or state-sponsored militant cyber warfare, may have confusing effects upon defence options, though being followed or aware (Vashishth et al., 2024). Considering the ever-changing and ever-advancing influences of today's threats as a new cipher in the logic tellers on this subject will require, that obviously, means must be initiated of intelligent, adaptive, and predicative means of securing poses and permutations of attack risks, whether known or unknown. Inherent in the above concept is that industries effective AI intuitive programs, it becomes an absolute necessity where both automated factor interventions in the internet arena, fulfilling NCR, where changes in theft and fraud area can usefully be implemented and possibly incorporated in some factor format for the more advanced ongoing protection and face fact of online feasible transactions additionally through also instant predictive analysis intelligent reaction, for the better protection of technologies, digital exchanges, confronted with also lesser friction by such as identity theft, also online fraud - and also to enable trust in users (Gupta & Vashishth, 2024).

1.2 Limitations of Traditional Security Mechanisms

Traditional security implementations (firewalls, antivirus tools, and rule-based intrusion detection systems) have served as the backbone of digital security for years, but their limitations are starting to surface in an increasingly complex cyber environment. One of the most significant weaknesses is that they rely on static, signature-based detection to accomplish detection. Specifically, they depend upon previously defined patterns of attack which means that any new or unknown attack or (variation) of malware will circumvent detection until such time as the signatures are supported. This creates a significant window of exposure in particular when zero-day attacks are sponsored or polymorphic malware attacks that change too frequently for signature-based data bases to react adequately. Another limitation is that traditional security implementations have a reactive quality. Generally, they are able to discover and alleviate threats after they are initiated (or after event logs indicate suspicious activity). This is not a great amount of exposure; however, the time frames existent between attack and reaction could cause damage to systems, loss of data, and bait prohibitively expensive periods of down time until mitigation can take place. Additionally, it is a true challenge in Security Operations Center (SOC) spaces to address alert fatigue. Traditional security implementations create innumerable alerts; however, many are false alerts. SOC analysts spend a good amount of their time triaging alerts that are entirely irrelevant to the security of the environment and lack of adequate resources to address the actual threat models. This inefficiency is a barrier to incident response and permits hundreds of attack vectors to develop while cybersecurity analysts are busy dealing with false positives. Moreover, traditional approaches are constrained in scale for many organizations due to the hybrid and distributed environments in which they operate. The rise of cloud computing platforms, mobile ecosystems, and the Internet of Things has fostered a hybrid, heterogeneous attack surface which rule-based approaches could not adequately negotiate. More importantly, on a strategic level, traditional mechanisms were not always proactive; they did not prognosticate or anticipate the emerging threats nor were they capable of neutralizing potential vulnerabilities prior to their attack by the cyber adversary (Hussain et al., 2025).

1.3 Role of AI and Predictive Intelligence in Modern Cybersecurity

Artificial Intelligence (AI) and Predictive Intelligence are changing the way companies defend themselves against become increasingly sophisticated cyber-attacks. In contrast to convention systems that depend simply on static signatures and pre-determined rules, AI-based security solutions utilize machine learning (ML), deep learning, and advanced analytics to learn from trillions of past and current data trails. It can pick up known threats and see unknown threats - at an accuracy level never experienced before. For example, machine learning models can identify atypical login attempts, the lateral movements in a network, or unusually large files sent to unknown IP or user accounts, which are subtle changes that signature-based systems won't pick up. Based on continuous evaluation of the amassed evidence by identifying user behaviours that deviate from the norm, the patterns, systems, and entity behaviours, will transition from detection that is reactive to identification that is proactive. When paired with predictive intelligence, you can actually dis-invent emerging as threats before they actually become attacks. As AI uses historical and current threat intelligence feeds, along with behaviour analytics and contextual data based on global attack trends, it will begin to model for future attacks, zero-day exploits, and rapidly evolving attack vectors including ransomware variants.

2. FOUNDATIONS OF AI AND MACHINE LEARNING IN CYBERSECURITY

AI and machine learning are predicated on the fact that they can turn unrefined data into intelligence that can strengthen defences against the persistent evolution of cyber threats. AI endows systems with human-like decision making, and machine learning allows systems to learn and adjust with new experiences and information. In cybersecurity, AI and machine learning are applied to explain changes or anomalies, identify labels of malicious activity, and automate incident response faster and more accurately than traditional response models. Each machine learning approach—supervised, unsupervised, reinforcement, and deep learning—equips models to solve disparate problems in cybersecurity, such as the identification of phishing attacks or the prediction of zero-day attacks. The performance of AI/ML systems depend on the pool of data, and these data sources may include network logs, intrusion datasets, and threat intelligence feeds. AI and ML represent the foundation of next-generation cybersecurity frameworks that move organizations from a reactive defence posture, to a proactive, adaptive, and predictive form of security. Figure 1 depicts the block architecture of AI in cybersecurity which displays the flow of information being taken from input, AI-based threat detection, predictive analysis, and timely automated response systems (Prince et al., 2024).

Figure 1. Block Architecture of AI in Cybersecurity

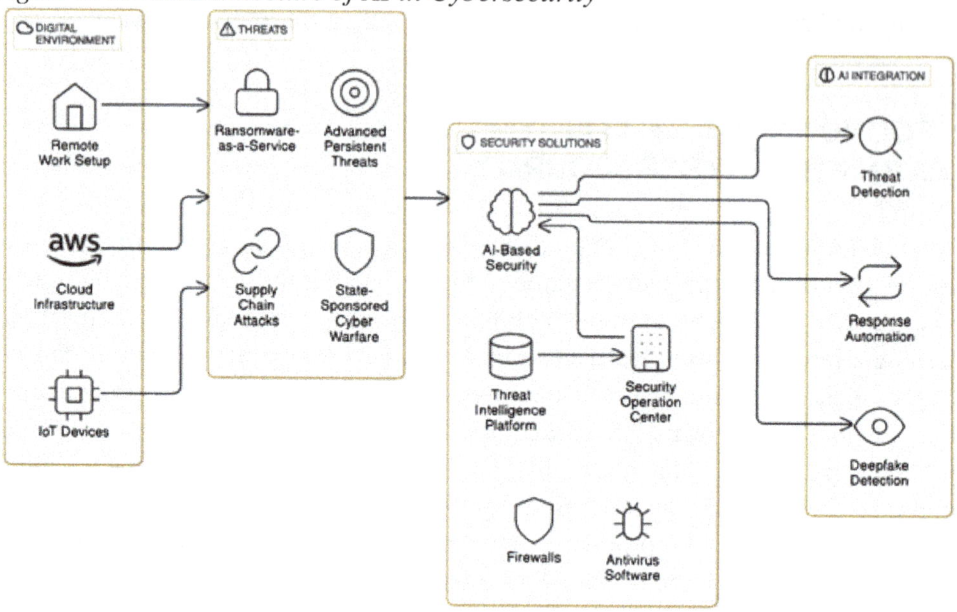

2.1 Overview of Artificial Intelligence and Machine Learning Concepts

Artificial Intelligence (AI), also known as AI, is the field of science that is focused on the construction of systems that perform tasks that normally require human intelligence, including reasoning, decision-making, and problem-solving. Machine learning (ML), a subdiscipline of AI, is specifically concerned with building algorithms that allow machines to learn regarding and improve also automatically from experience without being expressly programmed. Within cybersecurity, AI and ML provide organizations with effective means to analyze high volumes of network traffic, log files, user behaviour data, and threat intelligence data to help identify irregularities and predict possible attacks. ML models can be trained on historical data to distinguish between malicious versus benign activities. More sophisticated learning approaches, such as deep learning, provide an excellent tool that uses high-dimensional data to identify meaningful patterns, such as detecting malware variants or advanced persistent threat (APT) categories of attacks. In a similar manner, natural language processing (NLP) systems provide a great way to derive useful information from unstructured data, such as threat briefs, reports, or dark web forum discussions. At the same time, reinforcement learning can be developed as adaptive defences that learn the best series of responses through continual interaction to an evolving range of threats. Thus, all these concepts combined and applied to AI cybersecurity solutions create far greater than a rigid, rule-based capability that is aware of only limited, established rules-based conditions, but instead intelligent systems that can explore new behaviours and learn to detect, respond to, and even anticipate intelligent cyber-attacks in real time (Vashishth et al., 2024).

2.2 Relevance of AI to Threat Detection and Prevention

As cyberattacks continue to grow more sophisticated, more prolific, and more frequent, the relevance of Artificial Intelligence (AI) to threat detection, and prevention, continues to grow as defenders cannot keep up with threats using traditional security measures. Traditional security measures like signature-based detection or the use of static rules are very effective only for known threats. They will fail or be circumvented if attackers utilize polymorphic malware, zero-day exploits, or advanced persistent threats (APTs) where the attack is changing to evade detection. AI provides defenders with an adaptive and dynamic method of defense that detects both known and unknown threats while they are happening. AI-based technologies are powered by machine learning algorithms, anomaly detection models, and deep-learning networks that can digest and analyze heterogeneous multi-terabyte data from various sources such as firewalls, intrusion detection systems (IDS), logs, endpoints, cloud service systems, and Internet of Things (IoT) devices. Such analysis allows defenders to have very high levels of situational awareness. AI can also quantify each user or network's slight deviations from usual behavior, link attack campaigns with each other across different attack vectors and identify attack patterns that may be disguised or undetectable by human analysts or static tools. In prevention, the greatest benefit of AI is in its ability to automate and to provide predictive intelligence so that security systems may not only respond to an active attack but also be capable of detecting, anticipating, and neutralizing such a threat before it happens. For example, User and entity behavior analytics (UEBA) can establish baseline behaviours related to users and devices, and detect anomalies, such as strange login attempts, or the size of data transfer that may indicate insider threats or compromised accounts. AI-based malware detection solutions can leverage deep learning abilities to detect and classify files as malicious, including assisting in detection when no signatures are available for comparison. Similarly, AI is making Security Orchestration, Automation, and Response (SOAR) platforms smart, meaning it can automate alerts, isolating infected endpoints, deploying patches or half a dozen other tasks associated with triaging alerts and expanding the time frame an attack can be exploited. Less importantly, AI is helping to enhance accuracy and efficiency, thus significantly reducing false-positive alerts – one of the biggest limitations of traditional systems - consequently enabling human analysts to focus on high- priority threats, rather than issuing meaningless alerts about low-priority or benign issues (Gupta et al., 2024).

2.3 Types of Learning

Machine Learning (ML), as a major sub-set of Artificial Intelligence (AI), is being used in cybersecurity through the various learning paradigms each with their own characteristics, capabilities, and strengths when detecting and preventing cyber threats.

1. **Supervised Learning:** One of the most prevalent machine learning approaches to cybersecurity is supervised learning, which takes labelled data and trains a model to represent behaviours as either malicious or benign. By labelling previously harvested data with examples both of attacks and normal activity, the system learns to differentiate between multiple capabilities of cyber threats, such as distinguishing a phishing email to a malware attack, as well as a denial-of-service attempt, through unknown or new attacks as in the case of zero-day exploits. This type of approach has endured particularly momentum for IDS and anti-spam, due to the ability to have high-prevailed accuracy when trained with enough data. However, supervised learning is often bound to the training samples only and will only defend against labelled information, meaning that examples of attacks known as zero-day exploits, are previous labelled training information.
2. **Unsupervised Learning:** It mitigates the limitations of supervised techniques by searching for hidden structures, patterns, or outliers across unlabelled data-sets. An example of where unsupervised learning works best is with anomaly detection for cyber-situational awareness, specifically, identifying behaviours that deviate from the standard or normal. For example, maybe a user regularly logs into their account during the work day, yet frantically tries to remotely login at midnight multiple times. An unsupervised model of learning may capture the behaviours, and determine that they are undesired behaviours, allowing unsupervised learning to effectively address insider threats with no defined label, be it an APT or some other type of unlabelled or ground-truth attack. Unsupervised learning can identify unknown, unseen, or novel attack behaviours, making an adaptive security systems critical.
3. **Reinforcement Learning:** It **uses** a model of learning that is similar to the human experience, one agent interacts with their environment and learns the best action based on whether the agent has received a positive or negative reward for taking the action correctly or incorrectly. In cybersecurity, RL is being used in the realm of adaptive intrusion prevention, automated incident response, and

dynamic firewall rules. RL can figure out the best methods of blocking malicious traffic and limiting the impact to legitimate users by learning through its own "experience" in real time or the real world. Because of the adaptive learning involved, many of the applications of RL can operate unsupervised in unknown situations while the adversarial behaviour may, for instance, adapt its attacks, such as bot nets and DDoS campaigns (Ijiga et al., 2024).

4. **Deep Learning:** A specific variety of machine learning, where multiple layers of neural networks are employed to analyse large scale, high dimensional and unstructured data. Deep learning is especially useful in cybersecurity areas such as recognising complex attack signatures which other types of algorithms are apt to miss. For example, CNNs are specifically designed to discover patterns in malware binaries, while RNN can easily detect attacks which are in progress in the sequential data such as network traffic log files. Deep learning can be enhanced with NLP so that any relevant insight can be readily obtained from other unstructured types of information, such as serendipitous blogs about security issues, or dark web forums or system logs, so that any new threats may be predicted. By discovering the important features of the data automatically, deep learning minimises human bias and increases the rate of success when attacking the ever-changing nature of threats. In particular, deep learning is strong in the identification of zero-day attacks, polymorphic malware, and/or minor anomalies in large datasets.

3. AI-DRIVEN THREAT DETECTION APPROACHES

Artificial Intelligence (AI) has now become an integral part of the traditional cyber security toolkit. It provides new ways of detecting, analyzing, and responding to threats as they arise geometries in real time. AI-based systems are not simply rule-based systems, or signature-based systems that depend on previously determined attack patterns. Rather, it is more adaptable, digestible, and predictive systems. While it relies on a myriad of data-driven analytics, AI also frequently relies on machine learning algorithms, neural networks and other configured processes to process and identify files and attacks like zero-day attacks, insider threats, APTs and polymorphic malware assumptions better than static, first-drafting tools known as signatures and heuristics. The main benefit of AI associated with cybersecurity is that it has the capacity to continuously learn from changing threat information, create an awareness of hidden contextual relationships, and constantly develop its repertoire of defensive measures.

3.1 Signature-Based vs. Behavior-Based Detection

Signature-based detection is an older and one of the most common methods in cybersecurity, and used primarily in typical antivirus, and intrusion detection systems. Signature-based detection relies on taking files, traffic, or other system activities to compare them against malicious signatures or patterns stored in a database, such as byte sequences or hash values stored of the malware. Signature-based detection is good for well-established threats; however, it does not work for zero-day attacks or samples of malware we have never seen before, because there are no signatures for these threats. Conversely, behaviour-based detection looks at the actions and patterns of individual applications, users, or processes/modifies filters based on identifiable actions rather than a static identifier. Using AI, behaviour-based detection models can identify very complex and evolving attack behaviours that are not logic based on static rules. This raises the accuracy of the detection model as well as improving on raw adaptability. Together, signature and behaviour detection using AI creates a hybrid detection method for a more improved balance of accuracy, adaptability, and efficiency. This hybrid detection model creates an even stronger defence against both well-known threats, and the new advanced cyber-attacks we have yet to see.

3.2 Anomaly Detection with Machine Learning Models

Anomaly detection is an important AI-based methodology for cybersecurity in that it seeks to recognize behaviours or events that vary from the established norm. While rule-based mechanisms only recognize patterns which are defined as malicious based on a signature, anomaly detection that uses machine learning (ML) creates a baseline of normal behavior of a user, network, or systems. For instance, if an employee regularly logs in from a location during work hours, but at midnight challenges the system to access data from a foreign country, the ML-based anomaly detection model will be able to classify this behavior as anomalous. Additionally, the use of clustering techniques, statistical modeling and deep learning allows AI algorithms to sift through large volumes of logs; transaction history; and user behaviours to identify underlying abnormal patterns.

3.3 Intrusion Detection and Intrusion Prevention Systems (IDS/IPS)

Intrusion Detection Systems (IDS) and Intrusion Prevention Systems (IPS) are important security tools used to monitor and protect information resources against intrusion attempts - either unauthorized access or harmful incidents. An IDS provides a primarily passive sense of monitoring on the information resource, reviewing network traffic, system activity logs, and application traits to determine suspicious activity and inform administrators of its occurrence. An IPS acts as an active monitor with the ability to take action after discovering non-desired activity by blocking unallowed network traffic, closing, or killing deemed harmful sessions and isolating compromised systems interactively. Traditionally, IDS/IPS used signature-based approaches to detection which had a limited effectuality against new incidents and emergent threats. Integrating AI allows IDS/IPS to learn from an event; AI typically leverages machine learning and deep learning algorithms to improve detection rates and reduce false positives. An example of AI-based IDS/IPS could detect unusual traffic behavior and lateral movement around a network. Additionally, AI can improve the response to intrusions through contextualization by not only noting that an intrusion has occurred but also attempting to determine what the attack might be. In applying AI, IDS and IPS can be more proactive, adaptive, and scalable making them much more effective in increasing resilience against modern cyberattacks in complicated, high-speed networks. Figure 2 illustrates the integration of Intrusion Detection Systems (IDS) and Intrusion Prevention Systems (IPS), which shows some of the improvements in real-time detection and automated response provided by analytics from AI.

Figure 2. Integration of IDS and IPS

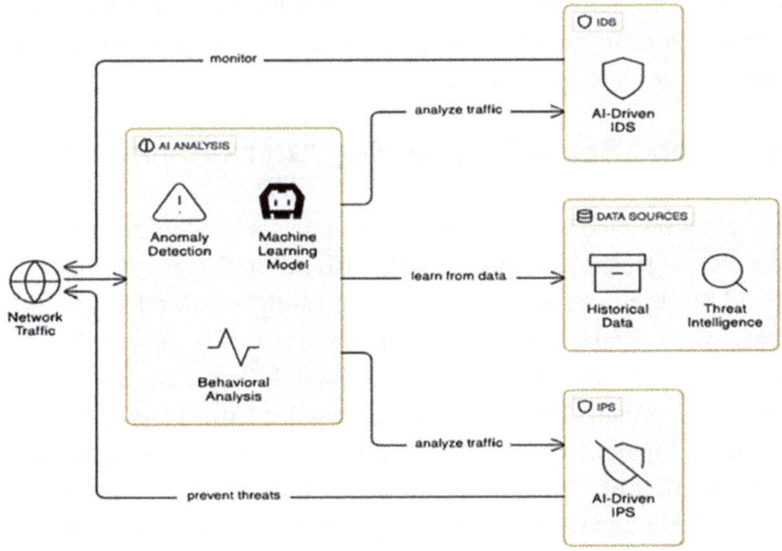

3.4 Malware and Ransomware Detection Using AI Models

Malware and ransomware rank as the top Cyber threats, offering unique capabilities of integrating data theft, service outages, and ransom payments to organizations. The typical signature detection is not able to keep up with the diverse range of threat actors creating malware variants and implementing obfuscation techniques. Unlike traditional methods that are limited to signature-based detection databases, AI-driven methods provide advantages of dynamic and adaptive defensive measures that rely on file, process, and network feature analysis. For ranger example, machine learning algorithms can check for system calls, APIs, or system structures to classify a program as malicious or benign. Deep learning capabilities can also evaluate large amounts of complex data like encrypted traffic or identify behaviours of polymorphic malware that changes after each execution. With regard to ransomware, ransomware detection can identify malicious behaviours and threats at the moment of the abnormal file access behaviours such as mass encryption or deletion of backups, preventing the "damage" that ransomware is designed to impose. Ransomware detection and malware forensics also benefit from AI advantages to cluster and categorize new strains of malware, allowing security analysts to better understand dove-tail malware threats. AI predictive analytics can provide higher levels of intelligence to cash out potential ransom campaigns by synthesizing data from global threat intelligence feeds. As a result, AI malware and ransomware detection capabilities can provide faster, accurate, more responsive, and predictive defense measures against one of the most serious forms of cyber-attack.

3.5 Phishing and Social Engineering Attack Prevention

Because phishing and social engineering attacks exploit human psychology instead of technology, they are particularly difficult to defend against and significantly expand phishing attack campaigns. A phishing attack may typically involve a fraudulent email, a fake web page, or impersonation to coerce the victim into divulging sensitive information, which may include login details or anything of monetary value. Generally, keyword blacklisting will not protect users from advanced phishing attack campaigns which often involve dynamic content, personalized content, and obfuscation of URLs while impeding traditional filtering measures. AI has a substantial role in developing phishing prevention measures as it uses Natural Language Processing (NLP), advanced learning skills, and computer vision models. NLP models assist in phishing prevention by analyzing the linguistic structure, tone, and intent of the emails to find affected content. For example, AI can find explicit instructions on URLs, subtle manipulations that are grammatically correct, urgency symbols or domain spoofing that people may not have noticed. Computer vision models can be trained to detect bogus web sites by examining the visual layout similarity of checked sites compared against legit portals. Likewise, supervised machine learning algorithms can be used to categorize questionable URLs having behavioural traits and structural elements. Furthermore, beyond that of content detection for purposes of fraudulent behavior, with the help of Artificial Intelligence, many awareness programs have applications directed towards providing real time training experiences or phish detection, detection remembrances made use of to assist users in realizing and avoiding a phish attempt. Remote defense technology and extensive user training techniques not only diminish the usefulness of attempting to pursue an act of phishing but subsequently develop that layer of human firewall used in profusion within the organization developing an additional layer of total security within the organization.

4. PREDICTIVE INTELLIGENCE FOR PROACTIVE CYBER DEFENSE

Predictive intelligence in cybersecurity is a major change from defence that reacts to security strategy that acts as an anticipation. Predictive intelligence differs from traditional methods in a further step; it is possible to predict the attack before it takes place. Traditional methods obtain knowledge only when the threat is developed.

4.1 Forecasting Emerging Threats and Zero-Day Exploits

The anticipation of emerging threats and the zero-day exploit is one of the best methods of use in the AI for the proactive defence of cyber. Traditional security instruments have readings of difficulty in exploiting zero-day vulnerability before the signature is available of the patch, since that they are only new exploits. AI and learning of the machine escape from this limitation giving itself an analysis of the system behaviour and the code situation, as well as of the anomalies in the context that can establish the probability of new exploits. The intelligence representatives process of separated nets of the NLP can cross an examination of forums on the dark net, communities of hackers and reports of intelligence of threats that show the current complies in the communities of the nefarious ones, so that they concern vectors of attack or vulnerability of unresolved software. The insights which appear from this analysis will enable the organizations to predict that there are the cyber-attacks before they occur. The analytics of machine learning like clustering, anomaly predictions and analytics when predicting will conclude into patterns referring to attack methods, then rather invent traffic patterns, an answer of corruption of privileges like methods to propagate the malware. The predications which result from the machine learning analytics will also help to gain benefits of the defender measures which helps to protect the enterprise. The types of responses can include anything such as prioritization of patches dependent on probability of vulnerability exploitation, hardening of those vulnerable systems, or efficient segmentation of network. Organizations can also leverage AI that can automatically simulate possible attack vectors on enterprise systems' digital twins to assist organizations in seeing exploitable vulnerabilities and remediating them in 'live action' scenarios. The primary benefit of forecasting is found in the mitigation of damage followed by the time it offers. Early warning flags allow defenders the opportunity to make fixes before a malicious actor can exploit vulnerabilities. The rise of cybercriminals leveraging automation and AI combined with an increasing need to forecast vulnerabilities related to emerging threats and zero-day exploits, will demand an ability to do so for strategic cyber defense thinking. Organizations that endorse a forecasting philosophy will defend themselves with a predictive shield that enables them to have resilience against both known and unknown attack vectors.

4.2 Behavioural Analytics and User Entity Behavior Analytics (UEBA)

Behavioural analytics, particularly through User and Entity Behavior Analytics (UEBA) is an innovative approach to identifying cyber threats by looking for deviations from baseline or normal patterns of behaviour. Where cybersecurity and security operations environments have relied on traditional rule-based detection systems that rely on known threats with pre-defined signatures, UEBA generates a "normal" baseline behaviour for users and systems through AI and Machine Learning. An employee may typically login during working hours, from a certain area, and perhaps work with a set of files. If suddenly that employee account is logging in overnight from an international IP address, or accessing or downloading large numbers of sensitive files, those actions could raise a concern. UEBA systems develop a usage model from structured logs, authentication logs, application-used logs, and network traffic logs, to create behaviour profiles for users and entities (servers or other devices, and applications) in the system. Then through machine learning, analysts look for minute deviations from normal usage that perhaps a human analyst might overlook; such as if an employee's behaviour is slightly becoming self-escalating privilege or detecting an insider threat where malicious activity blends into normal behaviour. UEBA is particularly strong against advanced persistent threats (APTs), internal fraud, or Account Take-Over (ATO) threats that are often invisible to standard monitoring controls. AI-enabled behaviour analytics also transcend detection, and can provide a predictive modelling capability. If UEBA is detecting anomalies across users, for example, it can create an analytical model to essentially predict a security breach before it occurs (Vashishth et al., 2025).

4.3 Threat Intelligence Platforms Enhanced by AI

AI-enabled Threat Intelligence Platforms (TIPs) are essential for proactive cyber defense and cyber threat intelligence as they aggregate, correlate, and contextualize cyber threat data from multiple dynamic sources all over the world. Traditionally, TIPs gather metadata and indicators of compromise (IoCs) in the form of IP addresses, malware signatures, or phishing domains. However, AI-enabled TIPs will analyze and contextualize these indicators into actionable intelligence applying machine learning (ML), natural language processing (NLP), and big data analytics (Patil, 2024). AI-enabled TIPs can assess threat reports, scrape hacker forums, and analyze malware repositories to determine and label an organization's emerging campaigns, and attack vectors. AI-enabled TIPs can assess risks and apply instant automation by correlating threat data with the telemetry of an organization, indicating risk and relevant prioritization in real-time. For example, if a new strain of ransomware is discovered targeting financial institutions all over the world, the TIP can search if similar attributes exist in the companies' infrastructure, and provide recommendations for patching or blocking. TIPs can also offer predictive modeling, aiding organizations in comprehending how attackers may strategically target them themselves, and what industries or regions may be next to garner future interest. Furthermore, AI gives TIPs the capacity to process terabytes of threat data applicable to threat intelligence or indicators of compromise (IoCs), while also lessening the noise data (Islam, et al., 2024).

4.4 Proactive Incident Response and Automated Mitigation

In the case of proactively responding to incidents and mitigating via automated means we are seeing the advent of a new era of cybersecurity defense where AI and automation allow organizations to contain and mitigate and remediate threats, all in real-time. Instead of the incident response models we have today where humans respond after an attack is detected, proactive incident response using AI encompasses predictive analytics and automated containment and remediation to be able to foresee and respond and remediate incidents in a moment's notice. This ability radically decreases the mean time to detect (MTTD) and mean time to respond (MTTR), which remain relevant measures for all effective modern cyber defense. Automated mitigation systems utilize pre-programmed actions from incident response playbooks which AI decides upon and star to mitigate anticipated threats. For example, in the case of a DDoS attack on a web property, prediction of anomalous traffic would immediately effect creation of new pathways for traffic, turn on additional firewalls, notify administrators, etc. If ransomware were detected actively encrypting files, the AI would quarantine the infected endpoint, blockade Command and Control (C2) communications, initiate recovery protocols, etc. without waiting for human authorization or deliberation. AI can also facilitate a proactive response by conducting "what-if" simulations based on its predictive modeling evaluation in determining the threat's potential attack path. This mechanism greatly expands an organization's choices in pre-positioning defences or, in some cases, making policy recommendations to resolve any vulnerabilities. By design, integrating automated responses with SOAR platforms ensures that an organization's documented policies and compliance requirements are appropriately reflected in the automated response, thus mitigating against the potential of an over-reaction or disruption to normal operations (Sarker, 2024).

5. ARCHITECTURES AND FRAMEWORKS FOR AI-BASED CYBERSECURITY

AI based cyber security solutions are based on strong architectures and frameworks that connect multiple data sources with machine learning; they aid and enhance human decision-makers - threat intelligence; and they enable automatic, automated, and human-made response to threats. Most, if not all contemporary frameworks are highly modular to enable rapid development, modification, scale, improvement and reduce complexity when enabling, enhancing or augmenting AI-assisted security.

5.1 End-to-End AI-Powered Security Architecture

An end-to-end AI-powered security architecture represents a complete solution comprised of all phases of cybersecurity defense from data collection to threat prediction and response automation, all integrated in a single operational platform. The design of end-to-end architecture incorporates measures for flow of information across data collection, preprocessing, AI/ML analytics, decision component, and feedback loops. The data collection phase integrates information across endpoints, network devices, cloud applications, and IoT, resulting in a complete picture of visibility on all of an organization's digital assets. The preprocessing component will remove noise, normalize, and structure data which will increase the accuracy of a model by eliminating irrelevant and non-contiguous signals. The analytics engine will process data utilizing supervised, unsupervised, reinforcement, and deep learning models to identify known and unknown threats, predict potential vulnerabilities, identify patterns and generate actionable outcomes to help cybersecurity teams. The decision layer is the phase where the suppression of outputs from the trained model will trigger an alert, determine the priority of the response, or self-automate response (which is often done with the integration of a SIEM and SOAR application), to mitigate unwanted digital incursions. The feedback loops will revisit previously made decisions and learn from past detection and outcomes from incidents (e.g. correct or incorrect identification of a threat) that reduce the "false positives" and improve predictive accuracy from one detection to the next. End-to-end architectures implementation phase also provides visualization dashboards, and reporting tools so that security teams have full visibility about threats, breach attempts, and the health of their systems.

Figure 3. Predictive Threat Intelligence System

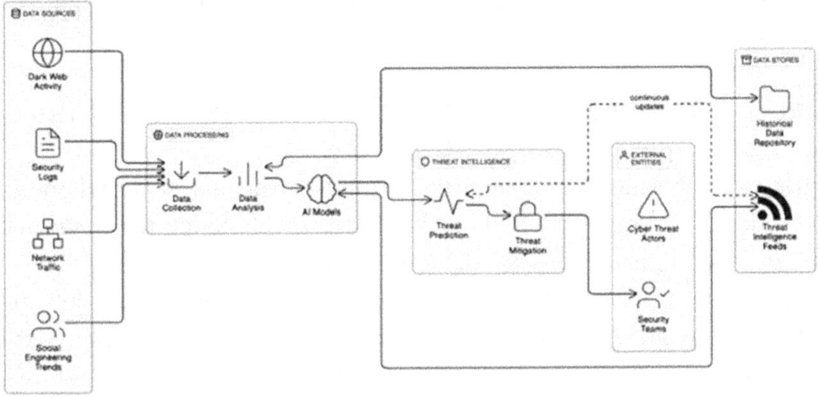

5.2 Cloud and Edge-Based Security Deployments

Cloud and edge deployments of security services span AI-driven cybersecurity capabilities across distributed and cloud-centric environments in recognition of, and response to, the ubiquitous deployment of cloud services, IoT-type devices, and remote infrastructures. Cloud-based deployments give AI and ML models access to virtually unlimited storage and computing to handle very large datasets, to ingest and analyze global threat intelligence feeds, and to enable real-time detection across globally distributed networks. Cloud applications can also host centralized operations of security tools, automated patching, and orchestration of security policies to provide optimized protection for enterprise workloads and reduce security processes for local IT teams (Vashishth et al., 2024). Cloud deployment grids also work in conjunction with edge deployments, as they allow AI models to be deployed in close proximity to sensors, instrumentation, or other endpoint devices to reduce latency and provide near real-time threat detection for IoT sensors, industrial control systems, or mobile endpoints. AI and ML models hosted at the edge can detect anomalous or outlier activities, prevent unauthorized access, and provide automated response capabilities without constant reliance on persistent connectivity to a cloud service. Cloud and edge deployments can also work together in a hybrid construct in a segmentation model, which allows for scalable, redundant, and low-latency prevention and protection for cybersecurity across central and distributed security and information technology services. These focused deployment strategies are particularly relevant for mission-critical applications in essential services, e.g. health care, manufacturing, smart cities, etc., where delays in threat identification or detection exposure can cause unacceptable levels of operational risk and/or safety concerns. Overall, the establishment of AI security frameworks in cloud and edge ecosystems enables resilient, responsive, flexible defences against threats to modern, distributed digital infrastructures (Sharma et al., 2025).

5.3 Hybrid Security Frameworks for Enterprise Networks

Integrated multi-framework security combines various artificial intelligence techniques, detections methods, and service deployment models to construct layered defences across complex enterprise networks. Integrated multi-framework security can include signature-based detection, anomaly detection, behavioural detection, and predictive intelligence. All of which safeguard against many types of cyber threats including traditional malware, advanced persistent threats (APTs), and insider attacks. Similar functional detection frameworks will yield better detection accuracy, even while reducing false positives, as well as a more comprehensive understanding of the attack vectors and vulnerabilities present in a targeted system. In the case of enterprise networks, which are usually a mix of on-premises servers, cloud services, and remote endpoints, integrated hybrid security frameworks acting across a heterogeneous technology stack are necessary. Integrated hybrid AI models, use telemetry from all parts of the network to profile anomalous behaviours, correlate those anomalies, and prioritize threats based, in part, on severity, potential business impact, the possibility of lateral movement, etc., as well as other variables. Additionally, an integrated hybrid security framework can also integrate the capability of automatic orchestration for defensive action through an integrated SIEM/SOAR type of toy platform by examining telemetry to automatically isolate a compromised endpoint, or prevent malicious connections, or initiate patch deployment, etc. Integration of threat or detection feedback loop can also be done to continually adjust and retrain the machine learning models using a variety of designed constructs to accommodate evolving attack patterns. The type of integrated hybrid enterprise security framework is designed to be adaptable, and scalable. An integrated multi-framework architecture is intended to be layered to create multiple levels of security to mitigate and defend against increasing complexity of cyber threats, and ultimately help organizations manage and maintain a secure operating posture, defensive capability, and regulatory compliance across all assets connected to all enterprise networks.

5.4 Role of Big Data Analytics in Cybersecurity Intelligence

Big data analytics is critical to the effective adoption of AI-enabled cybersecurity in that it serves the purpose of processing and analyzing large and disparate datasets to provide actionable intelligence to decision makers. Today's digital infrastructures are producing significant volumes of structured and unstructured data; including network logs, endpoint activity, system events, user activity, and threat intelligence feeds that all must be analysed in order to respond to more sophisticated cyber adversaries. Advanced data analytic platforms utilize big data technologies such as Hadoop, Spark, and NoSQL databases to stream and analyze big data in real-time to identify anomalous data and predict emerging threats. The integration of big data analytics utilizes the historical data from trends on incidents that are combined with the latest data streams, to remove the reliance on reactive responses to cyber adversaries. This provides security teams with the insights and information needed to identify more complex attack behaviours that include correlations of disparate events and gives security team members the information needed to prioritize incident responses based on risk assessment. Predictive modelling gives the organization(s) the ability to identify targeted vulnerabilities or zero-day exploits even before they become targeted. Clustering algorithms combined with classification algorithms will detect hidden behaviours and increasingly anomalous behaviours. Big data also improves upon existing threat intelligence collection and processing by enabling threat intelligence to utilize and contextualize more data sets in relation to one or more external information sets such as open-source intelligence (OSINT) feeds, dark web investigations, industry-specific databases on threats etc. (Adeyeye et al., 2024).

6. CASE STUDIES AND REAL-WORLD IMPLEMENTATIONS

The practical implementation of AI-driven cybersecurity strategies exemplifies how theory leads to quantifiable enhancements in threat detection, prevention, and response. The examples of real-world implementations can demonstrate how effective AI is in enterprise security, finance, healthcare, and critical infrastructure situations, with tangible information for the stakeholders pertaining to performance, scale, and return on investment.

6.1 AI in Enterprise Security Solutions

Enterprise-grade organizations receive huge volumes of security data each day, often mass amounts of logs originating from endpoints, servers, networks, and cloud services. Traditional SIEM platforms also struggle with alert fatigue and actor signal detections. An AI based solution is a must for overcoming this. Vendors such as IBM QRadar and Splunk Enterprise Security that leverage AI will now present AI driven analytics that can automatically derive anomalies, correlate multi-faceted events, and prioritize alerts on the risk of severity. For example, QRadar will correlate user and network events in millions in real-time performance to look for things like odd login patterns, not normal data transfers, odd behaviours at endpoints, etc. In addition to analyzing endpoint data and correlating behaviours to user identity data, being able to process this much data, allows it to eliminate false-positive incidents by up to 70 percent, allowing the analyst to prioritize for important company related risks. SOAR vendors add value to SIEM capabilities that leverage AI and can initiate automated remediation workflows to isolated compromised endpoints, block malicious IPs, and notify teams instantaneously; all while reporting to stakeholders including the complete incident investigation processes. Organizations employing these automated SIEM and SOAR solutions reported improvements of 50–60 percent in mean-time-to-detection (MTTD) per team and also improved efficiencies reduced much of the manual triaging. These enterprise grade implementations demonstrate, when AI augments enterprise security platforms to future-proof how we detect, respond, remediate, and respond to truly knowable but changing adversaries (Pulyala, 2024).

6.2 AI-Powered Threat Hunting in Financial Services

Financial services are prime targets for cybercriminals due to the sensitive monetary data and value of financial transaction. Institutions like Capital One are utilizing AI-enabled threat hunting on account behavior, network activity, and suspicious transactions. Machine learning models are utilized to detect trends in suspicious fund transfers, repeated failed login attempts, or unusual access to sensitive files and predict fraudulent activity in advance. For example, Capital One was able to identify an unseen malware variant targeting on-line banking systems which allowed its security team to stop accounts from being impacted and prevent the onslaught of financial loss. Similarly, JPMorgan Chase uses predictive analytics to detect insider threats, unusual employee behavior, and possible phishing attacks. Using AI, the machine-learning models are continually observing behaviours from new threats and incorporating this into its analytics relating to external intelligence feeds. The predictive outputs include real-time alerts, fewer false-positive alerts, and automated actions of mitigation. Financial organizations picked up trends that up to 30% of transaction attempts were fraud by issuing alerts and were able to act faster to ignore real fraud attempts. The use of AI shown that security is able provide proactive threat-hunting as opposed to reactive incidents where organizations had to react to an incident instead of protecting its assets and its customers' trust.

6.3 Predictive Analytics for Healthcare Cybersecurity

Healthcare systems often include sensitive patient data, together with connected medical devices, and crucial infrastructure that presents an enticing target for ransomware, insider threats, or data breaches. Organizations like Mount Sinai Health System and Cleveland Clinic are also utilizing AI analytics with predictive behavior in order to gain visibility into network traffic, endpoint traffic, and IoT devices. As a case in point, Mount Sinai's AI platform detected abnormal access behaviours to electronic health records (EHR), as well as anomalies with medical devices that could involve malware or insider tampering. Anomalies resulted in automated alerts and endpoint isolations that security teams could be mobilized on immediately. Darktrace's AI platform at Cleveland Clinic was put into play to objectively observed abnormal network behaviours in real time including suspected ransom campaigns in progress. The AI platform helped to reduce the likelihood of a security breach by 50% and a quicker reaction time to threats. These case studies exemplify the use of AI to identify and mitigate cybersecurity incidents as they occur, protect the integrity of patient data, HIPAA and other regulatory compliance, and clinical workflow.

6.4 Smart Cities and Critical Infrastructure Protection with AI

Smart cities and critical infrastructures are largely dependent upon interconnected devices, Internet of Things (IoT) sensors and networks, but are subject to many vulnerabilities. A successful attack can have a major impact on essential public services. Smart cities such as Singapore and Barcelona have harnessed artificial intelligence-enabled cyber security frameworks to enhance protection of the urban infrastructure of transportation, energy grids, and water management systems. Singapore's Smart Nation programme makes use of machine learning algorithms for the detection of anomalous behaviour of signals, energy consumption, and water distribution network systems. In a live simulation of a cyber-attack on traffic management the AI detected command signals that exhibited abnormal characteristics. The AI absorbed information relative to the signals and dynamically rerouted the traffic. Barcelona has used AI to monitor energy and water systems for the detection of anomalous patterns which might indicate the presence of a cyber-attack or the presence of a failure point within the system. The AI platforms notification systems provided in real time notifications, generated recommendations for maintenance and programmed service to enable operations to continue while lessening risk levels to necessary services. The use of AI within each study suggests that it is able to provide platforms that scale intelligence to the level necessary for complex city networks, providing situational awareness, predictive insight, and automated mitigation mechanisms for public safety for protection against cyber threats to critical urban infrastructure.

7. CHALLENGES AND LIMITATIONS OF AI-DRIVEN CYBERSECURITY

The use of AI-based cyber security measures can provide a transformative impact in the realms of the threats to be detected, predictive intelligence and automated response, and requires a number of challenges and limitations to be addressed to permit for effective deployment within the organizations.

1. **Data Quality and Availability:** AI systems require huge volumes of data that is accurate, diverse, labelled, etc. The AI needs large volumes of data to learn from to provide an accurate threat detection and/or predictive model. The quality of the data is extremely relevant, since bad datasets will lead to false positives and false negatives, etc, to put it crudely. However, for potential users of AI to make use of it, it may either be impossible or very difficult to find people who will agree to this enhanced level of training possible, particularly within acceptable timeframes, for example.
2. **Privacy and Regulatory Compliance:** AI-driven cybersecurity running on the cloud, combined with the need to collect and analyze personal or sensitive information, heightens the potential for privacy concerns. Organizations must also balance regulations (e.g., GDPR, HIPAA, PCI DSS) to ensure any processing of data does not breach the law or violate privacy regulations. AI can be implemented without an adequate compliance process, but organizations will face potential legal ramifications, brand attack, reduced trust, etc. Balancing a strong security posture, while favouring your data privacy concerns has always been a challenging undertaking (Vashishth et al., 2025).
3. **Model Complexity and Interpretability:** Most advanced models regarding AI are "black boxes" - large deep learning algorithms that the security team (or other stakeholders) cannot understand or decipher how it came to a particular decision. The lack of transparency reduces overall trust in the outputs of AI, and this runs the risk of delaying response in a critical incident. Understanding why a specific alert was raised, or how a model classified an event as malicious

or not, is critical to meet relevance (auditability) as they pertain to operational objectives.

4. **Adversarial Attacks and Model Evasion:** Cybercriminals are employing adversarial tactics to trick AI models. Some of these tactics include data poisoning and evasion attacks. Adversarial techniques and attacks look at the boundaries of the underlying Model, and these attacks can degrade model accuracy, and thus sophistication can expose the vulnerabilities associated with AI-based systems.
5. **Resource Constraints and Infrastructure Requirements:** AI generally requires additional computing resources (with specialized hardware, i.e., GPU's/TPU's) and/or personnel to either implement or maintain AI programs and resource costs may limit the access of small and medium enterprises (SME) organizations financially. Additionally, embedding AI capabilities into existing security systems, such as SIEM, SOAR and/or endpoint protection systems may not be easy to integrate and will come with additional configuring and interoperability tasks.

8. FUTURE DIRECTIONS AND RESEARCH OPPORTUNITIES

The realm of AI-driven cybersecurity is consistently changing to counter the complexities and growing number of cyber threats presented in today's digital ecosystem. Table 3 summarises key benefits from currently available AI systems available to generalize around Threat Detection, Predictive Intelligence, and Automation. However, the emergence of forthcoming challenges, such as technological advancements in AI create some opportunity for new scholarship and innovations from this chapter that will explore some directions that may offer opportunities for more effective, adaptable, and trustworthy AI-based cybersecurity solutions.

1. **Explainable and Transparent AI (XAI):** One of the most pertinent future pathways is to create explainable and transparent AI. Traditional machine learning, especially deep learning, approaches often function as "black boxes" that lack comprehensibility for security teams: for example, once a deep learning model provides a threat detection, it is challenging to understand how that threat was identified or why that specific alert was triggered. Explainable AI (XAI) research is dedicated to providing an understandable rationale for the decision-making process of the model, enabling an analyst to validate alerts, auditors can validate the reasoning for automated responses and defence organisations must comply with regulations. By producing interpretable AI decision-making, organizations will develop greater trust in autonomous systems, develop means for improving situational awareness, and support more rapid and accurate re-

sponses to complex cyber threats. XAI research will often consider the design of user-friendly dashboards or visualization tools to present AI findings in a way that makes them comprehensible to security analysts - enabling teams to bridge the gap between advanced analytics and a human nexus of expertise and experience.

2. **Integration with Emerging Technologies:** AI-driven cybersecurity will be closely integrated with multiple emerging technologies to improve defence capabilities. For example, quantum computing has the potential to reduce the time it takes to train an AI model - as well as develop more advanced cryptographic methods to better facilitate rapid and resilient automatable threat & vulnerability analysis. Blockchain technology should allow defence organisations to produce immutable ledgers for sharing and co-creating a threat intelligence ecosystem, providing each organisation with a mechanism to trust their data use, and contributing towards trustworthy AI. Finally, as mentioned in previous sections, 6G deployments are on the horizon and with that comes ultra-low latencies and data volumes that would be very important for AI-based real-time threat detection & response, especially in distributed or mission-critical systems. The combination of these emerging technologies and the AI research path will ultimately mean adaptive, resilient, and future-ready frameworks for addressing all types of digital threats.
3. **Adaptive and Self-Learning Security Systems:** Future AI systems will be adaptive and have self-learning capabilities. Unlike traditional rule-based systems, however, the great virtue of AI systems will be evolved operationally by realising new dangers, changes in the environment, and also in the "enemy's" mode of attack, etc. There exists research work in this field today designed to discover techniques and procedures for providing algorithms which will make it possible for the system itself to self-learn detection patterns, and optimising mitigation patterns, learn trends in attacks, and generally to lessen human interaction with the machine systems itself, while advancing effectiveness in processes of threat detection and responses alike.
4. **AI for IoT, Edge, and Distributed Networks:** With the eruption of IoT devices, edge computing, and distributed networks, AI-based security should change and adapt itself to the requirements of this change in the nature of the threat environment, because it will have to continue functioning in hyper-dynamic frames. Deploying AI models at the edge, allows for anomaly detection at connected devices, leading to near real-time detection with the lowest possible latency, and allowing immediate isolation or mitigation when anomalies are found. Distributed AI frameworks can also monitor systems that are heterogeneous, distributed, (across cloud, on-premise, etc.) and across IoT, and can provide comprehensive visibility and protection across different IoT ecosystems. Future research aims to

work towards designing AI-based models that are light-weight and scalable to even the smallest or most constrained environments while being accurate, and responsible while providing for robust protection, (for smart cities, industrial IoT, etc.), or any large-scale distributed networks.

5. **Predictive Intelligence and Behavioural Analytics:** Predictive intelligence & behavioural analytics have emerged as promising research focus areas for some time. AI could use predictive intelligence to not only identify ongoing threats, but it could research potential attacks by identifying changes in user behavior, changes in network traffic, changes in system interaction, etc. Being proactive could empower organizations to mitigate risk in advance, identify insider threats, decrease the impact of cyber incidents before escalation occurs, and other critical functions for organizations. Future research will focus on developments of more advanced algorithms that combine heterogeneous datasets and identify qualitatively different behaviours, all while providing recommendations or actionable information in real time or, close to, real time.

9. CONCLUSION

AI-powered threat detection and predictive intelligence is transforming the paradigm of cybersecurity into proactive, adaptable, automatic defences for sophisticated cyber threats. This chapter covered the fundamentals of AI and ML in cybersecurity, the various aspects of threat detection and predictive abilities, and the areas of enterprise, finance, healthcare, and critical infrastructure. AI has proved to offer benefits in improved accuracy of detection, faster response time in the event of a major security incident, and decreased costs of operational processes; yet we also appreciate the challenges of data, complexity, attacks from the adversary, treatment of operating resources, and increasing regulation. Future areas of research—Explainable AIs, pairing and integration of AIs with emerging technologies, adaptive self-learning systems, and ethical AIs—will continue to furnish resilience, transparency, and efficacy in cybersecurity solutions. In conclusory, this chapter additionally makes the case for the strategic implementation not just of AIs, but also of the human element of expertise and experience, of continuous learning processes, and of the proper governance which are essential to hand us still more secure, intelligent, and future-proof digital ecosystems to mitigate the existing and emerging threats of the cyberspace.

REFERENCES

Adeyeye, O. J., Akanbi, I., Emeteveke, I., & Emehin, O. (2024). Leveraging secured AI-driven data analytics for cybersecurity: Safeguarding information and enhancing threat detection. *International Journal of Research and Publication and Reviews*, *5*(10), 3208–3223. DOI: 10.55248/gengpi.5.1024.2911

Gupta, M., & Vashishth, T. K. (2024). Blockchain-Assisted Machine Learning For Securing Mobile Ad-Hoc Networks against Black-Hole Attacks. *Frontiers in Health Informatics*, *13*(7). Advance online publication. DOI: 10.31893/multiscience.2024209

Gupta, M., Vashishth, T. K., & Verma, P. K. (2024). Machine learning and deep learning based intrusion detection for blackhole attacks in mobile ad-hoc networks. *Multidisciplinary Science Journal*, *6*(11), 2024209–2024209. DOI: 10.31893/multiscience.2024209

Hussain, H., Kainat, M., & Ali, T. (2025). Leveraging AI and Machine Learning to Detect and Prevent Cyber Security Threats. [DSSR]. *Dialogue Social Science Review*, *3*(1), 881–895. DOI: 10.5281/zenodo.14714679

Ijiga, O. M., Idoko, I. P., Ebiega, G. I., Olajide, F. I., Olatunde, T. I., & Ukaegbu, C. (2024). Harnessing adversarial machine learning for advanced threat detection: AI-driven strategies in cybersecurity risk assessment and fraud prevention. J. Sci. Technol, 11, 001-024. DOI: 10.53022/oarjst.2024.11.1.0060

Islam, S. M., Bari, M. S., Sarkar, A., Khan, A. O. R., & Paul, R. (2024). AI-Powered Threat Intelligence: Revolutionizing Cybersecurity with Proactive Risk Management for Critical Sectors. Journal of Artificial Intelligence General Science (JAIGS) ISSN: 3006-4023, 7(01), 1-8. DOI: 10.60087/jaigs.v7i01.291

Mahmud, F., Barikdar, C. R., Hassan, J., Goffer, M. A., Das, N., Orthi, S. M., Kaur, J., Hasan, S. N., & Hasan, R. (2025). AI-Driven Cybersecurity in IT Project Management: Enhancing Threat Detection and Risk Mitigation. *Journal of Posthumanism*, *5*(4), 23–44. DOI: 10.63332/joph.v5i4.974

Patil, D. (2024). Artificial Intelligence in Cybersecurity: Enhancing Threat Detection and Prevention Mechanisms through Machine Learning and Data Analytics. Available at *SSRN* 5057410. DOI: 10.2139/ssrn.5057410

Prince, N. U., Faheem, M. A., Khan, O. U., Hossain, K., Alkhayyat, A., Hamdache, A., & Elmouki, I. (2024). AI-powered data-driven cybersecurity techniques: Boosting threat identification and reaction. *Nanotechnology Perceptions*, *20*(S10), 332–353. DOI: 10.62441/nano-ntp.v20iS10.25

Pulyala, S. R. (2024). From detection to prediction: AI-powered SIEM for proactive threat hunting and risk mitigation. *Turkish Journal of Computer and Mathematics Education, 15*(1), 34–43. DOI: 10.61841/turcomat.v15i1.14393

Samuel, A. J. (2024). Advancements in Cybersecurity: Leveraging AI and Machine Learning for Threat Detection and Prevention. Journal of Science. *Technology and Engineering Research, 2*(3), 64–79. DOI: 10.64206/thwq1548

Sarker, I. H. (2024). Introduction to AI-Driven Cybersecurity and Threat Intelligence. In AI-Driven Cybersecurity and Threat Intelligence: Cyber Automation, Intelligent Decision-Making and Explainability (pp. 3-19). Cham: Springer Nature Switzerland. DOI: 10.1007/978-3-031-54497-2_1

Sharma, R., Sharma, V., Vashishth, T. K., Kumar, B., Sharma, B. K., & Chaudhary, S. (2025, February). Implementation of adaptive cloud security framework for cloud computing monitoring system applications. In AIP Conference Proceedings (Vol. 3224, No. 1). AIP Publishing. DOI: 10.1063/5.0246104

Vashishth, T. K., Sharma, V., Samania, B., Sharma, R., Singh, S., & Jajoria, P. (2025). Ethical and Legal Implications of AI in Cybersecurity. In Machine Intelligence Applications in Cyber-Risk Management (pp. 387-414). IGI Global Scientific Publishing. DOI: 10.4018/979-8-3693-7540-2.ch017

Vashishth, T. K., Sharma, V., Sharma, K. K., & Kumar, B. (2025). Enhanced Security and Privacy from Industry 4.0 and 5.0 Vision. In Building Embodied AI Systems: The Agents, the Architecture Principles, Challenges, and Application Domains (pp. 133-158). Cham: Springer Nature Switzerland. DOI: 10.1007/978-3-031-68256-8_6

Vashishth, T. K., Sharma, V., Sharma, K. K., Kumar, B., Chaudhary, S., & Panwar, R. (2024). Enhancing Cloud Security: The Role of Artificial Intelligence and Machine Learning. In Improving Security, Privacy, and Trust in Cloud Computing (pp. 85-112). IGI Global. DOI: 10.4018/979-8-3693-1431-9.ch004

Vashishth, T. K., Sharma, V., Sharma, K. K., Kumar, B., Chaudhary, S., & Panwar, R. (2024). Security and Privacy Challenges in Blockchain-Based Supply Chain Management: A Comprehensive Analysis. In Achieving Secure and Transparent Supply Chains with Blockchain Technology (pp. 70-91). IGI Global. DOI: 10.4018/979-8-3693-0482-2.ch005

Vashishth, T. K., Sharma, V., Sharma, K. K., Kumar, B., Chaudhary, S., & Panwar, R. (2024). Security and Privacy Considerations in Cloud-Based Data Processing Solutions for Sensitive Data. In *Developments towards Next Generation Intelligent Systems for Sustainable Development* (pp. 35–61). IGI Global., DOI: 10.4018/979-8-3693-5643-2.ch002

ADDITIONAL READING

Khan, M. I., Arif, A., & Khan, A. R. A. (2024). AI-Driven Threat Detection: A Brief Overview of AI Techniques in Cybersecurity. BIN. *Bulletin of Informatics*, *2*(2), 248–261.

Muppalaneni, R., Inaganti, A. C., & Ravichandran, N. (2024). AI-Driven Threat Intelligence: Enhancing Cyber Defense with Machine Learning. *Journal of Computing Innovations and Applications*, *2*(1), 1–11.

KEY TERMS AND DEFINITIONS

Artificial Intelligence (AI): refers to the development of computer systems that can perform tasks that typically require human intelligence, such as learning, problem-solving, decision-making, and natural language understanding.

Internet of Things (IoT): The Internet of Things (IoT) is a concept that refers to the connection of everyday objects to the internet, allowing them to send and receive data. These objects can include devices like smartphones, thermostats, wearables, home appliances, and even vehicles. The idea behind IoT is to create a network where these objects can communicate with each other, collect and share data, and perform tasks more efficiently.

Machine Learning (ML): is a subset of artificial intelligence (AI) that involves the development of algorithms and statistical models that enable computer systems to improve their performance on a specific task through learning from data, without being explicitly programmed.

Natural Language Processing (NLP): is a field of artificial intelligence that focuses on enabling computers to understand, interpret, and generate human language in a way that is both meaningful and contextually relevant.

Chapter 4
Anomaly Detection With Machine Learning

T. K. Shaik Shavali
Lords Institute of Engineering and Technology, India

Sunita Vinod Mahale
Independent Researcher, India

S. Manikandan
https://orcid.org/0009-0005-7387-3739
Kongunadu College of Engineering and Technology, India

Sachin Vasant Chaudhari
https://orcid.org/0009-0005-8856-8905
Sanjivani College of Engineering, Ahmednagar, India

Fateh Bahadur Kunwar
https://orcid.org/0009-0007-5749-9892
Rajasthan Technical University, India

C. S. Sandeep
Jawaharlal College of Engineering and Technology, India

V. Bhoopathy
https://orcid.org/0000-0003-2175-6328
Sree Rama Engineering College, India

ABSTRACT

The structures know how to observe activity utilizing actual data thanks for cutting intelligence procedures. In order for systems to demonstrate action that is derived from previous interactions, procedures that are founded on those interactions can be developed. In order to identify out-of-the-ordinary occurrences in certain networks, predictive methods are employed. The encryption techniques can detect net abuse and are able to develop with various types of inputs. Machinery supervision and recognizing fraud are two applications of this concept. Whenever tackling multifaceted, extremely complicated, nonlinear information dividends, traditional techniques for statistics can be ineffective. Advancements in recognizing anomalies have been substantial via the introduction of ML, especially DL and unstructured

DOI: 10.4018/979-8-3373-2252-0.ch004

learning methods. In order to provide light on the present modern facilities and upcoming study areas, this part delves through the core ideas, methods, methods, and practical uses of finding anomalies via artificial intelligence.

1. INTRODUCTION

Structures in statistics whose vary from what is anticipated are sometimes called anomalous or abnormalities and the task of detecting them is known as discovery of anomalies. Because outliers provide crucial details regarding a good's well-being, finding them plays a crucial role in PHM. A large number of techniques for recognizing anomalies work by first creating a record of typical occurrences, prior to looking for outliers (Le & Zhang, 2022). Inevitably an illustration, what was utilized to describe the healthful position of a BGA was derived according to its rotating. The investigators identified the BGA's unusual behavior by recording gaps across the projected results together with observed data. Different approaches to discovering anomalies fall into one of four main categories: distance-based, classification-based, clustering-based, or statistics. When analyzing information provided by clean consumer goods, distance-based approaches take into account the type of aberrations that are distant (Chatterjee & Ahmed, 2022). The information collected gained from good formally goods are a long way the location of irregularities. Regular sightings will get assumed to relate for each comparable population or grouped using clustering-based algorithms. A freshly acquired sighting shall be considered anomalous when its location is located far removed from the cluster of containers centre or centers. Differentiating abnormal from ordinary conclusions is the job of classification-based algorithms like neural networks with the k-most neighbors, and one-class SVM. Furthermore, mathematical techniques make using anomaly statistics (Sayed, 2023).

2. UNDERSTANDING ANOMALIES

2.1 Types of Anomalies

The broader definition of a phenomenon is an event that is different to the usual expected behavior. There mainly consist of a trio of inconsistencies, are stated in references

2.1.1 Point Dissimilarities

Endpoint anomalies are the most basic kind of anomalies; they occur when a particular data occurrence stands out from the rest of the information being transmitted (Nassif et al., 2021).

2.1.2 Abnormalities in Contextual

A contextualize anomalies occurs when a set of data is considered abnormal in one setting but not another location. Situational abnormalities can be characterized by both context-specific factors and behavioral characteristics. The surroundings of a case is determined by applying the rstattribute. Location dependent properties in maps include things like latitude and longitude measurements(Pang et al., 2021) (Zaigham Zaheer et al., 2022). In addition, the spot of a single point on the whole timeline is determined by time and energy, a context property in data collected over time. Under the subsequent component, which describes an instance's no contextual qualities, we find what are known as behavior variables. Given an instance of a behavioral property, consider an area-based database that describes the common global rainfall and the quantity of moisture that falls at every location. If the background irregularities in the object of investigation area are significant, then contextually finding anomalies is a good method to use. A further significant variable is the readily available of higher-order qualities. When the environment is readily apparent, a contextually spotting method is the best course of action. However, there are cases where creating an environment where particular strategies are difficult to utilize is just not feasible (Chandola, 2009).

Figure 1. Grouping irregularities into three primary groups: individual, situational, and group-based.

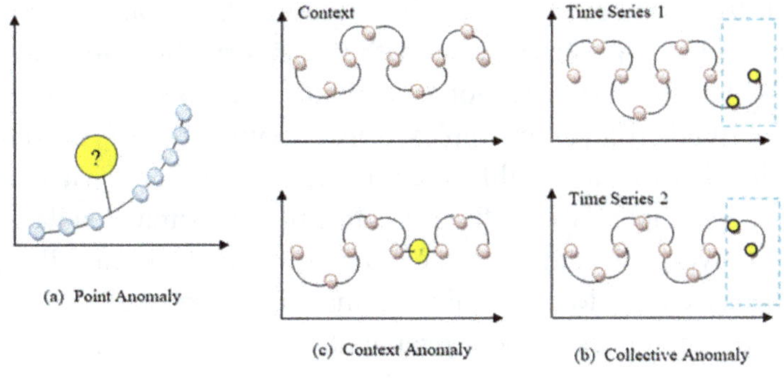

Exceptions are classified into two primary categories: particular, relevant and aggregate. Collection samples are depicted by the yellow & green cylinders, respectively. Examples of data that is standard are represented by green cylinders, whilst examples of atypical information are represented by yellow hemispheres. Grouping irregularities into three primary groups shown in Figure 1.

2.1.3 Group anomalies

The group's an exception occurs when a group of related data examples deviates from the norm throughout the entire data collection. Statistically methods to detect anomalies are among the first strategies developed for this purpose (Stoian, 2020). A mathematical equation describing the typical behavior of the given data is constructed using statistics techniques. The next step is to determine if a specific situation is a part of the model, using an inferential statistic check. When it comes to statistically anomalous identification, it utilizes a few different approaches. Nearby, parameterized, inelastic, & semi-parametric approaches are all part of this category. Among the multitude of techniques applied to spot outliers, ML algorithms have grown in popularity. Learning using scenarios, or ML, is an attempt to streamline the method (Ariyaluran Habeeb et al., 2019). Using this method, one can construct an algorithm that can differentiate from regular and out-of-the-ordinary categories. So, according to the sample data functioning, there are additionally three primary forms of identification of anomalies. Here is each of the main categories

Supervised identification of anomalies: There are labeled cases throughout both the typical and out-of-the-ordinary instructional kits for this subject. Making an estimator for the usual category plus another for that anomalous university to contrast the results is the main idea behind this technique (Golomb et al., 2018). Nevertheless, two complications arise in that way. A reduced amount of outliers relative to typical examples is the initially noticeable difference in the instructional batch. In addition, finding reliable and accurate names is difficult, especially when dealing with the abnormality subclass.

Semi-supervised identification of anomalies: In this instance instruction is limited to standard course examples. Consequently, anomaly is used to describe everything that does not qualify as common. The usual classification is the only one that semi-supervised methods assume that the simulated data has labeled representatives. They have become more prevalent than controlled approaches partly because they do not require anomalous group labelling.

Detecting anomalies without oversight: Here, the techniques can function without data sets used for training. Hence, according to those methodologies, regular cases are quite numerous in datasets used for testing than abnormalities (Liu et al., 2021). The procedure at hand, nonetheless, has a significant probability of false alarms in the event that its presumption is incorrect.

3. LEARNING SCENARIOS OF ANOMALY DETECTION

Here we will go over some typical instructional scenarios that involve AD methods. The research studies examined different AD strategies and their implications in depth, and they proposed classifying AD strategies into a trio of instruction situations: 1. AD methods that are supervised. 2. AD methods that is semi-supervised. 3. AD strategies that is unattended Instructional experiences. Following is a condensed version of the presentation (Fahrmann et al., 2024).

3.1. Supervised

Classify algorithms which separate data samples into "average" and "anomalous" examples form the basis of automated AD approaches. Managed category learning, in the other hand, necessitates data to train and fundamental truths marked on them (Chalapathy & Chawla, 2019). A widespread problem is that controlled AD techniques are suspicious. During the training set, there is frequently a disconnect between the quantity specimens labeled "average" against the amount of instances assigned the "anomalous" category. The amount of typical to samples that are not normal in the data being trained is typically substantially smaller. Another rarity is labeled real-life data sets suitable for AD algorithm building.

3.2. Semi-Supervised

The educational program data examples must consist solely of usual observers in order for semi-supervised AD approaches to work. Given information used for learning, an equation of normality is constructed (Schmidl et al., 2022). Sample instances are categorized as either typical or aberrant based on the possibility of the test case being created by the simulated model. Atypical phenomenon is defined as an occurrence that does not match the learnt paradigm. Since semi-supervised approaches are less usually useful, there are a great many of them than supervisory ones.

3.3. Unsupervised

When retraining their models, unattended AD approaches lack examples of annotations. Rather, these methods seek to autonomously discover the true make-up of the information as well as thereafter employ this information in identifying data events that have the highest unlike a large number of some cases, in order to determine data scenarios that are strange (Chambolle & Poret, 2005).

4. MACHINE LEARNING TECHNIQUES FOR ANOMALY DETECTION

There are a number of subfields within aberration methods for detection, including statistics, mental processes, and deep learning (Kaur et al., 2013). These days, a lot of real-world issues are being solved using data mining approaches. When trying to classify the trends that are studied, neural network approaches rely on either implied or explicit models. Many types of machine learning fall under this umbrella, including Genetic the algorithms, Statistical networking, Cognitive Networks, and fuzzy reasoning (Taha & Hadi, 2019). Categories of Machine learning based techniques shown in Figure 2.

Figure 2. Categories of Machine learning based techniques

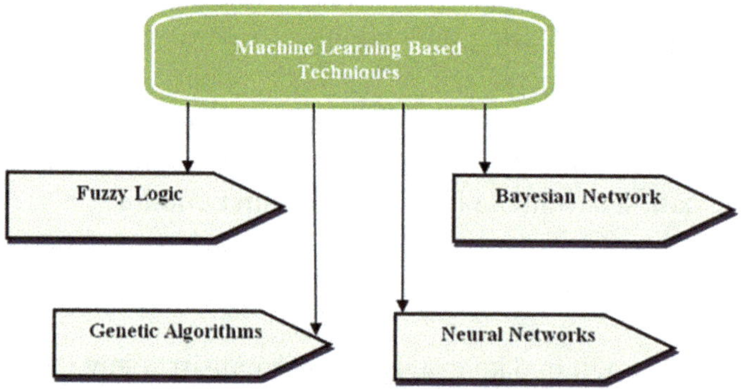

4.1. Fuzzy Logic

Fuzzy sets theory, whereby argumentation approximates while not directly deriving it using conventional proposition rationality, is the source of implausible reasoning. Although the attributes that need to be taken into consideration can be thought of as fuzzy elements, fuzzy approaches have thus been used in the finding anomalies discipline (Ravikumar & Govindarasu, 2024). The most significant drawback of fuzzy thinking is the significant amount of resources needed, despite the fact that it has demonstrated effectiveness, especially for scans for ports & monitors.

4.2. Genetic Algorithms

Crossover, which is descent, variation, choice, and other mathematical approaches are used in DNA algorithms, which have biological basis discovery methods. Thus, neural networks can choose the best values for the identifying operation and derive categorization principles. The application of Genetic Algorithm to the network data consist primarily of the following steps

Data on the data moving via a specific network is gathered by the system that detects attacks.

Following that, the intranet detection system uses neural networks that have been trained using the categorization criteria discovered from the data gathered via the framework's inspection of networks.

Determining these patterns, the firewall's intrusion detection system subsequently classifies the traffic that arrives as either regular or abnormal using a variety of criteria.

4.3. Neural Networks

The power of a neuronal network to generalize using sparse, loud, and unfinished data. This capacity to recognize unrecognized sequences—that is, sequences that are not precisely replicated and deviate within the specified frameworks of the prior output patterns—is made possible by this generalization expertise. Since good invasion detection system has to be able to identify both previously detected and undiscovered intrusions in future periods, artificial brains have been acknowledged as a viable method for identifying anomalies (Patel et al., 2020).

4.4. Bayesian Networks

An equation that captures probable correlations between the parameters that matter is called a network based on Bayesian analysis. The result method is typically applied to detecting breaches in conjunction at random projects a process that has various benefits, such as the capacity to encode interconnections within elements, indicate occasions, and integrate information from previous information (Bhuyan et al., 2016). Numerous methods to detect anomalies shown in Table 1.

Table 1. Numerous methods to detect anomalies utilize neural networks

Techniques	Pros/Cons
Logic with Fuzzy	✓ Instead of being exact, thinking is approximated. ✓ Efficient, particularly when it comes about port inspections & monitors. ✓ There is a significant use of resources.
The DNA Algorithm	✓ Built around principles from biology and using algorithmic evolution. ✓ Provides use of features including crossovers evolution, and chosen. ✓ Capability to choose the best characteristics and derive categorization procedures.
A neural network	✓ Being able to draw broad conclusions given sparse, chaotic, and imperfect evidence. ✓ It's capable of identifying correlations that will not be visible in future periods.
The Bayesian structure	✓ Captures each parameter of fascination with probable associations. ✓ The capacity to integrate facts and past experience.

5 OUTPUT OF ANOMALY DETECTION

Usually, methods for identifying anomalies produce a few of both basic formats

5.1 Labels

Methods using the results give the evaluation databases tags. Typically, this is the result of trained methods for finding anomalies (Systems, n.d.).

5.2 Scores

Methods using the result give each occurrence in the entire database a score based on how much of an abnormality a particular case is deemed to represent. Thus, a prioritized collection of irregularities might be the result. Through this output, neither a certain point in time is utilized to select unusual patterns nor are some top errors examined. Both semi-supervised and unstructured approaches frequently produce values (Musa & Bouras, 2022). Various finding anomalies techniques Shown in Figure 3.

Figure 3. Various finding anomalies techniques depending on the dataset's labelling supply.

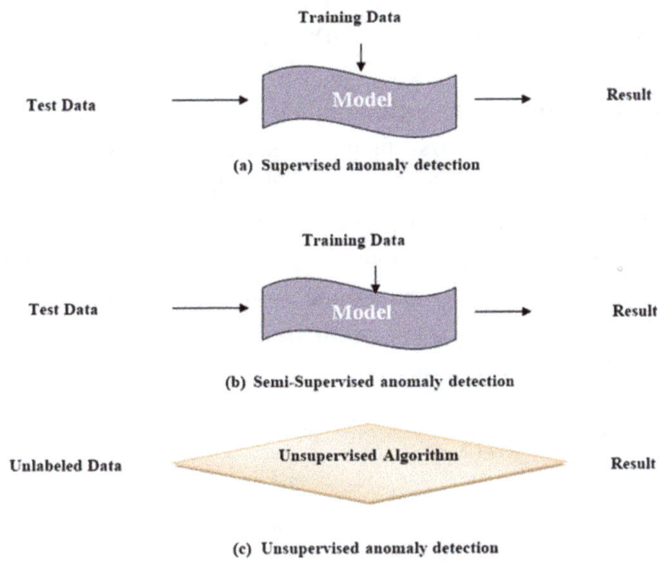

6. APPLICATIONS OF ANOMALY DETECTION

A number of identifying anomalies techniques are covered in this part of the article.

6.1 Identification of Intrusions

Detecting criminal activity in a technology-related system is known as the detection of intrusions. Through terms of security on machines, these malevolent actions or incursions are intriguing. Since a threat differs from the computer's typical behavior, methods to identify anomalies can be used in the detection of attacks field. Separates intrusion detection systems under two categories: network-based versus host-only (Republic, 2022).

6.1.1 Algorithms that identify intrusions on the host

These gadgets handle call traces from the Linux kernel. The signs contain abnormal consequences that represent the incursions. Unauthorized behavior, worms, and violations of laws are all results of the abnormal consequences. Although each record includes events that follow a single language, what really differentiates typical behavior from abnormal is when these instances occur together (Gupta et al., 2021).

6.1.2 Network intrusion detection and prevention Systems

The detection of intrusions that manipulate network data is the main focus of these platforms. While most incursions manifest as out-of-the-ordinary themes, or "points irregularities," certain methods can describe the data sequentially and identify out-of-the-ordinary consequences, or "a common goal aberrations". This unusual behavior is mostly attributable to intrusion attempts made by other individuals who intend to steal data or cause additional connectivity disruptions (Siniosoglou et al., 2021). An example of a common setup would be an enormous collection of desktops linked to the global web through the web.

6.2 Anti-Fraud Measures

When illegal acts are detected in businesses like credit card issuers, banks, insurance coverage companies, mobile device companies, stock markets, etc., this is called discovering fraud. Criminals may be the company's legitimate consumers or they may be impersonating buyers. Once those users engage in unauthorized consumption of the company materials, embezzlement happens. In an effort to avoid losing money, the organizations are keen on the quick identification of these kinds of scams. As we can see further down, the identification of fraud has several specific uses (Marino et al., 2022).

6.2.1 Recognizing Payment Card Fraud

Payment card illicit activity, including bogus enquiries and use, is a common problem in this industry, and methods for recognizing anomalies can help identify it. Finding instances of insurance deceit is comparable to finding instances of dishonest payment card registrations.

6.2.2 Identifying a mobile device Fraud

One common issue with tracking activities is identifying instances of mobile/cellular cheating. It is your job to look through a huge database of finances, analyze their work behaviors, and trigger an alert if any of them seem to have actually been compromised.

6.2.3 Insured Claiming Abuse Identification

Given an example, the claims fraud is a major issue in the land and accident industries. Automobile coverage deception. The payment management system is manipulated by a number of producers and applicants for the purpose of filing fraudulent and unlawful complaints. In order to prevent losses in money, it has become crucial for the related businesses that they identify this type of crime (Kumar et al., 2020).

6.2.4 Internal Trading Surveillance

One further area where identifying anomalies algorithms have recently found use is in the detection and prevention of fraud by insiders (Fernandes et al., 2019). The global stock markets are home to the phenomena known as interior trading, in which individuals engage in illicit profiteering by relying on proprietary data prior to its public disclosure. According to there are various shapes that insider knowledge might take. The details that can affect the value of stocks in a certain field could include things like impending mergers or acquisitions, terrorist attacks, regulations, or an additional relevant event. One way to spot insider dealing is to look for unusual transactions.

6.3 Medical and Public Health Anomaly Detection

Clients' neither clinical nor healthcare databases act as the usual starting point for finding anomalies efforts (Steenwinckel et al., 2021) (Bartolini et al., 2024). Exceptions in data might arise from a number of sources, including unusual patient conditions, mistakes in the instruments used or in the manner in which it was collected. The detection of disease epidemics in a specific area has also been the subject of various methodologies. Consequently, achieving a significant degree of efficiency in detecting anomalies is an extremely important challenge in this field.

6.4 Industrial Damage Detection

Constant use and regular deterioration cause machinery to deteriorate. In order to stop the injury from getting worse and more expensive, it needs to be found quickly. Knowledge acquired for assessment in that field is often called sensing information due to the fact that it captures information utilizing different sensors (Mokhtari et al., 2021). These losses have been detected widely in this category using methods for locating anomalies Industry the recognition of damage can be further polarized into two areas: one area addresses problems with building construction, the other one focusses on equipment like vehicles or generators. The first area is recognized as health care administrative systems.

7. APPROACHES OF ANOMALY DETECTION

Within the following paragraphs, we will go over the fundamentals of detection algorithms and techniques, with a focus on those used in digital safety. Distance, density, and rank are the main categories into which these methods fall (Raina & Krishnamurthy, 2022).

- Using height as a criterion, greater unusual endpoints are those situated further apart.
- Density-based: Points that are in relatively low density regions are considered more anomalous.
- Ranking: Out of all the points awarded, those that are out-of-the-ordinary ones are the ones where neighbors also have additional neighbors.

Under observation, semi-supervised, or uncontrolled information could be used in any of the above processes.

- Under the supervising scenario, every difference and assessments are relative to the given classifying designations on a collection of "instruction" samples.
- Since these distinctions are unknown in the unattended scenario, every evaluation and similarities are made relative to the full database.
- Keywords have been determined for specific information in semi-supervised tasks, yet they are believed over the majority of the information (Bogdoll et al., 2022). For example, a semi-supervised educational system could try to identify further probable cases of spyware that fall within a specific classification based on a small number of known occurrences of this type of malware. Confiding approximate categories to unlabelled info is a common first step in the iterative process that computers commonly follow.

The skills that follow must be included in an undetected anomaly finding technique

- It is necessary to set out typical conduct dynamically. It is not necessary to have an initial set of data or an analogous data set for typical behavior (Borghesi et al., 2022).
- Despite the lack of knowledge about the data transportation, it is nevertheless necessary to effectively recognize outlier.

- In order to find outliers in many domain names the technique needs to be flexible enough to respond to their unique properties, and it shouldn't necessitate extensive knowledge of the subject (Farzad & Gulliver, 2020).

8. EMPLOYMENT-RELATED ACTIVITY

Although techniques of deep learning have taken great strides in solving several AI issues and finding anomalies is still one area where deep-learning methods are still scarce. Offer an in-depth examination of catching fraud technologies that utilize neural networks. You will find here a detailed discussion of cyber-intrusion detection methods using DAD. The health-related domain's use of DAD strategies is thoroughly reviewed. In this article, we provide a high-level outline of DAD methods for IOT or large-scale identification of anomalies (Wang et al., 2021). An investigation of identifying anomalies in neural networks of sensors was conducted. We have shown the most cutting-edge approaches for film recognition of anomalies that employ neural networks, broken down into distinct categories (Hamamoto et al., 2018). We lack comparable evaluations of the design of deep learning used for the exception identification, despite the fact that we have few articles in utilizing DAD approaches. Aforementioned deep automatic encoding systems have been the subject of a great deal of new investigation, yet it has been no effort to compile a thorough evaluation of the many complicated designs that would work well with any particular datasets or group of applications. The context of an effort to fill this knowledge dearth, we have compiled the following questionnaire to serve as a resource for technical professionals interested in using deep programming for aberration identification. Displays the range of studies and areas of implementation that our study encompasses (Chalapathy & Chawla, 2019). Important parts of the finding anomalies method that shown in Figure 4.

Figure 4. Important parts of the finding anomalies method that uses deep neural networks.

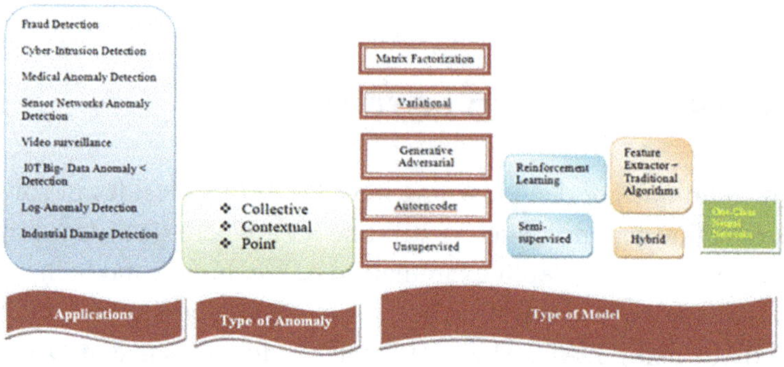

9. EVALUATION METRICS

9.1 The precision

Precisely a parameter to abnormality detection gadgets, efficacy is a metric for comparing or assessing what's actually to be anticipated. That indicates which of the equipment's productivity is up to par with the benchmarks (Nassif et al., 2021). Prejudices derived from the overall model are crucial to the computer's certainty; departing from these preconceptions reduces its precision.

$$Accuracy = (TP + TN)/(TP + TN + FP + FN) \tag{1}$$

$$Other\ measures\ FPR = FP/(FP + TN) and \tag{2}$$

$$Precision = TP/(TP + FP) \tag{3}$$

$$Recall = TP/(TP + FN), Sensitivity = TP/(TP + FN) \tag{4}$$

$$Specificity = TN/(TN + FP) \tag{5}$$

Whenever the proportion of FAR is low, it suggests that the reliability and expectation for DR are both good, which is a crucial metric for determining correctness. Through creating a matrix of errors for ADS, which is as illustrated in Figure 5, it becomes apparent that the precision of detection of anomalies is dependent on a number of characteristics, including FP, FN, TP, and TN (Jidiga & Sammulal, 2015).

Figure 5. Confusion matrix on anomalies.

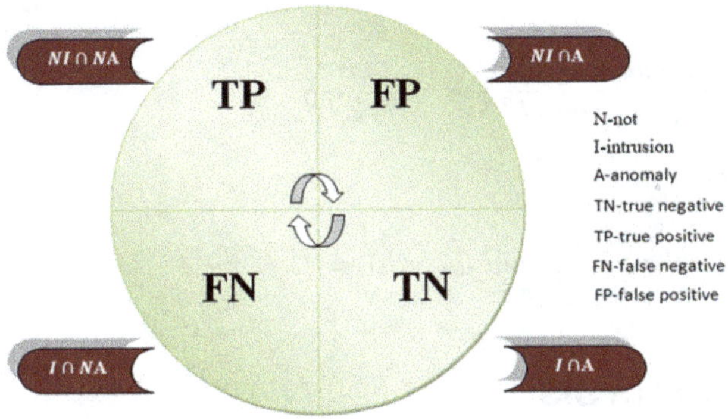

9.2 Rate of Error

The percentage of errors is defined as the average number of alarming errors triggered for a given set of variables. You may also acquire a lower percentage of errors by adjusting this variable by modifying the input data. The tolerance selections in the identification of anomalies typically determine the mistake ratio. One reliable method for finding outliers is to do a statistical assessment on a given series of incorrect answers. Towards the completion of the day, consistency and rates of error are mutually dependent (Gómez et al., 2019).

$$Error\ rate\ =\ (FP + FN)/(TP + TN + FP + FN)\ (6)$$

9.3 Ratio of False Positives

In accordance with the software being used, various metrics can be included in addition to the negotiation settings for the FPR and DR for evaluating the efficiency of system for identifying anomalies. In this instance, the FPR takes the history of counts asR_n, whereR_n, is the normal count and R_r is the false count, afterwards

$T_{p,p-}$ Documents as typical input and output (7)

$T_{p,h-}$ *Documents as typical input and output as untrue* (8)

$$T_{h,p-} \text{ Entries as erroneous data and results ad typical} \quad (9)$$

$$T_{h,h-} \text{ Paperwork as typical input and output} \quad (10)$$

$$T_{p,p} = T_p - T_{p,n} \text{ and } T_{h,h} = T_h - T_{h,p} T \quad (12)$$

$$FPR = \frac{T_{p,h}}{T_h} = \frac{no.of\ false\ positives}{no.of\ FP + no,of\ TN} = \frac{FP}{FP + TN} \quad (13)$$

$$and\ DR = TP = T_{p,p} \quad (14)$$

$$Let\ Example\ normal(p) = 3\ and\ false(h) = 2 \quad (15)$$

10. RESULT ANALYSIS

Keeping the point of equilibrium time to training constant for the 50-period scenario while ensuring agreement of suitable data were both achieved. Continuing across the page, in Figure 6, you can observe the graphical representations of the examination and instruction accuracy. A suggested LSTM All model of a precise curvature is shown in this Figure 6 (Ma et al., 2023).

Figure 6. Accuracy Curve for All Models

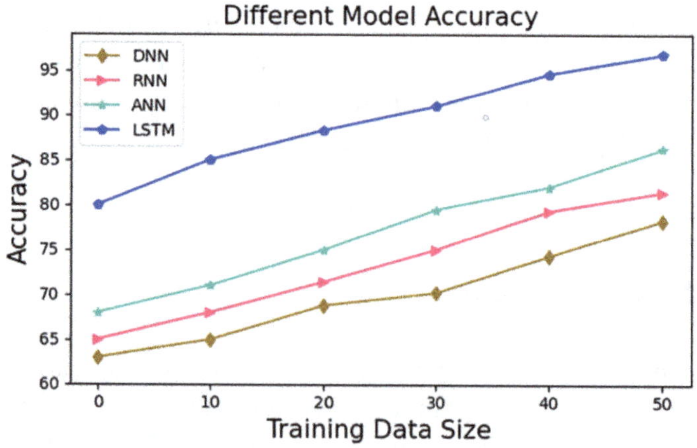

Figure 7 displays the Bewildered Matrix results of a classified binary algorithm. As a representation of the confusion matrix, the blue color scale uses darker hues to indicate greater values. The technique performs admirably under most circumstances, especially when it comes to accurately distinguishing class number 1, and it seldom fails to detect positive instances because of its low rate of incorrect results (Goix, 2016). We may see the matrix of disarray in Figure 7. There is a significant performance gap between the LSTM model and its rivals (Elmrabit et al., 2020).

Figure 7. Confusion Matrix

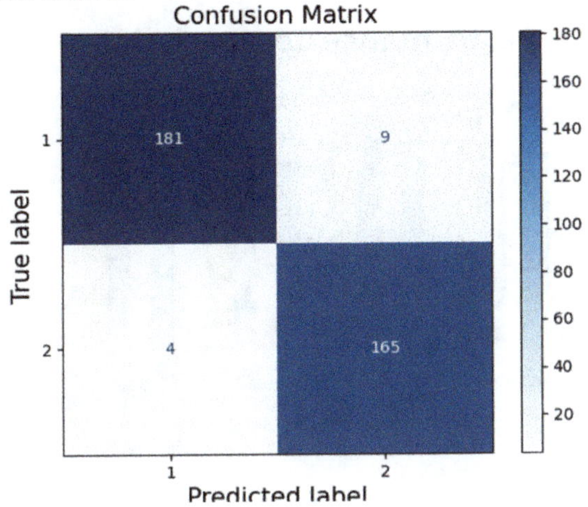

Figure 8 is a sample ROC curve that shows the relationship between the three parameters; the graph labels the FP Level and TP Rate as the axes of the horizontal and vertical directions, as well, reflecting the association between the three factors. The LSTM model outperforms its competitors, according to its ROC.

Figure 8. ROC Curve

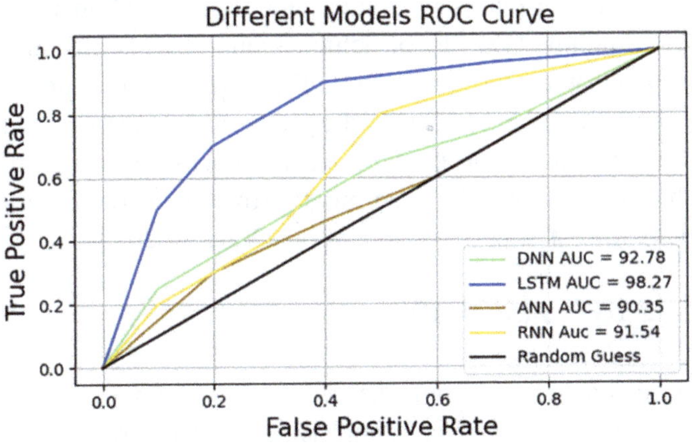

Researchers tested neural network models for predicting the weather using Accuracy, Precision, Recall, and F1-Score evaluation metrics. You can see the variations between the six deep learning scenarios in Figure 9, where is an array. As can be seen in the graphic, the LSTM model outperforms either method (Yang et al., 2023).

Figure 9. Performance Comparission

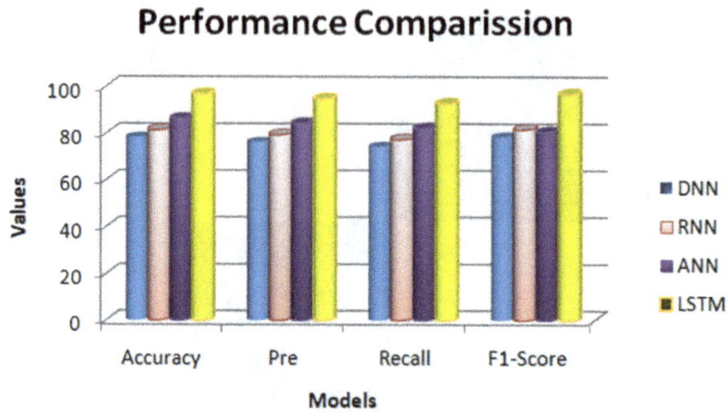

11. CHALLENGES

11.1 Measuring Improvements in effectiveness:

We find it challenging to quantify the extent to which items improve as a result from the strategy. Examining team tactics and adaptations models in order complicates matters, leading to muddled ratings of achievement. That is difficult to establish uniform measurements when the designs are subject to frequent changes. It becomes harder to assess their effectiveness in detecting anomalies due to feature (Shaukat et al., 2020). To attempt to tackle these issues, a comprehensive evaluation approach is required, one which considers both the cumulative impact of collaboration strategies and the dynamic nature of adaptive frameworks (Yaseen, 2023).

11.2 Obstacles to Collaboration:

Significant issues arise when our current protection approach is expanded to include adaptable approaches with collaborative techniques. Attempts to employ an especially sophisticated as well as intelligent method of locating peculiarities may encounter certain challenges. The proposed structure emphasizes change and collaboration, which may be challenging to implement in traditions that were originally developed for configuration methods. Ensuring ensures anything works smoothly, maintaining the framework is helps with discovering problems, and imagining old pieces are all necessary for success at integrating merchandise.

11.3 Data Privacy and Security Concerns:

Concerns about information's confidentiality and safety are inherent to algorithmic learning and complex product creation. There are ethical considerations when using personal information in order to spot anomalies (Sana et al., 2024). Maintaining data safety while still maintaining an eye on everything is challenging. Utilizing complex approaches also makes things tougher (Maseer et al., 2021). Robust methods of maintaining confidential details safe, ensuring all appropriate regulations adhere to and helping accessibility while managing information about oneself are all necessary in order to deal with these issues. For one's desired espionage weird event identification plan to gain trust, it must align combined with the latest thinking while still doing what was correct (Preuveneers et al., 2018).

12. CONCLUSION

Phenomenon mined is a fascinating field of study with many potential practical applications. There is a detailed review of methods for detecting outliers in data from time-series. Also contained is a nomenclature that sorts the techniques into different buckets based on the information being provided type, the degree of abnormality, and the characteristics of the way to detect it. The current part begins with a brief overview of the methods under consideration, before moving on to provide the findings within the taxonomy's directions. Development on finding anomalies could go in a number of interesting ways. What follows is an outline a few concrete proposals for studies to be conducted in the near future (Shaukat et al., 2021).

Programs for the web almost all modern practical problems use cases provide ever-changing data. In order to run the identification method on the entire extending datasets in real-time as more information comes in, it is necessary to mine these dynamical datasets for abnormalities using internet-based methods(Lin et al., 2019). The information grows exponentially over the years, making it impractical to perform online tasks on a regular schedule. While there are only a handful of uncontrolled digital phenomenon detectors, the overwhelming majority of them rely on some form of monitoring. Therefore, it would be a fascinating area to explore in the future to develop web-based forms of both our multidimensional and cooperative schools of learning (Xu et al., 2023).

Flexibility in scaling because more and more media is generated in everyday life, data gathering and archives are constantly improving. To handle massive amounts of information thousands of gigabyte of hard drive room is required (Munir et al., 2019). Consequently, adaptability is an important consideration while designing an info mining program. The accurateness of a method used to be the primary concern while designing one. Study participants today, nonetheless, are concerned with both precision and runtime, since techniques presently must handle material that cannot be stored in main memory during execution. Designing effective approximating procedures which involve constant time along with space could thus be an intriguing area for research to come. Additionally, it could be worthwhile to create abnormality group approaches that take advantage of complexity for future study (Landauer et al., 2023).

Complex heterogeneous graph anomaly ensemble Considering straight-forward, unsupervised homogeneity maps, most of the prior art in graphing abnormal analysis was developed. On the other hand, actual topologies are far more complicated, featuring a wide variety of edge nodes, edges properties, weights, etc. There is a lot of knowledge lost when communication graphs like Interest, Twitter, and social media sites are represented as simple graphs without direction because of their diverse nature. Anomaly detection on such complicated networks is an area that has received little attention. Consequently, an intriguing area for further inquiry could be the development of efficient and reliable ensembles methods for complicated heterogeneity topologies(Du et al., 2019).

REFERENCES

Ariyaluran Habeeb, R. A., Nasaruddin, F., Gani, A., Targio Hashem, I. A., Ahmed, E., & Imran, M. (2019). Real-time big data processing for anomaly detection: A Survey. *International Journal of Information Management*, *45*, 289–307. DOI: 10.1016/j.ijinfomgt.2018.08.006

Bartolini, A., Lombardi, M., & Milano, M. (2024). Alma Mater Studiorum Università di Bologna Archivio istituzionale della ricerca Borghesi, A ., et al . " A Semisupervised Autoencoder-Based Approach for Anomaly Detection in High Performance Computing Systems ." Engineering Applications of at : Rights / . June.

Bhuyan, M. H., Bhattacharyya, D. K., & Kalita, J. K. (2016). A multi-step outlier-based anomaly detection approach to network-wide traffic. *Information Sciences*, *348*, 243–271. DOI: 10.1016/j.ins.2016.02.023

Bogdoll, D., Nitsche, M., & Zollner, J. M. (2022). Anomaly Detection in Autonomous Driving: A Survey. IEEE Computer Society Conference on Computer Vision and Pattern Recognition Workshops, 2022-June, 4487–4498. DOI: 10.1109/CVPRW56347.2022.00495

Borghesi, A., Molan, M., Milano, M., & Bartolini, A. (2022). Anomaly Detection and Anticipation in High Performance Computing Systems. *IEEE Transactions on Parallel and Distributed Systems*, *33*(4), 739–750. DOI: 10.1109/TPDS.2021.3082802

Chalapathy, R., & Chawla, S. (2019). Deep Learning for Anomaly Detection. *Survey (London, England)*, •••, 1–50. https://arxiv.org/abs/1901.03407

Chambolle, C., & Poret, S. (2005). Keywords : 1 Introduction. 22(December), 1–22.

Chandola, V. (2009). Anomaly Detection for Discrete Sequences: A Survey Varun Chandola, Arindam Banerjee, and Vipin Kumar. https://www.cs.umn.edu/sites/cs.umn.edu/files/tech_reports/09-015.pdf

Chatterjee, A., & Ahmed, B. S. (2022). IoT anomaly detection methods and applications: A survey. *Internet of Things : Engineering Cyber Physical Human Systems*, *19*(June), 100568. DOI: 10.1016/j.iot.2022.100568

Du, M., Chen, Z., Liu, C., Oak, R., & Song, D. (2019). Lifelong anomaly detection through unlearning. *Proceedings of the ACM Conference on Computer and Communications Security*, 1283–1297. DOI: 10.1145/3319535.3363226

Elmrabit, N., Zhou, F., Li, F., & Zhou, H. (2020). Evaluation of Machine Learning Algorithms for Anomaly Detection. International Conference on Cyber Security and Protection of Digital Services, Cyber Security 2020. DOI: 10.1109/CyberSecurity49315.2020.9138871

Fahrmann, D., Martin, L., Sanchez, L., & Damer, N. (2024). Anomaly Detection in Smart Environments: A Comprehensive Survey. *IEEE Access : Practical Innovations, Open Solutions*, *12*(February), 64006–64049. DOI: 10.1109/ACCESS.2024.3395051

Farzad, A., & Gulliver, T. A. (2020). Unsupervised log message anomaly detection. *ICT Express*, *6*(3), 229–237. DOI: 10.1016/j.icte.2020.06.003

Fernandes, G.Jr, Rodrigues, J. J. P. C., Carvalho, L. F., Al-Muhtadi, J. F., & Proença, M. L.Jr. (2019). A comprehensive survey on network anomaly detection. *Telecommunication Systems*, *70*(3), 447–489. DOI: 10.1007/s11235-018-0475-8

Goix, N. (2016). How to Evaluate the Quality of Unsupervised Anomaly Detection Algorithms? https://arxiv.org/abs/1607.01152

Golomb, T., Mirsky, Y., & Elovici, Y. (2018). CIoTA: Collaborative Anomaly Detection via Blockchain. February. DOI: 10.14722/diss.2018.23003

Gómez, Á. L. P., Maimó, L. F., Celdrán, A. H., & Clemente, F. (2019). On the Generation of Anomaly Detection Datasets in Industrial Control Systems. *IEEE Access : Practical Innovations, Open Solutions*, *7*, 177460–177473. DOI: 10.1109/ACCESS.2019.2958284

Gupta, D., Kayode, O., Bhatt, S., Gupta, M., & Tosun, A. S. (2021). Hierarchical Federated Learning based Anomaly Detection using Digital Twins for Smart Healthcare. Proceedings - 2021 IEEE 7th International Conference on Collaboration and Internet Computing, CIC 2021, 16–25. DOI: 10.1109/CIC52973.2021.00013

Hamamoto, A. H., Carvalho, L. F., Sampaio, L. D. H., Abrão, T., & Proença, M. L.Jr. (2018). Network Anomaly Detection System using Genetic Algorithm and Fuzzy Logic. *Expert Systems with Applications*, *92*, 390–402. DOI: 10.1016/j.eswa.2017.09.013

Jidiga, G. R., & Sammulal, P. (2015). Anomaly detection using machine learning with a case study. *Proceedings of 2014 IEEE International Conference on Advanced Communication, Control and Computing Technologies, ICACCCT 2014*, 2(978), 1060–1065. DOI: 10.1109/ICACCCT.2014.7019260

Kaur, H., Singh, G., & Minhas, J. (2013). A Review of Machine Learning based Anomaly Detection Techniques. *International Journal of Computer Applications Technology and Research*, *2*(2), 185–187. DOI: 10.7753/IJCATR0202.1020

Kumar, V., Choudhary, V., Kumar, V., & Sahrawat, V. (2020).. . *Anomaly Detection in Networks Using Different Machine Learning Algorithms.*, *8*(4), 1145–1151. DOI: 10.5281/zenodo.15271016

Landauer, M., Onder, S., Skopik, F., & Wurzenberger, M. (2023). Deep learning for anomaly detection in log data: A survey. *Machine Learning with Applications*, *12*(May), 100470. DOI: 10.1016/j.mlwa.2023.100470

Le, V. H., & Zhang, H. (2022). Log-based Anomaly Detection with Deep Learning: How Far Are We? In Proceedings - International Conference on Software Engineering (Vols. 2022-May, Issue 1). Association for Computing Machinery. DOI: 10.1145/3510003.3510155

Lin, P., Ye, K., & Xu, C. Z. (2019). Dynamic network anomaly detection system by using deep learning techniques. Lecture Notes in Computer Science (Including Subseries Lecture Notes in Artificial Intelligence and Lecture Notes in Bioinformatics), 11513 LNCS(June), 161–176. DOI: 10.1007/978-3-030-23502-4_12

Liu, Z., Nie, Y., Long, C., Zhang, Q., & Li, G. (2021). A Hybrid Video Anomaly Detection Framework via Memory-Augmented Flow Reconstruction and Flow-Guided Frame Prediction. *Proceedings of the IEEE International Conference on Computer Vision*, 13568–13577. DOI: 10.1109/ICCV48922.2021.01333

Ma, X., Wu, J., Xue, S., Yang, J., Zhou, C., Sheng, Q. Z., Xiong, H., & Akoglu, L. (2023). A Comprehensive Survey on Graph Anomaly Detection With Deep Learning. *IEEE Transactions on Knowledge and Data Engineering*, *35*(12), 12012–12038. DOI: 10.1109/TKDE.2021.3118815

Marino, D. L., Wickramasinghe, C. S., Rieger, C., & Manic, M. (2022). Self-Supervised and Interpretable Anomaly Detection using Network Transformers. 1–9. DOI: 10.1109/TII.2025.3534443

Maseer, Z. K., Yusof, R., Bahaman, N., Mostafa, S. A., & Foozy, C. F. M. (2021). Benchmarking of Machine Learning for Anomaly Based Intrusion Detection Systems in the CICIDS2017 Dataset. *IEEE Access : Practical Innovations, Open Solutions*, *9*, 22351–22370. DOI: 10.1109/ACCESS.2021.3056614

Mokhtari, S., Abbaspour, A., Yen, K. K., & Sargolzaei, A. (2021). A machine learning approach for anomaly detection in industrial control systems based on measurement data. *Electronics (Basel)*, *10*(4), 1–13. DOI: 10.3390/electronics10040407

Munir, M., Siddiqui, S. A., Dengel, A., & Ahmed, S. (2019). DeepAnT: A Deep Learning Approach for Unsupervised Anomaly Detection in Time Series. *IEEE Access : Practical Innovations, Open Solutions*, *7*, 1991–2005. DOI: 10.1109/ACCESS.2018.2886457

Musa, T. H. A., & Bouras, A. (2022, January). Anomaly Detection: A Survey. *Lecture Notes in Networks and Systems*, *217*, 391–401. DOI: 10.1007/978-981-16-2102-4_36

Nassif, A. B., Talib, M. A., Nasir, Q., & Dakalbab, F. M. (2021). Machine Learning for Anomaly Detection: A Systematic Review. *IEEE Access : Practical Innovations, Open Solutions*, *9*, 78658–78700. DOI: 10.1109/ACCESS.2021.3083060

Pang, G., Shen, C., Cao, L., & Van Den Hengel, A. (2021). Deep Learning for Anomaly Detection: A Review. *ACM Computing Surveys*, *54*(2), 1–36. DOI: 10.1145/3439950

Patel, D., Srinivasan, K., Chang, C. Y., Gupta, T., & Kataria, A. (2020). Network anomaly detection inside consumer networks—A hybrid approach. *Electronics (Basel)*, *9*(6), 1–12. DOI: 10.3390/electronics9060923

Preuveneers, D., Rimmer, V., Tsingenopoulos, I., Spooren, J., Joosen, W., & Ilie-Zudor, E. (2018). Chained anomaly detection models for federated learning: An intrusion detection case study. *Applied Sciences (Basel, Switzerland)*, *8*(12), 1–21. DOI: 10.3390/app8122663

Raina, V., & Krishnamurthy, S. (2022). Anomaly Detection. Building an Effective Data Science Practice, 91–112. DOI: 10.1007/978-1-4842-7419-4_8

Ravikumar, G., & Govindarasu, M. (2024). Anomaly Detection and Mitigation for Wide-Area Damping Control using Machine Learning. *IEEE Transactions on Smart Grid*, *15*(6), 5939–5951. Advance online publication. DOI: 10.1109/TSG.2020.2995313

Republic, P. S. (2022). Anomaly Detection. *Survey (London, England)*, *151*, 704062220701–704062220703.

Sana, L., Nazir, M. M., Yang, J., Hussain, L., Chen, Y. L., Ku, C. S., Alatiyyah, M., Alateyah, S. A., & Por, L. Y. (2024). Securing the IoT Cyber Environment: Enhancing Intrusion Anomaly Detection With Vision Transformers. *IEEE Access : Practical Innovations, Open Solutions*, *12*(May), 82443–82468. DOI: 10.1109/ACCESS.2024.3404778

Sayed, A. K. (2023). Anomaly Detection Using Machine Learning. *International Journal of Advanced Research in Computer and Communication Engineering*, *12*(1), 131–162. DOI: 10.17148/IJARCCE.2023.12103

Schmidl, S., Wenig, P., & Papenbrock, T. (2022). Anomaly Detection in Time Series: A Comprehensive Evaluation. *Proceedings of the VLDB Endowment International Conference on Very Large Data Bases, 15*(9), 1779–1797. DOI: 10.14778/3538598.3538602

Shaukat, K., Alam, T. M., Luo, S., Shabbir, S., Hameed, I. A., Li, J., Abbas, S. K., & Javed, U. (2021). A Review of Time-Series Anomaly Detection Techniques: A Step to Future Perspectives. Advances in Intelligent Systems and Computing, 1363 AISC(April), 865–877. DOI: 10.1007/978-3-030-73100-7_60

Shaukat, K., Luo, S., Varadharajan, V., Hameed, I. A., Chen, S., Liu, D., & Li, J. (2020). Performance comparison and current challenges of using machine learning techniques in cybersecurity. *Energies, 13*(10), 2509. Advance online publication. DOI: 10.3390/en13102509

Siniosoglou, I., Radoglou-Grammatikis, P., Efstathopoulos, G., Fouliras, P., & Sarigiannidis, P. (2021). A Unified Deep Learning Anomaly Detection and Classification Approach for Smart Grid Environments. *IEEE Transactions on Network and Service Management, 18*(2), 1137–1151. DOI: 10.1109/TNSM.2021.3078381

Steenwinckel, B., De Paepe, D., Vanden Hautte, S., Heyvaert, P., Bentefrit, M., Moens, P., Dimou, A., Van Den Bossche, B., De Turck, F., Van Hoecke, S., & Ongenae, F. (2021). FLAGS: A methodology for adaptive anomaly detection and root cause analysis on sensor data streams by fusing expert knowledge with machine learning. *Future Generation Computer Systems, 116*, 30–48. DOI: 10.1016/j.future.2020.10.015

Stoian, N. A. (2020). *Machine Learning for Anomaly Detection in IoT networks: Malware analysis on the IoT-23 Data set*. University of Twente.

Systems, I. C. (n.d.). Computers in Industry Light-Weight Federated Learning-based Anomaly Detection for Time-Series data in Industrial Control Systems.

Taha, A., & Hadi, A. S. (2019). Anomaly detection methods for categorical data: A review. *ACM Computing Surveys, 52*(2), 1–35. Advance online publication. DOI: 10.1145/3312739

Wang, S., Balarezo, J. F., Kandeepan, S., Al-Hourani, A., Chavez, K. G., & Rubinstein, B. (2021). Machine learning in network anomaly detection: A survey. *IEEE Access : Practical Innovations, Open Solutions, 9*, 152379–152396. DOI: 10.1109/ACCESS.2021.3126834

Xu, H., Sun, Z., Cao, Y., & Bilal, H.XSu. (2023). A data-driven approach for intrusion and anomaly detection using automated machine learning for the Internet of Things. *Soft Computing, 27*(19), 14469–14481. DOI: 10.1007/s00500-023-09037-4

Yang, Y., Zhang, C., Zhou, T., Wen, Q., & Sun, L. (2023). DCdetector: Dual Attention Contrastive Representation Learning for Time Series Anomaly Detection. *Proceedings of the ACM SIGKDD International Conference on Knowledge Discovery and Data Mining*, 3033–3045. DOI: 10.1145/3580305.3599295

Yaseen, A. (2023). The Role of Machine Learning in Network Anomaly Detection for Cybersecurity. Sage Science Review of Applied Machine Learning, 6(8), 16–34. https://journals.sagescience.org/index.php/ssraml/article/view/126

Zaigham Zaheer, M., Mahmood, A., Haris Khan, M., Segu, M., Yu, F., & Lee, S. I. (2022). Generative Cooperative Learning for Unsupervised Video Anomaly Detection. Proceedings of the IEEE Computer Society Conference on Computer Vision and Pattern Recognition, 2022-June, 14724–14734. DOI: 10.1109/CVPR52688.2022.01433

Chapter 5

Comprehensive AI-Driven Approach to Cybersecurity in Fifth-Generation Networks

Ashok P.
https://orcid.org/0000-0002-5859-6041
Symbiosis Institute of Digital and Telecom Management, India

Sandeep Prabhu
https://orcid.org/0000-0002-2146-1960
Symbiosis Institute of Digital and Telecom Management, India

Srushtee Bhalerao
Symbiosis Institute of Digital and Telecom Management, India

Prathamesh Prabhu
George Washington University, USA

ABSTRACT

The AI-enabled risk management framework for 5G networks represents a significant advance in telecommunications security, in particular addressing the challenges posed by next-generation 5G networks. The key aspect of this article is to integrate established risk management principles with state-of-the-art artificial intelligence (AI). This new integration facilitates a dynamic approach to 5G security, allowing the system to evolve as new threats emerge. Unlike static security systems, AI-enabled risk management systems use adaptive controls, using AI to analyze real-time threat intelligence and adjust its security accordingly. Integrating AI enables the system to

DOI: 10.4018/979-8-3373-2252-0.ch005

intelligently address complex security challenges specific to 5G, combats multiple vulnerabilities. In doing so, risk AI-enabled planning for 5G networks not only protects against current threats but unexpected security. The approach, marks a significant step forward in the effort to secure the next generation of mobile networks mark, highlighting the critical role AI plays in shaping the future of network security.

1. INTRODUCTION

The evolution of cellular networks from the first generation (1G) to the fifth generation (5G) (as in Fig. 1, Table 1) has been a remarkable journey characterized by continuous innovation and technological advancement by each generation there are significant improvements in speed, capacity and connectivity, with which we communicate and communicate with mobile devices and businesses. There have also been new and complex security challenges to be addressed. In the early days of 1G networks in the 1980s, telecommunications were basically limited to voice calls, facilitated by analog technology. Although there were security concerns, these networks much less compared to the next generation because of their limited digital capacity.

Table 1. Characteristics of Different Generation Networks

Generation	Year	Description of Breach	Impact and Consequences
1G	1980s	Limited digital capabilities; minimal reported security breaches	Because of their analog nature, security risks were mainly physical, such as stolen equipment or unauthorized voice calls.
2G	1990s-2000s	SIM card cloning, eavesdropping on digital calls, SMS spoofing	Flaws in encryption algorithms (e.g., A5/1) allowed attackers to interrupt communications and impersonate SIM cards, enabling impersonation attacks and phishing scams using fake SMS access without granting access way and they are fraudulent.
3G	Early 2000s	Packet sniffing, man-in-the-middle attacks, SMS vulnerabilities	Weaknesses in protocol implementation and end-to-end encryption allowed attackers to intercept and manipulate data traffic, compromising user privacy and communication integrity SMS vulnerabilities that allowed SMS flooding and remote code execution attacks.
4G	Late 2000s	LTE protocol vulnerabilities, mobile app security flaws	The exploitation of LTE protocol vulnerabilities (e.g., IMSI catcher attacks) allowed data and voice communications to be hijacked. Mobile app security flaws (e.g., insecure data storage, inadequate trust) exposed user data to unauthorized access and use
5G	2020s	Network slicing vulnerabilities, IoT device security concerns	Network slicing vulnerabilities can allow universal access to fragmented network resources, resulting in data breaches and service disruptions. IoT device security concerns include vulnerabilities in device firmware, weak authentication methods, and susceptibility to botnet attacks, which compromise network integrity and the user privacy is threatened.

However, vulnerabilities such as listening to analog voice calls and simulating mobile devices still existed, underscoring the need for basic security measures. With the transition to 2G networks in the 1990s, which included digital voice calls and SMS. The emergence of techniques such as weak encryption algorithms and SIM card cloning posed serious threats to user privacy and network security. As mobile networks continued to evolve with the introduction of 3G in the early 2000s and 4G in the late 2000s, security concerns expanded to include threats such as packet sniffing, man-in-the-middle attacks, and weaknesses of the mobile app ecosystem. The advent of fifth-generation (5G) networks delivered an era of unprecedented connectivity, high data rates, low latency, and, like, the ability to seamlessly integrate an immense number of connected devices (Fakhouri et al.,). However, the rapid evolution of communication network architectures with software-centric, virtualized approaches, has literally given rise to intricate security challenges. The influx of vulnerabilities through wireless communication, and especially with the onset of the 5G network, has opened gates for an abundance of security threats. These range from identity manipulation and denial of service attacks to high-levels of complexity in the supply chain, and highly sophisticated cyber penetrations (Rajawat et al., 2023). It is in this context that the use of machine learning (ML) as a tool in strengthening 5G security is seen as highly promising. Of course, the physical layer is a veritable treasure trove of detailed information that can be exploited for security (Elapanda et al., 2020). Conventional encryption techniques have always made a strong base to justify security, but with the pace at which technology is accelerating, it puts a big question on the sustainability of such encryption with increased computational capabilities.

Figure 1. Evolution of Communication Networks

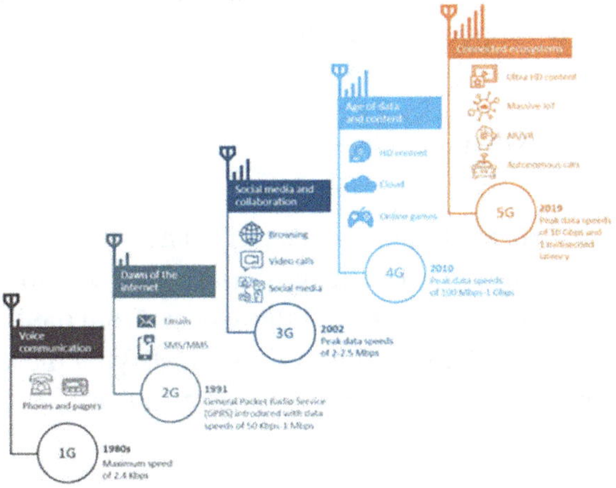

From 2G all through to the modern 5G era, the evolution of security protocols has matched the growing intricacy of wireless networks. The need for mutual authentication, verification of the integrity of the data packets, and protection against various forms of cyber threats such as man in the middle and rogue node attacks has been multiplied (Jiang et al., 2022). With the ambition of 5G networks in providing peerless speed, simplicity, and user experience altogether, an integrated security approach with encryption, authentication, and less onerous security practice becomes an indispensable ingredient (Apruzzese et al., 2022). The approach of the most critical inherent 5G network-related security challenges tries to tread through this study by offering a superior risk management framework—powered by Artificial Intelligence (AI). So much information with harnessing of ML algorithms available at the physical layer, it is our plan to develop security in dynamic and responsive nature and would respond even to new threats (Ahmed et al., 2023). That is a major transition toward more software-defined, cloud-based, and virtualized 5G networks, requiring forward-looking and resilient security posturing achievable through the synergistic application of AI and ML technologies. This paper discusses the architectural framework proposed, the usability, and the expected advantages of establishing an AI-enhanced risk management system for the protection of assets and infrastructure of 5G networks in order to increase the future wireless communications security (Le & Shetty, 2022). Moreover, the data breach landscape is daunting, given that the frequency and financial fallouts from data breaches are on the rise. The growth in cloud computing and digital transformation initiatives are also driving the cost of data breaches (Ramezanpour & Jagannath, 2022). A very common and potential hazard that a business faces when attacked by DDoS (as in Fig. 2) is infrastructure outages. With such challenges, businesses need to up their security on threats posed by cyber by having strong security protocols, instilling awareness about cyber security within staff, and all-inclusive strategies in place against incidents (Ramezanpour & Jagannath, 2022).

2. LITERATURE REVIEW

The integration of Artificial Intelligence (AI) in a risk management framework for the purpose of securing 5G networks has drawn the attention of academia and industry likewise. The article discusses all the aspects from the literature review in detail that are to be known related to the subject, identifying the key themes, methodologies, and findings that are surfacing in these recent years (Haider et al., 2020).

Figure 2. Number of DDoS attacks (From 2018-2023)

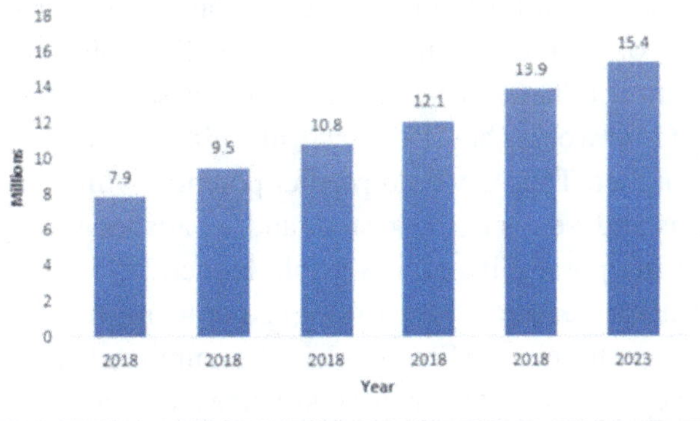

5G technology will set up a new generation of connectivity with speeds and bandwidth never before seen. But with the new development also comes to the fore a myriad of security challenges, thus requiring new-fangled solutions. On the contrary, AI emerges to be a powerful tool in increasing the security of the 5G networks with its capability of learning from data and predicting future outcomes (Polese et al., 2023). One of the very fast-growing topics of the usage of the machine learning (ML) algorithms is the anomaly detection inside the 5G networks. In addition, the researchers adopted various ML techniques, including supervised and unsupervised learning, in researching abnormal patterns, which could indicate security threats. These studies stress the potential role of ML in avoiding large-scale damage (IEEE Communications Society & Institute of Electrical and Electronics Engineers, 2015) (as in Fig. 3). The other key dimension to take into account is the capability of AI to automate responses when threats are detected. In the dimension of conventional security systems, this would consist of a time-consuming manual interference process and would possibly be fallible. On the other hand, AI-based systems could quickly analyse threats and bring in predefined actions. Thus, this considerably improves response time to threats (Nguyen et al., 2020). Not to mention the place that AI has in identity and access management in 5G networks. The AI systems (as in Fig. 4), for instance, through biometric data and the behaviour patterns, will give improved ways of making the authenticating processes. By this, a security becomes not only made robust but made better in general to the way service is being delivered (Qiu, 2021). Moreover, AI techniques have also been used in securing network slicing—one of the prominent features of 5G, where it offers the creation of multiple virtual networks atop a single physical network infrastructure. AI, in turn, can help in the optimal sharing of these slices and guaranteed isolation of these slices so as to prevent any cross-slice attacks (Ziegler et al., 2021). Another research direction concerns the application of AI for providing stronger methods of encrypting 5G networks. The strength of AI makes it possible to develop modern types of encryptions with ultra-high protection from classic methods, surpassing traditional methods of counteraction to technologically sophisticated cyber threats by orders of magnitude (Chamola et al., 2021). On the same issue of predictive risk management of 5G networks, heuristics and machine learning aside, AI is going to take it a notch higher. The AI would predict potential vulnerability by doing an analysis of patterns and trends in the system and, in advance, suggest pre-emptive measures to avert the possibility of a possible breach before it occurs (Chamola et al., 2021). Furthermore, the paper also looked at using AI in combination with blockchain technology to secure 5G networks. The combined offers improved integrity and transparency of data that provides resilience mechanisms against tampering and unauthorized access (Chamola et al., 2021).

Figure 3. Top 5G Network Security Concerns

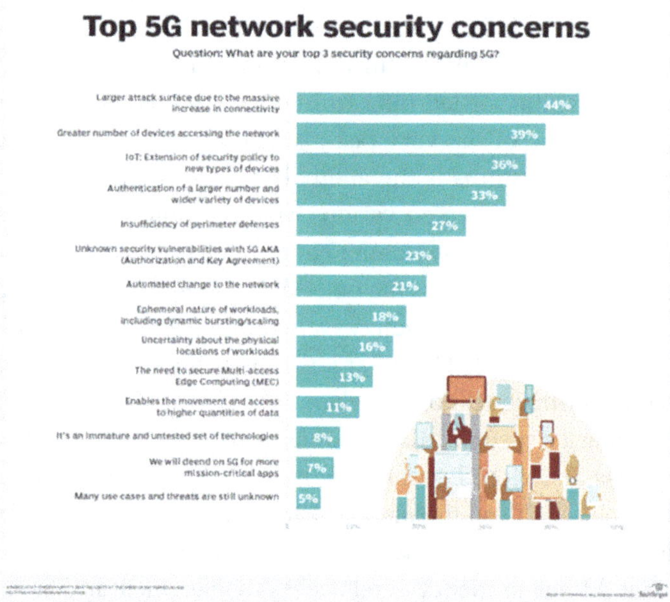

Perhaps the most critical contribution of AI has been in securing the devices connected to 5G networks belonging to the Internet of Things (IoT). It would certainly bring with it a vast number of diversified natured IoT devices, for which AI may, indeed, prove a very good solution to manage and secure them more efficiently than the traditional way (Afaq et al., 2021). The data privacy of the 5G network remains one of the biggest concerns for AI-based security measures. In this sense, the huge data volumes by AI systems make the importance of preserving and protecting data vital. The research to be carried out in this space would also be pertaining to the development of privacy-preserving AI algorithms (Afaq et al., 2021). Moreover, one big issue to concern with AI-enabled security solutions in 5G networks is scalability. During the scaling up of 5G networks however the great worry is whether the security systems are also going to scale up together with the networks. On this basis, other researchers undertook research in view of some number of options available so that AI-based security controls could remain useable despite an expansion in the network (Elapanda et al., 2020). Second, the AI studies in 5G networks ought to also consider the flexibility of the AI systems to modifications in the security threats. Cyber threats are not static and therefore the AI systems ought to adapt to the new developments of the cyber threats in order to present protection (Elapanda et al., 2020).

Figure 4. Key AI Components in Cybersecurity Space

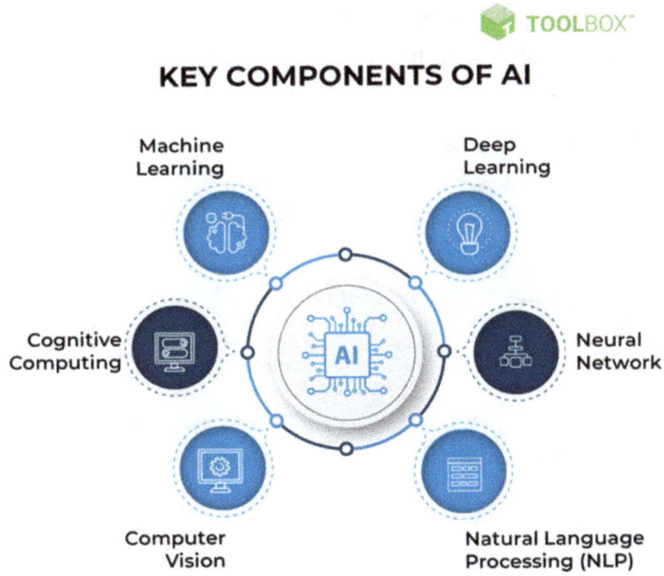

Artificial intelligence (AI) has transformed the industry to risk management, because it allows us to provide the advanced mechanisms and methods to enhance the decision-making process in terms of a single strength of AI is its functionality in processing large quantities of information rapidly and precisely. With highly considered data analytics and forecasting the AI has the ability to discover patterns, trends, and associations that could determine potential threats. The organizations will be able to develop risk mitigation measures and formulate risk management packages faster by learning more about the risk patterns and occurrences by adopting machine learning algorithms. The other major aspect of risk management that artificial intelligence stands out is anomaly detection. AI systems have the capability of detecting abnormalities in the anticipated behavior or unusual patterns in the data, which may display a threat or a security breach. Through real-time monitoring of abnormalities, organizations are able to detect and react rapidly to the risks emerging thus having less possibility of creating a negative effect. The process allows organizations to know their possible threats and weaknesses, thus enabling their general risk resilience. The NLP technology also complements risk management by allowing AI to carry out an analysis on unstructured data sources like the texts of the documents, emails, social media posts. NLP-powered AI emerging risks, market trends, clients through information and relevant insights extracted from these sources. It can also provide valuable emotional intelligence and this enables organizations to make more informed decisions and develop proactive risk mitigation strategies a based on real-time data and insights. Reliability of AI-based security system in 5G network has also been reviewed. Since the 5G networks are necessary (as in Fig. 5), AI systems used must have high reliability to be employed under different conditions.

Figure 5. Security Challenges in 5G

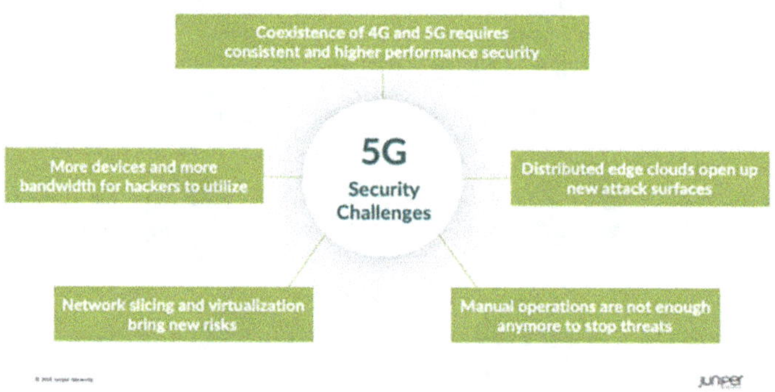

A major theme in 5G network security is the potential for collaboration between AI and human experts. AI can take care of a lot of things on its own, still human intervention is required in order to take on complex decisions and mitigate the fallacy of AI. The economic aspects of AI-driven security solutions implemented within 5G networks were offered. However, while there may be an initially taken high cost of investment, long-run benefits are seen, which relate to reduced downtime and prevention against costly breaches (Rastogi et al., 2023). The regulatory environment pertaining to the use of AI in 5G network security is changing. There is a real difficulty for policymakers to strike the right balance between creating an enabling environment for innovation and ensuring that, at the same time, AI is used responsibly, given the profound impact on privacy and security (Hallur et al., 2023). The debate on ethics within the AI domain, whether this is related to 5G security, is getting greater momentum. The other debate on AI, alongside its potential for bias, is that of the ethical use of the collected data (Hallur et al., 2024). A major practical problem is the interoperability of the AI-driven security systems to the installed network infrastructure, that should enable integration without disruption in the actual operation. With the rising tide of AI, the threat of adversarial AI attacks is growing, and robust defences are in need (Vankadara et al., 2024). Another important contribution to be made by AI is in regard to disaster recovery if 5G network attacks occur. AI will be able to automatically bring operations to the condition as they were just prior to the attack or collapse of the system, which will allow a company to lose minimal time and money on downtime and restoration (Hallur et al., 2024).

The interest in this context is based on the impact of AI for high energy efficiency in 5G networks as applied. The challenge is that the optimization of energy is required in AI-driven security systems in order to bring sustainability in the operations of the network (Hallur et al., 2024). On the other hand, AI may provide for a paradigm shift to proactive security means rather than reactive means against threats to the 5G network. Threat prediction offers to revolutionize the security landscape of these networks. But herein lies the very role of AI, making sure mobile edge computing in 5G networks is secure. Thus, the edge is the computing closer to the source of the data (Srivastava et al., 2024). The emergence of 5G technology that is hyper-connected ecosystem and unmatched speed poses immense security challenges. It is hard for traditional security solutions to catch up with the changing nature of threat landscape in which advanced attacks are launched and network environments change dynamically (Hallur et al., 2024). ML algorithms are able to analyse zettabytes of network data in real-time and detect anomalies or suspicious patterns that might escape signature-based detection. This facilitates early warning of emerging threats including zero-day attacks and Advanced Persistent Threats (APT) before they become big problems. Furthermore, AI can use anomaly detection and behavioural analysis to detect previously unknown vulnerabilities and misconfigurations within the network infrastructure that would otherwise have gone undetected with conventional security mechanisms (as in Fig. 6 and Fig. 7) (Hallur et al., 2024).

Figure 6. AI Use Cases

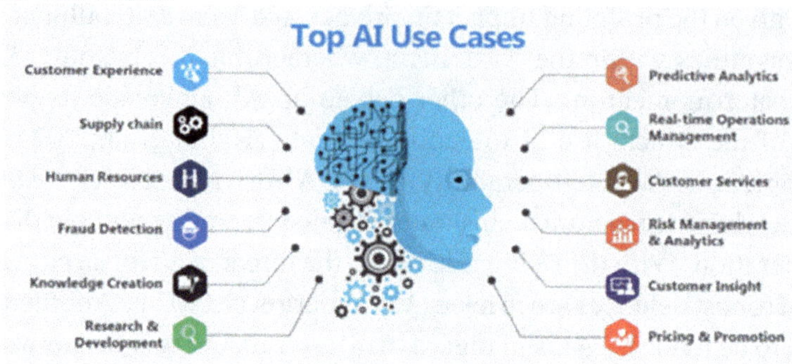

The automation features of AI contribute significantly to the optimization processes in incident response. AI-enabled systems can process security alerts, provide threat prioritization based on severity and potential damage, start containment and mitigation actions automatically. This dramatically cuts down the time-to-response which therefore minimizes greatly the amount of damage that cyberattacks can cause. In addition, AI can perform tasks such as log analysis and forensic investigation that frees human analysts to concentrate on complicated incidents and strategic threat assessment (Patil et al., 2024).

Figure 7. Role Of AI in Risk Management

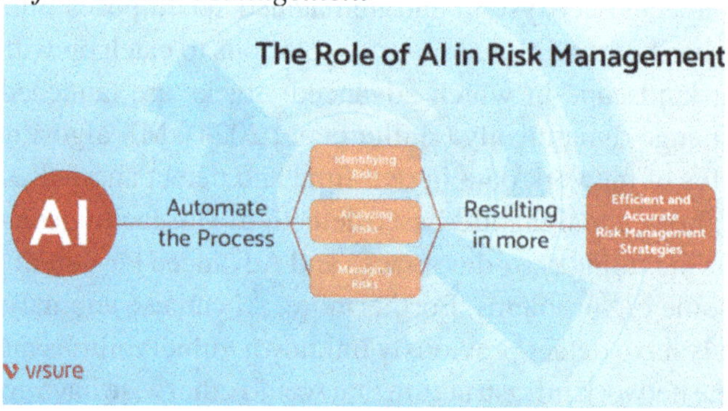

5G networks are designed to be dynamic and this is because of the fact that traffic patterns also change while device behaviours vary. Many static security configurations are not dynamic enough to meet advanced threats and configuration requirements for network defense have gaps. Unlike the human, AI in turn is capable of continuously monitoring network activity and can respond to it dynamically adjusting security policies instantly allowing for ultimate protection under ever-changing threats. AI-driven systems can analyse historical attack trends and approach of the network to forecast probable situations future risks, that need to be promptly covered with optimization security settings. This dynamic variant guarantees for the best 5G system security to change and adapt quickly (Anand et al., 2023). Although this may prove to be difficult, it is impossible not to accept the advantages of putting artificial intelligence into practice for 5G security. Through the integration of AI-based solutions along with conventional security techniques let's build a multi-layered defense system that can adapt according to rapidly changing and sophisticated nature of attacks on 5G network secure working. The cooperation between cybersecurity specialists, AI researchers and up-to date network operators will help develop further innovations in this emerging field promote efficacy of the emergent cutting AI security algorithms that may be able to protect 5G connectivity (Ravindranathan et al., 2024). Finally, continuous development in the area of AI technologies poses a moving target for researchers and practitioners within the 5G security area. Surely, the awareness of these developments and knowing what kind of implications they bring to security is crucial (Patil et al., 2024).

3. APPROACHES TO THE PROBLEM

Establishing a robust framework for implementing AI-driven risk management in 5G networks requires several critical steps. First, it is necessary to clarify the role of AI in risk managements, its parts, uses and applications. This is to be in the form of anomaly, threat prediction, and vulnerability scanning (Saxena et al., 2024). There are various network designers and AI developers, regulators, and security planners of the network in question, which have varied interest and responsibilities to address. It is also vital to abide by the current regulations and policies, especially those pertaining to cybersecurity, privacy, and the governance of AI, because compliance will help carry out AI risk management responsibly and lawfully. Risk management goals ought to be centered on 5G security, resilience, reliability and responsible AI use (Maiti et al., 2024). Threat intelligence based on AI, scenario design computations using AI, and human expertise are also important elements to successful risk assessment Attackers with AI in use should diversify into risks based on impact, likelihood, and application. The AI must be applied to measure the risk, model the attack operations and find AI-specific risk like bias, data poisoning, and malicious attack (Jain et al., 2024). Once risks are analyzed, prioritized and evaluated, their appropriate treatment is essential. This includes using AI-enhanced controls for intrusion detection, threat hunting, and automation of response actions. Implement dynamic security intelligence that adapts resources based on emerging threats (Ghosh et al., 2024). Descriptive AI must be used to ensure reliability and transparency in AI-based decisions, while continuous monitoring and enhancement of AI models is required to maintain the network in safety and efficiency. In communication and collaboration, transparency and the ability to explain are essential to building trust among stakeholders. Collaboration and knowledge sharing between AI system developers, security professionals and network operators should be encouraged through collaboration processes (Patel et al., 2024). Ethical considerations and governance frameworks must be adhered to, ensuring responsible use of AI in security applications and addressing potential ethical challenges. Regular communication and dialogue with stakeholders will help address concerns, foster consensus, and ensure consistency with ethical and legal standards (Bhalerao et al., 2024) (as in Fig. 8).

3.1. Establish the Context

Define Scope: List at least five points concerning 5G network components, services and applications that will implement AI's risk management.

Identify Stakeholders: Network operators, AI developers, regulators as well as security designers.

Consider Existing Policies & Regulations: Comply with standards laid down by cybersecurity, privacy and AI governance.

Establish Risk Management Objectives: Give focus to 5G security, resilience and reliability as well as responsible use of AI.

3.2. Identify Risks

Leverage AI for Threat Intelligence: Leverage AI – enabled anomaly detection, vulnerability scanning and threat prediction tools.

Conduct Scenario Planning: Use AI-based simulations for predicting possible attack vectors and resulting scenario

Incorporate Human Expertise: Work in conjunction with the security analysts to refine AI-generated risk insights and proper emphasis on context awareness.

Categorize Risks: Group risks as per impact, likelihood and exploitability by AI powered attackers.

Figure 8. AI Enabled Cybersecurity Framework

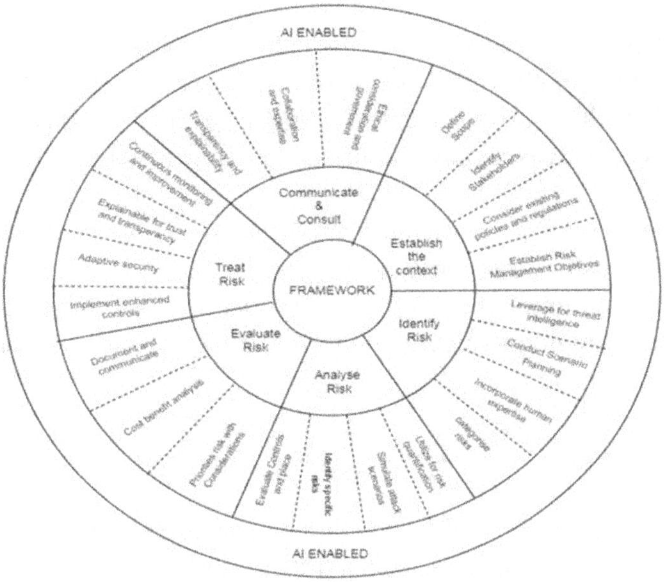

3.3. Analyze Risks

Utilize AI for Risk Quantification: Apply AI models to evaluate the level and possible consequences of detected risks.

Simulate Attack Scenarios: When running simulations to test the strength of existing controls, use AI-powered methods focused on targeted attacks.

Identify AI-Specific Risks: Study risks brought about by bias, data poisoning and adversarial attacks on AI security models.

Evaluate Controls in Place: Conduct an analysis of present security mechanisms, practices and technologies in their application efficiency coinciding with features AI contains.

3.4. Evaluate Risks

Prioritize Risks with AI Considerations: Concentrate on risks where the effects would be increased or income-able with AI.

Cost-Benefit Analysis: Compare how much to invest in AI-based prevention tactics relative to their potential security gain.

Document & Communicate Risks and Decisions: Provide stakeholders with the risk assessment results focusing on AI-related risks and mitigation measures.

3.5. Treat Risks

Implement AI-Enhanced Controls: Include AI-enabled systems for intrusion detection, threat hunting and automation of response actions.

Adaptive Security with AI: Deploy adaptive security intelligence that learns from incidents and dynamically modifications control measures depending on emerging threats.

Explainable AI for Trust and Transparency: Make AI-based decisions clear and comprehensible to allow the stakeholders to trust you.

Continuous Monitoring & Improvement: Trace machine learning so as to use it at the constant round-the-clock monitoring of network safety and risk status, perfecting its efficiency.

3.6. Communicate & Consult

Transparency & Explainability: Encourage conversation with stakeholders on AI as they pertain to risk management and their limits.

Collaboration & Expertise Sharing: Set up working platforms for AI program developers, security professionals as well the network operators.

Ethical Considerations & Governance: Ensure adoption of ethical guidelines and governance frameworks on responsible AI use in security applications.

4. INDUSTRY USE CASES

The industry use cases are neatly tabulated in Table 2.

Table 2. Industry use Case, its scope, stakeholders' involvement, risk identification, treatment of risk, communication and dialogue

Domain	Use Cases
5G Network Slice Security	Scope: AI-powered risk management was used to protect various parts of 5G network slices, including radio access networks (RAN), core networks, and service platforms. Stakeholders: Network operators, AI developers, regulators, and security designer work together to ensure the security and reliability of network slices. Identified risks: AI benefits from threat intelligence to find anomalies in network slices, plan for possible attack scenarios for slices, and classify risks based on their impact on slice performance. Risk treatment: AI-enhanced controls are used for intrusion detection and adaptive security intelligence is used to dynamically change security policies for each network slice. Communication and dialogue: Stakeholders communicate openly about the role of AI in securing network slices, share expertise in AI-powered security solutions, and adhere to ethical guidelines for AI deployment.
AI-Driven IoT Security	Scope: Use AI-based risk management to secure integrated IoT devices and applications and 5G networks. Stakeholders: Network operators work together with AI operators, IoT device manufacturers, regulators and security experts to mitigate the risks associated with IoT deployments. Threat detection: AI is used to identify and quantify the risk posed by IoT devices, create potential attack scenarios targeting IoT users, and assess the effectiveness of existing security measures works well. Risk management: AI-enhanced controls are being used to mitigate IoT-related security threats and automate threat hunting response actions. Communication and collaboration: Stakeholders openly communicate about the use of AI in the security of IoT devices, collaborate on AI-driven security solutions for IoT, and ensure compliance with ethical guidelines for IoT security in the field.
AI-powered network traffic analysis	Scope: Use AI-powered risk management to analyze network traffic and identify potential security threats in real time. Stakeholders: Network operators, AI professionals, cybersecurity experts, and regulators work together to ensure the accuracy and reliability of network traffic analysis. Threat identification: Use AI to identify risks associated with network traffic, simulate attack scenarios to test the effectiveness of traffic analysis tools, and identify specific AI-related risks such as bias in traffic search algorithms. Risk management: Use AI-enabled controls to continuously monitor and improve network traffic analysis tools, leveraging scalable security intelligence to strategically integrate analytical approaches based on emerging threats through the snow. Communication and dialogue: Stakeholders openly communicate the role of AI in network traffic analysis, share expertise in AI-powered traffic analysis solutions, and follow ethical guidelines for the use of AI for network security.

continued on following page

Table 2. Continued

Domain	Use Cases
AI-Powered Threat Intelligence	Scope: Using AI-based risk management systems to facilitate the sharing of threat intelligence between telecommunications providers and cybersecurity organizations. Stakeholders: Network operators are partnering with AI developers, cybersecurity firms, government agencies and industry associations to increase threat intelligence sharing. Risk identification: AI prioritizes threats based on potential impact on telecommunications networks, uses them to conduct cost-benefit analyzes to invest in AI-based threat intelligence, and documents risk a it contains and communicates to stakeholders. Risk Treatment: Threat intelligence sharing sessions use AI-enhanced controls for interpretable AI, allowing participants to trust and understand the decisions made by AI algorithms. Communication and dialogue: Stakeholders communicate openly about the use of AI in threat intelligence, collaborate on AI-powered ways to share threat intelligence, and ensure ethical guidelines are followed in using AI for threat intelligence sharing.
AI-powered network capability system	Scope: Apply AI-driven risk management to optimize network capacity planning and resource allocation in 5G networks. Stakeholders: Network developers partner with AI developers, equipment vendors, regulators, and capacity planners to ensure efficient use of network resources. Identified risks: AI is used to identify risks associated with congested networks, simulate capacity consumption to identify potential bottlenecks, and assess capacity consumption the old function works fine. Risk Treatment: Dynamic allocation and dynamic capacity planning are implemented using AI-enhanced controls, enabling networks to scale on demand and reducing the risks of service disruption the bottom of the table. Communication and collaboration: Stakeholders clearly communicate the role of AI in networking capabilities, collaborate on AI-driven solutions to optimize resources, and ensure compliance pa strategies on AI programming of communication systems.

continued on following page

Table 2. Continued

Domain	Use Cases
AI-Driven Customer Experience Management	Scope: Use AI-based risk management to enhance customer experience and satisfaction in 5G networks. Stakeholders: Network operators collaborate with AI developers, customer service teams, regulators and quality assurance experts to improve service quality and reliability. Risk identification: AI benefits from quantifying the risks associated with service disruptions and breakdowns, simulating different scenarios to predict customer experience in different interaction scenarios, and according to existing customer service practices works well. Risk Treatment: AI-enhanced controls are used for real-time monitoring of service performance and proactive troubleshooting, ensuring faster resolution of issues and maintaining high customer satisfaction. Communication and dialogue: Stakeholders clearly communicate the role of AI in customer experience management, collaborate on AI-enabled solutions to improve service quality, and ensure ethical guidelines are adhered to in using AI for customer service.
AI-enabled fraud detection and prevention	Enhancements: Implement AI-powered risk management to detect and prevent fraud in payment, service and identity management systems on 5G networks. Stakeholders: Network developers collaborate with AI developers, fraud analysts, law enforcement and law enforcement agencies to protect against fraudulent activities. Identified risks: AI is used to identify risks associated with fraudulent activities, simulate attack scenarios to test fraud detection techniques, and identify AI-specific risks such as methods which fraudsters evade. Risk Treatment: AI-enhanced controls are used to monitor transactions and user behavior in real-time, using adaptive fraud detection algorithms to identify emerging fraudulent patterns and prevent financial loss. Communication and collaboration: Stakeholders communicate openly about the role of AI in fraud detection and prevention, collaborate on AI-enabled solutions to prevent fraud, and ensure ethical behavior on the use of AI for fraud management.

5. CONCLUSION

As a conclusion, the introduction of AI to risk management frameworks in 5G networks signifies an innovative move that has improved on security, reliability and resilience over this emerging technological arena. This article indicates that there is a need for 5Gs smart networks be anchored on thin AI-driven strategies to counter integrated threats from cellular security tracks. This dependence on AI offers several benefits since organizations will be able to hire the services of threat intelligence, risk analysis and use adaptive security measures that could make their defense mechanisms much more effective in countering dynamic dynamism and highly advanced cyber threats. A comprehensive risk management system which is AI driven requires such cooperation as the interaction of network operators in general and AI developers in particular, regulators, and security designers. This strategy of leaning a thorough understanding of the innovation 5G networks components services and applications and the threats that accompanies the same ensures a global response that consider all the issues in the event of security challenges reaction. In addition, the orientation to alignment with existing policy processes and guidelines is what makes AI compliance in 5G security governance of critical importance. As we move on in the future, AI driven Security systems will have to be monitored with the objective of assessing it and making the necessary changes where possible to ensure security against emerging threats. The role of human supervision needs to be stressed because there is a necessity to have someone monitoring reliability and ethical behavior of AI technologies. Moreover, when it comes to issues like explainability and transparency as well as ethics, we must trust AI implementation. Lastly, our ability to align progress and accountability will be the determinant as to whether we will embrace the adoption of an AI-based risk management framework in 5G networks or not. With respect that AI comes with potential and limitations in place, through being vigilant, one can be able to move the 5G ecosystem to a safe efficient secure one. This initiative however goes beyond binging security with the safety of our digital infrastructure but it also involves the assurance that the 5G technology will do what it is meant to do to all stakeholders involved.

REFERENCES

Afaq, A., Haider, N., Baig, M. Z., Khan, K. S., Imran, M., & Razzak, I. (2021). Machine learning for 5G security: Architecture, recent advances, and challenges. *Ad Hoc Networks*, *123*, 102667. DOI: 10.1016/j.adhoc.2021.102667

Ahmed, I., Anisetti, M., Ahmad, A., & Jeon, G. (2023). A multilayer deep learning approach for malware classification in 5G-enabled IIoT.

Anand, A., ... (2023). Mitigating cyber-security risks using cyber-analytics. In 2023 7th International Conference on Trends in Electronics and Informatics (ICOEI) (pp. 630-635). IEEE. https://doi.org/DOI: 10.1109/ICOEI56765.2023.10126001

Apruzzese, G., Vladimirov, R., Tastemirova, A., & Laskov, P. (2022). Wild networks: Exposure of 5G network infrastructures to adversarial examples.

Bhalerao, S.. (2024). AI enabled risk management framework for enhanced security in 5G networks. In *2024 International Conference on Innovation and Novelty in Engineering and Technology (INNOVA)* (pp. 1-6). IEEE. https://doi.org/DOI: 10.1109/INNOVA63080.2024.10847018

Chamola, V., Jolfaei, A., Chanana, V., Parashari, P., & Hassija, V. (2021). Information security in the post quantum era for 5G and beyond networks: Threats to existing cryptography, and post-quantum cryptography. *Computer Communications*, *176*, 99–118. DOI: 10.1016/j.comcom.2021.05.019

Elapanda, S., Adinarayana Rao, U. V., & Sravan Kumar, E. (2020). Application of artificial intelligence in improving operational efficiency in telecom industry.

Elapanda, S., Rao, U. V. A., & Kumar, E. S. (2020). Application of artificial intelligence in improving operational efficiency in telecom industry. *International Journal on Emerging Technologies*, *11*(3), 65–69.

Fakhouri, H. N., Alawadi, S., Awaysheh, F. M., Hani, I. B., Alkhalaileh, M., & Hamad, F. (Year). A comprehensive study on the role of machine learning in 5G security: Challenges, technologies, and solutions.

Ghosh, S.. (2024). Scalable blockchain architecture for organ allocation in large-scale healthcare systems. In *2024 International Conference on Cybernation and Computation (CYBERCOM)* (pp. 732-736). IEEE. https://doi.org/DOI: 10.1109/CYBERCOM63683.2024.10803210

Haider, N., Baig, M. Z., & Imran, M. (2020). Artificial intelligence and machine learning in 5G network security: Opportunities, advantages, and future research trends. https://arxiv.org/abs/2007.04490

Hallur, G.. (2023). *Demystifying domain-specific key drivers in telecom technologies. In 2023 Intelligent Computing and Control for Engineering and Business Systems (ICCEBS).* IEEE., DOI: 10.1109/ICCEBS58601.2023.10449118

Hallur, G., ... (2024a). Empowering connections: Trailblazing technologies in telecom communication infrastructure. In 2024 5th International Conference on Image Processing and Capsule Networks (ICIPCN) (pp. 759-763). IEEE. https://doi.org/DOI: 10.1109/ICIPCN63822.2024.00131

Hallur, G.. (2024b). Navigating the infotainment landscape: Status and regulations in the digital age. In *2024 International Conference on Advances in Data Engineering and Intelligent Computing Systems (ADICS)* (pp. 1-6). IEEE. https://doi.org/DOI: 10.1109/ADICS58448.2024.10533560

Hallur, G., ... (2024c). Seamless mobility: Innovating the digital service landscape in telecom industry. In Proceedings of Fifth International Conference on Computing, Communications, and Cyber-Security, IC4S 2023, Lecture Notes in Networks and Systems (Vol. 991). Springer. https://doi.org/DOI: 10.1007/978-981-97-2550-2_14

Hallur, G., ... (2024d). Synergy in action: Harnessing cloud services and wired broadband for seamless operations. In 2024 2nd World Conference on Communication & Computing (WCONF) (pp. 1-7). IEEE. https://doi.org/DOI: 10.1109/WCONF61366.2024.10691966

Hallur, G., ... (2024e). Wireless broadband unleashed: Charting regulatory pathways for broadband development. In 2024 2nd World Conference on Communication & Computing (WCONF) (pp. 1-6). IEEE. https://doi.org/DOI: 10.1109/WCONF61366.2024.10692209

IEEE. Communications Society & Institute of Electrical and Electronics Engineers. (2015). 2015 IEEE/CIC International Conference on Communications in China - Workshops (CIC/ICCC).

Jain, S.. (2024). Emerging technologies for cybersecurity in healthcare: Evaluating risks and implementing standards. In *2024 International Conference on Cybernation and Computation (CYBERCOM)* (pp. 725-731). IEEE. https://doi.org/DOI: 10.1109/CYBERCOM63683.2024.10803219

Jiang, C., Xu, H., Huang, C., & Huang, Q. (2022). An adaptive information security system for 5G-enabled smart grid based on artificial neural network and case-based learning algorithms.

Le, T., & Shetty, S. (2022). Artificial intelligence-aided privacy preserving trustworthy computation and communication in 5G-based IoT networks.

Maiti, P., ... (2024). Decentralized defenses: A framework for 5G IoT security in Industry 4.0 using blockchain crowdsourcing. In 2024 3rd International Conference on Sentiment Analysis and Deep Learning (ICSADL) (pp. 534-538). IEEE. https://doi.org/DOI: 10.1109/ICSADL61749.2024.00093

Nguyen, D. C., Pathirana, P. N., Ding, M., & Seneviratne, A. (2020). Blockchain for 5G and beyond networks: A state of the art survey. *Journal of Network and Computer Applications*, *166*, 102693. DOI: 10.1016/j.jnca.2020.102693

Patel, K. N., ... (2024). Cybersecurity risks and countermeasures in the threat landscape of IoT devices. In 2024 4th International Conference on Technological Advancements in Computational Sciences (ICTACS) (pp. 875-883). IEEE. https://doi.org/DOI: 10.1109/ICTACS62700.2024.10841210

Patil, A., ... (2024a). 5G monetization strategies and business models: An insightful analysis for telecommunications service providers. In 2024 5th International Conference on Data Intelligence and Cognitive Informatics (ICDICI) (pp. 16-23). IEEE. https://doi.org/DOI: 10.1109/ICDICI62993.2024.10810884

Patil, A., ... (2024b). Cyber resilience: Safeguarding India's markets in the post-pandemic cyber landscape. In 2024 4th International Conference on Innovative Practices in Technology and Management (ICIPTM) (pp. 1-5). IEEE. https://doi.org/DOI: 10.1109/ICIPTM59628.2024.10563229

Polese, M., Bonati, L., D'Oro, S., Basagni, S., & Melodia, T. (2023). Understanding O-RAN: Architecture, interfaces, algorithms, security, and research challenges. *IEEE Communications Surveys and Tutorials*, *25*(2), 1376–1411. DOI: 10.1109/COMST.2023.3239220

Qiu, W. (2021). Enterprise financial risk management platform based on 5G mobile communication and embedded system. *Microprocessors and Microsystems*, *80*, 103594. DOI: 10.1016/j.micpro.2020.103594

Rajawat, A. S., Goyal, S. B., Bedi, P., Kautish, S., & Shrivastava, D. P. (2023). Analysis assaulting pattern for the security problem monitoring in 5G-enabled sensor network systems with big data environment using artificial intelligence/machine learning.

Ramezanpour, K., & Jagannath, J. (2022). Intelligent zero trust architecture for 5G/6G networks: Principles, challenges, and the role of machine learning in the context of O-RAN.

Rastogi, . (2023). Reimagining telecom industry using blockchain technology. In *2023 International Conference on Sustainable Computing and Data Communication Systems (ICSCDS)* (pp. 1261-1265). IEEE. https://doi.org/DOI: 10.1109/ICSCDS56580.2023.10104989

Ravindranathan, P.. (2024). Illuminating the dark: Gaining insights and managing risks with dark analytics. In *2024 International Conference on Intelligent and Innovative Technologies in Computing, Electrical and Electronics (IITCEE)* (pp. 1-6). IEEE. https://doi.org/DOI: 10.1109/IITCEE59897.2024.10467380

Saxena, Y.. (2024). Cloud renaissance: Thriving in the post-pandemic digital landscape. In *2024 Fourth International Conference on Advances in Electrical, Computing, Communication and Sustainable Technologies (ICAECT)* (pp. 1-6). IEEE. https://doi.org/DOI: 10.1109/ICAECT60202.2024.10469149

Srivastava, A., ... (2024). 5G network fusion: Exploring the interplay of edge and cloud computing. In 2024 5th International Conference on Image Processing and Capsule Networks (ICIPCN) (pp. 821-825). IEEE. https://doi.org/DOI: 10.1109/ICIPCN63822.2024.00142

Vankadara, Y.. (2024). 6G revolution: Redefining communication systems. In *2024 International Conference on Smart Systems for Applications in Electrical Sciences (ICSSES)* (pp. 1-6). IEEE. https://doi.org/DOI: 10.1109/ICSSES62373.2024.10561292

Ziegler, V., Schneider, P., Viswanathan, H., Montag, M., Kanugovi, S., & Rezaki, A. (2021). Security and trust in the 6G era. *IEEE Access : Practical Innovations, Open Solutions*, *9*, 142314–142327. DOI: 10.1109/ACCESS.2021.3120143

KEY TERMS AND DEFINITIONS

Adaptive Security Controls: Adaptive security controls are dynamic defense mechanisms that use Artificial Intelligence (AI) to continuously adjust and respond to new and evolving threats in 5G networks. They ensure ongoing protection by learning from data and adapting security policies in real time. Such controls move beyond static rules, enabling more robust and flexible network security. Their main goal is to minimize vulnerabilities by proactively countering sophisticated cyber-attacks.

AI Ethics and Governance: AI ethics and governance involve establishing transparent, fair, and accountable frameworks for the use of AI in 5G security systems. These frameworks address concerns about bias, privacy, and misuse of AI-driven decisions. They ensure that AI technologies are used responsibly, with clear guidelines for transparency and accountability. Implementing such governance builds trust and helps prevent unintended consequences in automated security operations.

Anomaly Detection: Anomaly detection refers to the use of machine learning algorithms to identify unusual patterns or behaviors within network traffic. In 5G cybersecurity, it helps detect potential threats or breaches by flagging deviations from established norms. AI-driven anomaly detection enables real-time monitoring and rapid response to emerging risks. This proactive method reduces the impact of attacks by identifying them before they escalate.

Network Slicing: Network slicing is a core feature of 5G technology that allows multiple virtual networks to be created on a single physical infrastructure. Each "slice" can be customized for specific applications, users, or services, with tailored security and performance requirements. AI plays a role in optimizing resource allocation and ensuring the isolation and security of each slice. This approach enhances flexibility, efficiency, and the ability to defend against cross-slice attacks.

Chapter 6

Leveraging Artificial Intelligence for Advanced Threat Detection and Autonomous Response in Cybersecurity

Venkata Ramana Kaneti
VNR Vignana Jyothi Institute of Engineering and Technology, India

D. Jayasutha
Kathir College of Engineering, India

B. Yamini
https://orcid.org/0000-0003-3531-108X
SRM Institute of Science and Technology, India

M. G. Dinesh
https://orcid.org/0009-0009-7643-5338
Easa College of Engineering and Technology, India

L. A. Anto Gracious
https://orcid.org/0000-0003-2386-9182
R.M.K. College of Engineering and Technology, India

P. Girija
https://orcid.org/0009-0000-1691-8180
Panimalar Engineering College, India

ABSTRACT

The increasing complexity and volume of cyber threats demand advanced solutions beyond traditional methods. This chapter explores the integration of emerging Artificial Intelligence (AI) technologies in cybersecurity, highlighting their transformative role in threat detection, prevention, and response. Key AI techniques such as machine learning, deep learning, natural language processing, and reinforcement learning are explored for their applications in malware detection, phishing prevention, network security, and autonomous defense systems. The chapter also discusses challenges

DOI: 10.4018/979-8-3373-2252-0.ch006

like data privacy, model bias, and resource requirements, alongside future directions involving IoT, 5G, cloud integration, and quantum computing. In summary, AI holds significant potential to drive the development of intelligent, adaptive, and proactive cybersecurity systems that can safeguard digital infrastructure in a continuously evolving threat landscape.

1. INTRODUCTION

1.1 Overview of Cybersecurity and Its Importance in the Digital Age

Since we live in a strongly connected digital world, cybersecurity is now a key element of developing technology, ensuring businesses remain open and protecting a country (Azizi, N & Haass, O 2023). Because of the wide use of digital platforms for business, government and communication, cyber assets are now necessary for both work and everyday activities. Because of cloud computing, IoT and smart devices, the risk of cyberattacks has grown much bigger. Cybersecurity involves the use of different techniques, tools and methods to stop unauthorized people from accessing, harming or stealing networks, systems and data. The recent world depends on the safety, privacy and access to information systems and any problems in these areas can lead to important consequences. Because cyber threats are occurring more and becoming increasingly advanced, cybersecurity is extremely important (Kour, R. 2020; Prabhu, D et al., 2025). More people and organizations across the globe are suffering from data breaches, ransomware attacks, identity theft and denial-of-service (DoS) attacks. Because healthcare, energy and transportation are regularly attacked, cybersecurity becomes an issue that concerns public safety and the economy. Since society is now more digital, having strong cybersecurity is necessary for a business to thrive, protect people's privacy and gain worldwide trust (Priyadarshini, I. 2017).

1.2 Challenges in Traditional Cybersecurity Methods

Modern cyber threats usually break through traditional cybersecurity arrangements, regardless of improvements in firewalls, antivirus software and IDS. The main drawback is that they do not foresee problems themselves. Traditional systems follow rules and mostly use known patterns of attacks to find threats. Therefore, they do not work when dealing with brand-new vulnerabilities and unusual attacks. Also, standard security tools find it hard to handle the high amounts and different types of data that are common in today's IT settings, especially in large companies and cloud systems.

Limits that humans have create a major problem. Security analysts usually face too many alerts from traditional systems and most of them turn out to be false positives. Because there is so much information, people may become tired and miss or react to important alerts late. Besides, the lack of skilled cybersecurity staff makes the problem worse by leaving gaps in the process of detecting, addressing and investigating incidents. Moreover, bad actors in cybercrime are getting smarter, making use of polymorphic malware, tricking people with social engineering and attacks that involve AI. Because of these new tactics, it is getting harder for traditional systems to respond. It is not enough to depend only on fixed rules in situations where threats are constantly changing. It is urgent to have systems that can adjust to new information, identify unusual situations in real time and act ahead of possible threats.

1.3 Introduction to the Role of AI in Improving Cybersecurity

Many of the challenges in traditional cybersecurity can be solved by using Artificial Intelligence (AI). Some of the technologies used in AI such as machine and deep learning, NLP and data mining, are effective in making cybersecurity operations more secure (Apruzzese et al., 2023). AI is able to analyze past records, recognize difficult patterns and foresee future security problems which is very useful for detecting and dealing with complex cyberattacks. The main advantage of AI in cybersecurity is that it can review a lot of information in real time which is not possible for people or traditional security solutions. With machine learning, it is possible to detect little changes in a system's behavior that could signal a cyberattack. Examples of anomalies are sudden changes in user actions, unusual access to the system or abnormal traffic in the network which may hint at a breach (Bharadiya, J., 2023). AI systems are able to update their models with new data which makes it easier for them to respond to new threats than traditional ways. AI helps take care of many cybersecurity tasks which lowers the workload for analysts and allows threats to be detected more quickly. Such systems collect information from many sources, point out indicators of attacks and suggest how to solve the problem. It is possible to use natural language processing to read through cybersecurity reports, blogs and threat databases and immediately find out about new threats. Thanks to AI, organizations are able to use predictive models to find out about possible weaknesses and ways attackers may enter the system, allowing them to act ahead of any breach. It is a major change from the old method of cybersecurity which usually reacted after an attack. With AI included in their security systems, organizations can protect themselves from threats that are already known as well as those that have not been identified yet (Yildirim, M. 2021; Yamini et al., 2024).

1.4 Purpose of the Survey

The survey chapter focuses on how AI technologies are changing the way cyber defense is done in the future. This work looks into how AI can improve different areas of cybersecurity such as spotting threats, responding to incidents, assessing weaknesses and handling risks. The goal of the chapter is to look at what AI can do now and where it falls short, as well as its usefulness in the real world, deployment problems and its future possibilities. This survey is meant to find the relationship between AI research and cybersecurity, showing how up-to-date AI technologies are used to deal with real security issues. It involves examining several AI-based tools and methods already being used, as well as judging how well they work in protecting against cyber threats. Besides, it looks at the moral, legal and practical issues involved in using AI in areas where the decisions of AI systems are very important.

All in all, this chapter aims to explain how artificial intelligence is being used in cybersecurity to protect digital platforms. The chapter uses recent works, case studies and experiments to explain both the advantages and the shortcomings of AI in cybersecurity, thus preparing for further research and action in this area.

2. BACKGROUND

2.1 Brief History of AI and Its Evolution in Various Fields

The history of Artificial Intelligence (AI) which involves developing machines that act intelligently like people, goes back several decades. For a long time, people imagined intelligent machines, but AI as a field did not begin until the 1950s. The year 1956 saw the Dartmouth Conference which established AI as a field and made researchers imagine machines that could learn and think. At the beginning, experts worked on symbolic reasoning and problem-solving which resulted in expert systems that mimicked people's decisions in specific areas. In the 1960s and 1970s, there were only small steps forward in AI, as it helped computers play games and do basic mathematical calculations. Yet, because of technical challenges and extremely high goals, interest and investment in AI dropped which is known as the "AI winter." Starting in the 1980s, AI was revived when algorithms for knowledge-based systems became better and its growth continued in the 1990s when ML techniques developed. Thanks to strong growth in computing, access to huge data sets and improvements in statistics, AI made significant progress in the 21st century. Deep learning which is based on the human brain, brought about major changes in image and speech recognition, natural language processing (NLP) and autonomous systems. Healthcare, finance, transportation, education and manufacturing industries have quickly started using AI to make their operations more efficient, improve what users get and make smart predictions[Thiyagarajan, P. 2020]. Specifically, AI is now necessary for tasks that involve spotting patterns, making predictions and making up decisions. Today, AI is used to identify fake banking actions as well as to help diagnose medical problems through images (Kashyap, R. 2021). Currently, AI is able to create music, write texts that sound like people, translate from one language to another and steer vehicles on their own. Because AI keeps getting better, it is becoming more important in all fields, including cybersecurity.

2.2 Overview of Current Cybersecurity Trends

Rapid changes in cybersecurity are happening because of new technologies, growing digital use and many advanced cyber threats[Murugan T., 2023]. Over the past few years, cyberattacks have evolved from one-off events to regular threats that may damage important infrastructure, take private data and endanger the country's safety. Recent attackers depend on ransomware-as-a-service, phishing, zero-day exploits and social engineering to get into systems without permission. Because more companies are using cloud services and allowing remote work, security risks have increased and new problems have arisen. It is now the job of organizations to protect multi-cloud systems, networks that mix public and private resources and a wide range of endpoints which makes cybersecurity much more difficult. Therefore, organizations are paying more attention to Zero Trust Architecture (ZTA) which believes that risks can be found inside and outside the network and requires everyone to be properly identified and given the smallest amount of access possible.

Cyber-physical systems and IoT devices are new developments that create security concerns because they lack enough computing power, do not use encryption and have weak communication methods. Because of the increasing number of these devices, there are now many chances for attackers to gain access. Also, companies are changing their security strategies because of regulations Cybersecurity Framework. Attention is also rising on exchanging threat information, analyzing activities and using machines to respond to incidents. Cybersecurity is now a main business concern that requires the attention of top-level leaders. Besides, machine learning and data analytics are now needed for threat detection, not just an extra benefit. In order to address threats that develop more rapidly than usual, organizations should use real-time monitoring, predictive analytics and anomaly detection. Such developments point out that intelligent, flexible cybersecurity is now required which makes AI all the more important.

2.3 Integration of AI with Cybersecurity: Past, Present, and Future

Because the threats in cybersecurity keep increasing, AI was adopted in security gradually, not all at once. At first, AI only helped with basic automation such as IDS systems that looked for suspicious actions by following set rules. The first systems were beneficial, but they were inflexible and sometimes produced wrong results. When machine learning advanced, AI became helpful for catching more serious threats, mainly by spotting malware and unusual events in a network[Das, R & Morris, T. H 2017]. With the help of both supervised and unsupervised learning algorithms, systems could spot novel threats by reviewing old data which resulted in better detection and fewer false alarms. With behavioral analytics, security platforms were able to spot unusual actions on a system which could mean a breach had occurred.

In today's world, NLP is used to analyze threat intelligence reports, chat conversations and phishing emails to obtain useful security information. The effectiveness of reinforcement learning and deep learning models is being examined to find out if they can assist in creating automatic defenses and choosing the right strategies in fake cyber scenarios (Ganapathi, P & Shanmugapriya, D 2019). In the days to come, there are great opportunities and obstacles for AI in cybersecurity. The development of AI should result in better prediction of threats, automation of incident response and even running tests to check how systems react to attacks. Still, the same AI technologies could be used by attackers to cause harm. There are serious risks from AI-powered malware, robots that use social engineering and attacks that affect AI models. That's why future studies should concentrate on developing AI systems in cybersecurity that are clear, dependable and ethical. Combining AI with blockchain for better data tracking, using federated learning to keep security analytics more private and coming up with AI systems that cooperate with human analysts are promising options. All in all, instead of just following simple rules, AI in cybersecurity has developed to handle threats in real time and respond effectively. Though AI can greatly improve cyber defense, it brings new risks that should be handled by designing carefully, creating proper rules and always innovating.

3. AI TECHNIQUES USED IN CYBERSECURITY

3.1 Machine Learning (ML)

Many experts in cybersecurity use Machine Learning (ML) because it is a leading branch of artificial intelligence. It allows systems to find patterns in past records and make choices or predictions on their own. Cybersecurity relies on supervised, unsupervised and reinforcement learning, as these are the basic kinds of ML approaches. In supervised learning, data that has been labeled is used to train algorithms capable of classifying or predicting things. It proves to be particularly useful when it comes to sorting malware, since the training is based on sample files that are either malicious or not. The model is able to detect new malware even without knowing its exact signature. A number of typical algorithms are support vector machines (SVM), decision trees and random forests. On the other hand, unsupervised learning does not depend on data that has been labeled. The main role of data mining is to locate unusual or hidden patterns in large sets of data. With IDS, this technique is used to notice unusual activity in the network that could mean an intrusion. With the help of clustering algorithms, it is possible to find outliers that could be threats. Through reinforcement learning, systems discover the best way to behave by going through the process of trial and error and getting feedback. In cybersecurity such a process is used in systems that can respond to new dangers by changing their settings or using resources more effectively. All in all, machine learning makes it possible to detect threats before they happen, assess risks that change over time and verify user behavior which is crucial in today's cybersecurity solutions(Prabhu, D et al., 2025).

3.2 Deep Learning (DL)

Deep Learning (DL) which is part of machine learning, applies artificial neural networks with several layers to study complex patterns in data (Boopathi, S. 2023; Sundari, V. M et al., 2024). They are built like the human brain and are very helpful in studying large and unorganized data, including images, audio and network logs. Threat detection and response are being improved by deep learning which can detect small and unnoticeable changes that other systems fail to spot. In cybersecurity, the Convolutional Neural Network (CNN) is one of the most popular models, as it is used to identify malware by analyzing each software application's binary file like an image (Kumar, P. R et al., 2023). The approach enables features to be automatically identified, so humans do not have to make many rules for detection. RNNs in general and especially LSTM networks, are good for studying information that comes in a sequence such as system logs or what users do over time. They detect suspicious actions by users by studying the changes in their behavior over time. This technology helps respond to threats right away by sorting events and advising actions as they take place. Because they use a lot of security data, DL-based systems can both detect and predict cyber incidents in advance. For example, some predictive analytics tools use DL models to notice signs of phishing and detect ransomware using their actions (Chinnasamy et al., 2023). Even though deep learning is very strong, it must be used wisely in cybersecurity because it is complex and open to attack. Still, it is expected to greatly improve the creation of smart, automatic and highly successful cyber defense systems (Raut et al., 2023).

3.3 Natural Language Processing (NLP)

Cybersecurity benefits a lot from Natural Language Processing (NLP), as it helps detect and address phishing and scam attempts. NLP makes it possible for machines to work with human language, so it is perfect for studying emails, messages and content found online. Phishing email detection is one of the main areas where NLP is very useful. Even if a phishing email is written in fancy language to look real, NLP-based systems can still detect it by examining the structure, tone and the content of the message. Such techniques as sentiment analysis, named entity recognition and keyword spotting are used to spot signs of danger like urgent requests, suspicious URLs or unanticipated attachments. NLP helps with processing a lot of threat intelligence data, including reports, advisories and forum discussions, so that useful information can be gained. Systems are able to detect new threats, frequent security weaknesses and recent changes in threat actors' methods by analyzing unstructured information. Besides, NLP supports the creation of chatbots and virtual assistants that assist incident response teams by giving quick responses to questions and speeding up the documentation process. Since language-based attacks are becoming more frequent, NLP is now more important in defending us (Lalitha, R et al., 2025).

3.4 Reinforcement Learning

Reinforcement Learning is an AI approach that helps an agent find the best strategies by interacting with its environment all the time. RL is becoming more popular in cybersecurity since it helps develop defenses that respond to changing threats as they happen. By using RL, intrusion response systems can now be set to act automatically. By considering cybersecurity as a competition, RL agents adjust their strategies by separating nodes, blocking IPs or deploying honeypots depending on the outcomes they get from the environment. RL is also applied in dynamic firewall configuration by updating the rules depending on changes in the network. Also, it can be applied to automated penetration testing, as an RL agent learns to exploit vulnerabilities as an attacker might which helps defenders identify and fix any problems ahead of time. RL is valuable because it can adapt as time goes on which makes it usable in places where set rules do not work well. Still, setting up successful reward programs and dealing with the difficulty of cyber environments are main issues that researchers are trying to solve(Anusha, S et al., 2024).

3.5 AI in Encryption and Decryption

Encryption and decryption are key to data security, since they keep information safe and confidential at all times while it is stored and sent. Cryptographic methods usually depend on mathematical equations, but now AI is being studied to improve, perfect and in some cases challenge ways of encrypting information. AI can make it easier to develop strong cryptographic keys, mainly when a fast and secure key exchange system is needed. Machine learning helps encryption levels to be changed based on how it is being used and by what threats. AI is also applied to understand the risks in cryptographic algorithms by launching attacks and spotting any issues in the production of keys or encryptions. In some cases, attackers use deep learning to study electromagnetic or power data to find out the keys used in encryption. AI helps in creating systems that can resist the possible threats from future quantum computers. Using reinforcement learning, algorithms are being made to update encryption methods on the go, making data protection better in variable conditions. Even though the process is just beginning, the connection between AI and cryptography has the potential to improve data security with smarter and stronger methods.

4. EMERGING AI TECHNOLOGIES IN CYBERSECURITY

4.1 AI-Driven Threat Intelligence

AI has greatly improved how proactive cybersecurity works. Usually, traditional ways of gathering threat intelligence use manual work and fixed databases of threats. Even so, as cyber threats keep evolving rapidly, these methods are not effective enough. AI makes it easier to gather, relate and analyze a lot of information from networks, security alerts, dark web sites and social networks. By using AI, threat intelligence systems can find unusual behaviors and patterns in real time and may stop attacks from happening. NLP algorithms are able to read security bulletins and conversations on hacker forums to detect possible threats in advance. With machine learning, IP addresses, phishing domains and malware signatures can be sorted out based on their history and the way they function (Singh et al., 2021). AI is especially helpful in this situation through predictive analytics. Looking at past attacks and threats, AI technology can predict the chances of future events. As an example, with predictive models, organizations can know which vulnerabilities are more likely to be used by attackers and thus focus on fixing them first. This capability allows cybersecurity to anticipate problems, giving a better and faster response to any threat.

4.2 Autonomous Security Systems

With autonomous security systems, AI is able to recognize threats, analyze them and deal with them without any human help. They keep learning from more data and experience and change their responses as new cyber threats emerge. Being able to respond instantly to any incidents is an important characteristic of autonomous security systems. If a threat is noticed, the system can separate infected computers, stop traffic from dangerous IPs or close down sessions of users who have been compromised automatically. They help respond to cyberattacks faster which is needed to avoid major damage. Besides, these systems can learn and adjust when new information is given to them. If a ransomware attack involves an unidentified variant, the system can isolate the affected environment and make sure to detect it in the future. With time, the constant process of learning strengthens and improves the defense infrastructure. Since autonomous AI takes care of typical issues, human analysts are able to work on more important and complex matters. Yet, monitoring and control are still necessary, mainly when dealing with sensitive systems, as incorrect actions might result in problems or data loss.

4.3 AI in Blockchain Security

Blockchain is famous for the security features it has such as being decentralized and unchangeable. Even so, its security is not perfect and it can be attacked by double-spending, 51% attacks and weak smart contracts. AI is important for improving blockchain security by adding intelligent tools for surveillance, analysis and finding fraud. AI helps a lot in the detection of fraudulent purchases. Machine learning programs are able to detect odd transaction activity right away and report it as suspicious. This way is especially helpful in financial systems based on blockchain because money laundering or exploiting loopholes often involves small and frequent transactions. AI is applied to better the processes used to gain agreement. Sometimes, AI algorithms are used to change the size of blocks, the number of transactions handled and how nodes are validated depending on what's happening in the network. It makes the blockchain environment both more efficient and secure. Furthermore, AI can locate problems or weaknesses in the code of smart contracts. Using natural language processing and symbolic reasoning, it is possible to check if smart contracts follow well-known best practices and legal rules which decreases the chance of exploitation. Thus, by merging AI with blockchain, the two technologies help improve security by using the strong decentralized structure of blockchain and the adaptability of AI.

4.4 AI for Secure Authentication

Proper verification of identities is important in cybersecurity and AI is now dramatically transforming this area. Passwords and PINs are not enough to ensure safety these days. The use of AI has made it possible for the latest generation of biometrics to rely on facial recognition, fingerprint scanning, iris detection and voice authentication.

Machine learning techniques are used by these systems to spot users using their biological features. An example is that facial recognition uses deep learning to analyze the face and its features, making authentication possible under many different situations. NLP and audio signal processing are used in voice recognition systems to find out the patterns in speech. In addition to biometrics, AI helps with authentication by studying a person's behavior. It depends on analyzing people's actions such as how fast they type, use their mouse, swipe and walk. If the behavior of a user is very different from what is usual, the system may ask for more information or refuse to allow access. AI is used to improve MFA by looking at where the login is happening which device is used and the login time to decide how risky it is. Because of this, the system can have flexible authentication, giving users a good balance between security and easiness. As these advanced techniques are being used, AI-based authentication has to improve continuously to ensure safety and block unauthorized entry.

4.5 Adversarial AI in Cybersecurity

Attackers in cybersecurity now use adversarial machine learning to trick AI systems by giving them inputs, that make the AI give the wrong answer. An example would be that a malware sample can avoid detection by an antivirus if it targets the process of picking out relevant information from the data. In the same way, attackers may fool facial recognition by using altered photos. As a result, AI which is meant to increase safety, can end up creating new risks. On the other hand, AI is employed to handle challenges caused by adversarial AI. To make AI models more secure, techniques such as adversarial training, model hardening and anomaly detection are put into use. In adversarial training, the model comes across adversarial examples which helps it become better at classifying them. GANs are also being used by cybersecurity researchers to create simulations of cyberattacks which helps defenders improve their systems against recent threats. Basically, AI is being taught to act like an attacker so that it can strengthen the defenses. When we look at it from another angle, adversarial AI creates a new race in cybersecurity, where those involved are always trying to stay ahead of each other. Trust and effectiveness in AI-based security systems are possible only if there is continuous innovation, openness about AI models and teamwork among different fields.

5. USE CASES OF AI IN CYBERSECURITY

5.1 Malware Detection

Malware is still a major problem in the cyber world and can attack everything from a home computer to a company's network and important infrastructure. Signature-based methods for detecting malware are successful against older threats, but find it hard to deal with new and fast-changing malware. In such cases, systems that use AI to detect malware are more reliable and smart. AI systems that use machine learning and deep learning are fed with lots of data containing both safe and harmful software. With this knowledge, they can spot and stop threats, even if there are no signatures for them. Unlike the older methods, AI-based systems check a file's structure, the way it behaves and its execution patterns to find malware. As an illustration, CNNs are used to process malware binaries as images and gain visual skills that can tell them apart from legitimate software. Also, RNNs are helpful in exploring sequential data such as execution logs to detect anything suspicious. Threat groups in malware classification are made by AI which organizes them according to their behavior and resemblance. As a result, security experts can decide what to address first and use the right defenses. In addition, AI models are able to update themselves with new information which helps them get better and more versatile over the years. So, AI helps a lot in the fight against malware that changes frequently and becomes more sophisticated.

5.2 Phishing Detection

Most cybercriminals use phishing to convince people to hand over their private information. Usually, these attacks are carried out by creating fake emails, websites and messages that try to look real. Traditional approaches to spotting phishing usually cannot detect the most advanced and quickly changing phishing methods. In this case, AI technology is a better and more flexible way to detect phishing attempts. NLP algorithms check emails and messages for signs that may indicate phishing such as a feeling of urgency, threats or requests for personal details. AI models are able to find unusual details in email metadata, for example, the sender, the legitimacy of the domain and links in the message and then warn about possible risks before the user reads them. Apart from analyzing emails, AI can also find phishing websites by checking their layout, style, URLs and where they have been hosted. Decision trees and support vector machines are usually used by machine learning systems to tell apart legitimate from malicious websites based on SSL certificates, scripts and the way the page is set up. With AI, we can detect phishing attacks as they happen and the system can update its detection process whenever it sees new forms of phishing attacks. As a result, organizations can respond fast to new phishing techniques as they appear every day. Since phishing is the main reason for many data breaches and credential thefts, using AI in phishing detection boosts an organization's protection.

5.3 Fraud Detection

Banks, e-commerce companies, insurance firms and people who use these services are all greatly concerned about financial fraud. It is usually hard to find fraud using rules alone, since scams like identity theft, money laundering, payment fraud and account takeovers often follow complex steps. AI has made it possible to detect fraud in real time which is useful for fighting financial crime. Artificial intelligence systems go over a lot of transactional data to detect anything that stands out from the normal patterns. They use methods like clustering which do not need predefined labels, to spot unusual behavior. As an example, a big increase in how money is spent, unusual places where it's used or a change in the rate of transactions may bring up alerts for more attention. Also, supervised learning uses old fraud data to estimate the chances that a new transaction is fraudulent. Due to AI, each transaction gets a risk score, so financial institutions can decide whether to let it through, stop it or send it for manual review. AI is used particularly well in real-time fraud detection, where the algorithms check the validity of a transaction in just a few seconds. AI also makes it possible for the system to learn all the time, so it can deal with new types of fraud such as synthetic identity fraud and coordinated attacks. Customer behavior modeling also relies on AI, so individual profiles can be made from previous data. If there is a big change such as logging in from a new device in a different location, the system may require authentication. All in all, AI supports an active and smart method of spotting fraud which reduces errors and builds trust among users.

5.4 Network protection

Any digital organization relies on its network infrastructure, so making it secure from cyber threats is very important. Because of AI, network security is improved by offering extra visibility, detection and automatic responses that are stronger than those from IDS and firewalls. AI is used to watch network traffic and spot any unusual signs of intrusions, theft of data or C2 activities. With autoencoders and graph neural networks, these instruments can detect attacks that involve several network servers. AI is useful in detecting intrusions by studying the regular activities of network devices and users. Any difference from the baseline such as a sharp increase in data or an attempt to enter the system without permission, is noticed for further review. It is most helpful for spotting threats from within and APTs which usually manage to evade detection by standard signature-based solutions. AI makes it possible for security analysts to automatically spot suspicious traffic and match it with information about threats. This speed ups the process of finding and analyzing threats. Because AI can manage large datasets on its own, it is a key element in today's network defense.

5.5 Endpoint Protection

Laptops, mobile gadgets and IoT devices are usually the most likely targets in cybersecurity since they are used by many and are easily attacked. AI technology in endpoint protection helps these devices stay safe from ransomware, spyware and unapproved access by being more flexible and smart. AI-powered endpoint protection looks at how a program behaves rather than depending on pre-made signatures, unlike regular antivirus. Such systems keep an eye on all activities of applications and processes to catch any suspicious behavior. Should the AI detect that a process is encrypting a lot of files as ransomware usually does, it will block the process to stop it from causing additional harm. Besides, AI makes it possible for the system to automatically reverse changes, get rid of dangerous files or cut the device off from the network if a threat is found. It helps to avoid long periods with no work and prevents the infection from reaching more people. AI makes mobile devices more secure by keeping an eye on how they are used which apps run and the user's location. In IoT, AI algorithms manage authentication of devices and watch for strange communications from devices which could point to a hacking attempt. Since AI keeps learning and changing, it is a perfect fit for protecting endpoints against new types of threats. When employees work remotely and use their own devices, AI guarantees that organizations keep their security strong everywhere (Kayan et al., 2022).

6. BENEFITS OF AI IN CYBERSECURITY

AI has greatly improved the methods organizations use to catch, block and deal with cyber threats. Most cybersecurity solutions are not fast enough to deal with new threats because they depend on human analysts and rules. It helps by automating processes, analyzing a lot of data in a short time and taking smart actions that boost security in real time. This part explains the various positive effects of AI in cybersecurity.

6.1 Speed and Accuracy in Threat Detection

Because AI works fast and accurately, it is a great tool for identifying security threats. It usually takes traditional systems a long time to detect and respond to advanced attacks and damage is often done before they act. AI is created to look through a lot of data quickly which makes it possible to find potential security issues immediately. ML algorithms which have been trained with previous information and patterns, are fast at spotting unusual activity in the network, a user's actions or file activity. Because these algorithms keep learning, they improve in detecting malware, phishing tricks or attempts to gain access unlawfully. When AI is used in security tools, unusual activities like access from a distant location or moving files are noticed and responded to within a short period. In addition, since AI can detect threats that have not yet been identified, it is better than using old definitions of known threats. With the help of behavioral analysis and pattern spotting, AI can point out risks before they become clear through a known indicator.

6.2 Proactive Defense Mechanisms

Before, cybersecurity was mostly reactive, but AI has changed that to being proactive. AI makes it possible for systems to notice potential threats and stop them before they occur. This way of working is crucial now because cyberattacks keep changing and often go unnoticed. Predictive analytics in AI uses past and current information to spot any signs that suggest a future attack. If the AI notices something strange in the scanning activity on a web server, it can expect a DDoS attack and take preventive measures such as limiting the rate and blacklisting suspicious IPs. AI is used in threat hunting to search for indications of compromise by itself, finding threats that could escape the notice of people. Because of these abilities, businesses can strengthen their defenses and prevent attacks by cybercriminals. AI is also able to imitate different attack scenarios using adversarial models to find out where defenses can be improved. As a result, cybersecurity systems are strong and able to respond to new risks as they happen.

6.3 Reducing Human Error and Fatigue

Human analysts are key in cybersecurity, but they are likely to make mistakes and feel tired when they handle the same tasks over and over again. With AI, many routine jobs do not require human help which cuts down chances of error and improves the efficiency of operations. For instance, AI can go through security alerts and arrange them in order of their importance. Because of this, analysts can concentrate on serious incidents that should be handled right away. When such tasks are automated, time is saved and all significant alerts are noticed, unlike when people might forget them after a long day. Furthermore, AI makes sure that response procedures are standardized by relying on pre-set plans which guarantees actions are done right each time. It brings consistency to the process and guarantees that people follow the company's rules. Since AI takes care of repetitive tasks, analysts can work on key aspects of cybersecurity like analyzing threats, drafting policies and updating cybersecurity systems. The combination of AI and human knowledge increases how accurate and effective cybersecurity operations become.

6.4 Enhancing Scalability and Efficiency

When a company expands, its IT infrastructure becomes more and more complicated. Since networks, endpoints, cloud services and IoT devices are getting more numerous, managing cybersecurity for all of them is becoming harder. Because it can automate many tasks, AI makes it possible for cybersecurity operations to grow and stay efficient. Using AI, these tools can watch over millions of connections and streams of data at once, so security remains the same for all types of systems. Cybersecurity can easily match the needs of a company, due to AI's ability to oversee remote teams, secure applications in the cloud and manage mixed environments. Besides, AI technology allows resources to be managed flexibly according to threat situations and the business's most important needs. For instance, if a data center gets attacked more often, AI can change the monitoring system to pay extra attention there. AI is able to quickly go through massive amounts of data to find useful information, so organisations do not have to spend much time using human resources. As a result, security teams can quickly catch more threats with less effort.

6.5 Minimizing False Positives and Negatives

One challenge in cybersecurity is that some harmless activity is mistakenly marked as dangerous and at the same time, some actual threats are missed. False positives might cause the system to be shut down or probed unnecessarily and false negatives could let attackers take advantage of the system. AI cuts down on these errors by using advanced techniques and analyzing the situation. AI understands the situation before making any action as wrong which is different from rule-based systems. In this case, the model will understand that the late-night access to a server is usual for a system admin but could be suspicious if a junior employee takes that action. When AI continues to learn, it becomes better at judging what is normal behavior in a certain environment. Because of this, threats can be sorted more clearly which helps security teams deal with less misleading information. Besides, using deep learning, it's possible to combine user actions, data on networks and application activity to make more precise decisions (Salloum et al., 2020). With this type of analysis, we depend less on one indicator and make threat detection more accurate. When AI eliminates both false positives and false negatives, it makes cybersecurity more reliable and also improves how users work and experience security.

7. CHALLENGES AND LIMITATIONS OF AI IN CYBERSECURITY

Even though Artificial Intelligence has greatly improved cybersecurity by detecting threats, analyzing them in real time and automating many tasks, there are some problems with it. It is necessary to deal with various technical, ethical and operational issues caused by AI to make sure its use is secure and fair. This part examines the main problems and issues that come with using AI in cybersecurity.

7.1 Data Privacy Concerns

AI models that work with machine learning and deep learning require huge datasets to be trained and improved (Khang et al., 2024). People in cybersecurity may be given access to user logs, communication records, system activities and even personal identity details. For this reason, gathering, storing and managing this information brings up major privacy problems. A main issue is that there is a risk of accidentally sharing data. If training data is not properly made anonymous, there is a possibility that AI could disclose or keep private or confidential details. This is most worrying in healthcare, finance and government, since data privacy breaches can result in both legal and ethical problems. It can also be tough for organizations to guarantee they are in line with privacy rules. The laws want data to be handled openly, for consent to be easy to give or take back and for data to be corrected or deleted. These rules are hard to manage in AI systems that are always changing. So, while AI makes cybersecurity better, it is important to have strict rules for data governance to make sure privacy is not affected by better security.

7.2 Bias and Fairness in AI systems

How well an AI system works depends on the data it has learned from. If the information used to train the AI is not fair, the AI may end up being biased and may cause results that are not fair. Because of this, AI tools in cybersecurity could consider some users, devices or actions to be threats due to historical data that is not accurate. Such an AI model may not work effectively when used outside of the corporate world such as in education or public institutions. In the same way, if previous reports are flawed or biased, AI could single out those groups by mistake during anomaly detection. Organizations may face damage to their reputation and legal issues because of AI bias. If people are blocked unfairly, wrongfully blamed for malicious actions or given strict security measures when they do not need them, trust can be destroyed and may result in problems with the law or regulators. Therefore, cybersecurity experts should pay attention to having different types of data, checking AI models and checking for fairness to guarantee that AI decisions are both clear and fair. Using human review and models that can explain their decisions can further assist in spotting and resolving bias as things happen.

7.3 High Resource Requirements for AI-Based Systems

It usually takes a lot of resources to implement AI-based cybersecurity technology. Such systems use a lot of computing power, storage space and network resources, mainly when monitoring and analyzing large companies in real time. To train machine learning models, you may have to work with huge amounts of data and this can be done using GPUs or TPUs. In addition, it is often necessary to keep updating and retraining deep learning systems to maintain their effectiveness as threats develop. It may be hard for SMEs to meet the financial needs of installing AI-based security systems. Besides, using AI in current systems often needs advanced knowledge which leads to more demand for cybersecurity and data science experts than the world can provide. Still, using AI in the cloud can help reduce these problems, but it brings up issues regarding where data is stored and how much we can trust third parties. This means that the heavy resource demands keep holding back the use of AI in cybersecurity.

7.4 The Risk of AI Systems Being Exploited by Attackers

Unfortunately, AI systems meant to protect against cyber-attacks may be used or attacked by those with bad intentions. People with evil intentions can use adversarial machine learning to feed specially designed inputs into an AI system and cause it to misread threats. As an example, attackers may create malware that works like legitimate software to avoid being spotted by AI. In some cases, people with bad intentions can learn the logic behind AI models and use this information to take advantage of their weaknesses. Another issue is that AI is making it easier for attackers to launch phishing campaigns, identify holes in security and organize big cyberattacks against many targets. Because of AI such threats are quicker, more flexible and more difficult for traditional security tools to spot. Another risk is that insiders within the company could infect the AI training data with misleading or wrong information which may affect the model's accuracy. As a result of this type of data poisoning, the system might become less effective and leave it open to serious security breaches. To fight these risks, one needs to use security measures for AI such as adversarial training, making models stronger, controlling access to the training data and regularly checking AI results.

7.5 Ethical Concerns Regarding the Deployment of AI Technologies

Using AI in cybersecurity leads to ethical issues that need to be handled. It is hard to trust politics when decisions are not clear to the public. A lot of AI models, including deep learning ones, are difficult to understand, so it's often hard to say why something happened such as blocking a website, barring a user or turning off the system. Because of this lack of transparency, accountability may be a problem. Should an AI system classify a legitimate action as malicious and cause problems for the business or damage the company's reputation, it may be difficult to determine whose mistake it was that of the software vendor, the cybersecurity team or the leaders of the organization. Another challenge is the amount of surveillance that AI technology can do. Cybersecurity AI tools can closely watch how people use systems which may go against the privacy of employees or customers. Even though security is a reason for surveillance, it must not infringe on people's rights and freedoms. In addition, people are concerned that AI might be used to launch cyber-attacks or disrupt other systems rather than for defense. This makes us consider the role of AI in international disputes and the rightness of letting AI decide on warfare actions. Therefore, companies should use ethical AI tools, strive to be clear and responsible and bring together ethicists, legal professionals and technologists.

8. FUTURE DIRECTIONS

Although Artificial Intelligence (AI) is changing cybersecurity, what we have today is only the first step. Because IoT, 5G networks and cloud technology are growing, cybersecurity using AI should also develop. This section discusses how AI will change cybersecurity in the future by using new technologies, shaping security systems, launching new studies and encouraging global partnership.

8.1 AI Integration with Emerging Technologies

Digital transformation has made it possible for many people to use IoT products, 5G networks and cloud platforms. Although these technologies make communication and performance easier, they also create many and complicated vulnerabilities. It is necessary to use AI together with these new technologies to handle their particular security problems. There are millions of devices in the IoT system that constantly produce data and most of their security is missing. Real-time monitoring by AI allows it to spot any unusual device activity, respond automatically and thus help secure these environments. When a smart thermostat connects to an IP address that is not recognized, AI-based systems can isolate the device and look into the issue as soon as possible. Even though 5G makes network speed and latency much better, it also adds more challenges to securing distributed edge nodes. AI is useful for managing and safeguarding edge computing environments since traditional security tools cannot function properly there. AI algorithms can be used to check network traffic at the edge and identify threats early, so they do not spread across the whole infrastructure. AI in the cloud can guarantee flexible and adaptive security by always checking how users operate, their access habits and the resources they use. When companies use multi-cloud and hybrid-cloud platforms, AI will ensure security stays consistent, find any mistakes in setup and address threats immediately.

8.2 The Role of AI in Next-Gen Cybersecurity Frameworks

Security in the future will rely on new architectures that are intelligent, capable of working on their own and adaptable. The transformation is powered by AI which is changing zero-trust systems, self-healing systems and risk management approaches. Zero trust is a system that supposes that risks might be present within and beyond the network. AI helps implement zero-trust by regularly checking user identities, watching their accesses and putting in place changing policies. Rather than sticking to set access rules, AI reviews behavior and data at the time of access to decide what to do. AI could also be applied in cybersecurity to find problems and handle them on its own in the future. They can spot infected computers, separate them, update security measures or restore the system's settings automatically. As a result, there is a faster response and the business can continue as usual. With AI, it will be possible to adapt security measures according to the constantly changing risks. AI technology can use things like device status, where a device is, its previous actions and risk information to adjust security levels automatically. AI will gradually shift cybersecurity so that companies can foresee and stop threats before they happen.

8.3 Research Areas and Innovations

Since cybersecurity threats keep advancing, we will need innovative research to remain safe from hackers. A number of new research fields may change the way AI is used in cybersecurity. A promising area is when quantum computing and AI come together. Quantum computing could make breaking modern encryption easier which would seriously affect data security. At the same time, AI can be used to design encryption systems that cannot be broken by quantum computers and to find out early about any quantum-related threats. Such algorithms may also help identify threats much faster than regular AI systems can. One more important field of innovation is explainable AI (XAI). With AI making more important decisions, it should be easy for people to understand why it acts the way it does. Researchers in XAI want to make sure AI models can be explained, so cybersecurity professionals trust and check the outcomes of AI systems. More and more, federated learning is considered a leading method for privacy in AI. Models in federated learning are developed by using data from many devices, not by sharing it directly. By using this approach, organizations can share threat information safely which is very important in highly regulated fields such as healthcare and finance.

Moreover, because of NLP, AI will be able to analyze threat intelligence reports, dark web messages and security documents, so analysts are always informed about the latest risks and weaknesses.

8.4 Collaborative AI Approaches to Enhance Global Cybersecurity Efforts

Since cybersecurity affects all regions, it calls for people from different places to join forces. AI can help countries and organizations share important information on threats, weaknesses and strategies safely and in an organized way. In the near future, we may witness more cases where several organizations cooperate and gain from the same security models. Since they are usually developed by federations or consortia, these platforms help people train models using similar data without giving up their privacy or ownership of the data. When experts team up, the training data becomes richer which helps create models that work well and can detect threats from different sources. Some organizations decide to participate in AI-based cyber threat intelligence (CTI) exchanges. They can apply AI to gather, study and share information about malware, phishing attacks and new methods of cyber-attacks as soon as they happen. AI helps in spotting similar patterns in different parts of the world so that proper responses can be taken globally. AI can be used by governments and international organizations to keep an eye on cyber warfare, enforce digital agreements and find out about cyberattacks supported by governments. AI-assisted monitoring systems can detect cyber-related issues in global politics and guide their stakeholders on taking suitable actions. However, to stop misusing the information and build trust, all such collaborations must rely on ethics, proper structures and set rules for sharing data. AI is expected to play a big role in cybersecurity, but its development may be complex. Since cyber threats are becoming more serious and advanced, AI provides an effective and intelligent way to protect digital systems. With the help of IoT, 5G and cloud computing, as well as its impact on upgrading security frameworks, it will play a big part in strengthening systems. Research in the fields of quantum computing, explainable AI and federated learning will increase what is possible in the future. In addition, working together using AI will be important to fight cybersecurity problems that affect many countries. Cybersecurity is clearly headed in the direction of AI which will be smart, active and ready to face challenges.

9. CONCLUSION

The use of Artificial Intelligence has greatly changed the process of spotting, analyzing and handling threats on the internet. AI technology such as machine learning, deep learning, natural language processing and reinforcement learning have given cybersecurity systems better abilities to detect threats in real time, analyze them in advance and respond automatically. Thanks to these measures, companies can better anticipate and respond to advanced cyber threats, spot them faster and need less manual help. It was revealed in this survey that AI is used in many cybersecurity areas like detecting malware, preventing phishing scams, securing networks and safeguarding endpoints. Also, AI-powered solutions including self-operating security, smart blockchain security and authentication based on behavior have shown their ability to change traditional security setups. Although there have been great achievements, AI still faces some issues when used for cybersecurity. To gain the most advantage and minimize the risks, issues relating to data privacy, AI bias, computational needs and possible abuse should be managed. As things continue, AI will play a major yet complicated role in cybersecurity. When AI combines with IoT, 5G and cloud computing, security will become more advanced. The development of quantum computing, explainable AI and federated learning is believed to solve existing issues and introduce tougher defense solutions. Moreover, collaboration on AI at a global level will help everyone exchange information on threats and work together to address them. All in all, AI is a key driver in cybersecurity, supplying solutions that are smart, flexible and can be used on a large scale. Since cybersecurity threats are constantly changing, AI needs to keep up, so that cybersecurity becomes proactive and can run on its own.

REFERENCES

Anusha, S., Nithyanandhan, R., Anish, T. P., Girija, P., & Nalini, M. (2024, October). Deep Reinforcement Learning: Key Algorithms, Applications, and Future Challenges. In *2024 2nd International Conference on Self Sustainable Artificial Intelligence Systems (ICSSAS)* (pp. 565-571). IEEE.

Apruzzese, G., Laskov, P., Montes de Oca, E., Mallouli, W., Brdalo Rapa, L., Grammatopoulos, A. V., & Di Franco, F. (2023). The role of machine learning in cybersecurity. *Digital Threats : Research and Practice*, *4*(1), 1–38. DOI: 10.1145/3545574

Azizi, N., & Haass, O. (2023). Cybersecurity issues and challenges. In *Handbook of research on cybersecurity issues and challenges for business and FinTech applications* (pp. 21–48). IGI Global.

Bharadiya, J. (2023). Machine learning in cybersecurity: Techniques and challenges. *European Journal of Technology*, *7*(2), 1–14. DOI: 10.47672/ejt.1486

Boopathi, S. (2023). Deep learning techniques applied for automatic sentence generation. In Promoting Diversity, Equity, and Inclusion in Language Learning Environments (pp. 255-273). IGI Global. DOI: 10.4018/978-1-6684-3632-5.ch016

Chinnasamy, P., Sathya, K. S., Jebamani, B. J. A., Nithyasri, A., & Fowjiya, S. (2023). Deep learning: algorithms, techniques, and applications—a systematic survey. In *Deep learning research applications for natural language processing* (pp. 1–17). IGI global.

Das, R., & Morris, T. H. (2017, December). Machine learning and cyber security. In 2017 international conference on computer, electrical & communication engineering (ICCECE) (pp. 1-7). IEEE.

Ganapathi, P., & Shanmugapriya, D. (Eds.). (2019). *Handbook of research on machine and deep learning applications for cyber security*. IGI Global.

Kashyap, R. (2021). Sensation of deep learning in image processing applications. In *Research Anthology on Artificial Intelligence Applications in Security* (pp. 1615–1639). IGI Global Scientific Publishing.

Kayan, H., Nunes, M., Rana, O., Burnap, P., & Perera, C. (2022). Cybersecurity of industrial cyber-physical systems: A review. *ACM Computing Surveys*, *54*(11s), 1–35. DOI: 10.1145/3510410

Khang, A., Singh, Y., & Barak, D. (2024). Review of the Literature on Using Machine and Deep Learning Techniques to Improve IoT Security. Revolutionizing Automated Waste Treatment Systems: IoT and Bioelectronics, 273-300.

Kour, R. (2020). Cybersecurity issues and challenges in Industry 4.0. *Advances in Civil and Industrial Engineering*, *4*(0), 84–101. DOI: 10.4018/978-1-7998-3904-0.ch005

Kumar, P. R., Meenakshi, S., Shalini, S., Devi, S. R., & Boopathi, S. (2023). Soil Quality Prediction in Context Learning Approaches Using Deep Learning and Blockchain for Smart Agriculture. In Effective AI, Blockchain, and E-Governance Applications for Knowledge Discovery and Management (pp. 1-26). IGI Global. DOI: 10.4018/978-1-6684-9151-5.ch001

Lalitha, R., Dhinavallesan, P. V., & Ponugoti, S. (2025, March). A Comprehensive Survey on NLP-based Approaches for Summarizing Lengthy Research Papers. In *2025 International Conference on Machine Learning and Autonomous Systems (ICMLAS)* (pp. 1501-1507). IEEE. DOI: 10.1109/ICMLAS64557.2025.10967868

Murugan, T. (Ed.). (2023). *Handbook of Research on Data Science and Cybersecurity Innovations in Industry 4.0 Technologies*. IGI Global. DOI: 10.4018/978-1-6684-8145-5

Prabhu, D., & Sudha, L. MR, P. K., Adaikkammai, A., Aparna, P., & Sathya, V. (2025). Machine Learning in Cybersecurity: Challenges, Applications, and Future Directions. *Exploiting Machine Learning for Robust Security*, 25-48.

Prabhu, D., Tejasri, M. V. S. L., Saratha, B., & Anish, T. P. (2025, April). Future Horizons: Key Trends Shaping the Evolution of Machine Learning. In *2025 8th International Conference on Trends in Electronics and Informatics (ICOEI)* (pp. 1091-1099). IEEE.

Priyadarshini, I. (2017). Cyber security risks in robotics. In *Detecting and mitigating robotic cyber security risks* (pp. 333–348). IGI Global Scientific Publishing. DOI: 10.4018/978-1-5225-2154-9.ch022

Raut, R., Pathak, P. D., Sakhare, S. R., & Patil, S. (Eds.). (2023). *Generative adversarial networks and deep learning: theory and applications*. CRC Press. DOI: 10.1201/9781003203964

Salloum, S. A., Alshurideh, M., Elnagar, A., & Shaalan, K. (2020, March). Machine learning and deep learning techniques for cybersecurity: a review. In *The International Conference on Artificial Intelligence and Computer Vision* (pp. 50-57). Cham: Springer International Publishing. DOI: 10.1007/978-3-030-44289-7_5

Singh, R., Singh, A., & Bhattacharya, P. (2021). A machine learning approach for anomaly detection to secure smart grid systems. In *Advancements in Security and Privacy Initiatives for Multimedia Images* (pp. 199–213). IGI global. DOI: 10.4018/978-1-7998-2795-5.ch008

Sundari, V. M., Rose, R. M., Sassirekha, S. M., Nalini, M., & Girija, P. (2024, November). Deep Learning: Techniques, Taxonomy, Applications, and Future Directions. In *2024 International Conference on Smart Technologies for Sustainable Development Goals (ICSTSDG)* (pp. 1-5). IEEE.

Thiyagarajan, P. (2020). A review on cyber security mechanisms using machine and deep learning algorithms. Handbook of research on machine and deep learning applications for cyber security, 23-41. DOI: 10.4018/978-1-5225-9611-0.ch002

Yamini, B. MAY, P. M. A., Shobana, R., TP, A., & Nalini, M. (2024, December). Cybersecurity: Strategies, Sector-Specific Challenges, and Future Prospects. In *2024 4th International Conference on Ubiquitous Computing and Intelligent Information Systems (ICUIS)* (pp. 1338-1345). IEEE.

Yildirim, M. (2021). *Artificial intelligence-based solutions for cyber security problems. In artificial intelligence paradigms for smart cyber-physical systems.* IGI Global Scientific Publishing.

Chapter 7
Utilization of Packet Tracer for Strengthening Network Security:
Methods, Implementation, and Assessment

Krishanu Kundu
https://orcid.org/0000-0003-1057-4713
G.L. Bajaj Institute of Technology and Management, Greater Noida, India

ABSTRACT

DHCP servers play a crucial role in dynamically allocating IP addresses and optimizing resource utilization. When a user types a domain name into their web browser, DNS servers translate it into IP addresses and point users to the relevant server. A web server's main job is to store, process, and provide users requested websites or information. In modern network security practices, tools like Cisco Packet Tracer have been implemented to enhance system security. This work discusses the integration of DHCP, DNS, and web servers to fortify network infrastructure. Enforcing strong password policies is essential for preventing unauthorized access and data breaches. Requiring complex passwords strengthens security measures and minimizes vulnerabilities associated with password use. The study also looks at how DNS servers resolve IPv4 addresses and URLs, providing a thorough grasp of internet communication procedures.

DOI: 10.4018/979-8-3373-2252-0.ch007

1 BASICS AND DIFFERENT TYPES OF NETWORK SECURITY

Computer networks (Ahlan et al., 2015) consist of interrelated computing devices which share resources. Such devices communicate using physical and wireless technologies based on predefined rules called communication protocols. Initially developed in the late 1950s for defence and military purposes, early computer networks had limited commercial and scientific use. Growth of internet technology (Liandani et al., 2020) transformed computer networks essential for businesses. Core network functions have evolved significantly, incorporating advancements in automation, programmability, and security. Network security encompasses the measures taken to protect a computer network and the data it contains. It is crucial for safeguarding confidential information from online threats while ensuring network reliability and performance. Effective network security strategies involve various technologies to defend against attacks.

Network security professionals or teams devise strategies and protocols to keep networks secure and compliant with standards and regulations. Every user must follow these security guidelines. Any point in the network accessible to an authorized user could become an entry point for malicious actors or careless or misinformed users, potentially compromising data. Security policies and tool selection vary across networks (Lubis et al., 2019). A robust security approach, often called defence in depth or layered security, uses multiple layers of protection to offer comprehensive security (Lubis et al., 2020).

The following are typical types of network security technologies:

- **Access control**, which restricts the ability of specific users to access network systems, preventing unauthorized access.
- **Antivirus and antimalware software**, designed to detect, remove, or block viruses as well as malware (e.g., Trojan horses) that can affect individual computers and networks.
- **Application security**, which protects business-critical software, whether developed in-house or purchased. Emerging malware often targets open-source code and container-based applications.
- **Cloud security** measures offered by cloud providers to secure cloud services and assist customers in protecting their data within the cloud infrastructure (Mason & Newcomb, 2001)
- **Data loss prevention (DLP)** systems (Feng, 2009) which monitor and prevent data breaches by tracking data in use, in transit, and at rest. DLP identifies critical data and promotes safe handling practices, such as avoiding email attachments containing sensitive information.

Email remains a significant vulnerability, as phishing and malware attacks can occur when employees unknowingly click on malicious links. Emails can also be a risky way to share files and sensitive data. **Intrusion detection systems (IDS)** flag suspicious activities but do not block them, while **intrusion prevention systems (IPS)** actively prevent unauthorized access.

A security technique known as multifactor authentication (MFA) requires users to enter more than one verification factor in addition to their password in order to access a resource.

2. METHODOLOGY

First and foremost, mastering network simulation requires a deep comprehension of the tool's features and capabilities. The next step in creating simulations is to specify the parameters, goals, and scope of each scenario. Variables including device setups, network topology, and security measures are taken into account throughout this procedure. To investigate various security policies and practices, such as improved password prerequisites, DHCP configuration, and subnetting, specialized simulations are created, such as those that concentrate on IP address administration and password management (Lubis et al.,2020).

2.1. SETUP

A DHCP server, a DCN server as well as a web server are all part of the topology of the Cisco Packet Tracer network configuration. Units on the network are allocated IP addresses dynamically by DHCP server. Active Directory services, comprising DNS for name resolution, are installed on the DCN server, which has a static IP address. Furthermore, a website accessible inside the local network is hosted by the web server. (Bhamare et al., 2019).

2.2. NETWORK TOPOLOGY

As depicted in Figure 1, two switches are connected via a centralized router in this network arrangement. One PC, a DHCP server, a DNS server, as well as a web server are connected to the right switch, whereas three PCs are connected to the left switch. Effective communication among all devices is guaranteed by this topology. When necessary, the router grants access to outside networks and efficiently controls traffic between the switches. Within their respective sectors, the switches make communication easier. The servers oversee crucial functions including IP address assignment as well as website hosting, guaranteeing smooth network operation.

Figure 1. Complete Topology

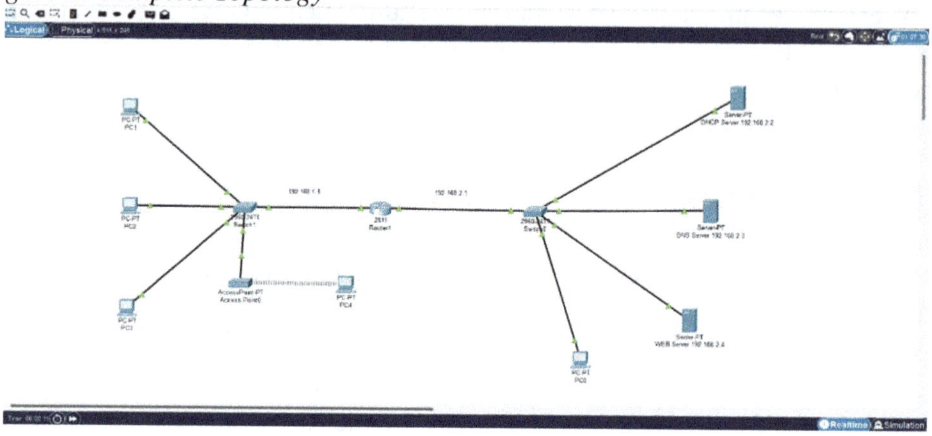

3. RESOURCES

3.1. Router

Routers serve as sophisticated post offices for the Internet. When you transmit or request data, the router scans the target machine's "address" and sends it into the world wide web. The data is conveyed in a series of tiny packets, each containing the address of its destination Router of Packet tracer supports protocols like RIP and OSPF for ensuring proficient data transmission paths. Network address translation (NAT) and DHCP like functionalities are also offered by Cisco Packet tracer (Chimphlee & Chimphlee, 2023)

3.2. LAN Switch

As a pivotal part of Local area network, a LAN switch permits multiple devices to connect effortlessly. Compared to existing hubs, switches basically function at data link layer of OSI model, which permits them to choose which MAC address to utilize for forwarding of data packets. LAN switches also support VLAN that partitions a network in multiple virtual LANs for enhancing security as well as maximizing efficiency.

3.3. DHCP Server

The client/server DHCP automatically assigns an IP host's IP address as well as other configuration settings like the subnet mask as well as default gateway. Each device requires an exclusive unicast IP address for linking to a TCP/IP network including its resources.

3.4. DNS Server

DNS is a TCP/IP standard protocol in which the Client and Server work together to offer name resolution as well as computer name-to-IP address mapping amenities for users and machines. DNS is used by PCs to discover Active Directory domain controllers and perform critical active directory functions.

3.5. Web Server

A web server is a system that stores both server software and the component files for a website. A web server communicates to the Internet and enables the exchange of physical data among web-connected devices.

3.6 Wireless Modem Device

Wireless modems (Platt, 2015) can work at rates equivalent to dial-up modems but cannot match the speed of broadband internet connections. Some newer mobile phones, smartphones, and PDAs even include built-in wireless modems. This allows them to function as data modems, providing wireless internet access via a wireless personal computer network connection.

4. CONNECTIVITY

In this Cisco Packet Tracer network configuration, various computers are used to demonstrate seamless connectivity across the different nodes of the network topology. The simulation setup features a centrally placed router within the workspace, providing direct access to gateways positioned on either side. A LAN switch efficiently distributes data to various points and nodes within the virtual network.

The DNS server is configured to handle domain name resolution. A web server is included in the network, meeting the needs of internal computers (Widjajarto et al., 2019).

4.1. LAN SETUP

Cisco Packet Tracer provides a wide range of interfaces and an extensive library of networking devices, making it easy for users to design and simulate a local area network (Ganesh & Sharma, 2020).

The first step in creating a LAN with Cisco Packet Tracer (Mattsson, 2006). is to open the program (which can be downloaded via Cisco Netacad) and configure the network topology you want. Four PCs, one router, and two LAN switches must be dragged and dropped into the workspace. Next, use Ethernet cables to connect the devices and nodes, making sure that every computer is linked to a switch and that both switches are linked to the main router. There should be a designated gateway for every LAN switch (Ceccarelli et al., 2018).

4.2. ADDING A DHCP SERVER TO A LAN

The Simulation workspace as depicted in figure 2-5, consists of a DHCP server which is one of the essential requirements of this paperwork to automate the process of IP Address allocation to different Networking devices that are present in the network. (It can be, computers, laptops, smartphones, tablets, etc) The role of Dynamic Host Configuration Protocol is important not only in providing the Ips to different sections of the network but also in maintaining smooth flexibility in the network.

By setting up the DHCP server (Eloff & Eloff, 2005) with such parameters, this will dynamically assign IP addresses to network-connected devices, beginning with 192.168.2.20, and permit up to 100 units to get IP addresses.

Figure 2. LAN Simulation

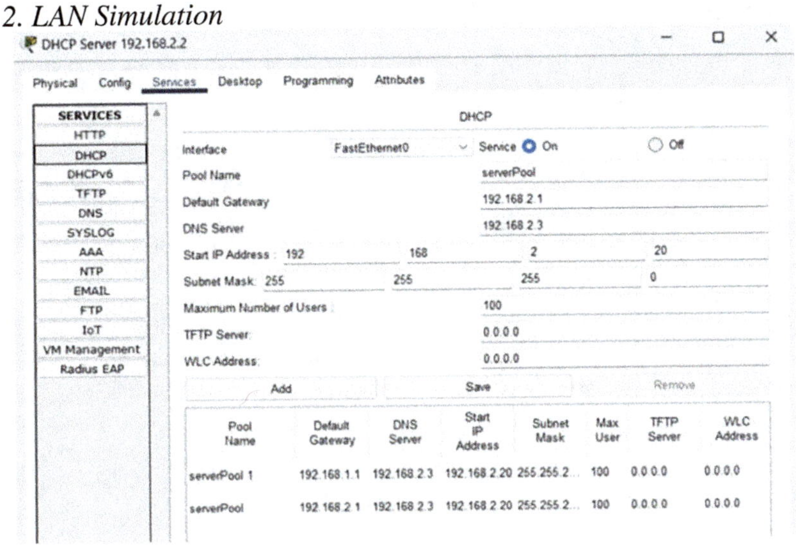

Figure 3. IP Configuration with Settings

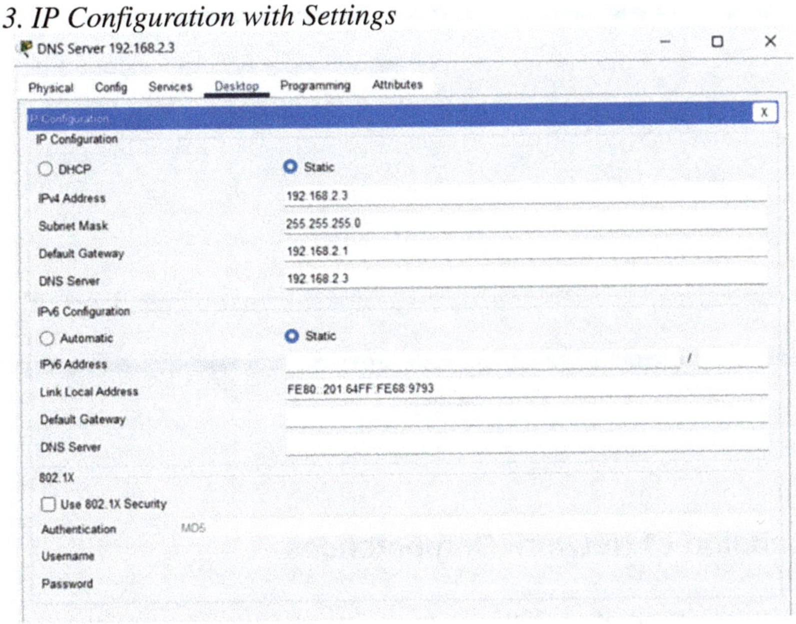

Figure 4. Setting of DNS Services

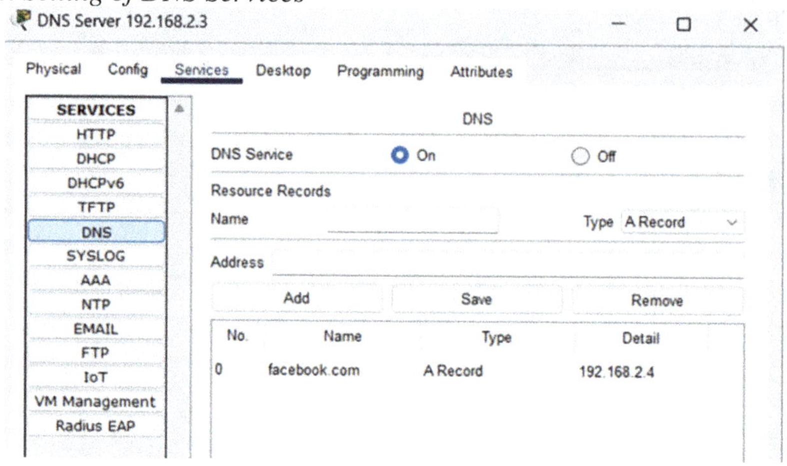

Figure 5. Ip Configuration

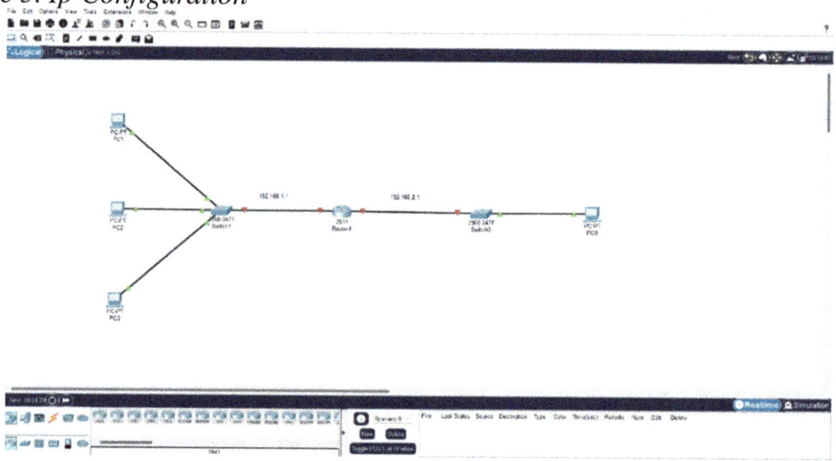

4.4 Expansion of Network Competences

A web server (Lau et al.,2002) is an essential component of the internet; it stores world-wide web data, processes different requirements, and delivers the information online to users all over the world. Add a web server to a Cisco packet tracer on the right side of the switch, as shown in the figure, and first attach it to the current switch via the Ethernet network. Make correct network traffic routing, access the web server configuration interaction, further add the IPv4 address as IP 192.168.2.4, and choose 192.168.2.1 as the default gateway. Save those changes to keep them preserved in the packet tracer-simulated environment. By connecting the web server using the LAN's right-side switch, users may communicate with the server via its assigned IP address, improving network functioning. Refer to Figure 6, shown below, for further setting requirements (Beigh, 2014).

Figure 6. IP Configuration w.r. to Web Server

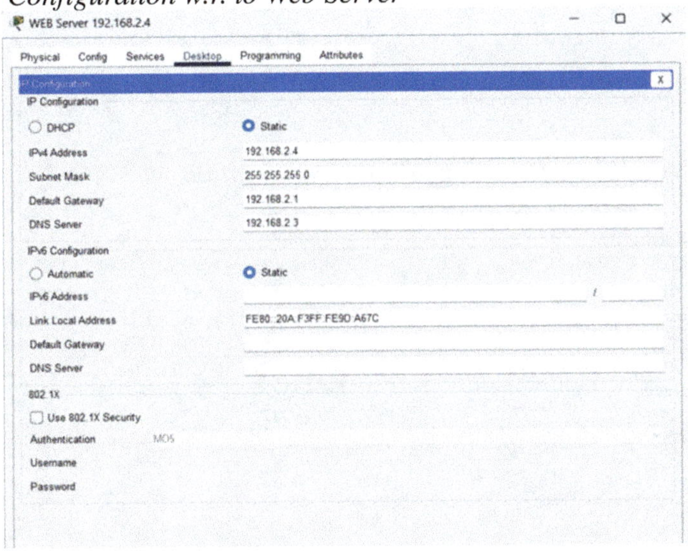

4.5 OPTIMIZATION OF NETWORK ROUTING

To improve network connectivity (Goos et al., 2011) and performance efficiency, router settings need to be correctly adjusted. The very first step is to enter the network router's configuration interface; therefore, assign a unique hostname, such as “DE00.” This native hostname improves order and clarity through network design, which results in more effective network management and administration. This optimisation enhances the network's overall effectiveness and stability by providing uninterrupted data transfer across different elements of the network (Neuman & Ts'o, 1994).

Initially, priority should be placed on setting up the Gigabit Ethernet 0/0 and 0/1 interfaces, both of which have separate IP addresses and gateway configurations. The Gigabit Ethernet 0/0 interface is assigned the IPv4 address 192.168.2.1. Refer to Figure 7, Figure 8, and Figure 9 shown below for further setting requirements.

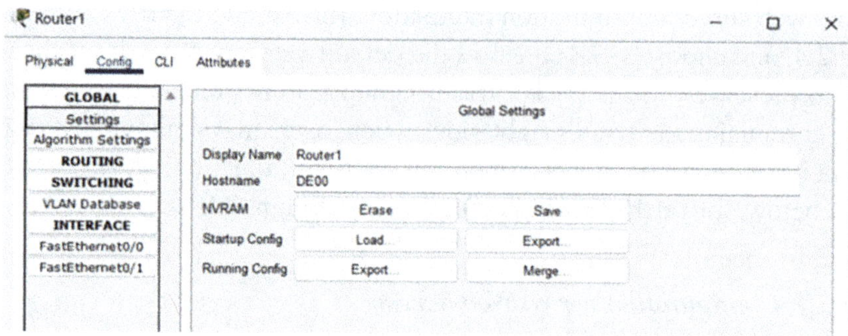

Figure 8. Speedy Ethernet having 0/0 IP Configuration

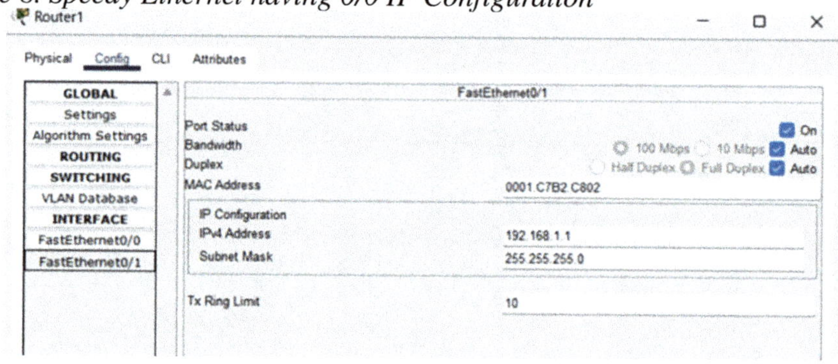

Figure 9. Speedy Ethernet having 0/1 IP Configuration

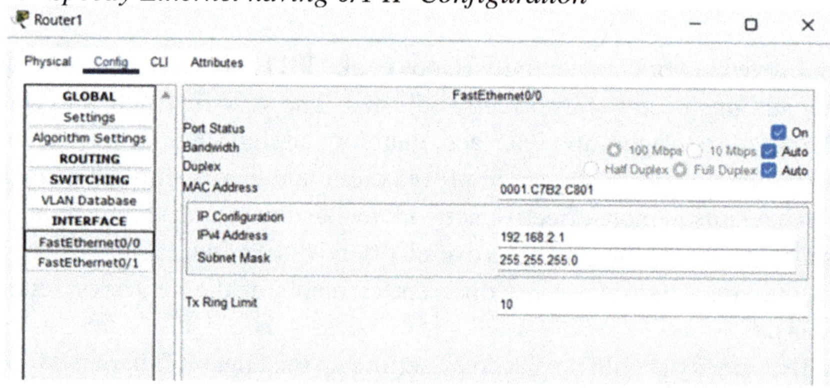

4.6 DNS Transformation Simulation

Cisco Packet Trainer highlights the importance of DNS translation. The text provides an in-depth review of DNS resolution procedures, focusing on the setting of a DNS server on multiple devices. This description emphasizes DNS's essential function and its role in enabling network communication. Refer to Figures 10, 11, and 12 for setting up the configurations.

Figure 10. Opening of Browser in PC0

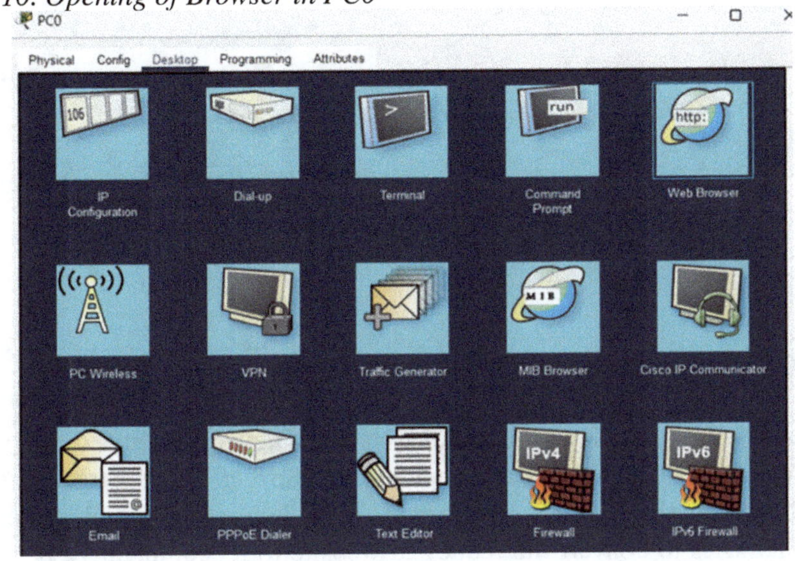

Figure 11. Typing on URL and then press Enter

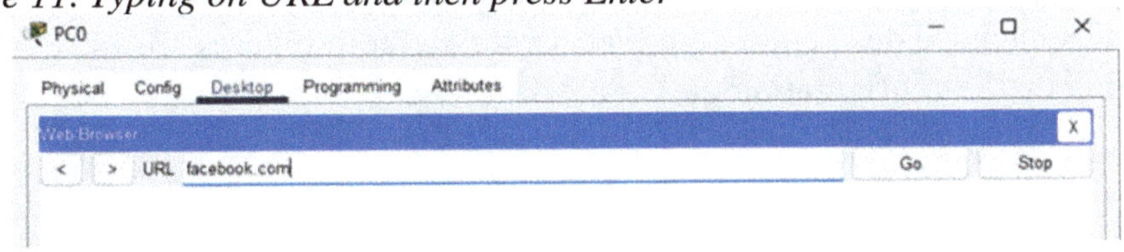

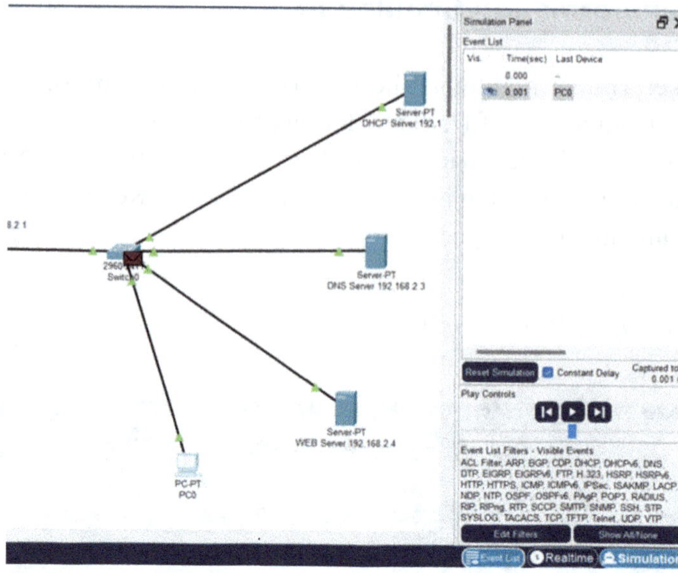

4.6.1. Insights

The data packet's journey in the simulation of this network (Waheed & Ali, 2018) starts by checking the pings on the computers, and further, the data travels up to the LAN switch in the simulation software. At LAN switch zero, the packet goes to the DNS, which tries to convert the requested website to its comparative IP address. After an effective fix by the website's DNS server, the data packet resumes sending its way back to the computer. This return path serves to validate the availability of the IP address concerned with the anticipated URL and marks the end of ongoing network communications cycle. With this confirmation, the data packet proceeds to go to its intended destination: the Web server. Refer to Figures 13, 14, 15and 16 for setting up the configurations.

Figure 13. Emulation Concerning DNS toward Switch 0

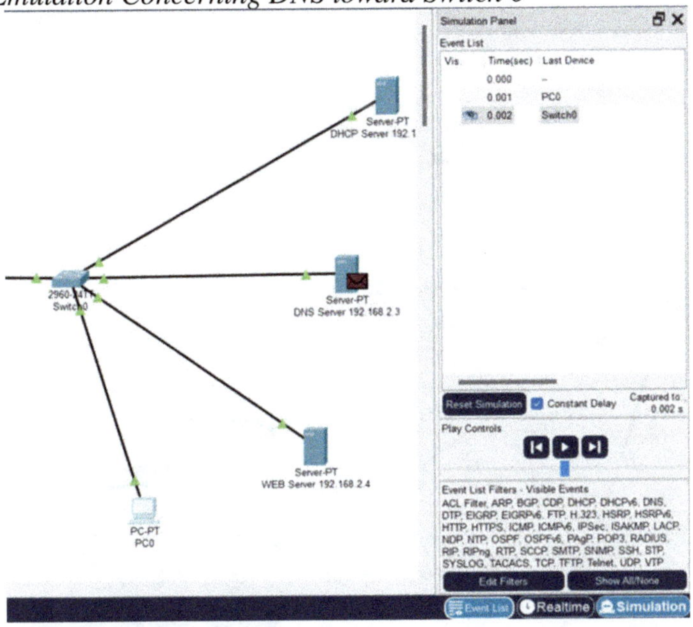

Figure 14. Simulation w.r. to Switch 0 towards PC0

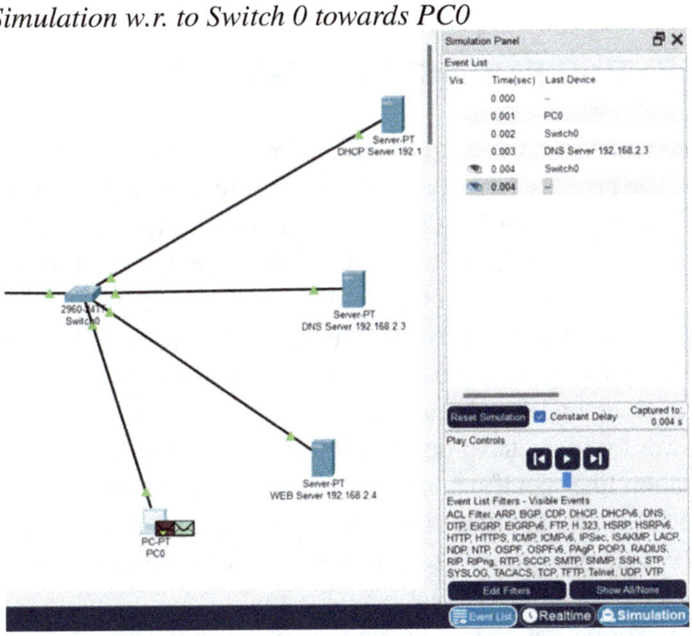

Figure 15. Emulation Concerning PC0 towards web server

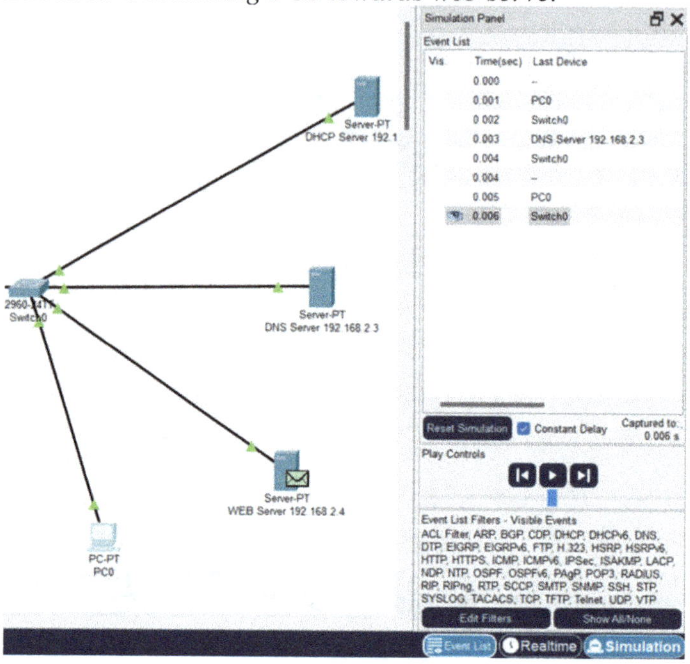

5. IMPLEMENTING PASSWORD STRATEGY

A password strategy is the basic and most important building block of the Network security. The primary function of the policy is to protect the systems, networks and devices form digital attacks aiming to steal and destroy sensitive information and personal data. These policies also compel the users to go through multi-factor authentication process and protect their data with strong passwords. Therefore, these polices provide overall safety and privacy to the systems, data, and networks by making it compulsory for the users to use robust and strong passwords thar are less prone to hacking and data breaches.

Such password polices have defined set of rules for setting strong passwords and authentication like specific numbers of upper and lower case alphabets, use of minimum special characters and digits. Also guide the users to avoid the usage of common and simple passwords like name and date of birth as they are more prone to cyberattacks and unauthorised access.

Therefore, the organisation can add up an extra layer of defence against the unauthorised access by installing techniques like Multi factor Authentication, limiting the access to vulnerable third-party applications and by following the safety measures and guidelines of such password policies. Also, by obeying the standard set of rules and guidelines of the password policies users can protect their systems.

The industries include further sectors like banking, healthcare, Information technology, manufacturing and many more which consist of cognizant and oversensitive data. So, they require more password related management and security standards. Therefore overall, these security measures help the organisation to create a secure and safe environment.

5.1 Importance

A password policy is important in network security foundation because it protects and safeguard the sensitive information from unauthorised access and vulnerable attacks. It compels the users to authenticate by following the standards and guidelines and create strong passwords that are less prone to attacks like dictionary attack and rainbow table assault. Hence, it increases the security of the organisation and reduces the risk of cyber-attacks, scams and frauds. Further, the password policies help the organisation to maintain accountability and create a safe and secure environment by reducing the risk of data breaches and password hacking. Some major and strong password policies are like expiry of passwords, minimum password length, history of the previous password. Therefore, the password policies not only help the users to safeguard their systems from data breaches, but also helps the users to build trust and reassure that the website uses password polices to maintain the security of sensitive information.

Figure 16. Ultimate Implemented Network

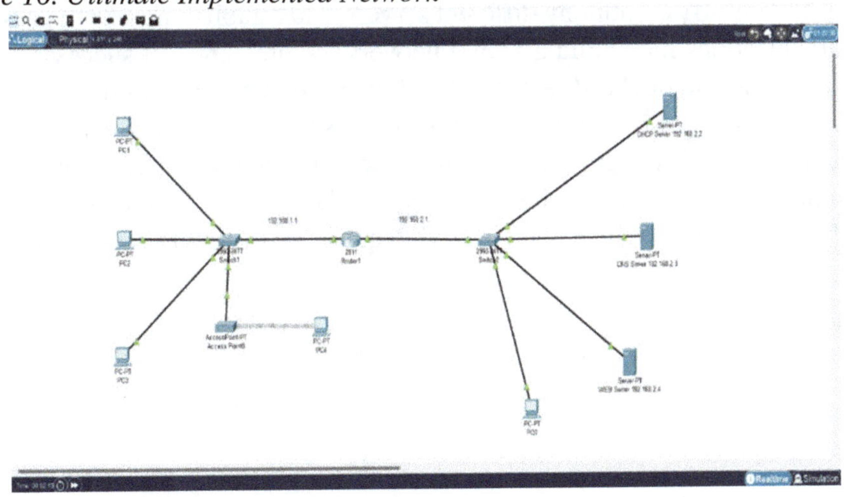

6 MERITS

The network security protects the sensitive and important data of an organisation from data breaches and cyber-attacks that can harm the company's dignity and can cause financial losses. Organisation can compete by keeping such ideas that linked to jobs, goods, and plans. In today's modern era, network security has become essential aspect because it guarantees the safety of our sensitive data and information from unauthorised access and cyber-attacks (Watkins & Wallace, 2008). Networks security measures are important and advantageous because firstly, it protects the sensitive and personal data like financial records, client details, companies trade records and many more. Secondly, it built the trust and credibility of organisation in the eyes of the stakeholders. Thirdly, network security guarantees proper functioning of the system by protecting it from unwanted threats, malware, and viruses. However, there are lot of problems and hurdles faced to provide safe and secure network. With the growing technology the attackers are changing and adopting sophisticated techniques to harm the privacy. The more issues include how complex the infrastructure of network is the need to keep them safe and secured from the data breaches; shortages of cybersecurity professionals to implement the safety measures, and the continuous requirement for the updates on new threats. But the organisation even though find it hard to pay for such big costs for network security, particularly the small and medium sized groups with low funds.

7 CONCLUSION

Cisco Packet Tracer is an effective tool for modeling and enhancing network security systems. By combining different servers, and establishing secure password rules, organizations may build a secure network architecture that successfully defends against shifting cyberthreats while allowing for smooth communication and collaboration. The study also looks at how DNS servers translate URLs into IPv4 addresses, which sheds light on the complicated mechanics that underpin internet communication. It emphasizes the significance of DNS in maintaining seamless and dependable internet access by tracing DNS requests from client to server and back.

REFERENCES

Ahlan, A. R., Lubis, M., & Lubis, A. R. (2015). Information Security Awareness at the Knowledge-Based Institution: Its Antecedents and Measures. *Procedia Computer Science*, *72*, 361–373. DOI: 10.1016/j.procs.2015.12.151

Beigh, B. M. (2014). A new classification scheme for intrusion detection systems. *International Journal of Computer Network and Information Security*, *6*(8), 56–70. DOI: 10.5815/ijcnis.2014.08.08

Bhamare, D., Zolanvari, M., Erbad, A., Jain, R., Khan, K., & Meskin, N. (2019). Cybersecurity for industrial control systems: A survey. *Computers & Security*, *89*, 101677. DOI: 10.1016/j.cose.2019.101677

Ceccarelli, A., Zoppi, T., Vasenev, A., Mori, M., Ionita, D., Montoya, L., & Bondavalli, A. (2018). Threat analysis in Systems-of-Systems. *ACM Transactions on Cyber-Physical Systems*, *3*(2), 1–24. DOI: 10.1145/3234513

Chimphlee, W., & Chimphlee, S. (2023). Hyperparameters optimization XGBoost for network intrusion detection using CSE-CIC-IDS 2018 dataset. *IAES International Journal of Artificial Intelligence*, *13*(1), 817. DOI: 10.11591/ijai.v13.i1.pp817-826

Eloff, J., & Eloff, M. (2005). Information security architecture. *Computer Fraud & Security*, *2005*(11), 10–16. DOI: 10.1016/S1361-3723(05)70275-X

Feng, J. (2009, May). Analysis, implementation and extensions of RADIUS protocol. *2009 International Conference on Networking and Digital Society*. Presented at the 2009 International Conference on Networking and Digital Society (ICNDS), Guiyang, Guizhou, China. https://doi.org/DOI: 10.1109/ICNDS.2009.44

Ganesh, V., & Sharma, M. (2020). Intrusion Detection and Prevention Systems: A review. Lecture Notes in Networks and Systems, 835–844. https://doi.org/DOI: 10.1007/978-981-15-7345-3_71

Goos, G., Hartmanis, J., Van Leeuwen, J., Hutchison, D., Kanade, T., Kittler, J., Kleinberg, J., Kobsa, A., Mattern, F., Mitchell, J., Naor, M., Nierstrasz, O., Pandu, C., Steffen, B., Sudan, M., Terzopoulos, D., Tygar, D., Weikum, G., Lin, D., . . . Wang, X. (2011). Cryptology and network security. In Lecture notes in computer science. https://doi.org/DOI: 10.1007/978-3-642-25513-7

Lau, F., Rubin, S. H., Smith, M. H., & Trajkovic, L. (2002). Distributed denial of service attacks. *SMC 2000 Conference Proceedings. 2000 IEEE International Conference on Systems, Man and Cybernetics. 'Cybernetics Evolving to Systems, Humans, Organizations, and Their Complex Interactions' (Cat. No.00CH37166).* Presented at the IEEE International Conference on Systems, Man, and Cybernetics, Nashville, TN, USA. https://doi.org/DOI: 10.1109/ICSMC.2000.886455

Liandani, P., Lubis, M., & Witjaksono, W. (2020). Exploring the relationship of individual indicator as the critical factor in information security awareness. *Selected Papers from the 1st International Conference on Islam, Science and Technology, ICONISTECH-1 2019, 11-12 July 2019, Bandung, Indonesia.* Presented at the Selected Papers from the 1st International Conference on Islam, Science and Technology, ICONISTECH-1 2019, 11-12 July 2019, Bandung, Indonesia, Bandung, Indonesia. https://doi.org/DOI: 10.4108/eai.11-7-2019.2297836

Lubis, M., Fauzi, R., & Hasibuan, M. A. (2019). Categorization for the Security Awareness Domain and Resource (SADAR) model in the organization: A clustering statistical analysis. *Journal of Physics: Conference Series*, *1235*(1), 012041. DOI: 10.1088/1742-6596/1235/1/012041

Lubis, M., Fauzi, R., Liandani, P., & Lubis, A. R. (2020, July 17). Information security awareness (ISA) towards the intention to comply and demographic factors. *Proceedings of the 8th International Conference on Computer and Communications Management.* Presented at the ICCCM'20: 2020 The 8th International Conference on Computer and Communications Management, Singapore Singapore. https://doi.org/DOI: 10.1145/3411174.3411196

Lubis, M., Novalia, D., & Puspita. (2020, September 3). Development of security awareness domain and resources (SADAR) framework: Capacity metrics to evaluate enterprise resource planning (ERP) implementation. *2020 4rd International Conference on Electrical, Telecommunication and Computer Engineering (ELTICOM).* Presented at the 2020 4rd International Conference on Electrical, Telecommunication and Computer Engineering (ELTICOM), Medan, Indonesia. https://doi.org/DOI: 10.1109/ELTICOM50775.2020.9230523

Mason, A., & Newcomb, M. (2001). *Cisco secure internet security solutions.* Cisco Press.

Mattsson, U. T. (2006). Best practice for enterprise database encryption solutions. SSRN Electronic Journal. https://doi.org/DOI: 10.2139/ssrn.934271

Neuman, B., & Ts'o, T. (1994). Kerberos: An authentication service for computer networks. *IEEE Communications Magazine*, *32*(9), 33–38. DOI: 10.1109/35.312841

Platt, F. (2015). Physical threats to the information infrastructure. In *Computer Security Handbook* (p. 22.1-22.28). https://doi.org/DOI: 10.1002/9781118851678.ch22

Waheed, F., & Ali, M. (2018). Hardening CISCO Devices based on Cryptography and Security Protocols - Part II: Implementation and Evaluation. *Annals of Emerging Technologies in Computing*, 2(4), 11–27. DOI: 10.33166/AETiC.2018.04.002

Watkins, M., & Wallace, K. (2008). *CCNA security official exam certification guide*.

Widjajarto, A., Lubis, M., & Yunan, U. (2019). Architecture Model of Information Technology Infrastructure based on Service Quality at Government Institution. *Procedia Computer Science*, *161*, 841–850. DOI: 10.1016/j.procs.2019.11.191

Chapter 8
Machine Learning in Cyber Security:
A Literature Review

Pooja Dehankar
Ajeenkya D.Y. Patil School of Engineering, India

Sudipta Banerjee
Symbiosis Institute of Technology, Symbiosis International University, Pune, India

Susanta Das
https://orcid.org/0000-0002-9314-3988
Ajeenkya D.Y. Patil University, India

ABSTRACT

Rise in cyber-attacks has prompted organizations to change to a smarter & more proactive approach to cyber security. ML is a component of a larger AI ecosystem, & has really disrupted our thinking around cyber security. This chapter will examine the application of ML in the domain of cyber security to describe its strengths & its weaknesses. We will investigate how ML algorithms can sift through substantial datasets to find patterns, & irregular behavior, and detect threats that could point to advanced persistent threats (APT). It will explain how to achieve this by utilizing traditional isolation- & detection-based cyber security frameworks & understanding their limitations which we can then move to ML approaches. We will see that the approach of ML to cyber security could greatly transform the field because it has the potential to provide automated incident response, enables detection of threats in real time, & is capable of improving security visibility significantly. However, it is important to note that ML success will depend on having sufficient and quality training data.

DOI: 10.4018/979-8-3373-2252-0.ch008

1. INTRODUCTION

The speed of technological change has placed cyber security as a high priority challenge for the global community. People, businesses, and governments face a persistent threat due to the ongoing sophistication of cyber threats. Cyber security tools are necessary to monitor, detect, and respond to any security risks that may exist in our digital ecosystem. These useful tools can help to both protect our information and prevent breaches (unauthorized access) to sensitive materials. However, traditional approaches to cyber security can often prove insufficient against the complexity and pace of changes to cyber-attacks. That is where machine learning can be an important asset for enhancing cyber security responses. Using machine learning (ML) models, organizations can explore large amounts of data, identify unusual behavior, and potentially develop models that allow for the anticipation of attacks. By combining machine learning with cyber security tools, enterprises can have an additional resource to counter risks like identity theft, data compromises and unauthorized access. ML can be included in selecting and updating cyber security tool collections for enterprise IT solutions. In addition, the study notes the significant need for effective practitioners that can leverage ML technologies and develop security-enhanced solutions. Through understanding existing knowledge, trends to inform where we should be heading, and consideration of future needs, valuable insight is presented on ways in which machine learning can enhance cybersecurity practices for the increasing digital safety of the global community (Ahmad et al., 2025).

Machine learning approaches have gained prominence in identifying security threats due to the notable uptick in cyber-attacks over time. Establishing meaningful security benchmarks is paramount to ensure we are using the appropriate and best security mechanisms, providing adequate security by embedding security metrics. From this perspective, these benchmarks are required for various areas of cybersecurity research, including those designed for intrusion detection. While some researchers have looked into specific datasets, it is rare to consider the broader landscape of the overall security datasets. There exist numerous cybersecurity research papers that rely on varying datasets (Buczak & Guven, 2015; Thuraisingham et al., 2008; Meshram & Haas, 2017; Feily et al., 2009, Salem et al., 2008).

Because cyber threats and attacks are becoming more common and complicated very quickly, old ways of detecting them are not working well anymore. Machine learning offers a solution by creating smart and automatic systems that is able to examine vast volumes of data and identify trends and spot security issues right away. Many uses of machine learning in cybersecurity, like detecting intrusions, viruses, and spam, are explored. ML techniques are used by these software uses to improve threat discovery and response times. Cyber threats and attacks can be identified by using ML algorithms that are trained on labelled datasets to learn to differentiate between dangerous and legitimate behavior. However, integrating machine learning with cyber security presents challenges. The value and variety of the training data greatly affects performance of ML models. It can be challenging to locate relevant and meaningful information, particularly considering how rapidly cyber hazards are evolving. Additionally, ML models must be efficient and retrained continuously to enhance their effectiveness, adapt to new attack techniques, and confirm their accuracy. Privacy and security concerns are also brought up by the use of ML in conjunction with big data and IoT security. Data privacy and confidentiality must be maintained when using big data to increase effectiveness of ML models. It is now feasible to work together on threat intelligence while maintaining confidentiality of raw information thanks to advent of techniques like federated learning (Bharadiya, 2023).

2. LITERATURE REVIEW

2.1 Application of ML Algorithms in Cyber security

It is used to distinguish between DoS, Probe, U2R, and R2L assaults. It might also be used in conjunction with ANN and FCM clustering to create a system for detecting network intrusions, as well as with PSO or KNN to create an intrusion detection system. It is employed to set up a system for identifying intrusions into networks. Decrease of false alarms as well. Additionally, it might be combined with clustering or K-Means to create a system for detecting intrusions and established a system for anomalous intrusion detection with Decision Trees (Dai et al., 2019).

Internet of Things (IoT) has enabled linking of multiple devices that are capable of gathering enormous quantities of data due to development of sophisticated technology. Therefore, IoT security necessities are critical. Network access control, data integrity, secrecy, and authentication are protected by cryptography. However, outdated cryptographic protocols are not suitable for all IoT setups, including smart cities, because of the numerous limitations of IoT devices. In order to secure data on IoT networks, researchers have been putting out a number of lightweight cryptographic algorithms and protocols. A comparison of common modern ciphers is provided, along with a discussion of lightweight cryptographic protocols for Internet of Things networks. Additionally, the security of several recently developed block cipher and stream cipher algorithms is evaluated (Rana et al., 2022).

Resource constraints of IoT make it vulnerable to security breaches. Among these breaches, the Distributed Denial-of-Service (DDoS) attack has ability to disrupt network services for customers in many ways, including by using up server resources and overloading link capacity. In critical Internet of Things scenarios, these distributed denial-of-service attacks can lead to deadly consequences. The research addressed a DDoS attack targeting IoT servers that was caused by malicious wireless IoT devices. Cloud computing and software-defined networking approaches help shield IoT servers from these DDoS threats. LEDEM, which stands for learning-driven detection mitigation, represents a novel method that employs a semi-supervised machine learning approach to spot and reduce DDoS attacks. After putting LEDEM through testing in a controlled environment and running simulated network configurations, the findings were measured against cutting-edge existing systems (Ravi & Shalinie, 2020).

2.2 Methods to improve or enhance cyber security

Machine learning models can dig into massive amounts of data - things like system logs, network traffic, and how users typically behave. By doing this analysis, these models get pretty good at spotting weird stuff and potential threats. Basically, machine learning figures out what "normal" looks like for any given network. Knowing that baseline enables it to identify and flag anything that appears suspicious or dangerous, greatly improving the system's ability to identify and address security issues (Mane et al., 2022).

As new malware types appear, ML is essential for identifying and detecting them. Machine learning can detect malicious programs that traditional antivirus software frequently overlooks by looking at how files behave and analyzing what code actually does. In the ever-evolving realm of online security, this proactive approach provides us with a better means of adapting and defending against new cyberthreats (Chowdhury et al., 2023).

By examining online behavior, verifying website addresses, and sifting through email messages to identify questionable patterns, ML systems are able to identify and stop phishing attacks. These intelligent systems monitor user behavior and highlight any unusual activity. UEBA, or user and entity behavior analytics, is a technology that can be very useful for businesses looking to identify compromised accounts or potentially malicious employees (Kőrösi, 2022).

Machine learning keeps a constant eye on how users behave to spot any suspicious or illegal activities. When companies set up and train these smart threat detection systems properly, they can stop sophisticated ongoing attacks, catch brand-new security flaws that nobody knew about before, and quickly pick up on complicated threats. This hands-on approach makes everything more secure by catching and fixing potential problems fast and effectively (He et al., 2020).

As more and more businesses rely on cloud computing, it's becoming essential to build machine learning security tools right into these cloud systems. This approach makes it easier to spot and deal with cyber attacks that older security methods - the ones that just focused on protecting the network's edges - simply can't handle effectively. By using cloud-based machine learning, administrations can increase their skill to recognize and react to changing cyber security threats in a dynamic and scalable manner (Yan & Au, 2019; Pavithra & Samy, 2022).

2.3 Adversarial machine learning in cybersecurity

Adversarial Machine Learning (AML) focuses on evaluating and refining ML models through use of adversarial samples or attack methods. ML shows a lot of potential when it comes to cybersecurity, helping to spot and stop various threats like malicious software, cyber attacks, and stolen identities. But it's not without its challenges - things like struggling to create effective test scenarios for security systems, not having enough privacy protection, and having trouble making security approaches that work well across different situations and can adapt when needed. The relationship between adversarial attacks and defenses is dynamic; attackers are constantly developing new techniques, and defenders need to constantly improve their strategies. AML technology is rapidly evolving and growing in importance in cyber security as a result of this relationship. By carefully analyzing the relationship between adversarial attacks and defenses, the groundwork for future AI advancements in cyber security can be established to increase the robustness and reliability of cyber security systems (Xu et al., 2025).

Machine learning algorithms, particularly deep learning algorithms, have become increasingly popular in cyber security. However, ML systems' susceptibility to hostile attacks restricts their use, especially in dynamic, combative contexts like the cyber security space where actual adversaries are present (Rosenberg et al., 2021).

Protecting computer networks from online dangers is known as cyber security, and it is becoming more and more important in the Information Age. Machine learning presents itself as a viable cure since outdated signature-based attack detection techniques are often inadequate due to growing rate at which fresh assaults are created. The study of creating and classifying adversarial instances—inputs specifically designed to trick classifiers—is known as adversarial machine learning. It has been particularly studied in field of image recognition, wherever small changes are made to pictures that result in erroneous predictions from a classifier. However, research into such techniques is continuously expanding in other domains, such malware and intrusion detection (Martins et al., 2020).

Machine learning has been remarkably accepted in an extensive range of fields over past several years. Deep learning in particular has been widely deployed in applications and services in domains such as computer vision, natural language processing, machine translation, and cyber security, with outcomes comparable to or superior to those of human specialists. However, adversarial attacks can target machine learning systems, particularly in nonstationary contexts like cybersecurity where real opponents are present (Macas et al., 2024).

2.4 Applications of machine learning in network security

One revolutionary area of cyber security is the use of machine learning in network security. Real-time network behavior analysis, anomaly detection, and threat identification are all made possible by these systems' sophisticated algorithms. Machine learning models that are trained on previous data are able to adjust to changing attack tactics, improving intrusion detection and prevention's overall effectiveness. Mobile health text misinformation detection is a problem that is similar to the investigation of adversarial machine learning in network security. Self-reconfigurable misinformation detection systems may provide novel ways to counteract hostile attacks in machine learning-based security systems. Additionally, these programs are excellent at spotting trends that point to criminal activity, allowing for preventative defenses. Machine learning adds to a more resilient and dynamic network security infrastructure by identifying anomalous network traffic patterns and highlighting possible vulnerabilities. The use of machine learning into network security not only fortifies defenses but also offers a scalable and clever method of protecting digital assets as cyber threats continue to change (Pillai et al., 2022).

Numerous decision support systems are now quicker, more accurate, and more effective thanks to machine learning models. In contrast to other sectors, network security applications of machine learning are more vulnerable to active adversarial attacks. This is due to the fact that machine learning applications in network security, such spam filtering, intrusion detection, and malware detection, are inherently hostile. Adversaries continuously test machine learning systems with inputs specifically created to go around the system and produce an incorrect prediction, in what could be described as an arms race between attackers and defenders. A computer network or system's dynamic event monitoring requires the use of intrusion detection systems, or IDS. IDS basically come in two varieties: anomaly-based and signature-based. By correlating threats with a

repository of established attack patterns, signature-based intrusion detection systems mitigate the generation of unnecessary alerts. Nonetheless, a drawback of these systems is their vulnerability to evasion when cybercriminals employ novel attack techniques that are not yet cataloged in their database (Ibitoye et al., 2019).

Using ML in network security has created a new generation of smart, flexible security systems that can change and improve over time. Old security methods, which depended on fixed rules and known attack signatures, often struggled to keep up with the fast-changing and complex nature of modern threats (Chaabouni et al., 2019).

Machine learning has transformed network security by helping systems better spot threats, stop attacks before they happen, and handle issues quickly when they arise. This improvement comes from machine learning's ability to study large amounts of data and find complex patterns that are hard for humans to detect. Different machine learning approaches, like deep learning, supervised learning, and unsupervised learning, let security systems change on their own and stay ahead of hackers who are always coming up with new ways to attack. This adaptability is essential for dealing with new types of attacks that have never been seen before. Security systems enhanced by machine learning can oversee internet traffic, scrutinize user interactions with networks, and examine system activity logs to identify any anomalous behavior. When they spot these red flags, they can quickly alert security teams about potential problems before they turn into major breaches. Additionally, threat intelligence analysis, virus detection, and the recognition of questionable network activity are all made more effective by machine learning (Bakhsh et al., 2023).

2.5 Machine learning in analyzing cyber security attacks

In field of cyber security, identifying cyber-anomalies and threats is becoming increasingly important. These problems can be solved with help of artificial intelligence understanding, especially ML techniques. However, security features and data characteristics might affect how successful a learning-based security model is. A thorough empirical investigation of the efficacy of several ML-based security models is provided together with CyberLearning, an ML-based cyber security modeling with correlated-feature selection. Cyberlearning modeling, a binary classification model for identifying abnormalities, and a multi-class classification model for different kinds of cyberattacks were all taken into account. The security model was built using ten popular machine learning classification techniques: stochastic gradient descent, adaptive boosting, eXtreme gradient boosting, logistic regression, naive Bayes, K-nearest neighbors, support vector machines, decision trees, random forests, and linear discriminant analysis. An artificial neural network-based security model that considers multiple hidden layers was unveiled. Numerous research tested the effectiveness of these learning-based security models using the two most popular security datasets, UNSW-NB15 and NSL-KDD (Sarker, 2021).

2.6 Machine Learning Algorithms

The main goal of ML is to develop models that accept input data and use statistical exploration to predict an output value within an appropriate series.

One of the quickly expanding fields in computer science with wide-ranging applications is machine learning (Yavanoglu & Aydos, 2017). Supervised, unsupervised, and reinforcement learning are the three categories of machine learning algorithms. Supervised algorithms are the well-known processes utilized in machine learning algorithms. Moreover, two other subcategories of supervised algorithms are regression and classification (Feily et al., 2009; Salem et al., 2008). Among the frequently used machine-learning algorithms are Random Forest (Hasan et al., 2016), K-Means, KNN (Yusof et al., 2016), Naive Bayes (Xie et al., 2014), SVM, Decision Tree (Gallagher & Eliassi-Rad, 2009), and Logistic Regression (Bhamare et al., 2016).

Cyber security primarily guards against external attacks on the data, software, and hardware that are part of a system with an active internet connection. Businesses mostly use cybersecurity to guard against unwanted access to their databases and systems. Machine learning methods are incorporated into deep neural networks, allowing the network to learn from unstructured input and resolve challenging issues. It is evident from the experimental analysis that the deep learning model enhanced the cyber security apps' performance, accuracy, scalability, and dependability when used in real-time (Dixit & Silakari, 2021).

Several machine learning algorithms have been used to analyze code patterns and similarities in order to detect malicious code in its various forms. The first studies on this topic that were discovered in the Scopus database were published in 2005 and examined computer access using an unsupervised machine learning system (Stolfo et al., 2005) and virus dissemination using Markov models (Chen & Ji, 2005). Clustering techniques were later used to identify software as malicious (Lin, 2008; Li et al., 2010; Nakazato et al., 2011), and SVM was evaluated on Symbian-OS mobile phones (Bose et al., 2008) and computer systems (Shafiq et al., 2008).

2.7 Cyber security in Blockchain Networks

Machine learning algorithms have demonstrated efficacy in augmenting blockchain security through anomaly detection, cyber threat mitigation, and authentication mechanism improvement.

Although federated learning, deep learning, and reinforcement learning present potential solutions, they also present computational and security issues. Enhancing model interpretability, guaranteeing strong adversarial defensive mechanisms, and optimizing machine learning models for real-time threat detection should be the main goals of future research. Decentralized networks will need to be protected by incorporating AI-driven security mechanisms as blockchain technology develops (Mukesh, 2025).

The connection between machine learning and securing blockchain networks has attracted significant attention from researchers over the past few years. Before 2024, researchers looked into different ways to make blockchain systems more secure. For example, in 2020, Conti and his team studied how supervised machine learning could spot strange patterns and find dishonest activities in blockchain networks. Then, in 2021, Feng and his group focused on using deep learning to find Sybil attacks by looking at how networks behave. In 2022, Liu's research team took a different approach by using reinforcement learning to make smart contracts work better and protect against reentrancy attacks. Federated learning has a lot of promise for security in decentralized systems. Adversarial machine learning can help protect AI systems that are built on blockchain. Even with all these improvements, researchers still face issues like scalability, the high computational needs of these systems, and the need to make models simpler so they are easier to understand and use. Digital banking has revolutionized the financial industry, enabling lightning-fast transactions and significantly improving the customer experience. The problem is that banks have made themselves far more vulnerable to cyberattacks, such as identity theft, fraud, and hackers breaching their systems, as a result of their hasty digital transformation. That's where machine learning comes in as a real game-changer for keeping digital banks safe. These smart ML systems can spot fraud before it happens, catch weird activity that doesn't look right, and stop threats as they're happening. What's really cool is that these systems get smarter over time by learning from new types of attacks, so they don't cry wolf as much with false alarms and can react way faster when something actually goes wrong (Yusuff et al., 2025).

These days, people don't really use pen and paper for banking anymore since everything's gone digital - you just use your phone or go online to handle your banking stuff. The occurrence of several security issues is one of the main issues with the financial system. The unlawful activities of hackers and scammers who want to steal people's money are the cause of these risks. Data encryption, authentication processes, and multiple verifications are all necessary components of an efficient security system that can combat such a danger (Alzoubi et al., 2022).

3. CHALLENGES

The world is becoming more and more data-rich. Data has become an essential component of everyday life due to digitization, and as a result, its value has grown. Storage and security issues were brought on by the increasing amount and importance of data. Government and corporate activities are at risk from data breaches, and cybercriminals make huge sums of money.

A contemporary arsenal, advanced techniques, and technological breakthroughs, in addition to the growing attack surface, ensure that cybercriminals always have an advantage. Particular consideration should be given to the phishing and ransomware attacks that were showcased. By deliberately following the described defense measures and cyber hygiene based on the principle of homogeneity, exposure can be greatly decreased (Huszár, 2022).

In the realm of cybersecurity, AI and ML models are especially vulnerable to hostile attacks. In order to fool AI algorithms, these assaults entail altering the input data they process, which results in inaccurate threat detection. For example, by making minor changes to its code signature, attackers may produce malware that evades detection but is still harmful.

The main worry here is that AI-driven security systems' dependability and credibility may be compromised. These systems may not be able to identify actual threats, which could result in security breaches, or they might wrongly interpret normal activities as threats, which would cause needless interruption and inefficiency (Pooyandeh et al., 2022).

The performance of artificial intelligence and machine learning systems really depends on how good and how much training data you have. When the data is wrong or has built-in biases, you end up with models that don't work well or that unfairly discriminate against certain groups. There's also the issue that these complex algorithms need tons of data to learn properly, which brings up serious concerns about keeping that information private and secure. If the training data has gaps or is tilted in certain directions, AI systems can develop blind spots where they miss specific types of cyber threats entirely. On top of that, when organizations collect and store massive amounts of sensitive information, they basically paint a target on their backs for hackers, making them more vulnerable to cyber attacks (Muneer et al., 2023).

As artificial intelligence takes on bigger roles in making cybersecurity decisions, we're starting to worry more about the ethical side of things. When AI systems decide to block someone's access or keep a closer eye on certain online activities, it can really mess with people's privacy and basic freedoms. This gets us thinking about whether these AI systems are being held responsible for their choices, whether we can actually understand how they work, and whether they're treating everyone fairly. We really need to figure out some clear rules about how AI should make these decisions, who's to blame when things go wrong, and how to make sure these systems aren't trampling on people's rights or making existing biases even worse. Businesses that ignore these elements risk not only technical and security challenges but also legal and reputational repercussions (Sontan & Samuel, 2024).

4. FUTURE RESEARCH

Data storage and sharing confidentiality is crucial. Various kinds of security procedures have been proposed in order to preserve the confidentiality of the data. These procedures, however, fall short if there is a design defect or a zero-day assault occurs. Therefore, there is room for improvement because hackers and online attackers are becoming more sophisticated and using more sophisticated techniques to compromise system security. Therefore, new security protocols that can withstand zero-day vulnerabilities and have additional security and functionality characteristics are needed. A variety of methods and tools are used in the "unification of cyber security and ML" (i.e., different sorts of security approaches, such as encryption algorithms, hashing algorithms, signature creation and verification algorithms, and machine learning algorithms, such as CNNs, clustering, and classification). They also need different setups and types of hardware. There might be some problems with these mechanisms and tools' compatibility in such situations. As was previously said, we employ a variety of methods when combining cyber security and machine learning. We require additional resources in order to execute these numerous algorithms. The chores won't be carried out correctly otherwise. As a result, combining and using different algorithms could overburden the system, which could further impact how the system functions. As a result, we should choose our algorithms carefully and work to develop new, lightweight algorithms that use fewer system resources, whether they be in machine learning or security. Certain datasets are necessary for the ML models to function; errors in the dataset or in the ML model's settings may result in issues. For instance, the system might anticipate something incorrectly or the acquired accuracy might not be entirely accurate. In order to address such circumstances, researchers should try to develop new techniques for identifying flaws in datasets or enhancing system accuracy (Wazid et al., 2022).

Quantum-resistant cryptography technology should be developed in order to identify and counteract any assaults associated with the development of quantum computers, which has also presented issues for cyber security of current cryptographic methods. To ensure the long-term security of sensitive cryptographic material, future scholars should focus on developing encryption algorithms that are resistant to quantum computer attacks. Shortage of skilled personnel and people's unawareness of cyber security and its threats are the other major concerns surrounding cyber security tasks (Admass et al., 2024).

5. CONCLUSION

Computational statistics, data mining, and data science are all strongly related to machine learning (ML), a branch of artificial intelligence. Teaching robots to learn from data is its main goal. ML models are composed of a number of rules, procedures, or intricate "transfer functions" that aid in identifying patterns in data and forecasting behavior. This is very helpful in the cybersecurity industry. Data science is at the forefront of significant technological and operational advancements in cybersecurity. A crucial component of artificial intelligence, machine learning (ML) is helping to extract insightful information from data. It was discovered that machine learning is improving cybersecurity after reviewing earlier research and evaluating the findings. The chapter emphasizes the importance of machine learning in this field by relating key algorithms to various cyberattacks and talking about how successful each algorithm is against particular attacks.

REFERENCES

Admass, W. S., Munaye, Y. Y., & Diro, A. A. (2024). Cyber security: State of the art, challenges and future directions. *Cyber Security and Applications*, *2*, 100031. DOI: 10.1016/j.csa.2023.100031

Ahmad, S., Haque, M. A., Abdeljaber, H. A., Eljialy, A. E. M., Nazeer, J., & Mishra, B. K. (2025). Machine Learning Approaches in Cybersecurity to Enhance Security in Future Network Technologies. *SN Computer Science*, *6*(4), 1–18. DOI: 10.1007/s42979-025-03853-1

Alzoubi, H. M., Ghazal, T. M., Hasan, M. K., Alketbi, A., Kamran, R., Al-Dmour, N. A., & Islam, S. (2022, May). Cyber security threats on digital banking. In *2022 1st International Conference on AI in Cybersecurity (ICAIC)* (pp. 1-4). IEEE. DOI: DOI: 10.1109/ICAIC53980.2022.9896966

Bakhsh, S. A., Khan, M. A., Ahmed, F., Alshehri, M. S., Ali, H., & Ahmad, J. (2023). Enhancing IoT network security through deep learning-powered Intrusion Detection System. *Internet of Things : Engineering Cyber Physical Human Systems*, *24*, 100936. DOI: 10.1016/j.iot.2023.100936

Bhamare, D., Salman, T., Samaka, M., Erbad, A., & Jain, R. (2016, December). Feasibility of supervised machine learning for cloud security. In *2016 International Conference on Information Science and Security (ICISS)* (pp. 1-5). IEEE. DOI: DOI: 10.1109/ICISSEC.2016.7885853

Bharadiya, J. (2023). Machine learning in cybersecurity: Techniques and challenges. *European Journal of Technology*, *7*(2), 1–14. DOI: 10.47672/ejt.1486

Bose, A., Hu, X., Shin, K. G., & Park, T. (2008, June). Behavioral detection of malware on mobile handsets. In *Proceedings of the 6th international conference on Mobile systems, applications, and services* (pp. 225-238). DOI: 10.1145/1378600.1378626

Buczak, A. L., & Guven, E. (2015). A survey of data mining and machine learning methods for cyber security intrusion detection. *IEEE Communications Surveys and Tutorials*, *18*(2), 1153–1176. DOI: 10.1109/COMST.2015.2494502

Chaabouni, N., Mosbah, M., Zemmari, A., Sauvignac, C., & Faruki, P. (2019). Network intrusion detection for IoT security based on learning techniques. *IEEE Communications Surveys and Tutorials*, *21*(3), 2671–2701. DOI: 10.1109/COMST.2019.2896380

Chen, Z., & Ji, C. (2005). Spatial-temporal modeling of malware propagation in networks. *IEEE Transactions on Neural Networks*, *16*(5), 1291–1303. DOI: 10.1109/TNN.2005.853425 PMID: 16252834

Chowdhury, N. U. R., Haque, A., Soliman, H., Hossen, M. S., Fatima, T., & Ahmed, I. (2023, September). Android malware detection using machine learning: A review. In *Intelligent Systems Conference* (pp. 507-522). Cham: Springer Nature Switzerland. DOI: DOI: 10.1007/978-3-031-47715-7_35

Conti, M., Kumar, E. S., Lal, C., & Ruj, S. (2018). A survey on security and privacy issues of bitcoin. *IEEE Communications Surveys and Tutorials*, *20*(4), 3416–3452. DOI: 10.1109/COMST.2018.2842460

Dai, H. N., Zheng, Z., & Zhang, Y. (2019). Blockchain for Internet of Things: A survey. *IEEE Internet of Things Journal*, *6*(5), 8076–8094. DOI: 10.1109/JIOT.2019.2920987

Dixit, P., & Silakari, S. (2021). Deep learning algorithms for cybersecurity applications: A technological and status review. *Computer Science Review*, *39*, 100317. DOI: 10.1016/j.cosrev.2020.100317

Feily, M., Shahrestani, A., & Ramadass, S. (2009, June). A survey of botnet and botnet detection. In *2009 third international conference on emerging security information, systems and technologies* (pp. 268-273). IEEE. DOI: DOI: 10.1109/SECURWARE.2009.48

Feng, Q., He, D., Zeadally, S., Li, N., & Wang, H. (2021). A survey on privacy protection in blockchain system. *Journal of Network and Computer Applications*, *169*, 102807. DOI: 10.1016/j.jnca.2018.10.020

Gallagher, B., & Eliassi-Rad, T. (2009). *Classification of http attacks: a study on the ECML/PKDD 2007 discovery challenge* (No. LLNL-TR-414570). Lawrence Livermore National Lab.(LLNL), Livermore, CA (United States). DOI:DOI: 10.2172/1113394

Hasan, M. A. M., Nasser, M., Ahmad, S., & Molla, K. I. (2016). Feature selection for intrusion detection using random forest. *Journal of information security, 7*(3), 129-140.

He, Y., Meng, G., Chen, K., Hu, X., & He, J. (2020). Towards security threats of deep learning systems: A survey. *IEEE Transactions on Software Engineering*, *48*(5), 1743–1770. DOI: 10.1109/TSE.2020.3034721

Huszár, M. (2022). Current state of IT security awareness–challenges, risks and effects globally.

Ibitoye, O., Abou-Khamis, R., Shehaby, M. E., Matrawy, A., & Shafiq, M. O. (2019). The Threat of Adversarial Attacks on Machine Learning in Network Security—A Survey. *arXiv preprint arXiv:1911.02621*. /arXiv.1911.02621DOI: 10.48550

Kőrösi, G. (2022). *Machine Learning based analysis of users' online behaviour* (Doctoral dissertation, Szegedi Tudomanyegyetem (Hungary)).

Li, P., Liu, L., Gao, D., & Reiter, M. K. (2010). On challenges in evaluating malware clustering. In *Recent Advances in Intrusion Detection: 13th International Symposium, RAID 2010, Ottawa, Ontario, Canada, September 15-17, 2010. Proceedings 13* (pp. 238-255). Springer Berlin Heidelberg. DOI: 10.1007/978-3-642-15512-3_13

Lin, J. (2008, December). On malicious software classification. In *2008 International Symposium on Intelligent Information Technology Application Workshops* (pp. 368-371). IEEE. DOI: DOI: 10.1109/IITA.Workshops.2008.106

Liu, Y., Lin, X., Shen, X., & Liang, X. (2022). Securing blockchain-based IoT with deep reinforcement learning. *IEEE Internet of Things Journal, 9*(3), 1785–1797.

Macas, M., Wu, C., & Fuertes, W. (2024). Adversarial examples: A survey of attacks and defenses in deep learning-enabled cybersecurity systems. *Expert Systems with Applications, 238*, 122223. DOI: 10.1016/j.eswa.2023.122223

Mane, D. T., Sangve, S., Upadhye, G., Kandhare, S., Mohole, S., Sonar, S., & Tupare, S. (2022). Detection of anomaly using machine learning: A comprehensive survey. *International Journal of Emerging Technology and Advanced Engineering, 12*(11), 134–152. DOI: 10.46338/ijetae1122_15

Martins, N., Cruz, J. M., Cruz, T., & Abreu, P. H. (2020). Adversarial machine learning applied to intrusion and malware scenarios: A systematic review. *IEEE Access : Practical Innovations, Open Solutions, 8*, 35403–35419. DOI: 10.1109/ACCESS.2020.2974752

Meshram, A., & Haas, C. (2017). Anomaly detection in industrial networks using machine learning: a roadmap. In *Machine learning for cyber physical systems: selected papers from the international conference ML4CPS 2016* (pp. 65–72). Springer Berlin Heidelberg., DOI: 10.1007/978-3-662-53806-7_8

Mukesh, V. (2025). A Comprehensive Review of Advanced Machine Learning Techniques for Enhancing Cybersecurity in Blockchain Networks. *Journal ID, 8736*, 2145.

Muneer, S. M., Alvi, M. B., & Farrakh, A. (2023). Cyber Security Event Detection Using Machine Learning Technique. *International Journal of Computational and Innovative Sciences, 2*, 42–46.

Nakazato, J., Song, J., Eto, M., Inoue, D., & Nakao, K. (2011). A novel malware clustering method using frequency of function call traces in parallel threads. *IEICE Transactions on Information and Systems*, *94*(11), 2150–2158. DOI: 10.1587/transinf.E94.D.2150

Pavithra, J., & Selvakumara Samy, S. (2022). A comparative study on detection of malware and benign on the internet using machine learning classifiers. *Mathematical Problems in Engineering*, *2022*(1), 4893390. DOI: 10.1155/2022/4893390

Pillai, S. E. V. S., ElSaid, A. A., & Hu, W. C. (2022, May). A Self-Reconfigurable System for Mobile Health Text Misinformation Detection. In *2022 IEEE International Conference on Electro Information Technology (eIT)* (pp. 242-247). IEEE. DOI: DOI: 10.1109/eIT53891.2022.9813840

Pooyandeh, M., Han, K. J., & Sohn, I. (2022). Cybersecurity in the AI-Based metaverse: A survey. *Applied Sciences (Basel, Switzerland)*, *12*(24), 12993. DOI: 10.3390/app122412993

Rana, M., Mamun, Q., & Islam, R. (2022). Lightweight cryptography in IoT networks: A survey. *Future Generation Computer Systems*, *129*, 77–89. DOI: 10.1016/j.future.2021.11.011

Ravi, N., & Shalinie, S. M. (2020). Learning-driven detection and mitigation of DDoS attack in IoT via SDN-cloud architecture. *IEEE Internet of Things Journal*, *7*(4), 3559–3570. DOI: 10.1109/JIOT.2020.2973176

Rosenberg, I., Shabtai, A., Elovici, Y., & Rokach, L. (2021). Adversarial machine learning attacks and defense methods in the cyber security domain. *ACM Computing Surveys*, *54*(5), 1–36. DOI: 10.1145/3453158

Salem, M. B., Hershkop, S., & Stolfo, S. J. (2008). A survey of insider attack detection research. *Insider Attack and Cyber Security: Beyond the Hacker*, 69-90. DOIhttps://DOI: 10.1007/978-0-387-77322-3_5

Sarker, I. H. (2021). CyberLearning: Effectiveness analysis of machine learning security modeling to detect cyber-anomalies and multi-attacks. *Internet of Things : Engineering Cyber Physical Human Systems*, *14*, 100393. DOI: 10.1016/j.iot.2021.100393

Shafiq, M. Z., Khayam, S. A., & Farooq, M. (2008, July). Improving accuracy of immune-inspired malware detectors by using intelligent features. In *Proceedings of the 10th annual conference on Genetic and evolutionary computation* (pp. 119-126). DOI: 10.1145/1389095.1389112

Sontan, A. D., & Samuel, S. V.Adewale Daniel SontanSegun Victor Samuel. (2024). The intersection of Artificial Intelligence and cybersecurity: Challenges and opportunities. *World Journal of Advanced Research and Reviews*, *21*(2), 1720–1736. DOI: 10.30574/wjarr.2024.21.2.0607

Stolfo, S. J., Hershkop, S., Bui, L. H., Ferster, R., & Wang, K. (2005). Anomaly detection in computer security and an application to file system accesses. In *Foundations of Intelligent Systems: 15th International Symposium, ISMIS 2005, Saratoga Springs, NY, USA, May 25-28, 2005. Proceedings 15* (pp. 14-28). Springer Berlin Heidelberg. DOI:_DOI: 10.1007/11425274_2

Thuraisingham, B., Khan, L., Masud, M. M., & Hamlen, K. W. (2008, December). Data mining for security applications. In *2008 IEEE/IFIP International Conference on Embedded and Ubiquitous Computing* (Vol. 2, pp. 585-589). IEEE. DOI: DOI: 10.1109/EUC.2008.62

Wazid, M., Das, A. K., Chamola, V., & Park, Y. (2022). Uniting cyber security and machine learning: Advantages, challenges and future research. *ICT Express*, *8*(3), 313–321. DOI: 10.1016/j.icte.2022.04.007

Xie, M., Hu, J., & Slay, J. (2014, August). Evaluating host-based anomaly detection systems: Application of the one-class SVM algorithm to ADFA-LD. In *2014 11th International conference on fuzzy systems and knowledge discovery (FSKD)* (pp. 978-982). IEEE. DOI: DOI: 10.1109/FSKD.2014.6980972

Xu, J., Wang, Y., Chen, H., & Shen, Z. (2025). Adversarial Machine Learning in Cybersecurity: Attacks and Defenses. *International Journal of Management Science Research*, *8*(2), 26–33. DOI: 10.53469/ijomsr.2025.08(02).04

Yan, N., & Au, O. T. S. (2019). Online learning behavior analysis based on machine learning. *Asian association of open universities journal, 14*(2), 97-106. DOI: 10.1108/AAOUJ-08-2019-0029

Yavanoglu, O., & Aydos, M. (2017, December). *A review on cyber security datasets for machine learning algorithms. In 2017 IEEE international conference on big data (big data)*. IEEE., DOI: 10.1109/BigData.2017.8258167

Yusof, A. R. A., Udzir, N. I., & Selamat, A. (2016). An evaluation on KNN-SVM algorithm for detection and prediction of DDoS attack. In *Trends in Applied Knowledge-Based Systems and Data Science: 29th International Conference on Industrial Engineering and Other Applications of Applied Intelligent Systems, IEA/AIE 2016, Morioka, Japan, August 2-4, 2016, Proceedings 29* (pp. 95-102). Springer International Publishing. DOI: 10.1007/978-3-319-42007-3_9

Yusuff, M., Rankine, A., & Wicky, K. (2025). The Impact of Machine Learning on Cybersecurity in Digital Banking.

Additional Readings

https://www.cisco.com/site/us/en/learn/topics/security/what-is-machine-learning-in-security.html#:~:text=Machine%20learning%20is%20a%20domain,by%20uncovering%20suspicious%20user%20behavior

https://www.exabeam.com/explainers/ai-cyber-security/10-ways-machine-learning-is-transforming-cybersecurity/#:~:text=Machine%20learning%20(ML)%20in%20cybersecurity,to%20identify%20patterns%20and%20anomalies

https://gurucul.com/cybersecurity-101/what-is-machine-learning-in-cybersecurity/

https://www.darktrace.com/cyber-ai-glossary/machine-learning#:~:text=Machine%20learning%20plays%20a%20significant,Fraud%20detection

https://builtin.com/artificial-intelligence/machine-learning-cybersecurity

https://swimlane.com/blog/the-role-of-machine-learning-in-cybersecurity/

https://www.ninjaone.com/blog/machine-learning-in-cybersecurity/#:~:text=combat%20cyber%20threats.-,Introduction%20to%20machine%20learning%20in%20cybersecurity,actors%20to%20exploit%20system%20vulnerabilities

KEY TERMS AND DEFINITIONS

Decision tree: Decision tree models are often applied to spot and classify different types of cyberattacks.

Dimensionality reduction: Techniques for dimensionality reduction help clean datasets by stripping away noisy or irrelevant information.

K-means: K-means clustering can be used as a method to uncover malware patterns hidden in large volumes of data.

K-nearest neighbors: The k-nearest neighbors (kNN) approach is frequently adapted for facial recognition tasks that support secure authentication.

Linear regression: Linear regression provides a way to estimate or forecast outcomes tied to network security performance.

Logistic regression: Logistic regression has proven useful in identifying and preventing fraudulent activity.

Naïve Bayes: Naïve Bayes classifiers serve as a practical tool for intrusion detection systems.

Random forest: Random forest methods are commonly chosen when the goal is to detect and categorize phishing attempts.

Support Vector Machines: Support Vector Machines (SVM) are employed to classify, detect, and even predict suspicious IP or port addresses that may be blacklisted.

Chapter 9
Next Generation Firewall: A Comprehensive Analysis and Practical Applications

Brindha Subburaj
https://orcid.org/0000-0003-2173-5228
Vellore Institute of Technology, Chennai, India

T. Subbulakshmi
Vellore Institute of Technology, Chennai, India

M. Sidharth
https://orcid.org/0009-0004-6473-8482
Vellore Institute of Technology, Chennai, India

ABSTRACT

This chapter provides an extensive discussion on Next Generation Firewalls (NGFWs) and its significance in the recent security infrastructure. Tradition firewalls filters traffic using packet metadata, whereas NGFWs are bundled with security features like application and user awareness, Deep Packet Inspection, Intrusion Prevention System, Virtual Private Network, etc. which enables intelligent threat detection. The evolution of firewalls, the security profiles and configuring these security features are presented in this chapter. An experimentation using machine learning algorithm is carried out to filter traffic and make intelligent decision on whether to allow or deny a traffic. A log record dataset consisting of history of traffic logs is used to train the machine learning model namely XGBoost classifier. The classifier attains AUC Score of 0.998, which shows the significance of integrating machine learning capabilities with next generation firewalls for intelligent threat detection.

DOI: 10.4018/979-8-3373-2252-0.ch009

1. INTRODUCTION

Firewall is a device used to monitor the network traffic and protect an organisations network environment from threats of any forms. The traffic monitoring is based on a predefined rules. If the information in packet metadata is matching the rule, traffic is denied, else it is confirmed to be from/to trusted source and access is granted. Firewall (Bellovin & Cheswick, 1994) acts as a barrier between internal network of an enterprise from the unknown external network. Firewall can be in both hardware and software forms. Hardware firewalls are piece of equipment bundled with the duties of firewall. On the other hand, software firewalls are software codes installed on the computer to monitor incoming and outgoing traffic. Enterprises configure firewalls using a predefined rule set based on source IP address, destination IP address, port numbers, protocol types of the packets to make decision on access or denying the traffic.

Firewalls are configured to monitor and control incoming and the outgoing traffic to protect the enterprise from both external and internal threats.

Threats from external network can be a virus, malware, Denial of service attacks, trojans, phishing mail, etc. In this instance, firewalls monitor traffic flow by inspecting the packets and allows them by matching against the predefined rule list. Threats within the network might include restricting outgoing traffic towards botnets, command and control servers and even monitors the suspicious activity of internal users and their behavioural changes. Suspicious activities like suddenly downloading some sensitive files are potential threats.

The way traditional firewall operates is, it is rule based and it enforces access control policies by monitoring packet metadata like IP address, port numbers and protocol, operating at layer 3 of OSI layers, Network layer and layer 4 transport layer. The major drawbacks of this traditional firewall setup are, Attacks at application layer protocol level will not be handled. Deep packet monitoring is not performed. The evolution of sophisticated malwares demands advanced monitoring and detection systems.

Next generation firewalls are bundled with advanced and a number of security feature to overcome the above issues and it works by filtering at application layer level of OSI (Neupane et al., 2018). Next generation firewalls are Artificial Intelligence enabled and utilizes machine learning and deep learning algorithms to deliver modern and advanced security features to identify the latest cyber attacks and to combat the highly evolving threats (Noor et al., 2025).

(Ritu Rani, 2025) has presented machine learning based next generation firewalls for intrusion detection. Support vector machine and naïve bayes classifier are used for experimentation. A benchmark dataset namely NSL-KDD dataset is used to identify and classify the traffic as normal traffic or attack traffic. Dataset is subject to preprocessing, followed by feature selection and classification. SVM classifier attained highest accuracy of 97.29%.

AI enabled next generation firewalls for cloud environment, its capabilities and features are presented by (Sharma, 2021). The most required security features like deep packet inspection, intrusion detection and application awareness are ensured, and it lists the cloud applicability to deliver improved performance in dynamic environment like cloud. Next generation firewalls can handle the scalability issues in cloud computing environment such as, increase in network traffic volume. To ensure optimal performance dynamic allocation of resources is carried out effectively (Liang & Kim, 2022). ML techniques when integrated with firewall, improves its performance. For instance, ML algorithms like K-Nearest Neighbor (KNN), Guassian Naïve Bayes (GNB) and Random Forest (RF) are employed for DDoS attack detection based on traffic rules and the results are promising when tested on real-time dataset (Alam et al., 2023)

The AI revolution in Network security - The integration of artificial intelligence with firewall technology is not an easy task as it involves many complex steps that ensure that everything is done in a way that follows the CIA triad. AI-powered firewalls are capable of identifying both known and unknown threats within the network traffic. It works in real-time data through live network data, these firewalls keep improving their ability to differentiate between normal traffic and genuine threats.

AI enhances the firewall's working aspects through several mechanisms:

- **Advanced Threat detection**: AI algorithms identify threats in no time and neutralize threats broadly. It analyzes threat traffic patterns to detect patterns of ransomware, malware, and advanced persistent threats.
- **Real-time traffic analysis:** AI firewalls continuously monitor the activity, rapidly identifying abnormalities and addressing them in real-time, stopping attacks before they gain traction.
- **Automated response mechanisms:** These systems are build in such a way it is automated to block malicious traffic, enact security protocols, and isolate devices compromised devices with better precision, reducing response times and minimizing the burden on human interactions.
- **Adaptive learning:** AI systems evolve continuously, learning from new data to improve their threat detection capabilities and stay ahead of emerging attack vectors.

2. RELATED WORKS

The recent research work in the field of next generation firewalls are discussed in this section. The next generation AI based firewalls are reviewed and a comparative study or such recent firewalls are presented (Ahmadi, 2023). In the paper several firewalls are evaluated based on metrics such as adaptability, scalability, its robustness against adversarial attacks, and it is reported that such AI based firewalls provide a better protection against modern cyber threats.

Deep generative gaussian models are used with next generation firewalls to identify hard-to-detect threats (Gurijala et al., 2024). Machine learning plays a key role in intrusion detection to identify the recent cyber attacks and its patterns. New threats are constantly evolving, thus extending such machine learning algorithms improves the firewall capabilities by constantly learning about these threats. Further, machine learning can be used for better access control by creating intelligent systems that would learn from behavioural patterns of user.

A modern security architecture is designed to be suitable for enterprises of all sizes (Oussama et al., 2024). The configuration recommendation for next generation firewalls are presented and to evaluate the effectiveness it is tested using testbed with 2 frontend firewalls and a backend firewall. Firewall inspection test suite is used to conduct experiments, and the results show that malware are identified and blocked either in frontend or backend.

DDoS detection using various machine learning algorithms is experimented and presented using firewall traffic data. (Patel et al., 2024). Algorithms like XGBoost, binary decision tree and support vector machine are extended to identify DDoS attacks using packet header data. Features related to DDoS attacks such as standard deviation of flow packets and standard deviation of flow bytes are used. Accuracy of 99% is reported using binary decision tree. Time efficiency is also analyzed, where binary decision tree is reported with less computation time of about 1.1 milli second per packet on an average.

Intrusion detection using ML and DL algorithms are experimented and presented by Kant et al., (2024). Support Vector Machines (SVM), Convolutional Neural Networks (CNN) and Recurrent Neural Networks (RNN) were used for the study to detect intrusions. Experiments were conducted using multiple datasets, with the goal of classifying datasets as normal or suspicious. CNN outperforms other models and accuracy of 97.29% is reported. F1 score of normal traffic class is 96% and F1 score of attack traffic is 95%.

Algorithms like XGBoost (Chen & Guestrin, 2016), SVM (Cortes & Vapnik, 1995), CNN (LeCun et al., 2015), RNN (Zhang et al., 2019) are robust in handling large and complex datasets to detect intrusions and anomalies with good accuracy (Ozohu & Victor-Ime, 2023). CNNs with its spatial feature extraction capabilities and RNNs with ability to model temporal network events aid in behavior predictions. Thus, these ML and DL algorithms are integrated with latest firewalls to improve security.

AI based cyberattack detection and mitigation system named CYBRANA is recently proposed by (Rengarajan & Karpagam, 2024). Random forest is used for detecting threats using the logs of server and logs of firewall traffic. YAML rules are then mapped to detect if any known attack pattern is available. If attack is identified, its type and severity is classified using scoring system.

Performance test method for next generation firewalls is designed and tested (Wang & Song, 2022). Suggested the necessary values for parameters like network layer throughput, TCP concurrent connections, TCP connection establishment rate, application layer throughput and attack detection rate. With this test method design it is believed to have a better threat detection. The proposed design is verified by testing using six next generation firewalls, it is reported that the capability comparison of different firewalls is possible using the proposed test method design.

3. FIREWALL EVOLUTION

The Various stages of firewall over the period are discussed in this section. The First generation firewalls are called under the term "packet filter firewalls" during 1980 and 1990. The primary functioning of such firewalls is to inspect the incoming and outgoing packets in the network traffic. They inspect the packets by using the meta data like the source and destination IP address, port numbers and protocol. This information is assessed against the predefined access rule set to make decision on to grant or reject the traffic. The limitation is it works by evaluating the traffic only based on the metadata, failing to monitor the contents in the packets. The next major drawback of packet filter firewalls is they are stateless in nature, the state information of the session is not preserved. It doesn't store the information about previous traffic, so it won't compare the traffic in the same session, zero visibility on the packet sequencing. Treating the packets in isolation will fail to identify the threats in the traffic that could be identified if state information are stored and processed. When we check the history of firewalls, it began in the late 1980s with simple packet filtering mechanisms that examined basic characteristics like source and destination IP addresses to determine whether to allow or drop the packet. These elementary firewalls provided rudimentary protection but lacked in several aspects, which is very important in this era, leaving networks vulnerable to application layer attacks (George & George, 2021).

The second generation firewalls during the period of early 2000s are called "Dynamic packet filtering firewalls". They are also called stateful firewalls. As said, these firewalls are built with capability to maintain the state information through state table, and tracks the network connection using it. This state information can ascertain whether the new packet in the traffic is part of the session, by this way it can correlate the packets in a session and makes better decision on threat availability in the traffic. Since it tracks the entire session details, the advancements like context-ware security, enhanced threat detection were possible and which laid the foundation for next generation firewalls.

This firewall type is, it still operates at layer 3 and layer 4 of OSI Model, the network layer and transport layers respectively. It is called dynamic packet filtering firewalls as it can adapt and modify the access rules used for traffic filtering dynamically based on network conditions. The major limitations of second generation firewalls are, application level traffic inspection is not performed. Performance degradation when the traffic is high. Difficulty in handling dynamic IP environment.

In 1990s, we saw the emergence of firewalls, which maintained connections using state tables to track network sessions. These second-gen firewalls could distinguish between legit traffic and attempts to exploit existing connections, offering a much more secure environment, ensuring only packets belonging to established connections are permitted. As web applications became more prevalent, the need for firewalls with better capabilities grew, leading to the development of application-layer-based firewalls, also known as proxy firewalls. These systems operated with higher protocol layers, which go through the actual contents of packets to identify and block application-specific threats, enforcing more granular security policies based on application-level implementations.

Next, the era of third generation firewalls which includes application firewalls and Unified Threat Management (UTM). The very common application gateway or proxy firewalls was built and used from this era. These firewalls operate at layer 7, application layer as well. Thus, it is aware of traffic from/towards an application having better control. Inspection of packets beyond the metadata through deep packet inspection is a giant improvement to firewall capabilities. These deep packet inspection, inspects encrypted data as well, and better analyses the protocol behaviour. It is essential to improve the application level security as web based attacks have been evolved into more sophisticated form. It is in this generation where Unified Threat Management (UTMs) were introduced, and it's the early stage of UTMs. UTMs comes with multiple features like anti virus, URL Filtering, deep packet inspection, application filtering, etc. all together in a single device.

In the fourth generation (2000s to present), the next generation firewalls and UTM were built and are fully established. These fire walls are stateful as well. They are built with robust features to protect the enterprise network. The features include anti-virus, anti-malware, deep packet inspection (DPI), intrusion prevention (IPS), SSL Decryption and application awareness, Virtual private network, etc. User identity based security policies can be easily enforced in these type of firewalls. This can map the traffic activity with the associated user for better control. Behavioral changes can be easily tracked to find the threats. These firewalls are AI powered and are also cloud based. Remote access is feasible as well. These firewalls are equipped with machine learning algorithm based threat identification. The UTM and next generation firewalls are bundled with more or less similar features and detail discussion on the same is given in next section.

Next-Gen firewalls started their development and started implementing them in the mid-2000s, incorporating features of stateful firewalls with advanced capabilities like intrusion detection, application awareness, and deep monitoring of incoming and outgoing packets. It is designed to identify and block threats, including malware and ransomware, by examining traffic at multiple layers of the infrastructure.

The current Next-Gen firewalls can perform critical tasks similar to traditional firewall capabilities, including filtering Layer 7 applications, blocking malicious attachments and links, detecting known threats and device vulnerabilities, applying patches, preventing DDoS attacks, and providing web filtering for direct internet access. This approach of consolidating multiple functions into one has been revolutionary, as it has reduced cybersecurity complexity by integrating previously separate systems into unified solutions.

The evolution of firewalls is summarized in Table 1.

Table 1. Firewall types and its evolution

Year	Firewall type	Features
Early 1990s	Packet-filtering firewalls	• Operates at network layer • Controls traffic based on IP address and ports
Late 1990s	Stateful firewalls	• Connection state is monitored • Connection awareness, improved security, foundation for advanced features
Early 2000s	Application layer, web application firewalls	• Application gateway, proxy firewalls • Unified Threat Management
Late 2000s	Next-Generation Firewalls	• Advanced features like intrusion prevention
2020s	ML powered Next-Generation Firewalls	• Cloud-based • AI for enhanced security and adaptability

4. NEXT GENERATION FIREWALL AND UNIFIED THREAT MANAGEMENT

In this section Next Generation Firewalls (NGFWs) and Unified Threat Management (UTM) are discussed in detail. The similarities and differences between these devices are compared and contrasted as well.

UTM is a security hardware appliance that brings together multiple key security features in to a single device, for easier security management. As already discussed, it is evolved during fourth generation. UTMs can do basic packet filtering, stateful inspection is an added benefit. They can also be configured to enable VPN tunnels for establishing secure remote connections. The key features include, Intrusion detection and prevention system to detect and block the threats, SSL/TLS Inspection for deep packet inspection of encrypted traffic, antivirus and antimalware for identifying virus, malware and other related threats, web filtering and URL filtering to block malicious or traffic from/to unsafe website and URLS, spam filtering preventing against spam emails, application control to block unauthorised and unwanted applications for the enterprise, etc.

NGFWs further evolve and leverages the capabilities of the conventional firewalls. The aforementioned features like packet filtering, deep packet inspection, secure VPN connections are covered by NGFWs as well. Additionally, NGFWs are bundled with features such as, application control awareness, threat intelligence, user identity awareness, AI driven threat prevention, cloud and remote work protection. They offer more granular control over the network traffic, preventing against modern cyber threats.

UTMs as an integrated and bundled single security solution comes as all in one approach and are easy to manage as well. The increase in threat types and severity improvements demands a single yet efficient system. UTMs are suitable for moderate traffic environments and businesses of small to medium size. They are easy to manage with a single dash board.

NGFWs includes all the above features, but in a more advanced level and with more granular control on applications. They are optimized for high speed processing, with dedicated hardware acceleration. These are suitable for large enterprises with huge network traffic. NGFWs are usually more complex to configure and require skilled professionals to configure firewalls and the features.

The NGFWs vendors include Fortinet (Fortigate 100E/200E/500E/600E1000E /2000E), Palo Alto (400, 800, 1400, 3400 5400, 7000 series), Cisco, Check Point, Huawei, etc.

5. FEATURES OF NEXT GENERATION FIREWALLS

The next generation firewalls are loaded with multiple security features and policies to manage the threat effectively. The major features are listed and discussed in this section. Configuring these features as security policies will be discussed in the next section.

- Deep Packet Inspection (DPI)
- Application Awareness and Control
- Intrusion Prevention System (IPS)
- SSL/TLS Inspection
- Web/URL Filtering
- Threat Intelligence
- User Identity Awareness
- Managing remote work challenges

Deep Packet Inspection (DPI)

The usual packet filtering by inspecting the source and destination IP address and the source and destination port numbers. DPI does the above, and additionally it also inspects the packet bodies for the malware signatures and for other threats. The packet contents are analyzed and are compared against known threats.

Application Awareness and Control

It is possible in next generation firewall to have better application control. The enterprise could block traffic from a particular application. Any traffic from or towards risky applications could also be restricted by imposing appropriate security policy.

Intrusion Prevention System (IPS)

IPS includes real time intrusion detection and prevention. The network is monitored for malicious activity, and when such activity is detected, firewall will block and take preventive actions to overcome the intrusions. IPS can be performed in different ways, such as signature based, policy based and anomaly based. In Intrusion Detection System (IDS), the malicious activities are detected but not prevented. IPS can detect and prevent against the threats.

Threat Intelligence (TI)

TI is a record of potential cyberattacks. This is evidence based and are organized and analyzed by cyber security experts. TI includes IP reputation information as well. The attack mechanism, identification methods, its impact and the action to defend the same are all included in TI.

User Identity Awareness

The network activity of individual users can be recorded and maintained. This aids in user behavior analysis in an enterprise.

Web Filtering/URL Filtering

This security feature enables the enterprise to restrict traffic from and towards a specific URL. The traffic can be restricted based on URL, or even based on categories like News, entertainment, etc. Network is protected from threats, and security compliance are enforced and productivity is improved through it.

SSL/TLS Inspection

https traffics are mostly in encrypted form. It is difficult and computationally expensive to decrypt and inspect the same. Thus, it is essential to decrypt and inspect such encrypted traffic to identify malicious payload if any, that are hidden within such secure connections. Secure Socket Layer (SSL) are cryptography protocols that encrypts and transmits the data. Transport Layer Security (TLS) is now used instead of SSL for data encryption.

Managing remote work connections -VPN Support

Next generation firewalls support VPN protocols like IPSEC to enable secure remote access.

6. CONFIGURING SECURITY PROFILES

As we have already seen, the next generation firewalls are loaded with multiple security features for a better threat management. In this section the steps to configure the above security feature in next generation firewall is detailed. Fortigate firewall is used for the same.

Application control configuration

This security feature allows enterprises to manage access to a specific application. Through the next generation firewall we can better monitor and control network connections to a specific application or category of applications. This application control operates at layer 7, the application layer of OSI model to have better application control, regardless of other parameters like port, protocol and encryption techniques that are used. The policies are written by the organization, according to the requirements to block unauthorized or applications that are risky to the enterprise.

The steps to configure the application control policies are:

1. In the FortiGate User Interface-> click security profiles-> click application control
2. Next, we have to create application sensor, which is listing the categories and applications that we wish to restrict in various modes like fully block, monitor mode or allow mode
3. Select the application categories we wish to block like Gaming, Social media, etc
4. We can also give the specific application name that we wish to block, in this example we may block Facebook, Facebook messenger
5. Save the application sensor
6. Next, we have to configure this as policy. Click policies and objects -> create new policy
7. Here we may name the policy, Incoming Interface, Outgoing Interface, Source and destination IP (we mention all here)
8. Enable the application control and save

Now, the firewall is configured with the required application control, restricting access to the specified applications.

Figure 1. Enabling Application control

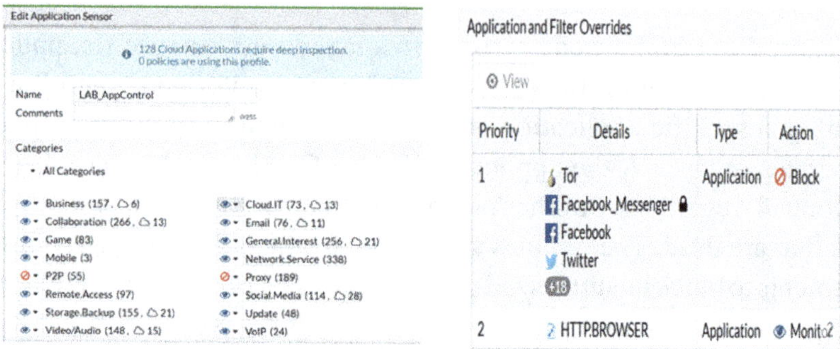

Figure 2. Configuring policy

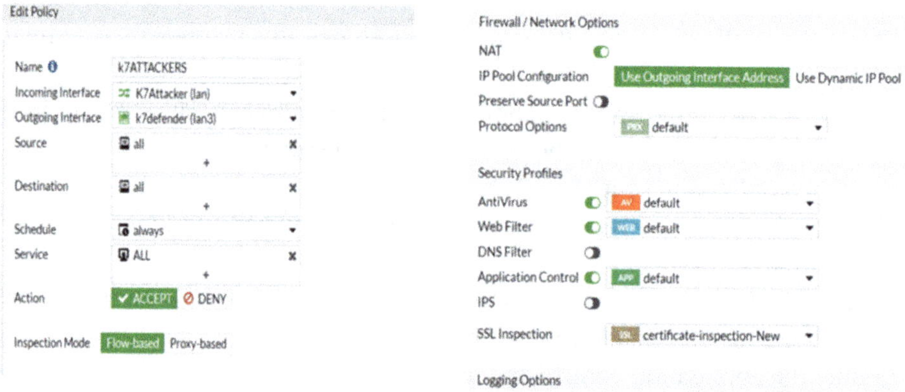

Web Filtering/ URL Filtering

It is possible to restrict access to a specific URL or website through predefined policies. In the previous case entire application is restricted. URL are filtered as category which are predefined or by specifying the URL. When a user tries to access a specific URL, it is verified against this list of URLs to filter traffic and prevent from cyber threats. Web filter lookup repository can be used to check the URL category.

The steps to configure the application control policies are:

1. In the FortiGate User Interface-> click security profiles-> click web filter
2. Select the categories appropriately to allow or block a particular website category

3. To block traffic from specific URL, we may click Edit URL Filter-> specify URL to filer and take specific action (Block, allow, monitor)
4. Next, configure the control policy appropriately and enable the WebFilter

Figure 3. Configuring Web Filter Profile

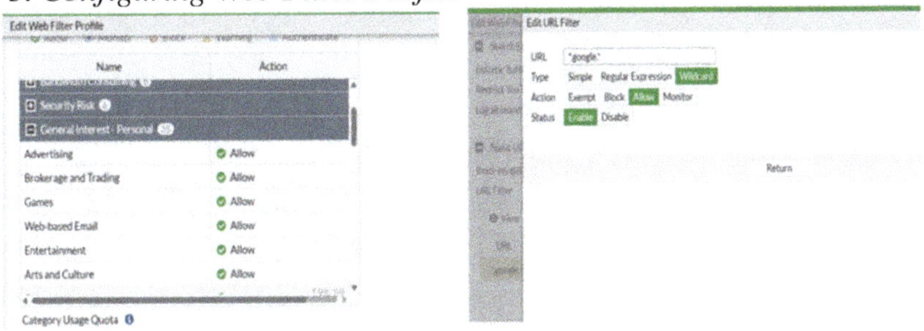

Intrusion Prevention System (IPS)

IPS ensures network integrity through its advanced security solutions to detect and prevent malicious activities. It works by filtering the incoming and outgoing traffic by comparing with a set of already known attack signatures to detect matches. Behavioural analysis is performed to further identify activities that deviate from the normal characteristics. IPS can be implemented in two ways, Signature based detection, Anomaly based detection.

In Signature based detection, this detection scheme works fine for known threat types. It uses a repository of already known threat attack patterns. Traffic is compared with these patterns to make intelligent decision. The major drawback is, this method highly relies on the already known threats.

Another detection method is Anomaly based detection, that works fine for unknown threats as well. A baseline is created using the normal network behavioural activities. If any user activity deviates from this baseline, flag is raised. An example for this is, an user from enterprise suddenly accesses sensitive files.

Through the above methods, IPS ensures real time prevention from threats. It ensures automated response action if any intrusion is identified. Its capability to identify known and unknown threats.

The steps to configure the application control policies are:

1. In the FortiGate User Interface-> click security profiles-> click IPS

2. Signatures of threats are selected based on severity, protocols, etc. and are included.
3. Botnet sites and traffic towards such C&C- Command and control nodes are filtered. Select such C&C IP definitions
4. Next, configure the control policy appropriately and enable the IPS

Figure 4. Configuring IPS

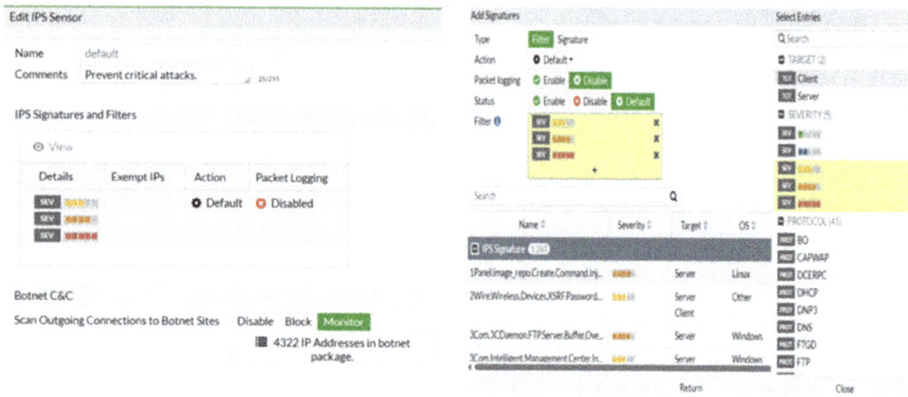

SSL Inspection (TLS/SSL Decryption)

Secure Socket Layer (SSL), Transport Layer Security (TLS) are security protocols used to provide secure communication across network. SSL is a older protocol. TLS is an evolved and recently used protocol than SSL.

In recent years, the internet traffics are highly encrypted, the https traffic are encrypted using TLS protocols. Threats like malware, phishing may intrude if the encrypted content are not analysed. SSL Inspection is used to confirm that such threats in the encrypted traffic are filtered. SSL inspection is a computationally expensive task, the encrypted HTTPS traffic is decrypted and are inspected for threats like malware (Deep packet inspection) and are re-encrypted and forwarded if found to be safe. Security profiles like URL filtering, application control required SSL inspection security profile to be enabled.

SSL certificate plays a key role in the above process. SSL/TLS certificate is a digital certificate used to verify and confirm a website's identity, and to further encrypt the communication session between the server and the user browser. This certificate is hosted at the website server. It holds the public key of the website. The certificate includes details domain name, to whom certificate is issued, Domain name, to whom, authority who issued, digital signature of issuing authority, issue date, expiry, public key. It is to be noted that SSL inspection has a high performance impact as it utilizes significant amounts of CPU and memory resources.

The steps to configure the application control policies are:

1. In the FortiGate User Interface-> click security profiles-> click SSL/SSH Inspection
2. Upload the CA certificate
3. Configure other SSL options as required
4. Next, configure the control policy appropriately and enable the SSL inspection option

Figure 5. Configuring SSL/TLS Inspection

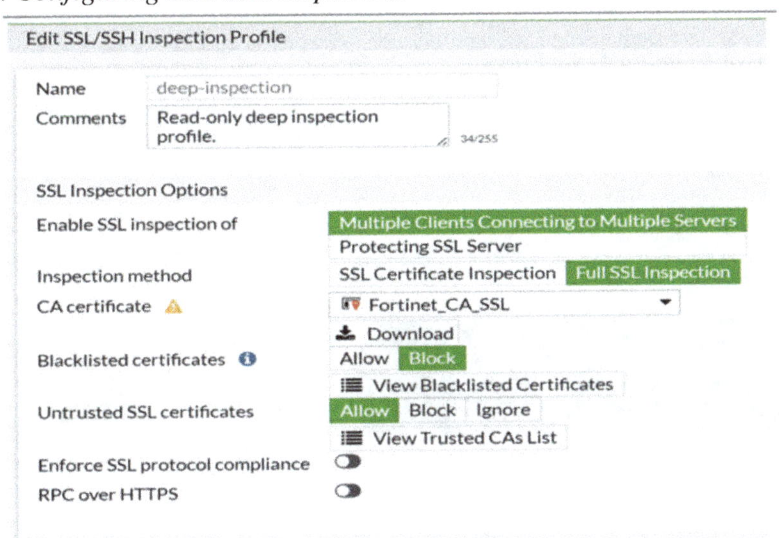

DNS Filter

Domain Name System (DNS) is used to map the URL with respective IP address, and DNS resolver is responsible for this mapping. These DNS mapping requests do face certain threats such as request access towards a suspicious or malicious domains. Such request need to be identified and filtered, in next generation firewall this is achieved through the DNS filter security policy. The working principle is, whenever a user initiates request to access a particular domain, the firewall intercepts this request and evaluates against the configured DNS filtering policies. Access to harmful domain is blocked and access to domain marked as safe is granted.

The steps to configure the application control policies are:

1. In the FortiGate User Interface-> click security profiles-> click DNS Filter
2. Enable FortiGuard Category Based Filter and select the categories to filter, such as domains with mature content, domain that are bandwidth consuming, etc
3. We may also configure static domain filter and mention domain access to be restricted
4. Configure and select the option of RedirectPortlIP to redirect traffic to a specified IP if DNS filter identifies access towards a restricted domain.
5. Next, configure the control policy appropriately and enable the DNS Filter option

Figure 6. Configuring DNS Filter

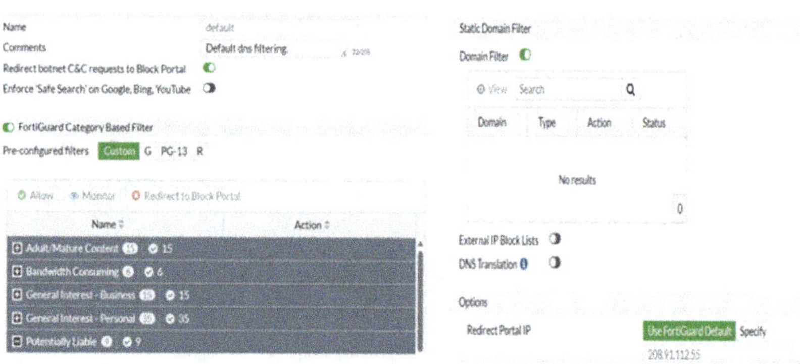

Antivirus

Antivirus security feature aids in detecting and protecting network from virus, malware, trojans and other malicious threats from intruding our network. Antivirus security policy can be configured either in proxy based or flow based pattern. We configure antivirus security profile through following steps.

1. In the FortiGate User Interface-> click security profiles-> click antivirus
2. Click the action to be taken if a virus is detected (block/monitor)
3. Specify the ports to be inspected

4. Select and upload the appropriate SSL inspection certificate
5. We can select and maintain the log record of traffic flow
6. Next, configure the control policy appropriately and enable the Antivirus option

Figure 7. Configuring Antivirus

7. Experiments and Results

Machine Learning-Powered Firewalls: Enhancing Network Security with XGBoost

Problem Statement

Network administrators always face the challenge of processing massive amounts of network traffic data to identify malicious activities or enforce security policies. The problem lies in distinguishing between legitimate and harmful traffic while ensuring minimal disruptions to normal operations. Traditional rule-based systems are often insufficient to handle the complexity and volume of modern network environments.

In this rapidly evolving cybersecurity space, traditional technologies aren't enough to meet the current requirements of our cyberspace. Firewall plays an essential role in securing the environment secured behind. It's not possible to meet the requirements of millions of requests with the fixed rules, automation is not a simple answer for this question. An algorithm that is flexible depending on the situation is required. A machine learning approach is one such thing that can be used for this, XGBoost

(Extreme Gradient Boosting) (Chen & Guestrin, 2016) have emerged as a powerful tool for enhancing firewall capabilities. This experiment is to examine how XGBoost algorithms are performing for threat detection, classification accuracy, and real-time protection. Current implementations show us that ML-powered firewalls are capable of accuracy up to 97.5% in detecting web attacks while processing over 100000 req / sec. The integration of AI enables us to have adaptive learning capabilities that continue improving the threat dataset while reducing false positives and providing more robust protection against evolving threats.

About the Dataset

The model was trained using a variety of features derived. The dataset (Firewall.csv) comprises records of network traffic with the following 12 attributes/features:

- Source Port and Destination Port: Indicating the source and destination ports involved in communication.
- NAT Source/Destination Port: Representing ports after Network Address Translation (NAT).
- Action: The target variable that specifies whether the traffic was allowed, denied, or dropped.
- Bytes, Bytes Sent, Bytes Received: Metrics representing data volume.
- Packets: The number of packets transmitted during communication.
- Elapsed Time (sec): The duration of the communication session in seconds.
- pkts_sent and pkts_received: Packet-level statistics for sent and received data.

The dataset provides a comprehensive view of network activity, enabling predictive modeling for traffic classification. A total of 65532 instances available in dataset.

Firewall data set is taken from: https://archive.ics.uci.edu/dataset/542/internet+firewall+data

XGBoost is an effective machine learning algorithm for cybersecurity applications. It is powered by a gradient boosting framework that optimizes the model's performance by minimizing the loss functions while it prevents overfitting through regularization techniques.

This powerful algorithm offers several advantages that make it well suited for our experiment. Its features include:

1. Efficiency: XGboost works in parallel processing and tree pruning to accelerate the model's training and improve performance, enabling rapid analysis of a large amount of network data.

2. Flexibility: It supports a large types of data types and can be processed with multiple hyperparameters to address specific needs.
3. Accuracy: XGBoost consistently works better than many other existing algorithms in classification tasks due to its capability to capture complex interactions between features, achieving impressive results in comparative analyses.

In a study a various classifiers for attack detection were conducted, XGBoost demonstrated excellent performance with a mean score of 96.2, compared to Random Forest (93.34), Decision Tree (96), and KNN (96.5). This high accuracy makes XGBoost a compelling choice for security applications requiring precise threat identification.

XGBoost for Network Intrusion Detection

Network Intrusion Detection Systems represent one of the most effective applications of XGBoost in cybersecurity.

The study focused on optimizing XGBoost for intrusion detection and identified key parameters that significantly influence its performance. The researchers discovered that XGBoost delivers results that are as good as, or even better than, other classifiers like Random Forests and Stochastic Gradient Boosting. Its ability to strike a balance between computational efficiency and detection accuracy makes it especially useful for real-time security applications.

Data Preprocessing and Model Training

The implementation of an XGBoost-based firewall solution follows a structured approach, its starts with thorough data checking to ensure the dataset is clean, consistent, and prepared for effective model training. The key steps involved in preprocessing are:

1. **Encoding categorical variables**: Firewall actions such as "allow," "deny," and "drop" are converted into numerical values so that its compatible with our machine learning model.
2. **Handling missing values**: Some data might be missing so it is addressed by replacing it with the median value of each column, ensuring uniformity across the dataset.
3. **Feature scaling**: Numerical features are standardized so that it ensure that all variables contribute equally to the model's performance, they prevent any single feature from disproportionately influencing the results.

4. **Feature and target separation**: The dataset is divided into input features (such as network attributes) and the target variable (firewall action) to simplify the training process.

After preprocessing, the dataset is split into training and testing subsets, into 80-20 ratio. This ensures that a sufficient portion of the data is available for training and validation purposes. The XGBoost classifier is then made into such a way that it uses optimized hyperparameters such as the number of estimators, maximum tree depth, learning rate, and subsampling ratio. The model is trained by fitting it to the preprocessed training data using XGBoost's advanced optimization techniques.

Model Evaluation and Performance

Once the model is trained, its performance is evaluated using multiple metrics to ensure its reliability and effectiveness:

1. **Confusion matrix**: This provides a detailed breakdown of true positives, true negatives, false positives, and false negatives for each class, helping identify areas where misclassifications occur.
2. **Classification report**: It offers insights into precision, recall, F1-score, and support for each class, providing a comprehensive view of how well the model performs across different firewall actions.
3. **ROC-AUC score**: This metric evaluates the model's ability to distinguish between classes, with scores closer to 1 indicating superior predictive power. AUC stands for "Area Under the Curve," it is referring to the ROC (Receiver Operating Characteristic) curve. It is a performance metric used to evaluate the ability of a classification model to find difference between different classes. The ROC curve plots the true positive rate (sensitivity) against the false positive rate (1-specificity) at various threshold levels. An AUC score of 1.0 indicates perfect classification, while a score of 0.5 suggests that the performance equivalent to random guessing. In this context, high AUC scores—such as 1.0000 for Class 0 and 0.9997 for Class 1—demonstrate that the model has excellent discriminatory power and can effectively differentiate between normal and malicious traffic.

Research findings have demonstrated XGBoost's exceptional capabilities in intrusion detection for firewall applications. For instance, multi-class ROC curves have shown high AUC values (e.g., Class 0: 1.0000, Class 1: 0.9997), indicating excellent separability between categories. Additionally, overall accuracy rates of up to 100% and weighted average F1-scores of 1.00 highlight XGBoost's potential as a reliable and efficient solution for real-time security applications.

Result:

Figure 8. Attained results

```
Confusion Matrix:
[[7543    2    0    0]
 [   0 2984    7    3]
 [   0    0 2562    0]
 [   0    2    0    4]]

Classification Report:
              precision    recall  f1-score   support

           0       1.00      1.00      1.00      7545
           1       1.00      1.00      1.00      2994
           2       1.00      1.00      1.00      2562
           3       0.57      0.67      0.62         6

    accuracy                           1.00     13107
   macro avg       0.89      0.92      0.90     13107
weighted avg       1.00      1.00      1.00     13107

ROC-AUC Score: 0.9988
```

Figure 9. ROC Curve

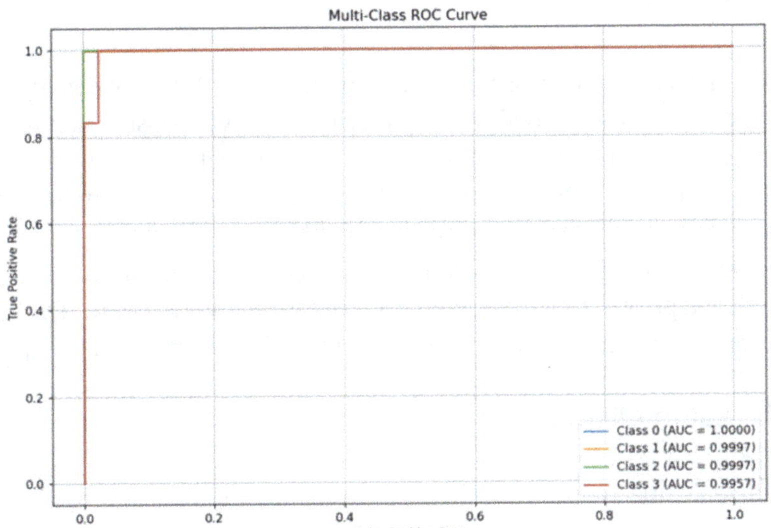

Multi-Class ROC curve

The Multi-Class ROC curve tells that the model's performance in distinguishing between each class. Each line represents a class, which shows the trade-off between the true positive rate (TPR) and false positive rate (FPR) at various thresholds. The high AUC values for all classes (e.g., Class 0: 1.0000, Class 1: 0.9997) indicate excellent separability and predictive power of the model across all categories.

Inference

1. Model Performance:
   - The XGBoost classifier has achieved high accuracy in predicting firewall actions based on historical data.
   - The ROC-AUC score demonstrated excellent class separation capabilities across all categories.
2. Feature Importance:
   - Information on Bytes, Packets, and Elapsed Time was found to be significant contributors to predictions.
3. Visualization Insights:
   - The multi-class ROC curve highlighted areas where certain classes (e.g., "deny") had slightly lower AUC scores compared to others ("allow").

Real-World Applications and Use Cases

Anomaly detection

Anomaly detection is a primary application area where ML-powered firewalls can be used. Its potential for recognition of patterns using XGBoost to identify unusual or potentially malicious network behaviors. This approach begins with establishing the baseline norms for network traffic, API calls, or logs, then employs statistical analysis to monitor system behavior continuously.

The model can trigger alerts when anomalous actions are detected, while also categorizing and prioritizing these events to keep the network secure. The intelligent prioritization ensures that critical threats are taken into care as soon as possible.

Cyber Threat Intelligence

Beyond real-time monitoring, ML-powered firewalls can be used to analyze patterns across global networks to identify emerging threats before they impact the organizations. These infrastructures collect and organize information about the attacks, security logs etc, for future references and training purposes.

While traditional CTI requires extensive manual analysis by security professionals, Xg boost can be used to automate routine tasks, organize information more efficiently, and provide deeper analytical insights, lessening human interaction.

This experiment tells how machine learning can revolutionize networks by automating big tasks like firewall action classification. By leveraging a model with training on detailed data, In the future we can achieve a highly predictive and accurate model.

Future work could involve integrating this model into a real-time monitoring system or exploring advanced techniques like deep learning for more accurate predictions in complex scenarios.

CONCLUSION

In this chapter we have presented an in depth discussion on next generation firewall, its evolution, features, benefits and challenges. Further machine learning based method to grant or deny traffic is discussed as well. Traditional firewalls lack the advanced security features and work by monitoring traffic at layers 3 and 4 of OSI model. They fail to identify the modern cyberattacks as well. To overcome this, Unified Threat Management and Next Generation Firewalls were designed and developed and are integrated and loaded with multiple security features ranging from deep packet inspection, intrusion prevention, antivirus, application awareness, user awareness, web filtering, VPN for remote access etc. All these features are loaded in a single device. Modern firewalls comes with sophisticated applications and user interface and can be accessed remotely as well. They are loaded with artificial intelligence capabilities, machine learning and deep learning algorithms are used for multiple purpose such as for intelligent threat detection, behavioural analysis, identifying DDoS attacks, adversarial attack detection using algorithms like support vector machine, CNN, RNN, etc. we have conducted a small experiment using XGBOOST classifier to filter traffic and make intelligent decision on whether to allow or deny a traffic. A log record dataset consisting of history of traffic logs is used to train the machine learning model namely XGBoost classifier. The classifier attains AUC Score of 0.998, which shows the significance of integrating machine learning capabilities with NGFWs for intelligent threat detection. NGFWs thus are resilient and provide highest level defence against modern cyber attacks, further remote monitoring, AI and cloud based solution makes them a more robust source for network security. NGFWs thus play a major role in the modern cybersecurity landscape, to combat the sophisticated and fast-evolving threats through proactive threat detection and response and granular control over applications and users.

REFERENCES

Ahmadi, S. (2023). Next Generation AI-Based Firewalls: A Comparative Study. *International Journal of Computer*, *49*, 245–262.

Alam, S., Alam, Y., Cui, S., & Akujuobi, C. (2023). Data-Driven Network Analysis for Anomaly Traffic Detection. *Sensors (Basel)*, *23*(19), 8174. DOI: 10.3390/s23198174 PMID: 37837004

Bellovin, S., & Cheswick, W. (1994). Network firewalls. *IEEE Communications Magazine*, *32*(9), 50–57. DOI: 10.1109/35.312843

Chen, T., & Guestrin, C. (2016). XGBoost: A scalable tree boosting system. In *Proceedings of the 22nd ACM SIGKDD International Conference on Knowledge Discovery and Data Mining* (pp. 785–794). ACM. https://doi.org/DOI: 10.1145/2939672.2939785

Cortes, C., & Vapnik, V. (1995). Support-vector networks. *Machine Learning*, *20*(3), 273–297. DOI: 10.1023/A:1022627411411

George, A., & George, A. (2021). A brief study on the evolution of next generation firewall and web application firewall. Zenodo *(CERN European Organization for Nuclear Research)*. DOI: 10.5281/zenodo.7027397

Gurijala, P., Avula, R., & Lekkala, S. (2024). Next-Gen Firewalls: Enhancing Cloud Security with Generative AI. *Journal of Artificial Intelligence & Cloud Computing.*, *3*(4), 1–9. DOI: 10.47363/JAICC/2024(3)404

Kant, V., Singh Gill, K., Kumar, M., & Rawat, R. (2024). The Future of Cyber Defence: ML and DL Enhanced Firewalls for Intrusion Detection. *2024 4th Asian Conference on Innovation in Technology (ASIANCON)*. 2024, 1-4. Doi: DOI: 10.1109/ASIANCON62057.2024.10838028

LeCun, Y., Bengio, Y., & Hinton, G. (2015). Deep learning. *Nature*, *521*(7553), 436–444. DOI: 10.1038/nature14539 PMID: 26017442

Liang, J., & Kim, Y. (2022). Evolution of firewalls: Toward securer network using next generation firewall. *2022 IEEE 12th Annual Computing and Communication Workshop and Conference (CCWC)*, 0752–0759. DOI: 10.1109/CCWC54503.2022.9720435

Neupane, K., Haddad, R., & Chen, L. (2018). *Next generation firewall for network Security: a survey*. SoutheastCon., DOI: 10.1109/SECON.2018.8478973

Noor, A., Tariq, N., Khan, F. A., & Ashraf, M. (2025). Evolution of Next-Generation firewall system for secure networks. In *CRC Press eBooks* (pp. 263–271). DOI: 10.1201/9781003497851-24

Oussama, L., Ismail, A., Mohamed, M. E., Fabien, C., & Lahcen, A. I. (2024). Toward a modern secure network based on next-generation firewalls: Recommendations and best practices. *Procedia Computer Science, 238*, 1029–1035. DOI: 10.1016/j.procs.2024.06.130

Ozohu Musa, M., & Victor-Ime, T. (2023). Improving Internet Firewall Using Machine Learning Techniques. *American Journal of Computer Science and Technology, 6*(4), 170–179. DOI: 10.11648/j.ajcst.20230604.14

Patel, M., Amritha, P. P., Sudheer, V. B., & Sethumadhavan, M. (2024). DDoS Attack Detection Model using Machine Learning Algorithm in Next Generation Firewall. *Procedia Computer Science, 233*, 175–183. DOI: 10.1016/j.procs.2024.03.207

Rengarajan, A., & Karpagam, G. R. (2024). Enhancing Cybersecurity Resilience with CYBRANA: A Cyber YARA/YAML-Based Resilience Firewall Solution Applied with Next-Gen AI. *2024 IEEE International Conference on Computer Vision and Machine Intelligence (CVMI)*. 2024, 1-7. DOI:DOI: 10.1109/CVMI61877.2024.10782249

RituRani. (2025). Next-Generation Intrusion Detection Systems with Machine Learning and Deep Learning-Based Firewalls. *2025 International Conference on Intelligent and Innovative Technologies in Computing, Electrical and Electronics (IITCEE)*. 1-4. DOI:DOI: 10.1109/IITCEE64140.2025.10915227

Sharma, H. (2021). Next-Generation Firewall in the Cloud: Advanced Firewall Solutions to the Cloud. *ESP Journal of Engineering & Technology Advancements.*, *1*(1), 98–111. DOI: 10.56472/25832646/JETA-V1I1P112

Wang, Z., & Song, H. (2022). Research on performance test method for the next generation firewall. *2022 IEEE International Conference on Advances in Electrical Engineering and Computer Applications (AEECA)*. 585-589. DOI: 10.1109/AEECA55500.2022.9919085

Zhang, A., Lipton, Z. C., Li, M., & Smola, A. J. (2019). *Dive into deep learning.*

ADDITIONAL READING

Garbis, J., & Chapman, J. W. (2021). Next-Generation firewalls. In *Apress eBooks* (pp. 135–142). DOI: 10.1007/978-1-4842-6702-8_10

Müller. Andreas C., & Guido, Sarah. (2016). Introduction to Machine Learning with Python: a Guide for Data Scientists (Pdf ed.). Sebastopol, CA: *O'Reilly*

KEY TERMS AND DEFINITIONS

Access Control List: These are set of rules used to permit or deny traffic towards an network by monitoring criteria like IP address, port number.

Application Layer Filtering: It is a technique to filter network traffic through contents of application layer protocols, thus it ensures control over application behavior and prevents threats associated specific to application level.

Deep Packet Inspection: An advanced security feature to control network traffic by inspecting the data part of packets for threats like viruses, spam, intrusions.

Next-Generation Firewall: It is a security device that includes the traditional firewall capabilities like packet filtering with advanced security features like deep packet inspection (DPI), intrusion prevention systems (IPS), application awareness, etc.

Packet Filtering: It is a firewall function, which controls network access by monitoring outgoing and incoming packets through metrics like source/destination IP, port, and protocol to make decision on allowing packets through or blocking packets.

Stateful Inspection: Firewall architecture variant that tracks the state information of active network connections. Decisions are made based on the context of the traffic, and not limited by just monitoring packets.

Threat Intelligence: The threat data collected in reality are integrated into NGFWs to identify and act to emerging threats based characteristics like attack patterns, malicious IPs, etc.

Chapter 10
The Phishing Epidemic: Threats, Techniques, and Countermeasures

Shalomo Agarwarkar
https://orcid.org/0009-0006-6728-1267
Gujarat University, India

Kiranbhai R. Dodiya
https://orcid.org/0009-0001-9409-7303
Gujarat University, India

Kapil Kumar
Gujarat University, India

ABSTRACT

Phishing scams, often seen as simple tricks, actually use complex tactics causing major financial, digital, and personal losses globally. Exploiting human behavior and urgency, attackers deceive victims through fake websites, messages, calls, and more. As technology evolves, phishing grows more advanced, using tools like scripts and malicious payloads. This chapter explores the causes, techniques, psychological impact, and countermeasures of phishing. It also analyzes two major phishing case studies to show the scale of harm. Lastly, it highlights effective prevention methods, combining technical defenses with awareness to help individuals and organizations stay protected.

DOI: 10.4018/979-8-3373-2252-0.ch010

1. INTRODUCTION

Phishing attacks continue to be one of the most common cybersecurity threats, where attackers are deploying highly sophisticated attacks with diverse tactics. This is how attackers create convincing clones of actual and official websites to lure users into giving their login credentials and other related sensitive information.(Lim et al., 2025). Such attacks have substantial consequences, leading to financial losses for victims. In this world full of technology and people with different mindsets. There are many different individuals living in it who have creative minds as well. With this developing era, people with high intelligence, when exposed to pressure, greed or under the influence of other individuals, perform crime. The reasons may be personal, financial or conditional. If we talk about this digital age the most portion of crime happens via the internet. The Internet has made it very easy for criminals to target people. We are going to learn about phishing, a very well-known and common cyber-attack that criminals use to lure people and fulfill their own greed.

1.1. Overview of Phishing Scams

Phishing is a form of online fraud in which hackers attempt to get your private information, such as passwords, credit cards, or bank account data. This is usually done by sending false emails or messages that appear to be from trusted sources like banks or well-known websites. In the current era of the internet, it is not very hard to clone a voice or clone a website to scam individuals. When we specifically talk about phishing, the techniques involving Emails, voice messages, and other ways are included. This is done after some criminals gather some minor information about the group or a specific targeted individual. Traditional phishing often involving making of counterfeit platforms, like that can be fake websites and software applications. (Chen et al., 2024). Then there are criminals targeting people to collect money and use it as funds in criminal activity. They gather the money, make partitions, and use it to brainwash individuals. The brainwashing could be in a way that the person is emotionally and mentally broken and feels like the whole world is wrong, and only 1 specific person can save them. This is how criminals are motivated for terrorist and criminal activity. Suppose you have a call from the bank asking for a KYC update, and suddenly, they ask for an OTP to confirm it. As soon as the OTP is given, the attacker gains access to the users'/victims' bank accounts. The money was transferred via more than 3 bank accounts, making it harder to trace the money. This led to a violation of bank policy, as the investigator cannot investigate more than 3 bank accounts due to security policy restrictions by the bank.

1.2. The Growing Threat of Phishing in the Digital Age

As technology evolves, there is a very big rise in the ease of crime. This crime may be easy to commit, but hard to detect as well. This technology helps to hide criminal location, identity and even clone someone's Identity as well. Things are not as hard as in the past. A random person can commit a crime and hide himself, and all this just in the blink of an eye. This sure raises concerns for the people, especially for parents who live alone and don't know how to use technology. This also includes the children who are unaware of the dangers of this technology. And nowadays, A.I. is also playing a major role as it helps to create and design social engineering attacks that look genuine. In a paper published in the year 2021, it is mentioned that over 90% of companies have faced the issue of getting phishing emails. (Alkhalil et al., 2021). The thing that is concerning is that over 88% of them had face, to be spear phishing mails, 83% of them had fake voice phishing, and 84% of them experienced SMS phishing.(Alkhalil et al., 2021).

1.3. A simple example

There are large numbers of individuals creating groups that gather people and individuals to perform phishing crimes. First, seek people who have a weak financial condition to do the job. A bond of policy is signed for the security of these groups. Then, as soon as the individual joins the group, they are forced to talk to people, send spam emails in bulk to find targets. They then keep sending this message until they find individuals willing to respond to their emails and messages. After this, based on the type of response they get from the victims, they use the "social engineering" techniques best suitable for them. Then, people are traditionally lured to give out their personal data. Then, as mentioned before, transfer of funds takes place. The gathered data and funds are broken into small parts and distributed to international accounts. To make the tracing harder, it is transferred via different local bank accounts before international transactions. This is how targeting people takes place. So, from this, we can say it is not that hard to set up a business in the name of call centers. This trend can be largely seen in South Asia and some other parts, such as Africa.

2. LITERATURE REVIEW

As we have discussed previously, there are many reasons that work from the formation of the attack till its execution. From the client side, the scenario that triggered the incident leading to the loss of resources also has various aspects. In Registration,

Detection and Deregistration, by author Lim, we viewed how attackers abuse DNS for phishing attacks (Lim et al., 2025). The study of proactive domain monitoring while timing the mitigations is shown in this paper. They examined detection methodologies based on registration patterns and mentioned some effective countermeasures that included strict domain policies and automatic abuse detection systems(Lim et al., 2025). In a paper named Multiscale Features and Graph Convolutional Networks for Ethereum Phishing Detection author Chen mentions an approach of detecting phishing scams in Ethereum transactions (Chen et al., 2024). They demonstrated how blockchain-based scams are different from traditional scams and how machine learning is used to enhance the detection power of these phishing techniques (Chen et al., 2024). Another paper, named Comprehensive Study and Anatomy of Phishing Attacks by Alkhalil the author has explains the overview of phishing attacks, their effects and discusses modern countermeasures (Alkhalil et al., 2021). This study deeply explained the results after examination of psychological tactics and stress reactions that affected users (Alkhalil et al., 2021). In 2015, Flamholz and Annaswamy proposed a mechanism to protect cyber-physical systems from stealth attacks. These attacks were intended to harm critical infrastructure like power grids and industrial control systems. The reason for their entering the critical infrastructure was that they operated under a threshold limit (Flamholz & Annaswamy, 2015). The author has mentioned techniques of detecting attackers by replicating false yet realistic signals into a system (Flamholz & Annaswamy, 2015). Using mathematical techniques and simulations, the author demonstrated a well-crafted technique that could force attackers to reveal their presence. They also discussed the problems one might face while implementing the technique (Flamholz & Annaswamy, 2015). This research highlighted the importance of integrating security with conventional intrusion detection systems to create a robust defense against CPC threats (Flamholz & Annaswamy, 2015). There was an interesting paper published in 2024 by author Tamal mention about, mentioning Unveiling Suspicious phishing attacks with feature vectorization and Machine learning (Tamal et al., 2024). It mentioned the detection of phishing attacks using a vectorization algorithm and supervised machine learning. The author argues that dynamic phishing attacks are not sufficient in detecting evolving phishing techniques (Tamal et al., 2024). There is a necessity for more robust and adaptive ML techniques. The study focuses on the limitations that current phishing detection mechanisms have. This includes techniques like signature-based detection and heuristic analysis. These techniques cannot detect zero-day or sophisticated attacks. In order to address these challenges, the author proposed a vectorization algorithm that helps to improve the data representation of ML models. Refining these features gives results with fewer false positives and thereby increases the overall efficiency of the phishing detection system. The author investigated various methods like deep learning architecture, random forests, support vector machines and even decision trees (Tamal et al., 2024). The results show that combining vectorization with ML helps to outperform traditional detection methods. The key feature that helped them to distinguish phishing content from legitimate sources required a study of URL structure, domain age, hyperlink patterns and email header analysis (Tamal et al., 2024). This was how one can introduce ML in order to safeguard their assets.

3. CAUSES AND MECHANISMS OF PHISHING

As phishing is a very common crime used by cyber criminals, it is rapidly spreading in very little time as well. For this reason, phishing is considered an easy-to-use, effective weapon for criminals. The base of attack consists of factors like technical vulnerabilities, human psychological flaws and the sophistication of the attack. The reason for the widespread nature of this attack is the wide availability of all this personal information on social media, public databases and data breach sets. Based on this, the attacks can be crafted more easily and effectively. The reliance on email and other digital communication mediums in a professional environment has widely increased the surface area, and helps criminals to remain undetected. Mostly many organizations lack all the essential security practices, such as multi-factor authentication, regular employee training and strict security protocols. These things make the architecture more vulnerable to phishing emails and attacks. Attackers commonly exploit human fear, greed, curiosity and panic when it comes to human emotions. Some examples are promising messages, refunds, rewards or exclusive offers, trying to exploit human behaviour to grab these kinds of opportunities. Many platforms are providing “Phishing as a Service” as well. These platforms have a user-friendly interface, event support, and custom phishing kits as well. The important thing one must understand is that psychological reasons could influence the behaviour of fraudsters. (Abroshan et al., 2018). These platforms enable simple people with minimal skills to launch highly sophisticated phishing campaigns. Some services provide the facility for securely receiving ransom payments. Nowadays, A.I. is also used to refine and automate phishing techniques. Common methods used are email spoofing, URL obfuscation, domain impersonation, DNS spoofing and SSL spoofing. Most frequently used malware is “Advanced Persistent Threat (APTs)”. They are used to escalate privileges, initiate vector access and exfiltrate sensitive data.

3.1. Social Engineering Techniques

When we talk about Social Engineering, the whole base of Phishing, there are many parts that play a major part while doing so. Social engineering is about manipulating techniques that cyber criminals use and lure and expose sensitive data and use they're for their own benefit. Cyber criminals usually craft convincing emails or websites, making it impossible to distinguish between legitimate and fake content. The thing to be noted is that even though social engineering attacks look different, they have some common patterns. (Salahdine et al., 2019).

Figure 1. Types of Phishing Attacks

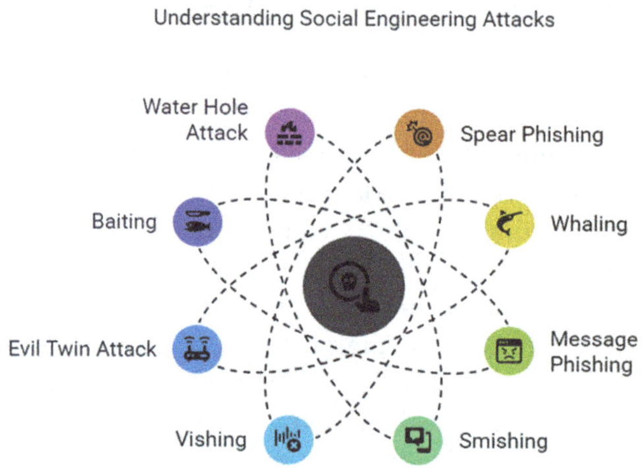

3.1. Types of Phishing Attacks

1) Spear Phishing and Whaling

Spear phishing involves specifying the target, which could be an individual or an organization whose information can be publicly available. Attackers conduct reconnaissance to craft specific attacks as per the data gathered. The attack might be related to a job role or could be a recent activity too. If the attacker goes more specific, then the attack is considered whaling. The attacker will show you urgency, trying to request all confidential reports from employees. Whaling is a word that comes from the English word whale, which refers to large sea creatures living in the sea. As it is related to fishing, these are the types of phishing that target large individuals or victims who are not ordinary and common people. Whaling is an attack that usually targets high-level professional or publicly popular figures, such as the company's CEO, to disrupt a specific company.(Putra et al., 2024). As Most people are unaware of this technique, it is very well done. Attackers change the way they communicate to match their target's characteristics, occupation, and contact list to make their attacks invisible or harder to detect. Nowadays, spear phishing attacks are getting more and more sophisticated by utilizing the information that is gathered from sources, including social media, to increase the efficiency of an attack. (Putra et al., 2024). Here, the main motive of attackers is the manipulation of dissension, gaining power over victims. Success here depends on the exploit of user trust and the authority of the sender.

2) Message and Email Phishing

These are some of the most common types of social engineering ideas that are used basically in phishing mail, which may include payloads such as malicious URLs and malicious payloads. Due to a very high availability of personal details by means such as social media, it has become simpler for attackers to draft social engineering attacks to gain restricted data that may require higher privileges. (Understanding and Mitigating Phishing Attacks in the Digital Era, n.d.).These emails are designed in a way that it looks like taking urgent action will solve the problem the phishing emails are talking about. The email sender might be claiming to be a bank recipient asking for KYC of your account, and to update your bank details, they may require your credentials. Additional attackers could use spoofed emails just by altering the FROM address, making it appear legitimate. Social media platforms prove effective in spreading this phishing email. The selling of sophisticated email marketing tools and other advertising automations has made it easy for an attacker to craft personalized mail on scale.

3) **Smishing**

Smishing, which is also known as SMS phishing. This is when an attacker sends phishing mail in text message format, requesting sensitive information. These messages include urgency, alerts and security warnings. The message may contain malicious QR codes, URLs and other payloads. Attackers usually distribute these codes via email, printed flyers, which could be in a public space, targeting victims to those phishing sites that capture login credentials or potential malware.

4) **Vishing**

Vishing, which is also known as Voice-derived Phishing. It is considered that attackers usually use VoIP [Voice over IP] technology to collect confidential data (Yeboah-Boateng et al., 2014). Here, the attacker calls a victim, impersonating a trusted entity like a government agency or technical support of an insurance company. They rely on redesigned scripts to evoke fear and confusion in victims. The attacker exploits authority in the name of impersonating a personality. Vishing attacks are effective in bypassing human intelligence. As with voice, it is not just limited to phone calls, as attackers can create fake social media IDs and could even be created in a professional network. It may require time to build trust and retrieve sensitive information, but it is still better than traditional phishing techniques. For example, the attacker might pose as a member of the HR team and try to either gather information or inject malicious payloads for exploitation.

5) Evil Twin Attack

This attack is also known as cloning. This type of attack involves the replacement of a legitimate email that victims might have previously received. Here, the attacker clones the email will makes sure it looks like a related, follow-up update of previous emails. An example is the pop-up of a new network is like having a Wi-Fi network known to your device, which will confuse you and make you insert the credentials into that network. In this kind of attack, the attacker creates a network similar to the victim's, prevents connection to the original network, interacts with network nodes and captures a handshake. (Agarwal et al., 2018).

6) **Baiting**

This attack is also known as baiting. Here, in this kind of attack, the attacker tries and fabricate an attack based on a plausible scenario and pretexting to extract the expected response. Unlike traditional phishing, these techniques depend on creating a convincing back story to gain trust. For example, a couple has opened a fundraising campaign in the name of their son. They are asking for funds to save the life of their son, who is suffering from cancer. They are collecting funds in their son's name, who has a very low chance of survival. This couple collects the funds and uses them to fulfill their own needs, and after a specific time, there are no related updates regarding the affected child. Physical baiting is also common, where the attacker might use USB drives to infect the victim's system, which could be in public places, hoping someone might plug them into their device. This shows that if an attacker tries to attack someone after finding a loophole into the system or environment, in such kind of inaccurate architecture, the attacker goes undetected. (Flamholz & Annaswamy, 2015).

7) Water hole attack

This attack usually contains pre-configured, compromised websites. The attacker makes sure the website is a clone of a well-known and well-visited website. Attackers inject a piece of malicious code into the site, which will further lead to the exploitation of browser vulnerabilities to install malware on the victim's devices. The website may contain redirection as well. Using URL hijacking, the exploitation of common typing errors while clicking URLs occurs. Attackers create malicious websites by cloning popular websites, while hoping to capture credentials or distribution malware when the user visits the site. As this attack is highly sophisticated, the detection and prevention of this attack in earlier stages is hard. (Allen et al., 2020).

8) Fear Appeals

A technique that is mainly known as quid pro quo, which involves the offering of services or benefits in exchange for information. Let's imagine an attacker might call employees while posing as the IT support team. In the name of resolving the issue, the attacker might take the required information from an employee. This technique usually exploits the willingness of people to gain benefits. They use fear appeals and show a hyper need for immediate response. They might even send email warnings to provoke legal action and other consequences, like account suspensions. This kind of thing bypasses human intelligence in a better way, triggering the required action.

3.2. Psychological Triggers

3.2.1. Exploiting Human Vulnerabilities

As we all know, phishing heavily relies on the exploitation of human emotions to bypass security measures and access sensitive data. Mainly, cyber criminals target psychological flaws like fear, trust, curiosity and a mind to follow the one with the authority without question. While using techniques like authority bias, confirmation bias, and scarcity effects, the attacker skillfully drafts these phishing campaigns. Because of these kinds of reasons, people are seen to be more forward towards sharing their personal information with others when a strong emotion has been triggered, and it's in human nature that when triggered this way, it is easier to be driven by unintentional processes. The methods used in training A.I. are also different, which include voice detection, image detection, and human nature identification. (Sallai et al., n.d.)The main problem is that the function of the subconscious mind is not something that is based on any logical or analytical behaviour; in fact, the reason that the attacker exploits in pursuing their motives. (Jari, 2022). For these reasons, understanding human emotions and skills is essential.

1) Authority and Trust

People are easier to trap when they are requested by an authorized person demanding information. They normally don't even question that person's legitimacy. Let's assume a company's IT department gets mail from an employee requesting a password reset, leading to exploit of credentials. The usage of official names, logos and signatures, which might be copied, leads to the creation of an illusion that the person asking for data is authorized. When using a digital signature on any document, there is a need for a public and private key, while the document is to be digitally certified as well. (Boonkrong, 2024).

Figure 2. Attack Psychology

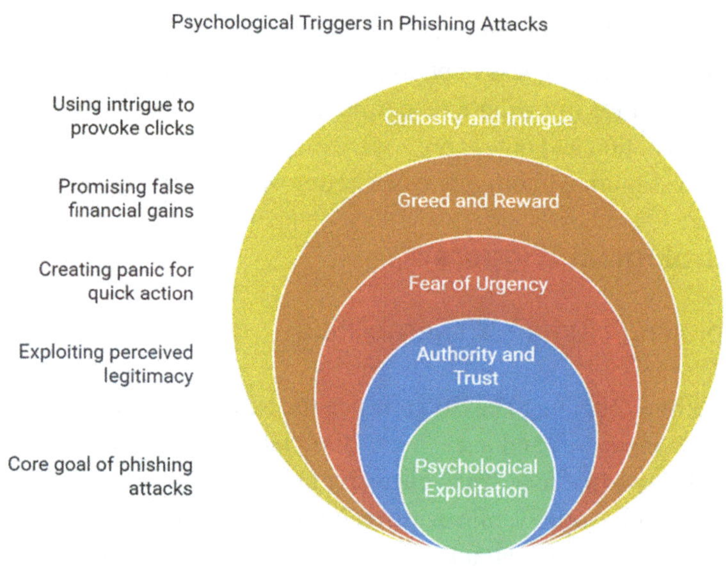

2) Fear of Urgency

Creating fear is still the best trick to get data with less work. The usage of fear tactics creates powerful psychological triggers that lead to immediate response. The attacker uses names of government officials or any other legal consequences to trigger fear. There are several phishing attacks that are specifically designed in a way to get a response. (Digitalcommons@uno et al., n.d.). They try to create a panic in the situation by using words like "very little time is remaining" or maybe "you are a bit too late". This kind of request leads the recipient to act as quickly as possible in the hope of avoiding danger. So, this way, by creating panic and using human anxiety, the attacker tries to get the information they need.

3) Greed and Reward

These kinds of tricks include promising fixed returns and financial gain. This kind of attack usually contains messages like "You have been selected for our limited-time offer" or maybe something like "You just won a lottery". Here, the victim may be motived by many incentive promises which could be financial, informational or political in some cases (Rajivan et al., 2018). These kinds of tricks normally trigger greed and desire in the hope of personal gain. These attacks are a bit complex as they also contain fake websites having malware and many fake investment schemes. This way, attackers try to lower the victim's defenses and make sure that they are more likely interested in those Ponzi schemes rather than in the authenticity of the message.

4) Curiosity and Intrigue

These kinds of tricks include many curious words that make kids, as well as older people, click on the URLs and get hacked. This can also be seen on many websites that have ads showing the download button, making it difficult for visitors to click on the ad. This also has many redirections as well as fake websites with embedded malware. Cyber-criminals also use some messages like "Importation document inside" and "You just got lucky". These kinds of tricks are usually used in office and corporate environments. Here, attackers use fuzzing. But unlike traditional fuzzing, they use techniques like Guided fuzzing to make the attack highly undetected and easy to trap an individual. (Huang et al., n.d.).

5) Sympathy and Helpfulness

Sometimes there could be messages from unknown numbers or accounts saying they know you. Then, the creation of a predesigned background story. This way, they try and demand mostly money and, in some cases, your personal credentials. They try to create sympathy like "I am really in trouble" and "I need Urgent Money". One of the common social media scams that comes under this case is "Romance scams and Honey Traps". It was found under research that Honey Traps use some special Computer Mediated Communication [CMC], and because of this, the victims tend to ignore negative information related to other people they are talking to (Yosiandra et al., 2024). As the backstory has previously created space in the victim's heart and mind, authentication may feel useless. This way, by leveraging empathy and desire, it is possible to lower the victim's guard.

6) Limited-Time Offers

Here, the phisher and criminals use the names of well-known entities to create trust. They show that a product is available for a limited time, or the price has dropped up to 80% for a limited time. This may be used in marketing strategy, but it is also used to phish people. The attacker usually requests money in order to deliver the product. E-commerce scams are some of the common scams that have cases where scammers falsely and forcefully advertise goods and wait for payment. (Shah et al., 2024). As soon as the money is transferred, the account from which the product was listed goes blank. Some of the attackers use AI for better usage, as when implementing AI, the ethical and legal considerations are ignored, with the sole aim of performing a clean and untraceable crime. (Naz et al., 2024). As there is usage of fake names and data is there, retrieval of money as well as criminal almost impossible. The urge to get something that is available for a limited time or may be financially beneficial may lead to becoming a victim, as mostly these schemes are either flawed or are phishing emails.

7) Social Proof

These attacks use already compiled emails that can benefit from Social Proof bias. For example, you get an email that claims that a large number of users have secure and safe accounts that are supposed to be on security alerts. As this looks like others are also using that specific media or feature, create a pressure to conform request, making the victim more likely to follow the instruction in the mail without authentication and investigation. Some massive attacks included social proof. In an incident, the attack was designed in a way that the mail generated use to configure itself as per the individual's name and customize itself based on social details gathered from their database. (Khadka, n.d.).

8) Distraction

These types of phishing attacks include complex and long messages drafted in a way that causes an overload and confusion. This may include several links, instructions, and other technical stuff. This type of attack is making a straightforward request, as the message/mail/website itself is made confusing enough that the viewer somehow even after not wanting to click on any unwanted stuff. This triggers actions leading a viewer to become a victim. The reason for not being able to detect a possible scam is due to a lack of presence of mind and critical thinking at the moment of the incidence. (Sarno et al., 2024).

3.2.2. Common Delivery Methods

Figure 3. Different methods of Phishing attack delivery

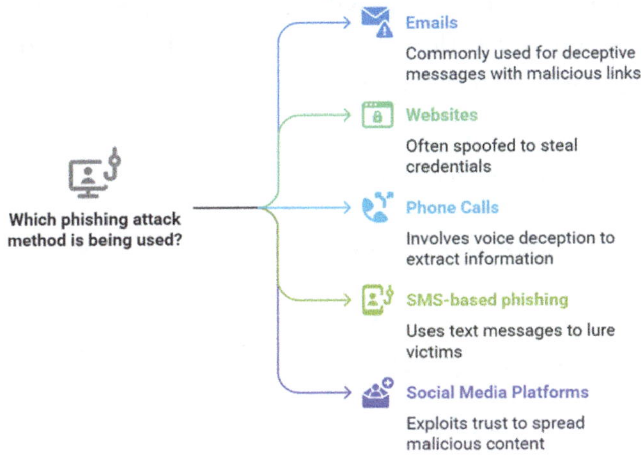

Usually, phishing attacks vary based on different delivery methods, each having different motives and methods as well. Emails are more commonly used that pretend to be coming from a trusted source, which may have malicious attachments. To prevent detection from anti-phishing tools, attackers have to change their tactics and regularly look for more creative ways to attack victims. (Tamal et al., 2024). Then the message consists of human exploits that leverage urgency, fear, greed or curiosity. Website spoofing is another major part where attackers usually try to spoof a legitimate website resembling the original website. There are attacks conducted using ads, websites, URLs, etc., led by small and large phishing campaigns. Phone call phishing use to be more common, like 5 years ago, as not everybody had access to the internet at that time. This way of bypassing human behaviours and flaws was also easy, but came with a risk of getting caught or leaving evidence. Another common one is SMS phishing. Then there come social media platforms, which are used by attackers and used to create fake accounts to befriend and exploit people.

4. IMPACT OF PHISHING SCAMS

There are several effects that occur at the time and after the attack is completed. A company or a person may experience monetary loss, which could hurt economic and social growth in major cases. There are a lot of phenomena responsible for the cause of action and loss of funds and data. These kinds of events are mostly not recorded by legal authorities, as the amount of loss from an individual is mostly so minor that it goes unnoticed. Here we will study some examples that what kinds of possible losses as well as the effects these kinds of incidents have on our daily life, and how big they can be (Ali et al., 2024).

Figure 4. Impact pg multifaceted threats

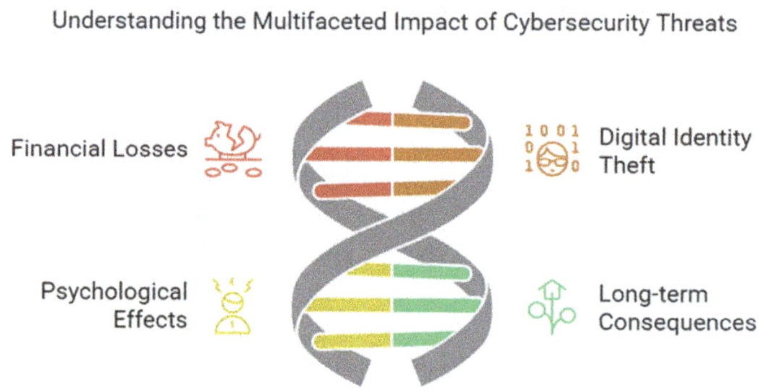

4.1. Financial Losses

Phishing scams do result in big financial losses for individuals as well as organizations. Attackers try to manipulate victims to provide them with data related to their financial assets, leading to fraud. Some places, like online marketplaces, have given a push to these scammers in performing attacks with ease. For the news reports, we found that phishing is starting to grow into a big financial loss to victims while working as a growing market for criminals. It has caused the loss of billions of dollars worldwide. These are the moments which lead to loss of services, demand for ransom payments, frequent data breaches and high costs of forensic investigation done to find remediation to the problems.

4.2. Digital Identity Theft and Data Breaches

Some of the scariest things that could happen to one is the theft of identity. In this kind of case, criminals use stolen credentials to hijack personal accounts, using them to commit fraud or sell illegal goods. There are some illegal marketplaces where scammers sell their collected data and other assets. (Yoganandham et al., n.d.). They sell stolen information, counterfeit goods and even illicit services. Large campaigns are there that are harvesting usernames, passwords, Social Security numbers and related personal data. By using the name of a known individual, this small mistake could lead to large-scale cyber scams. This type of condition could lead to legal consequences, leading to compliance penalties and loss of customers.

4.3. Psychological Effects on Victims

The Psychological Effects are some mental health problems caused by losing personal assets to phishing scams. This impacts mental health and could lead to distress and uneasy feelings of betrayal. Victims could experience stress, anxiety and cause them to isolate themselves from digital communication. People who experienced this incident at work have a very high guilt feeling and a constant fear of job loss. Even the usage of different tools that are not updated and are unable to detect the attack is also one of the causes. The impact here includes effects like loss of time, lowering of quality, loss of mental peace and loss of trust in other people. (Trisolvena et al., 2024). As these impacts are not just technical but also psychological issues, leading to mitigating problems while helping victims overcome the effects of the incident.

4.4. Long-term Consequences for Organizations

For organizations, phishing attacks could be devastating, leading to financial loss, reputation loss, as well as loss of trust. Rebuilding this reputation and trust will take a lot of time and planning, which can take years to stabilize. Also, enhancement of the security architecture and other security measures will be strongly needed. The formation of better security policies and under legal regulations like GDPR and CCPA for data protection will be highly needed. There is high usage of security systems in corporate environments. One of the major differences between personal and distributed security architecture is that it has logging, log monitoring, centralized management and other facilities as well, which helps to analyze the cause in case of an incident. (Ojima John et al., n.d.). This kind of decision will have a significant effect on rebuilding customer and market trust. Regular employee training gives employees more moral values that need to be conducted from time to time. Things like compliance, licensing and better production planning with high network security that safeguard and profit the organization in the long term.

5. PSYCHOLOGICAL FACTORS BEHIND PHISHING ATTACKS

5.1. Cognitive Biases and Human Error

Cognitive Biases and Human Error are some vulnerabilities that play a significant role when it comes to successful phishing. Cognitively Biased uses mental shortcuts that are irrational to the brain, making phishing easier while deceiving individuals. This trick makes people compromise with requests and make decisions. Likewise, in urgency bias, people are tricked into acting quick without thinking. For example, you are asked to play a game that has continuous questioning, and you are in a group. Some theory that helps attackers in implementing these attacks includes the usage of "Rational choice theory" (Itzhak et al., n.d.). There is a condition that the person who answers the most questions will win. Also, you have the authority to answer the question related to your group member. This leads to the hope of winning the competition, leading to confusion and the piling out of secrets in a hurry. Emotions play a big role in deciding how to react when responding to a phishing email. (Tian et al., 2024). This way a very simple but effective phishing technique that is used to reveal information. These kinds of tricks are mostly seen in Live TV shows and Game Shows. Knowing these tricks is very important for the improvement of awareness and securing an entity from phishing attacks.

5.2. Decision-Making Under Pressure

A common factor leading to exploit of human vulnerability is where urgency or pressure are the main factors. These tactics are used to impair the decision-making capability of the brain, leading to answering wrong questions. There could be attacks where attackers might be using threat consequences, such as suspension or loss of reputation.

5.3. The Emotional Impact of Falling Victim to Phishing

The emotional impacts after experiencing a phishing attack can be profound, leaving the victims in shock, embarrassment and guilt. This can also lead to loss of self-confidence and self-blaming. For example, in an incident, an older man gave bank-related data to scammers and suffered a loss of financial assets. This caused the man to experience sleepless nights and constant worry. An experience of negative emotions and long-term trust issues. The behaviour may be affected, and the mental scar may be so deep that it could lead to problems in performing simple household tasks. Also, the long flow of negative emotions could lead to forgetful behaviour. From this, we do recommend listening to calm music, a little bit of nature travel, some pet therapy, and if the case is still not improving, going to a Psychotherapist is always an option.

6. COMMON PHISHING PAYLOAD AND TOOLS

6.1. Spoofed Websites and Emails

As we previously viewed, spoofed websites and emails are also considered common phishing tactics. The fake website is full of spoofed URLs, malware, click-jacking and other information-stealing tactics. These tricks aim to steal important user information. The main reason for success is information gathering and spoofing websites and email. Well, think of it yourself, how much time will it take a person to use an unrecognized spare part in their vehicle, considering the high cost? It may not affect you now, but in case of an accident, when you go to claim your insurance, the agent who views your claim on the incident site views and says that there was a change in the condition of your vehicle. As the information was not provided to the company, your insurance will not be issued. For these reasons, only modifications are considered illegal in some countries.

6.2. Payloads, Scripts, and Malware

A payload, malicious script, as well as malware are some of the main components used in drafting phishing attacks. A payload could be injected into the viewer's device, and it may provide some essential information to the attackers. It could be your contacts, call logs, or maybe your browser's saved password list. The scripts do the same. They are designed in a way that may execute in the background and steal the required information from your device while a session is going on. There are attacks where the payload is designed in a way that goes undetected, bypassing the firewall and detonating on the victim's side. (Maroofi et al., 2020). So, while you are watching your favorite movie on an online pirated site, your passwords are being fetched, and you are being tracked in the name of a mandatory cookie on a website.

6.3. Social Engineering Tactics

These are sets of psychological tricks used by attackers to scheme and bypass all the possible checkpoints that may stop the required information or data flow they want to get. The technique could be Voice phishing, it can be pretexting, in some cases it could be baiting and others. Thus, when it comes to social engineering tactics, there is a way the criminal plays with the readers' or viewers' minds. They show how important things they are missing, or there can be just limited resources, or maybe something like "you have a lucky day" kind of message.

6.4. Phishing-as-a-Service and Organized Cybercrime

As there is development of technology and the need for the market, many illegal services are also hosted over the internet. Phishing-as-a-Service (PhaaS) comes under the same example. This is the center where the infrastructure, phishing kits and other support essential for phishing are provided. These services have a list of criminals providing services in their own specialized fields. The user might have to pay a fixed amount in case of an unsuccessful attempt, but a fixed percentage in case of a successful attack. There are even incidents of recent cases where the victims click on sponsored ads and get hacked (Huzairin et al., 2024). The medium that provided these services was like Google Ads and other ad services. (Huzairin et al., 2024). There are detailed tracking systems, high-quality control panels, and predefined spoofing material as well on these cloud services. This way, the goal of distributing the risk, increasing the usage and creating a higher chance of profit does lead to an easy and effective phishing center.

7. CASE STUDIES: LARGE-SCALE PHISHING INCIDENTS

As there is a very big need for improvement in security and awareness of human behavior, this is where a case study comes in handy. This study helps in finding the cause of incidents and helps to mitigate further possible attacks. Let's study some of the cases as well.

7.1. Case Study 1: Google and Facebook Phishing Scams

These scams are some of the most well-known scams that have been exposed to the market. These scams took place between 2013-2015. The incident resulted in the loss of $100 million. The attacker was identified as a Lithuanian man named Evaldas Rimasauskas, who drafted a sophisticated attack compromising the business email of the company. This took place by luring an Asia-based hardware manufacturer called Quanta Computer. The attacker spoofed the email of this hardware company using a fake email address. He then sent fraudulent invoices and payment requests to Google and Facebook. This led to the bypass of security systems and human intelligence. Due to this, without much authentication, a payment of $100 million was transferred to a criminal. Then this amount was distributed in multiple countries. After finding the criminal, an arrest was made in 2017, and Evaldas Rimasauskas was sent to prison for more than 60 months. (Kelley, 2022).

7.2. Case Study 2: Deep-fake Enhanced Phishing Scam Targets Thousands

In 2024, the use of deep-fake-based phishing operations by call centers led to fraud in which over 6000 individuals were found to be victims. They lost an estimated amount of $35 million. The structure consists of 3 main elements: Deep-fake, Call Centers and Financial transactions. Scammers first gathered information and then created a convincing deep-fake video featuring celebrities, such as British broadcaster Ben Fogle, to invest in cryptocurrency platforms named AdmiralsFX. Call centers operated from Tbilisi, Georgia. These people established a call center and hired a staff of 85 agents. These agents helped to spread phishing attacks, contacted the potential victims and had a policy using high-pressure sales tactics to make an investment in AdmiralsFX. Victims were told to transfer money through a new online bank mentioning application. The application for financial transactions via applications like Revolut and Kroo. This kind of act leads scammers to in coaching and misleading victims to provide information related to their banks. This way we can say that Deep-fake can create fraud, doing social engineering and creating trust to inject malicious payloads (de Rancourt-Raymond et al., 2023). Even some may have voice cloning, some may see their clothes in a deep-faked video and work effectively in exploiting the trust of bad actors in an organization. (de Rancourt-Raymond et al., 2023).

7.3. Analysis of Victim Impact and Consequences

Here we are talking about the analysis of the impact of both cases above. As we saw in the 1st well as in the 2nd case, the large-scale phishing scams lead to a profound impact on victims. As we saw in the case of the Google-Facebook scam, most fraud of $100 million and $35 million had occurred. This was made possible by monitoring the conversation between suppliers and companies. This taught the researcher about the technique criminals used for building trust. They analyze the techniques and messages used to draft. The breach was caused by a vulnerability that was considered low-level. We saw the impact on the victim's form in both cases. Emotional scenes of betrayal could be so intense that victims could experience other feelings like shame, anxiety and diminished trust when doing digital communication. This could lead to strict misbelief on the internet, online work, as well as in transactions using UPI. The mental health effect could lead to permanent shock. The person could face poor health conditions, while in some cases, due to continuous anger, there could be a hormonal imbalance. Thus, when we talk about Consequences other than mental health, there are cases of company shutdown. Legal consequences could take you to Jail, cause legal action, including heavy fines that could affect the company's profit. Then there comes a loss of customer trust, for which one would have to face criticism. To prevent this kind of case, one can try lowering their profit margin. Though R&D funds may have a cut out, you may not be able to launch a new product on the market for some time. From these results, we can say that phishing may look like a minor crime, but as soon as it takes up, this can lead to company shutdown, big financial losses, reputation damage and in some cases, debt.

8. DEFENSIVE MEASURES AND SECURITY PREPARATIONS

We have now studied phishing, and we have quite a good amount of knowledge regarding the topic. We studied the definition, the motives, the types and the techniques used by them. Now comes the most important part, the main reason for learning this whole chapter. The solutions and precautions needed for safety are discussed below. The techniques an organization can use include multi-layered security, real-time analysis and automated response mechanisms (Abbas, 2024). This is how an organization makes sure about the safety of its data as well as its customers and clients.

8.1. Technical Defences: Email Filters, Anti-Phishing Software, etc.

Figure 5. Migrations and Precautions

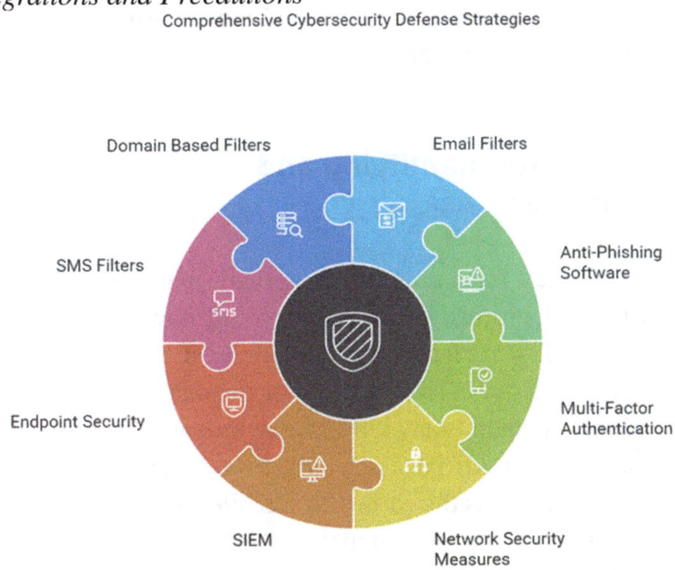

There can be a lot of mitigation depending on the type of security architecture the company uses. A company receives a lot of fake emails and spam mail. What they can do is use Spam and Phishing Filters in their Emails. These filters work on the detection of specific keywords, can analyze the payload in some cases and can detect its genuineness by analyzing the email header. Also, it can filter out malicious URLs from the content. The next thing one can use is AI-based filters, which work on targeting the behaviour pattern and language of the mail. They try to figure out if there are any anomalies present in it or not. This is an advance and heavy technique if executed on a local server. Using a remote service in these cases could be much better. Usage of secure browsers as well as browsing techniques also comes in handy sometimes. The user may face some unsatisfactory GUI experience, but unless and until you are secure, everything is safe. Using Multi-Factor Authentication (MFA) is one of the easiest and most secure practices. This will increase the security of your digital assets to 90%. And if you are in any case including your biometric data, the detection becomes more precise, which cannot be denied without a classified stealing and copying plan. One can implement DNS filtering on the network to prevent malicious websites and block suspicious IPs. Using Web Application Firewalls (WAFs) is a common practice, but it still lacks essential detection methods. Using IDS/IPS is highly recommended as it is capable of checking anomalies even in large data traffic. Some people can implement Security Information and Event Management environments in sensitive places. A control center is much requested. Creating a good defensive framework based on the organization's architecture may be a better way to safeguard assets (Sivakumar et al., 2023). Also, last but not least, the usage of common passwords in multiple accounts and not securing your account with a security key is a very common practice, which, in the end, leads to loss of assets and funds.

8.2. Best Practices for Identifying and Avoiding Phishing Scams

Each time you get mail from an unknown email, make sure to check its email address to confirm its legitimacy. The email could have suspicious names like "support@UPIs.com". Try to check the authenticity if there is a message related to urgent payments or transfers. The presence of mismatched URLs can be clearly visible in URLs. Suppose there is any kind of attachment like .exe, .zip, .docm, etc., never open such attachments. If necessary, try to open in a useless or old system with no data present in it. If it is the case with websites, try to check the presence of HTTPS. Training in phishing-based simulations and other practices might increase the chance of avoiding phishing mail just by applying human intelligence. Existing methods have created a solid base for the classification and detection of vulnerabilities within blockchain networks. Even after this, there is a good gap when it comes to crafting a combine solution that is equipped to adapt itself in this ever-changing nature of blockchain and the internet. As some related works have shown what could be the effects of this challenge, as they commonly lack an integrated architecture that combines vulnerability detection while classifying data in a manner that, when it's needed to adapt, it must be able to shift patterns of detection (Kang et al., 2024).

8.3. Employee Training and Organizational Policies

As there is a high rise and frequent change in technological use, it has become a problem. People unaware of the new technology, especially older adults, are required to be trained. They are most afraid when it comes to using new technology. Regular security training, specific sessions related to phishing awareness are needed. The employees must be trained properly in identifying phishing indications. The company must give Role-based training better suited to the different roles of employees. If we talk about policies Acceptable Use Policy (AUP), Password Management Policy, and Bring Your Own Device Policy (BYOD) must be enhanced regularly. The gaps in the policy must be analyzed every year. One must try to find the flaws, possible vulnerabilities and mistakes in the policy design. Changes in the policies can be frequent, so a team for policy designing must be on standby. And do regular research for secure policy implementation. This way, it will benefit the company and the security architecture.

8.4. The Role of Government and Legal Frameworks in Combating Phishing

When running a company, there is a constant check by the government. They check if the company is following the legal as well as social laws of the country. They check if there is a flaw in tax consumption or income whose tax has not been paid. Overall, the technical and IT departments have to commonly deal with problems related to end-to-end encryption and security problems (Yusif et al., 2021). Here, they check for the presence of vulnerabilities and loopholes in the policies and security architecture. If any finds any flaw, it is fined under legal regulations. Using Anti-Phishing laws is common in many countries. While some laws of Data Protection and Privacy laws, like GDPR and PDPA acts, are present in the system. The financial regulations supporting these laws help to decide on what level the mistake or crime is to be considered and what amount of fine is to be paid by the company. This is how government officials try to find all these flaws and legal regulations. Also, one thing that the user can do is add a limit to their bank account, which can help to reduce the risk of the whole account getting empty. Block your account and make sure no further transactions can be made. One must register an FIR within 2 hours of the incident, contact the central bank authority and add a note to the cyber helpline for security. There is no certainty that they will be able to catch the criminals and punish them, but the money that has been circulating in the country can be recovered within that period. The chances of your money getting back increase by 70%. This is how one can protect themselves as well as their organization in case of a phishing attack.

9. CONCLUSION

We saw how phishing scams take place, people cause trouble, criminals draft an attack, the psychological impact on the human mind and migrations related to phishing. Things we observed are that there is a constant increase in phishing campaigns, and there are new ways these scammers use to scam people. The flaw in the legal system makes it hard to catch criminals in different states and overseas. The key findings are mentioned below.

9.1. Summary of Key Findings

These topics are the ones that helped in performing a phishing attack. The main methodology is Information gathering, attack drafting, payload addition, trust building and exploitation. As there must be regular analyses of law and there must be an effort to make the process simpler, easy, fast and effective if taken overall. When it comes to catching these criminals, there is a serious need for an understanding of laws, as well as trying to find criminals who are the source of phishing mail. This is how the whole scenario from the start of phishing campaigns till the end, with the catching of criminals. Contacting the police to register an FIR and adding a request to the RBI in case the scam has happened in India.

9.2. The Path Forward: Education, Awareness, and Technology

As we have discussed before, there is a need to grow the environment and surroundings in a way that everyone has security awareness regarding digital fraud and phishing scams. Regular awareness programs are to be conducted in the city. Chapters regarding digital security and methods mentioning how to secure their digital assets are to be included in the education curricular. This will help future generations in finding and preventing this kind of scam. We have to make sure the environment that we live in is aware of rapidly growing technology. This is how we can secure and develop an environment secure for present and future generations.

REFERENCES

Abbas, A. (2024). *Evolving Phishing Defense: Innovative Defense Mechanisms and Effective Measurement Strategies*. DOI: 10.13140/RG.2.2.18505.97128

Abroshan, H., Devos, J., Poels, G., & Laermans, E. (2018). Phishing attacks root cause. *Lecture Notes in Computer Science (Including Subseries Lecture Notes in Artificial Intelligence and Lecture Notes in Bioinformatics), 10694 LNCS*, 187–202. DOI: 10.1007/978-3-319-76687-4_13

Agarwal, M., Biswas, S., & Nandi, S. (2018). An Efficient Scheme to Detect Evil Twin Rogue Access Point Attack in 802.11 Wi-Fi Networks. *International Journal of Wireless Information Networks*, *25*(2), 130–145. DOI: 10.1007/s10776-018-0396-1

Ali, M. M., & Mohd Zaharon, N. F. (2024). Phishing—A Cyber Fraud: The Types, Implications and Governance. *International Journal of Educational Reform*, *33*(1), 101–121. DOI: 10.1177/10567879221082966

Alkhalil, Z., Hewage, C., Nawaf, L., & Khan, I. (2021). Phishing Attacks: A Recent Comprehensive Study and a New Anatomy. In Frontiers in Computer Science (Vol. 3). Frontiers Media S.A. DOI: 10.3389/fcomp.2021.563060

Allen, J., Yang, Z., Landen, M., Bhat, R., Grover, H., Chang, A., Ji, Y., Perdisci, R., & Lee, W. (2020). Mnemosyne: An Effective and Efficient Postmortem Watering Hole Attack Investigation System. *Proceedings of the ACM Conference on Computer and Communications Security*, 787–802. DOI: 10.1145/3372297.3423355

Boonkrong, S. (2024). *Design of an academic document forgery detection system*. International Journal of Information Technology., DOI: 10.1007/s41870-024-02006-6

Chen, Z., Huang, J., Liu, S., & Long, H. (2024). Multiscale Feature Fusion and Graph Convolutional Network for Detecting Ethereum Phishing Scams. *Electronics (Basel)*, *13*(6), 1012. Advance online publication. DOI: 10.3390/electronics13061012

De Rancourt-Raymond, A., & Smaili, N. (2023). The unethical use of deepfakes. *Journal of Financial Crime*, *30*(4), 1066–1077. DOI: 10.1108/JFC-04-2022-0090

Digitalcommons@uno, D., House, D., & Raja, M. K. (n.d.). *Phishing: message appraisal and the exploration of fear and self-Phishing: message appraisal and the exploration of fear and self-confidence confidence Phishing: message appraisal and the exploration of fear and self-confidence*. Retrieved from https://digitalcommons.unomaha.edu/isqafacpub

Flamholz, D. B., & Annaswamy, A. M. (2015). *Baiting For Defense Against Stealthy Attacks on Cyber-Physical Systems Signature redacted Signature redacted.*

Huang, H., Zhou, A., Payer, M., & Zhang, C. (n.d.). *Everything is Good for Something: Counterexample-Guided Directed Fuzzing via Likely Invariant Inference.*

Huzairin, R. A., Multazam, M. T., Phahlevy, R. R., & Ahrorov, F. (2024). *Google's Legal Responsibility in Displaying Phishing Ads Through Google AdWords.*, DOI: 10.2991/978-2-38476-247-7_53

Itzhak, I., Stanovsky, G., Rosenfeld, N., & Belinkov, Y. (n.d.). *Instructed to Bias: Instruction-Tuned Language Models Exhibit Emergent Cognitive Bias.* doi: DOI: 10.1162/tacl

Jari, M. (2022). *An Overview of Phishing Victimization: Human Factors, Training and the Role of Emotions.* 217–228. DOI: 10.5121/csit.2022.121319

Kang, J., & Buu, S. J. (2024). Graph Anomaly Detection with Disentangled Prototypical Autoencoder for Phishing Scam Detection in Cryptocurrency Transactions. *IEEE Access : Practical Innovations, Open Solutions, 12*, 91075–91088. DOI: 10.1109/ACCESS.2024.3419152

Kelley, P. (2022). *Evolution of Cyber Attacks and Their Economic Impact.* DOI: 10.36227/techrxiv.21670718.v1

Khadka, K. (n.d.). *Persuasion and Phishing: Analysing the Interplay of Persuasion Tactics in Cyber Threats.*

Lim, K., Lee, K., Sommese, R., Jonker, M., & Mok, R. claffy, kc, & Kim, D. (2025). *Registration, Detection, and Deregistration: Analyzing DNS Abuse for Phishing Attacks.* Retrieved from https://arxiv.org/abs/2502.09549

Maroofi, S., Korczyński, M., & Duda, A. (2020). Are You Human?: Resilience of Phishing Detection to Evasion Techniques Based on Human Verification. *Proceedings of the ACM SIGCOMM Internet Measurement Conference, IMC*, 78–86. DOI: 10.1145/3419394.3423632

Naz, H., & Kashif, M. (2024). Artificial intelligence and predictive marketing: An ethical framework from managers' perspective. *Spanish Journal of Marketing - ESIC.* Advance online publication. DOI: 10.1108/SJME-06-2023-0154

Ojima John, M., Emmanuel Oche, O., & Blessing Toyin, E. (n.d.). MITIGATING THE IMPACT OF PHISHING ATTACKS ON THE E-LEARNING INFRASTRUCTURE. In Scientific and Practical Cyber Security Journal (SPCSJ) (Vol. 8, Issue 3).

Putra, F. P. E., Ubaidi, U., Zulfikri, A., Arifin, G., & Ilhamsyah, R. M. (2024). Analysis of Phishing Attack Trends, Impacts and Prevention Methods: Literature Study. *Brilliance: Research of Artificial Intelligence*, *4*(1), 413–421. DOI: 10.47709/brilliance.v4i1.4357

Rajivan, P., & Gonzalez, C. (2018). Creative persuasion: A study on adversarial behaviors and strategies in phishing attacks. *Frontiers in Psychology*, *9*(FEB), 135. Advance online publication. DOI: 10.3389/fpsyg.2018.00135 PMID: 29515478

Salahdine, F., & Kaabouch, N. (2019). Social engineering attacks: A survey. In Future Internet (Vol. 11, Issue 4). MDPI AG. DOI: 10.3390/fi11040089

Sallai, D., Cardoso-Silva, J., Barreto, M. E., Panero, F., Berrada, G., & Luxmoore, S. (n.d.). *Approach Generative AI Tools Proactively or Risk Bypassing the Learning Process in Higher Education.*

Sarno, D. M., & Black, J. (2024). Who Gets Caught in the Web of Lies?: Understanding Susceptibility to Phishing Emails, Fake News Headlines, and Scam Text Messages. *Human Factors*, *66*(6), 1742–1753. DOI: 10.1177/00187208231173263 PMID: 37127397

Shah, N. K. M. D., Ab Aziz, A. A., Juned, A. M., Anuar Yatim, A. I., & Wan Fakhruddin, W. F. W. (2024). Scheming in Syntax: Analysing Scammer-Victim Conversations in Malaysian E-Commerce Scams. *3L: Language, Linguistics. Literature*, *30*(4), 47–59. DOI: 10.17576/3L-2024-3004-04

Sivakumar, A. A. / P., Fahmi, A., Abdul, M., Ramli, J., Kastriafuddin, T., Yakob, T., Habee, E. A., & Affandy, B. (2023). ANALYSIS THE TYPES AND IMPACTS OF PHISHING ATTACKS ON INTERNET USERS. In Journal of Global Business and Social Entrepreneurship (GBSE) (Vol. 9, Issue 26). Retrieved from www.gbse.my

Tamal, M. A., Islam, M. K., Bhuiyan, T., Sattar, A., & Prince, N. U. (2024). Unveiling suspicious phishing attacks: Enhancing detection with an optimal feature vectorization algorithm and supervised machine learning. *Frontiers of Computer Science*, *6*, 1428013. Advance online publication. DOI: 10.3389/fcomp.2024.1428013

Tian, C., Jensen, M. L., Bott, G., & Luo, X. (2024). The influence of affective processing on phishing susceptibility. *European Journal of Information Systems.* Advance online publication. DOI: 10.1080/0960085X.2024.2351442

Trisolvena, M. N., & Saputra, N. H. (2024). Phishing Cyber Security Threats. *Jurnal Improsci*, *2*(1), 38–48. DOI: 10.62885/improsci.v2i1.440

Understanding and Mitigating Phishing Attacks in the Digital Era. (n.d.). DOI: 10.13140/RG.2.2.19619.98085

Yeboah-Boateng, E. O., & Amanor, P. M. (2014). *Journal of Emerging Trends in Computing and Information Sciences Phishing, SMiShing & Vishing: An Assessment of Threats against Mobile Devices Campus and a database administrator. 5*(4). Retrieved from http://www.cisjournal.org

Yoganandham, G., & Head, P. (n.d.). *THE ECONOMIC IMPACT OF PHISHING, VISHING, ONLINE MARKETPLACES, AND EMERGING CYBERCRIMES: EXPOSING THE CYBERCRIME ECONOMY AND SOCIAL COSTS IN THE MODERN ERA OF DIGITAL FRAUD-AN ASSESSMENT.*

Yosiandra, S. Y., & Sakariah, D. S. (2024). Unveiling the Romance Scam Scheme: Psychological Manipulation and Its Impact on Victims. *HUMANIKA, 31*(2), 185–199. DOI: 10.14710/humanika.v31i2.67604

Yusif, S., & Hafeez-Baig, A. (2021). A Conceptual Model for Cybersecurity Governance. *Journal of Applied Security Research, 16*(4), 490–513. DOI: 10.1080/19361610.2021.1918995

KEY TERMS AND DEFINITIONS

Cybersecurity: The practice of protecting networks, digital systems, and data from damage and attack by implementing solutions and security measures like monitoring, implementing a firewall and encrypting data.

Encryption: A process of converting plain text into ciphertext by using data security algorithms, which ensures the confidentiality of data while in storage or in transmission.

KYC: A process of confirming the identity of a client done by banks and many organizations by collecting documents like ID proof, photographs, and address proof.

OTP: An authentication method that shares a password or a key that is valid for a limited period of time, which can be used to cross-verify the authority of the person using the service.

Phishing: An attempt made fraudulently to gain sensitive information such as credit card details, contacts, passwords or personal data, done by one pretending to be a trustworthy source through emails, social media and fake websites.

Scam: A deceptive scheme or trick that is used with the intention to cheat someone to gain valuable information and money.

Compilation of References

Abbas, A. (2024). *Evolving Phishing Defense: Innovative Defense Mechanisms and Effective Measurement Strategies*. DOI: 10.13140/RG.2.2.18505.97128

Abidde, W. N., Eyidia, N., & Eme, E. S. J. (2023). CIA Triad: A review of the confidentiality, integrity and availability of data in a system of connected networks. *International Research Journal of Modernization in Engineering Technology and Science*, *7*(3), 12824–12828. https://www.irjmets.com/uploadedfiles/paper/issue_3_march_2025/68704/final/fin_irjmets1744339796.pdf

Abroshan, H., Devos, J., Poels, G., & Laermans, E. (2018). Phishing attacks root cause. *Lecture Notes in Computer Science (Including Subseries Lecture Notes in Artificial Intelligence and Lecture Notes in Bioinformatics), 10694 LNCS*, 187–202. DOI: 10.1007/978-3-319-76687-4_13

Achuthan, K., Ramanathan, S., Srinivas, S., & Raman, R. (2024). Advancing cybersecurity and privacy with artificial intelligence: Current trends and future research directions. *Frontiers in Big Data*, *7*, 1497535. Advance online publication. DOI: 10.3389/fdata.2024.1497535 PMID: 39703783

Adeyeye, O. J., Akanbi, I., Emeteveke, I., & Emehin, O. (2024). Leveraging secured AI-driven data analytics for cybersecurity: Safeguarding information and enhancing threat detection. *International Journal of Research and Publication and Reviews*, *5*(10), 3208–3223. DOI: 10.55248/gengpi.5.1024.2911

Admass, W. S., Munaye, Y. Y., & Diro, A. A. (2023). Cyber security: State of the art, challenges and future directions. *Cyber Security and Applications*, *2*, 100031. DOI: 10.1016/j.csa.2023.100031

Adriko, R., & Nurse, J. R. C. (2024). Does Cyber Insurance Promote Cyber Security Best Practice? An Analysis Based on Insurance Application Forms. *Digital Threats : Research and Practice*, *5*(3), 1–39. Advance online publication. DOI: 10.1145/3676283

Afaq, A., Haider, N., Baig, M. Z., Khan, K. S., Imran, M., & Razzak, I. (2021). Machine learning for 5G security: Architecture, recent advances, and challenges. *Ad Hoc Networks*, *123*, 102667. DOI: 10.1016/j.adhoc.2021.102667

Affendi, M. R. N., Hussin, M., & Hasan, D. (2025). A Study of the High-Performance Computing Parallelism in Solving Complexity of Meteorology Data and Calculations. *Journal of Advanced Research in Applied Sciences and Engineering Technology*, *54*(1), 16–26. DOI: 10.37934/araset.54.1.1626

Agarwal, M., Biswas, S., & Nandi, S. (2018). An Efficient Scheme to Detect Evil Twin Rogue Access Point Attack in 802.11 Wi-Fi Networks. *International Journal of Wireless Information Networks*, *25*(2), 130–145. DOI: 10.1007/s10776-018-0396-1

Ahlan, A. R., Lubis, M., & Lubis, A. R. (2015). Information Security Awareness at the Knowledge-Based Institution: Its Antecedents and Measures. *Procedia Computer Science*, *72*, 361–373. DOI: 10.1016/j.procs.2015.12.151

Ahmadi, S. (2023). Next Generation AI-Based Firewalls: A Comparative Study. *International Journal of Computer*, *49*, 245–262.

Ahmad, S., Haque, M. A., Abdeljaber, H. A., Eljialy, A. E. M., Nazeer, J., & Mishra, B. K. (2025). Machine Learning Approaches in Cybersecurity to Enhance Security in Future Network Technologies. *SN Computer Science*, *6*(4), 1–18. DOI: 10.1007/s42979-025-03853-1

Ahmed, I., Anisetti, M., Ahmad, A., & Jeon, G. (2023). A multilayer deep learning approach for malware classification in 5G-enabled IIoT.

Alam, S., Alam, Y., Cui, S., & Akujuobi, C. (2023). Data-Driven Network Analysis for Anomaly Traffic Detection. *Sensors (Basel)*, *23*(19), 8174. DOI: 10.3390/s23198174 PMID: 37837004

Ali, M. M., & Mohd Zaharon, N. F. (2024). Phishing—A Cyber Fraud: The Types, Implications and Governance. *International Journal of Educational Reform*, *33*(1), 101–121. DOI: 10.1177/10567879221082966

Aljohani, A. A. (2025). *Integrating AI-Driven predictive models for enhanced cyber threat detection and mitigation*. https://spast.org/ojspath/article/view/5347

Alkhalil, Z., Hewage, C., Nawaf, L., & Khan, I. (2021). Phishing Attacks: A recent comprehensive study and a new anatomy. *Frontiers of Computer Science*, *3*, 563060. Advance online publication. DOI: 10.3389/fcomp.2021.563060

Allen, J., Yang, Z., Landen, M., Bhat, R., Grover, H., Chang, A., Ji, Y., Perdisci, R., & Lee, W. (2020). Mnemosyne: An Effective and Efficient Postmortem Watering Hole Attack Investigation System. *Proceedings of the ACM Conference on Computer and Communications Security*, 787–802. DOI: 10.1145/3372297.3423355

Alzoubi, H. M., Ghazal, T. M., Hasan, M. K., Alketbi, A., Kamran, R., Al-Dmour, N. A., & Islam, S. (2022, May). Cyber security threats on digital banking. In *2022 1st International Conference on AI in Cybersecurity (ICAIC)* (pp. 1-4). IEEE. DOI: DOI: 10.1109/ICAIC53980.2022.9896966

Anand, A., ... (2023). Mitigating cyber-security risks using cyber-analytics. In 2023 7th International Conference on Trends in Electronics and Informatics (ICOEI) (pp. 630-635). IEEE. https://doi.org/DOI: 10.1109/ICOEI56765.2023.10126001

Ang, T. L., Choolani, M., See, K. C., & Poh, K. K. (2023). The rise of artificial intelligence: Addressing the impact of large language models such as ChatGPT on scientific publications. *Singapore Medical Journal*, *64*(4), 219–221. DOI: 10.4103/singaporemedj.SMJ-2023-055 PMID: 37006087

Ansari, M. F., Sharma, P. K., & Dash, B. (2022). Prevention of phishing attacks using AI-Based cybersecurity awareness training. *International Journal of Smart Sensor and Adhoc Network*, 61–72. https://doi.org/DOI: 10.47893/IJSSAN.2022.1221

Anusha, S., Nithyanandhan, R., Anish, T. P., Girija, P., & Nalini, M. (2024, October). Deep Reinforcement Learning: Key Algorithms, Applications, and Future Challenges. In *2024 2nd International Conference on Self Sustainable Artificial Intelligence Systems (ICSSAS)* (pp. 565-571). IEEE.

Apruzzese, G., Vladimirov, R., Tastemirova, A., & Laskov, P. (2022). Wild networks: Exposure of 5G network infrastructures to adversarial examples.

Apruzzese, G., Laskov, P., Montes de Oca, E., Mallouli, W., Brdalo Rapa, L., Grammatopoulos, A. V., & Di Franco, F. (2023). The role of machine learning in cybersecurity. *Digital Threats : Research and Practice*, *4*(1), 1–38. DOI: 10.1145/3545574

Ariyaluran Habeeb, R. A., Nasaruddin, F., Gani, A., Targio Hashem, I. A., Ahmed, E., & Imran, M. (2019). Real-time big data processing for anomaly detection: A Survey. *International Journal of Information Management*, *45*, 289–307. DOI: 10.1016/j.ijinfomgt.2018.08.006

Arnob, A. K. B., Chowdhury, N. R. R., Chaiti, N. N. A., Saha, N. S., & Roy, N. A. (2025). A comprehensive systematic review of intrusiondetection systems: emerging techniques,challenges, and future research directions. *Journal of Edge Computing*. https://doi.org/DOI: 10.55056/jec.885

Azeem, M., Khan, D., Iftikhar, S., Bawazeer, S., & Alzahrani, M. (2023). Analyzing and comparing the effectiveness of malware detection: A study of machine learning approaches. *Heliyon, 10*(1), e23574. DOI: 10.1016/j.heliyon.2023.e23574 PMID: 38187275

Azizi, N., & Haass, O. (2023). Cybersecurity issues and challenges. In *Handbook of research on cybersecurity issues and challenges for business and FinTech applications* (pp. 21–48). IGI Global.

Bakhsh, S. A., Khan, M. A., Ahmed, F., Alshehri, M. S., Ali, H., & Ahmad, J. (2023). Enhancing IoT network security through deep learning-powered Intrusion Detection System. *Internet of Things : Engineering Cyber Physical Human Systems, 24*, 100936. DOI: 10.1016/j.iot.2023.100936

Barredo Arrieta, A., Díaz-Rodríguez, N., Del Ser, J., Bennetot, A., Tabik, S., Barbado, A., Garcia, S., Gil-Lopez, S., Molina, D., Benjamins, R., Chatila, R., & Herrera, F. (2020). Explainable Artificial Intelligence (XAI): Concepts, taxonomies, opportunities and challenges toward responsible AI. *Information Fusion, 58*, 82–115. DOI: 10.1016/j.inffus.2019.12.012

Bartolini, A., Lombardi, M., & Milano, M. (2024). Alma Mater Studiorum Università di Bologna Archivio istituzionale della ricerca Borghesi, A ., et al . " A Semisupervised Autoencoder-Based Approach for Anomaly Detection in High Performance Computing Systems ." Engineering Applications of at : Rights / . June.

Beigh, B. M. (2014). A new classification scheme for intrusion detection systems. *International Journal of Computer Network and Information Security, 6*(8), 56–70. DOI: 10.5815/ijcnis.2014.08.08

Bellovin, S., & Cheswick, W. (1994). Network firewalls. *IEEE Communications Magazine, 32*(9), 50–57. DOI: 10.1109/35.312843

Benjamens, S., Dhunnoo, P., & Meskó, B. (2020). The state of artificial intelligence-based FDA-approved medical devices and algorithms: An online database. *NPJ Digital Medicine, 3*(1), 1–8. DOI: 10.1038/s41746-020-00324-0 PMID: 32984550

Bhalerao, S.. (2024). AI enabled risk management framework for enhanced security in 5G networks. In *2024 International Conference on Innovation and Novelty in Engineering and Technology (INNOVA)* (pp. 1-6). IEEE. https://doi.org/DOI: 10.1109/INNOVA63080.2024.10847018

Bhamare, D., Salman, T., Samaka, M., Erbad, A., & Jain, R. (2016, December). Feasibility of supervised machine learning for cloud security. In *2016 International Conference on Information Science and Security (ICISS)* (pp. 1-5). IEEE. DOI: DOI: 10.1109/ICISSEC.2016.7885853

Bhamare, D., Zolanvari, M., Erbad, A., Jain, R., Khan, K., & Meskin, N. (2019). Cybersecurity for industrial control systems: A survey. *Computers & Security*, *89*, 101677. DOI: 10.1016/j.cose.2019.101677

Bhandari, R. (2025). AI and Cybersecurity: Opportunities, challenges, and governance. *EDPACS*, 1–9. https://doi.org/DOI: 10.1080/07366981.2025.2544363

Bharadiya, J. (2023). Machine learning in cybersecurity: Techniques and challenges. *European Journal of Technology*, *7*(2), 1–14. DOI: 10.47672/ejt.1486

Bhuyan, M. H., Bhattacharyya, D. K., & Kalita, J. K. (2016). A multi-step outlier-based anomaly detection approach to network-wide traffic. *Information Sciences*, *348*, 243–271. DOI: 10.1016/j.ins.2016.02.023

Bogdoll, D., Nitsche, M., & Zollner, J. M. (2022). Anomaly Detection in Autonomous Driving: A Survey. IEEE Computer Society Conference on Computer Vision and Pattern Recognition Workshops, 2022-June, 4487–4498. DOI: 10.1109/CVPRW56347.2022.00495

Boonkrong, S. (2024). *Design of an academic document forgery detection system.* International Journal of Information Technology., DOI: 10.1007/s41870-024-02006-6

Boopathi, S. (2023). Deep learning techniques applied for automatic sentence generation. In Promoting Diversity, Equity, and Inclusion in Language Learning Environments (pp. 255-273). IGI Global. DOI: 10.4018/978-1-6684-3632-5.ch016

Borghesi, A., Molan, M., Milano, M., & Bartolini, A. (2022). Anomaly Detection and Anticipation in High Performance Computing Systems. *IEEE Transactions on Parallel and Distributed Systems*, *33*(4), 739–750. DOI: 10.1109/TPDS.2021.3082802

Bose, A., Hu, X., Shin, K. G., & Park, T. (2008, June). Behavioral detection of malware on mobile handsets. In *Proceedings of the 6th international conference on Mobile systems, applications, and services* (pp. 225-238). DOI: 10.1145/1378600.1378626

Buczak, A. L., & Guven, E. (2015). A survey of data mining and machine learning methods for cyber security intrusion detection. *IEEE Communications Surveys and Tutorials*, *18*(2), 1153–1176. DOI: 10.1109/COMST.2015.2494502

Cakir, M., Guvenc, M. A., & Mistikoglu, S. (2021). The experimental application of popular machine learning algorithms on predictive maintenance and the design of IIoT based condition monitoring system. *Computers & Industrial Engineering*, *151*, 106948. Advance online publication. DOI: 10.1016/j.cie.2020.106948

Camilleri, M. A. (2023). Artificial intelligence governance: Ethical considerations and implications for social responsibility. *Expert Systems: International Journal of Knowledge Engineering and Neural Networks*, *41*(7), e13406. Advance online publication. DOI: 10.1111/exsy.13406

Ceccarelli, A., Zoppi, T., Vasenev, A., Mori, M., Ionita, D., Montoya, L., & Bondavalli, A. (2018). Threat analysis in Systems-of-Systems. *ACM Transactions on Cyber-Physical Systems*, *3*(2), 1–24. DOI: 10.1145/3234513

Çetinkaya, H. F., & Yenidünya, A. F. çetinkaya, S., & Tüzün, B. (2024). Deep learning and machine learning and their application on computational chemistry. In *Emerging Engineering Technologies and Industrial Applications* (pp. 21–35). DOI: 10.4018/979-8-3693-1335-0.ch002

Chaabouni, N., Mosbah, M., Zemmari, A., Sauvignac, C., & Faruki, P. (2019). Network intrusion detection for IoT security based on learning techniques. *IEEE Communications Surveys and Tutorials*, *21*(3), 2671–2701. DOI: 10.1109/COMST.2019.2896380

Chalapathy, R., & Chawla, S. (2019). Deep Learning for Anomaly Detection. *Survey (London, England)*, •••, 1–50. https://arxiv.org/abs/1901.03407

Chambolle, C., & Poret, S. (2005). Keywords : 1 Introduction. 22(December), 1–22.

Chamola, V., Jolfaei, A., Chanana, V., Parashari, P., & Hassija, V. (2021). Information security in the post quantum era for 5G and beyond networks: Threats to existing cryptography, and post-quantum cryptography. *Computer Communications*, *176*, 99–118. DOI: 10.1016/j.comcom.2021.05.019

Chandola, V. (2009). Anomaly Detection for Discrete Sequences: A Survey Varun Chandola, Arindam Banerjee, and Vipin Kumar. https://www.cs.umn.edu/sites/cs.umn.edu/files/tech_reports/09-015.pdf

Chatterjee, A., & Ahmed, B. S. (2022). IoT anomaly detection methods and applications: A survey. *Internet of Things : Engineering Cyber Physical Human Systems*, *19*(June), 100568. DOI: 10.1016/j.iot.2022.100568

Chatterjee, S., Rana, N. P., Dwivedi, Y. K., & Baabdullah, A. M. (2021). Understanding AI adoption in manufacturing and production firms using an integrated TAM-TOE model. *Technological Forecasting and Social Change*, *170*, 120880. Advance online publication. DOI: 10.1016/j.techfore.2021.120880

Chen, T., & Guestrin, C. (2016). XGBoost: A scalable tree boosting system. In *Proceedings of the 22nd ACM SIGKDD International Conference on Knowledge Discovery and Data Mining* (pp. 785–794). ACM. https://doi.org/DOI: 10.1145/2939672.2939785

Chen, Z., Huang, J., Liu, S., & Long, H. (2024). Multiscale Feature Fusion and Graph Convolutional Network for Detecting Ethereum Phishing Scams. *Electronics (Basel)*, *13*(6), 1012. Advance online publication. DOI: 10.3390/electronics13061012

Chen, Z., & Ji, C. (2005). Spatial-temporal modeling of malware propagation in networks. *IEEE Transactions on Neural Networks*, *16*(5), 1291–1303. DOI: 10.1109/TNN.2005.853425 PMID: 16252834

Chimphlee, W., & Chimphlee, S. (2023). Hyperparameters optimization XGBoost for network intrusion detection using CSE-CIC-IDS 2018 dataset. *IAES International Journal of Artificial Intelligence*, *13*(1), 817. DOI: 10.11591/ijai.v13.i1.pp817-826

Chinnasamy, P., Sathya, K. S., Jebamani, B. J. A., Nithyasri, A., & Fowjiya, S. (2023). Deep learning: algorithms, techniques, and applications—a systematic survey. In *Deep learning research applications for natural language processing* (pp. 1–17). IGI global.

Chowdhury, N. U. R., Haque, A., Soliman, H., Hossen, M. S., Fatima, T., & Ahmed, I. (2023, September). Android malware detection using machine learning: A review. In *Intelligent Systems Conference* (pp. 507-522). Cham: Springer Nature Switzerland. DOI: DOI: 10.1007/978-3-031-47715-7_35

Conti, M., Kumar, E. S., Lal, C., & Ruj, S. (2018). A survey on security and privacy issues of bitcoin. *IEEE Communications Surveys and Tutorials*, *20*(4), 3416–3452. DOI: 10.1109/COMST.2018.2842460

Cortes, C., & Vapnik, V. (1995). Support-vector networks. *Machine Learning*, *20*(3), 273–297. DOI: 10.1023/A:1022627411411

Craigen, D., Diakun-Thibault, N., & Purse, R. (2014). Defining cybersecurity. *Technology Innovation Management Review*, *4*(10), 13–21. DOI: 10.22215/timreview/835

Dai, H. N., Zheng, Z., & Zhang, Y. (2019). Blockchain for Internet of Things: A survey. *IEEE Internet of Things Journal*, *6*(5), 8076–8094. DOI: 10.1109/JIOT.2019.2920987

Das, R., & Morris, T. H. (2017, December). Machine learning and cyber security. In 2017 international conference on computer, electrical & communication engineering (ICCECE) (pp. 1-7). IEEE.

Davenport, T. H., & Mittal, N. (2023). How companies can prepare for the coming "AI-first" world. *Strategy and Leadership, 51*(1), 26–30. DOI: 10.1108/SL-11-2022-0107

De Rancourt-Raymond, A., & Smaili, N. (2023). The unethical use of deepfakes. *Journal of Financial Crime, 30*(4), 1066–1077. DOI: 10.1108/JFC-04-2022-0090

Devadas, R. M., & T, S. (2025). Quantum Machine Learning: A Comprehensive Review of Integrating AI with Quantum Computing for Computational Advancements. *MethodsX, 14*, 103318. DOI: 10.1016/j.mex.2025.103318 PMID: 40331033

Digitalcommons@uno, D., House, D., & Raja, M. K. (n.d.). *Phishing: message appraisal and the exploration of fear and self-Phishing: message appraisal and the exploration of fear and self-confidence confidence Phishing: message appraisal and the exploration of fear and self-confidence*. Retrieved from https://digitalcommons.unomaha.edu/isqafacpub

Dixit, P., & Silakari, S. (2021). Deep learning algorithms for cybersecurity applications: A technological and status review. *Computer Science Review, 39*, 100317. DOI: 10.1016/j.cosrev.2020.100317

Dubey, R., Gunasekaran, A., Childe, S. J., Bryde, D. J., Giannakis, M., Foropon, C., Roubaud, D., & Hazen, B. T. (2020). Big data analytics and artificial intelligence pathway to operational performance under the effects of entrepreneurial orientation and environmental dynamism: A study of manufacturing organisations. *International Journal of Production Economics, 226*, 107599. Advance online publication. DOI: 10.1016/j.ijpe.2019.107599

Du, M., Chen, Z., Liu, C., Oak, R., & Song, D. (2019). Lifelong anomaly detection through unlearning. *Proceedings of the ACM Conference on Computer and Communications Security*, 1283–1297. DOI: 10.1145/3319535.3363226

Dwivedi, Y. K., Hughes, L., Ismagilova, E., Aarts, G., Coombs, C., Crick, T., Duan, Y., Dwivedi, R., Edwards, J., Eirug, A., Galanos, V., Ilavarasan, P. V., Janssen, M., Jones, P., Kar, A. K., Kizgin, H., Kronemann, B., Lal, B., Lucini, B., & Williams, M. D. (2021). Artificial Intelligence (AI): Multidisciplinary perspectives on emerging challenges, opportunities, and agenda for research, practice and policy. *International Journal of Information Management, 57*, 101994. Advance online publication. DOI: 10.1016/j.ijinfomgt.2019.08.002

Elapanda, S., Adinarayana Rao, U. V., & Sravan Kumar, E. (2020). Application of artificial intelligence in improving operational efficiency in telecom industry.

Elapanda, S., Rao, U. V. A., & Kumar, E. S. (2020). Application of artificial intelligence in improving operational efficiency in telecom industry. *International Journal on Emerging Technologies, 11*(3), 65–69.

Elmrabit, N., Zhou, F., Li, F., & Zhou, H. (2020). Evaluation of Machine Learning Algorithms for Anomaly Detection. International Conference on Cyber Security and Protection of Digital Services, Cyber Security 2020. DOI: 10.1109/CyberSecurity49315.2020.9138871

Eloff, J., & Eloff, M. (2005). Information security architecture. *Computer Fraud & Security, 2005*(11), 10–16. DOI: 10.1016/S1361-3723(05)70275-X

Fahrmann, D., Martin, L., Sanchez, L., & Damer, N. (2024). Anomaly Detection in Smart Environments: A Comprehensive Survey. *IEEE Access : Practical Innovations, Open Solutions, 12*(February), 64006–64049. DOI: 10.1109/ACCESS.2024.3395051

Fakhouri, H. N., Alawadi, S., Awaysheh, F. M., Hani, I. B., Alkhalaileh, M., & Hamad, F. (Year). A comprehensive study on the role of machine learning in 5G security: Challenges, technologies, and solutions.

Farzad, A., & Gulliver, T. A. (2020). Unsupervised log message anomaly detection. *ICT Express, 6*(3), 229–237. DOI: 10.1016/j.icte.2020.06.003

Feily, M., Shahrestani, A., & Ramadass, S. (2009, June). A survey of botnet and botnet detection. In *2009 third international conference on emerging security information, systems and technologies* (pp. 268-273). IEEE. DOI: DOI: 10.1109/SECURWARE.2009.48

Feng, J. (2009, May). Analysis, implementation and extensions of RADIUS protocol. *2009 International Conference on Networking and Digital Society*. Presented at the 2009 International Conference on Networking and Digital Society (ICNDS), Guiyang, Guizhou, China. https://doi.org/DOI: 10.1109/ICNDS.2009.44

Feng, Q., He, D., Zeadally, S., Li, N., & Wang, H. (2021). A survey on privacy protection in blockchain system. *Journal of Network and Computer Applications, 169*, 102807. DOI: 10.1016/j.jnca.2018.10.020

Fernandes, G.Jr, Rodrigues, J. J. P. C., Carvalho, L. F., Al-Muhtadi, J. F., & Proença, M. L.Jr. (2019). A comprehensive survey on network anomaly detection. *Telecommunication Systems, 70*(3), 447–489. DOI: 10.1007/s11235-018-0475-8

Flamholz, D. B., & Annaswamy, A. M. (2015). *Baiting For Defense Against Stealthy Attacks on Cyber-Physical Systems Signature redacted Signature redacted.*

Folorunso, N. A., Adewumi, N. T., Adewa, N. A., Okonkwo, N. R., & Olawumi, N. T. N. (2024). Impact of AI on cybersecurity and security compliance. *Global Journal of Engineering and Technology Advances, 21*(1), 167–184. DOI: 10.30574/gjeta.2024.21.1.0193

G, R. K. C. (2025). The Strategic role of AI in enhancing national cybersecurity frameworks. *Asian Journal of Research in Computer Science, 18*(6), 378–389. https://doi.org/DOI: 10.9734/ajrcos/2025/v18i6708

Gallagher, B., & Eliassi-Rad, T. (2009). *Classification of http attacks: a study on the ECML/PKDD 2007 discovery challenge* (No. LLNL-TR-414570). Lawrence Livermore National Lab.(LLNL), Livermore, CA (United States). DOI:DOI: 10.2172/1113394

Ganapathi, P., & Shanmugapriya, D. (Eds.). (2019). *Handbook of research on machine and deep learning applications for cyber security*. IGI Global.

Ganesh, V., & Sharma, M. (2020). Intrusion Detection and Prevention Systems: A review. Lecture Notes in Networks and Systems, 835–844. https://doi.org/DOI: 10.1007/978-981-15-7345-3_71

George, A., & George, A. (2021). A brief study on the evolution of next generation firewall and web application firewall. Zenodo *(CERN European Organization for Nuclear Research)*. DOI: 10.5281/zenodo.7027397

Ghosh, S.. (2024). Scalable blockchain architecture for organ allocation in large-scale healthcare systems. In *2024 International Conference on Cybernation and Computation (CYBERCOM)* (pp. 732-736). IEEE. https://doi.org/DOI: 10.1109/CYBERCOM63683.2024.10803210

Goix, N. (2016). How to Evaluate the Quality of Unsupervised Anomaly Detection Algorithms? https://arxiv.org/abs/1607.01152

Golomb, T., Mirsky, Y., & Elovici, Y. (2018). CIoTA: Collaborative Anomaly Detection via Blockchain. February. DOI: 10.14722/diss.2018.23003

Gómez, Á. L. P., Maimó, L. F., Celdrán, A. H., & Clemente, F. (2019). On the Generation of Anomaly Detection Datasets in Industrial Control Systems. *IEEE Access : Practical Innovations, Open Solutions, 7*, 177460–177473. DOI: 10.1109/ACCESS.2019.2958284

Goos, G., Hartmanis, J., Van Leeuwen, J., Hutchison, D., Kanade, T., Kittler, J., Kleinberg, J., Kobsa, A., Mattern, F., Mitchell, J., Naor, M., Nierstrasz, O., Pandu, C., Steffen, B., Sudan, M., Terzopoulos, D., Tygar, D., Weikum, G., Lin, D., . . . Wang, X. (2011). Cryptology and network security. In Lecture notes in computer science. https://doi.org/DOI: 10.1007/978-3-642-25513-7

Gupta, D., Kayode, O., Bhatt, S., Gupta, M., & Tosun, A. S. (2021). Hierarchical Federated Learning based Anomaly Detection using Digital Twins for Smart Healthcare. Proceedings - 2021 IEEE 7th International Conference on Collaboration and Internet Computing, CIC 2021, 16–25. DOI: 10.1109/CIC52973.2021.00013

Gupta, M., & Vashishth, T. K. (2024). Blockchain-Assisted Machine Learning For Securing Mobile Ad-Hoc Networks against Black-Hole Attacks. *Frontiers in Health Informatics*, *13*(7). Advance online publication. DOI: 10.31893/multiscience.2024209

Gurijala, P., Avula, R., & Lekkala, S. (2024). Next-Gen Firewalls: Enhancing Cloud Security with Generative AI. *Journal of Artificial Intelligence & Cloud Computing.*, *3*(4), 1–9. DOI: 10.47363/JAICC/2024(3)404

Haider, N., Baig, M. Z., & Imran, M. (2020). Artificial intelligence and machine learning in 5G network security: Opportunities, advantages, and future research trends. https://arxiv.org/abs/2007.04490

Hallur, G., ... (2024a). Empowering connections: Trailblazing technologies in telecom communication infrastructure. In 2024 5th International Conference on Image Processing and Capsule Networks (ICIPCN) (pp. 759-763). IEEE. https://doi.org/DOI: 10.1109/ICIPCN63822.2024.00131

Hallur, G., ... (2024c). Seamless mobility: Innovating the digital service landscape in telecom industry. In Proceedings of Fifth International Conference on Computing, Communications, and Cyber-Security, IC4S 2023, Lecture Notes in Networks and Systems (Vol. 991). Springer. https://doi.org/DOI: 10.1007/978-981-97-2550-2_14

Hallur, G., ... (2024d). Synergy in action: Harnessing cloud services and wired broadband for seamless operations. In 2024 2nd World Conference on Communication & Computing (WCONF) (pp. 1-7). IEEE. https://doi.org/DOI: 10.1109/WCONF61366.2024.10691966

Hallur, G., ... (2024e). Wireless broadband unleashed: Charting regulatory pathways for broadband development. In 2024 2nd World Conference on Communication & Computing (WCONF) (pp. 1-6). IEEE. https://doi.org/DOI: 10.1109/WCONF61366.2024.10692209

Hallur, G.. (2023). *Demystifying domain-specific key drivers in telecom technologies. In 2023 Intelligent Computing and Control for Engineering and Business Systems (ICCEBS).* IEEE., DOI: 10.1109/ICCEBS58601.2023.10449118

Hallur, G.. (2024b). Navigating the infotainment landscape: Status and regulations in the digital age. In *2024 International Conference on Advances in Data Engineering and Intelligent Computing Systems (ADICS)* (pp. 1-6). IEEE. https://doi.org/DOI: 10.1109/ADICS58448.2024.10533560

Hamamoto, A. H., Carvalho, L. F., Sampaio, L. D. H., Abrão, T., & Proença, M. L.Jr. (2018). Network Anomaly Detection System using Genetic Algorithm and Fuzzy Logic. *Expert Systems with Applications*, *92*, 390–402. DOI: 10.1016/j.eswa.2017.09.013

Hansen, E. B., & Bøgh, S. (2021). Artificial intelligence and internet of things in small and medium-sized enterprises: A survey. *Journal of Manufacturing Systems*, *58*, 362–372. DOI: 10.1016/j.jmsy.2020.08.009

Hasan, M. A. M., Nasser, M., Ahmad, S., & Molla, K. I. (2016). Feature selection for intrusion detection using random forest. *Journal of information security, 7*(3), 129-140.

He, Y., Meng, G., Chen, K., Hu, X., & He, J. (2020). Towards security threats of deep learning systems: A survey. *IEEE Transactions on Software Engineering*, *48*(5), 1743–1770. DOI: 10.1109/TSE.2020.3034721

Huang, H., Zhou, A., Payer, M., & Zhang, C. (n.d.). *Everything is Good for Something: Counterexample-Guided Directed Fuzzing via Likely Invariant Inference.*

Hussain, H., Kainat, M., & Ali, T. (2025). Leveraging AI and Machine Learning to Detect and Prevent Cyber Security Threats. [DSSR]. *Dialogue Social Science Review*, *3*(1), 881–895. DOI: 10.5281/zenodo.14714679

Huszár, M. (2022). Current state of IT security awareness–challenges, risks and effects globally.

Huzairin, R. A., Multazam, M. T., Phahlevy, R. R., & Ahrorov, F. (2024). *Google's Legal Responsibility in Displaying Phishing Ads Through Google AdWords.*, DOI: 10.2991/978-2-38476-247-7_53

Ibitoye, O., Abou-Khamis, R., Shehaby, M. E., Matrawy, A., & Shafiq, M. O. (2019). The Threat of Adversarial Attacks on Machine Learning in Network Security—A Survey. *arXiv preprint arXiv:1911.02621.* /arXiv.1911.02621DOI: 10.48550

IEEE. Communications Society & Institute of Electrical and Electronics Engineers. (2015). 2015 IEEE/CIC International Conference on Communications in China - Workshops (CIC/ICCC).

Ighofiomoni, M. O., Ojerinde, J. S., Iqmat, O., Issah, P. P., Similoluwa, A. O., Oluwaseun, O., David, E. T., Idowu, A., Emmanuel, I. M., & Chinonyerem, C. A. (2025). Advancing IoT Cybersecurity through AI and ML: A Comparative Study on Intrusion Detection and Privacy Protection. *Asian Journal of Advanced Research and Reports*, *19*(8), 159–174. DOI: 10.9734/ajarr/2025/v19i81122

Ijiga, O. M., Idoko, I. P., Ebiega, G. I., Olajide, F. I., Olatunde, T. I., & Ukaegbu, C. (2024). Harnessing adversarial machine learning for advanced threat detection: AI-driven strategies in cybersecurity risk assessment and fraud prevention. J. Sci. Technol, 11, 001-024. DOI: 10.53022/oarjst.2024.11.1.0060

Islam, S. M., Bari, M. S., Sarkar, A., Khan, A. O. R., & Paul, R. (2024). AI-Powered Threat Intelligence: Revolutionizing Cybersecurity with Proactive Risk Management for Critical Sectors. Journal of Artificial Intelligence General Science (JAIGS) ISSN: 3006-4023, 7(01), 1-8. DOI: 10.60087/jaigs.v7i01.291

Itzhak, I., Stanovsky, G., Rosenfeld, N., & Belinkov, Y. (n.d.). *Instructed to Bias: Instruction-Tuned Language Models Exhibit Emergent Cognitive Bias*. doi: DOI: 10.1162/tacl

Jada, I., & Mayayise, T. O. (2023). The impact of artificial intelligence on organisational cyber security: An outcome of a systematic literature review. *Data and Information Management*, *8*(2), 100063. DOI: 10.1016/j.dim.2023.100063

Jain, S.. (2024). Emerging technologies for cybersecurity in healthcare: Evaluating risks and implementing standards. In *2024 International Conference on Cybernation and Computation (CYBERCOM)* (pp. 725-731). IEEE. https://doi.org/DOI: 10.1109/CYBERCOM63683.2024.10803219

Jari, M. (2022). *An Overview of Phishing Victimization: Human Factors, Training and the Role of Emotions*. 217–228. DOI: 10.5121/csit.2022.121319

Javaid, M., Haleem, A., Singh, R. P., Suman, R., & Gonzalez, E. S. (2022). Understanding the adoption of Industry 4.0 technologies in improving environmental sustainability. *Sustainable Operations and Computers*, *3*, 203–217. DOI: 10.1016/j.susoc.2022.01.008

Jiang, C., Xu, H., Huang, C., & Huang, Q. (2022). An adaptive information security system for 5G-enabled smart grid based on artificial neural network and case-based learning algorithms.

Jidiga, G. R., & Sammulal, P. (2015). Anomaly detection using machine learning with a case study. *Proceedings of 2014 IEEE International Conference on Advanced Communication, Control and Computing Technologies, ICACCCT 2014*, 2(978), 1060–1065. DOI: 10.1109/ICACCCT.2014.7019260

Kang, J., & Buu, S. J. (2024). Graph Anomaly Detection with Disentangled Prototypical Autoencoder for Phishing Scam Detection in Cryptocurrency Transactions. *IEEE Access : Practical Innovations, Open Solutions*, *12*, 91075–91088. DOI: 10.1109/ACCESS.2024.3419152

Kant, V., Singh Gill, K., Kumar, M., & Rawat, R. (2024). The Future of Cyber Defence: ML and DL Enhanced Firewalls for Intrusion Detection. *2024 4th Asian Conference on Innovation in Technology (ASIANCON)*. 2024, 1-4. Doi: DOI: 10.1109/ASIANCON62057.2024.10838028

Kashyap, R. (2021). Sensation of deep learning in image processing applications. In *Research Anthology on Artificial Intelligence Applications in Security* (pp. 1615–1639). IGI Global Scientific Publishing.

Kaur, H., Singh, G., & Minhas, J. (2013). A Review of Machine Learning based Anomaly Detection Techniques. *International Journal of Computer Applications Technology and Research*, *2*(2), 185–187. DOI: 10.7753/IJCATR0202.1020

Kaur, R., Gabrijelčič, D., & Klobučar, T. (2023). Artificial intelligence for cybersecurity: Literature review and future research directions. *Information Fusion*, *97*, 101804. DOI: 10.1016/j.inffus.2023.101804

Kayan, H., Nunes, M., Rana, O., Burnap, P., & Perera, C. (2022). Cybersecurity of industrial cyber-physical systems: A review. *ACM Computing Surveys*, *54*(11s), 1–35. DOI: 10.1145/3510410

Kelley, P. (2022). *Evolution of Cyber Attacks and Their Economic Impact*. DOI: 10.36227/techrxiv.21670718.v1

Khadka, K. (n.d.). *Persuasion and Phishing: Analysing the Interplay of Persuasion Tactics in Cyber Threats*.

Khang, A., Singh, Y., & Barak, D. (2024). Review of the Literature on Using Machine and Deep Learning Techniques to Improve IoT Security. Revolutionizing Automated Waste Treatment Systems: IoT and Bioelectronics, 273-300.

Khan, M. M., Shah, N., Shaikh, N., Thabet, A., Alrabayah, T., & Belkhair, S. (2024). Towards secure and trusted AI in healthcare: A systematic review of emerging innovations and ethical challenges. *International Journal of Medical Informatics*, *195*, 105780. DOI: 10.1016/j.ijmedinf.2024.105780 PMID: 39753062

Kőrösi, G. (2022). *Machine Learning based analysis of users' online behaviour* (Doctoral dissertation, Szegedi Tudomanyegyetem (Hungary)).

Kour, R. (2020). Cybersecurity issues and challenges in Industry 4.0. *Advances in Civil and Industrial Engineering*, *4*(0), 84–101. DOI: 10.4018/978-1-7998-3904-0.ch005

Kumar, P. R., Meenakshi, S., Shalini, S., Devi, S. R., & Boopathi, S. (2023). Soil Quality Prediction in Context Learning Approaches Using Deep Learning and Blockchain for Smart Agriculture. In Effective AI, Blockchain, and E-Governance Applications for Knowledge Discovery and Management (pp. 1-26). IGI Global. DOI: 10.4018/978-1-6684-9151-5.ch001

Kumar, N. B. H., Nuka, N. S. T., Malempati, N. M., Sriram, N. H. K., Mashetty, N. S., & Kannan, N. S. (2025). Big Data in Cybersecurity: Enhancing Threat Detection with AI and ML. *Metallurgical and Materials Engineering*, *31*(3), 12–20. DOI: 10.63278/1315

Kumar, R., Grover, N., Singh, R., Kathuria, S., Kumar, A., & Bansal, A. (2023). Imperative role of artificial intelligence and big data in finance and banking sector. *2022 International Conference on Sustainable Computing and Data Communication Systems (ICSCDS)*, 523–527. https://doi.org/DOI: 10.1109/ICSCDS56580.2023.10105062

Kumar, V., Choudhary, V., Kumar, V., & Sahrawat, V. (2020)... *Anomaly Detection in Networks Using Different Machine Learning Algorithms.*, *8*(4), 1145–1151. DOI: 10.5281/zenodo.15271016

Kwentoa, I. K. (2025). AI-Driven Threat Intelligence for Enterprise Cybersecurity. *Journal of Next-Generation Research 5.0.* https://doi.org/DOI: 10.70792/jngr5.0.v1i4.125

Lalitha, R., Dhinavallesan, P. V., & Ponugoti, S. (2025, March). A Comprehensive Survey on NLP-based Approaches for Summarizing Lengthy Research Papers. In *2025 International Conference on Machine Learning and Autonomous Systems (ICMLAS)* (pp. 1501-1507). IEEE. DOI: 10.1109/ICMLAS64557.2025.10967868

Landauer, M., Onder, S., Skopik, F., & Wurzenberger, M. (2023). Deep learning for anomaly detection in log data: A survey. *Machine Learning with Applications*, *12*(May), 100470. DOI: 10.1016/j.mlwa.2023.100470

Lau, F., Rubin, S. H., Smith, M. H., & Trajkovic, L. (2002). Distributed denial of service attacks. *SMC 2000 Conference Proceedings. 2000 IEEE International Conference on Systems, Man and Cybernetics. 'Cybernetics Evolving to Systems, Humans, Organizations, and Their Complex Interactions' (Cat. No.00CH37166).* Presented at the IEEE International Conference on Systems, Man, and Cybernetics, Nashville, TN, USA. https://doi.org/DOI: 10.1109/ICSMC.2000.886455

Le, T., & Shetty, S. (2022). Artificial intelligence-aided privacy preserving trustworthy computation and communication in 5G-based IoT networks.

Le, V. H., & Zhang, H. (2022). Log-based Anomaly Detection with Deep Learning: How Far Are We? In Proceedings - International Conference on Software Engineering (Vols. 2022-May, Issue 1). Association for Computing Machinery. DOI: 10.1145/3510003.3510155

LeCun, Y., Bengio, Y., & Hinton, G. (2015). Deep learning. *Nature*, *521*(7553), 436–444. DOI: 10.1038/nature14539 PMID: 26017442

Lens, (2025). *Search results for "Artificial Intelligence (AI) in Cybersecurity".* The Lens. Retrieved September 22, 2025, from https://www.lens.org/lens/search/scholar/list?q=(%22Artificial%20Intelligence%22%20OR%20%22AI%22%20OR%20%22Machine%20Learning%22%20OR%20%22Deep%20Learning%22%20OR%20%22Neural%20Networks%22)%20AND%20(%22Cybersecurity%22%20OR%20%22Cyber%20Security%22%20OR%20%22Information%20Security%22%20OR%20%22Network%20Security%22%20OR%20%22Intrusion%20Detection%22%20OR%20%22Malware%20Detection%22)&p=0&n=10&s=_score&d=%2B&f=false&e=false&l=en&authorField=author&dateFilterField=publishedYear&orderBy=%2B_score&presentation=false&preview=true&stemmed=true&useAuthorId=false

Li, P., Liu, L., Gao, D., & Reiter, M. K. (2010). On challenges in evaluating malware clustering. In *Recent Advances in Intrusion Detection: 13th International Symposium, RAID 2010, Ottawa, Ontario, Canada, September 15-17, 2010. Proceedings 13* (pp. 238-255). Springer Berlin Heidelberg. DOI: 10.1007/978-3-642-15512-3_13

Liandani, P., Lubis, M., & Witjaksono, W. (2020). Exploring the relationship of individual indicator as the critical factor in information security awareness. *Selected Papers from the 1st International Conference on Islam, Science and Technology, ICONISTECH-1 2019, 11-12 July 2019, Bandung, Indonesia.* Presented at the Selected Papers from the 1st International Conference on Islam, Science and Technology, ICONISTECH-1 2019, 11-12 July 2019, Bandung, Indonesia, Bandung, Indonesia. https://doi.org/DOI: 10.4108/eai.11-7-2019.2297836

Liang, J., & Kim, Y. (2022). Evolution of firewalls: Toward securer network using next generation firewall. *2022 IEEE 12th Annual Computing and Communication Workshop and Conference (CCWC)*, 0752–0759. DOI: 10.1109/CCWC54503.2022.9720435

Lim, K., Lee, K., Sommese, R., Jonker, M., & Mok, R. claffy, kc, & Kim, D. (2025). *Registration, Detection, and Deregistration: Analyzing DNS Abuse for Phishing Attacks*. Retrieved from https://arxiv.org/abs/2502.09549

Lin, P., Ye, K., & Xu, C. Z. (2019). Dynamic network anomaly detection system by using deep learning techniques. Lecture Notes in Computer Science (Including Subseries Lecture Notes in Artificial Intelligence and Lecture Notes in Bioinformatics), 11513 LNCS(June), 161–176. DOI: 10.1007/978-3-030-23502-4_12

Lin, J. (2008, December). On malicious software classification. In *2008 International Symposium on Intelligent Information Technology Application Workshops* (pp. 368-371). IEEE. DOI: DOI: 10.1109/IITA.Workshops.2008.106

Liu, Y., Lin, X., Shen, X., & Liang, X. (2022). Securing blockchain-based IoT with deep reinforcement learning. *IEEE Internet of Things Journal*, *9*(3), 1785–1797.

Liu, Z., Nie, Y., Long, C., Zhang, Q., & Li, G. (2021). A Hybrid Video Anomaly Detection Framework via Memory-Augmented Flow Reconstruction and Flow-Guided Frame Prediction. *Proceedings of the IEEE International Conference on Computer Vision*, 13568–13577. DOI: 10.1109/ICCV48922.2021.01333

Lubis, M., Fauzi, R., Liandani, P., & Lubis, A. R. (2020, July 17). Information security awareness (ISA) towards the intention to comply and demographic factors. *Proceedings of the 8th International Conference on Computer and Communications Management*. Presented at the ICCCM'20: 2020 The 8th International Conference on Computer and Communications Management, Singapore Singapore. https://doi.org/DOI: 10.1145/3411174.3411196

Lubis, M., Novalia, D., & Puspita. (2020, September 3). Development of security awareness domain and resources (SADAR) framework: Capacity metrics to evaluate enterprise resource planning (ERP) implementation. *2020 4rd International Conference on Electrical, Telecommunication and Computer Engineering (ELTICOM)*. Presented at the 2020 4rd International Conference on Electrical, Telecommunication and Computer Engineering (ELTICOM), Medan, Indonesia. https://doi.org/DOI: 10.1109/ELTICOM50775.2020.9230523

Lubis, M., Fauzi, R., & Hasibuan, M. A. (2019). Categorization for the Security Awareness Domain and Resource (SADAR) model in the organization: A clustering statistical analysis. *Journal of Physics: Conference Series*, *1235*(1), 012041. DOI: 10.1088/1742-6596/1235/1/012041

Macas, M., Wu, C., & Fuertes, W. (2024). Adversarial examples: A survey of attacks and defenses in deep learning-enabled cybersecurity systems. *Expert Systems with Applications*, *238*, 122223. DOI: 10.1016/j.eswa.2023.122223

Madnick, B., Huang, K., & Madnick, S. (2023). The evolution of global cybersecurity norms in the digital age: A longitudinal study of the cybersecurity norm development process. *Information Security Journal a Global Perspective*, *33*(3), 204–225. DOI: 10.1080/19393555.2023.2201482

Mahmud, F., Barikdar, C. R., Hassan, J., Goffer, M. A., Das, N., Orthi, S. M., Kaur, J., Hasan, S. N., & Hasan, R. (2025). AI-Driven Cybersecurity in IT Project Management: Enhancing Threat Detection and Risk Mitigation. *Journal of Posthumanism*, *5*(4), 23–44. DOI: 10.63332/joph.v5i4.974

Maiti, P., ... (2024). Decentralized defenses: A framework for 5G IoT security in Industry 4.0 using blockchain crowdsourcing. In 2024 3rd International Conference on Sentiment Analysis and Deep Learning (ICSADL) (pp. 534-538). IEEE. https://doi.org/DOI: 10.1109/ICSADL61749.2024.00093

Malatji, M., Marnewick, A. L., & Von Solms, S. (2022). Cybersecurity capabilities for critical infrastructure resilience. *Information and Computer Security*, *30*(2), 255–279. DOI: 10.1108/ICS-06-2021-0091

Mane, D. T., Sangve, S., Upadhye, G., Kandhare, S., Mohole, S., Sonar, S., & Tupare, S. (2022). Detection of anomaly using machine learning: A comprehensive survey. *International Journal of Emerging Technology and Advanced Engineering*, *12*(11), 134–152. DOI: 10.46338/ijetae1122_15

Mansur, M. A. (2025). National security and cyber defense in the rise of artificial super intelligence. *European Scientific Journal*, *21*(10), 116. DOI: 10.19044/esj.2025.v21n10p116

Marino, D. L., Wickramasinghe, C. S., Rieger, C., & Manic, M. (2022). Self-Supervised and Interpretable Anomaly Detection using Network Transformers. 1–9. DOI: 10.1109/TII.2025.3534443

Maroofi, S., Korczyński, M., & Duda, A. (2020). Are You Human?: Resilience of Phishing Detection to Evasion Techniques Based on Human Verification. *Proceedings of the ACM SIGCOMM Internet Measurement Conference, IMC*, 78–86. DOI: 10.1145/3419394.3423632

Martins, N., Cruz, J. M., Cruz, T., & Abreu, P. H. (2020). Adversarial machine learning applied to intrusion and malware scenarios: A systematic review. *IEEE Access : Practical Innovations, Open Solutions*, *8*, 35403–35419. DOI: 10.1109/ACCESS.2020.2974752

Maseer, Z. K., Yusof, R., Bahaman, N., Mostafa, S. A., & Foozy, C. F. M. (2021). Benchmarking of Machine Learning for Anomaly Based Intrusion Detection Systems in the CICIDS2017 Dataset. *IEEE Access : Practical Innovations, Open Solutions*, *9*, 22351–22370. DOI: 10.1109/ACCESS.2021.3056614

Mason, A., & Newcomb, M. (2001). *Cisco secure internet security solutions*. Cisco Press.

Mat, N. I. C., Jamil, N., Yusoff, Y., & Kiah, L. M. (2024). A systematic literature review on advanced persistent threat behaviors and its detection strategy. *Journal of Cybersecurity*, *10*(1), tyad023. Advance online publication. DOI: 10.1093/cybsec/tyad023

Mattsson, U. T. (2006). Best practice for enterprise database encryption solutions. SSRN Electronic Journal. https://doi.org/DOI: 10.2139/ssrn.934271

Ma, X., Wu, J., Xue, S., Yang, J., Zhou, C., Sheng, Q. Z., Xiong, H., & Akoglu, L. (2023). A Comprehensive Survey on Graph Anomaly Detection With Deep Learning. *IEEE Transactions on Knowledge and Data Engineering*, *35*(12), 12012–12038. DOI: 10.1109/TKDE.2021.3118815

Meshram, A., & Haas, C. (2017). Anomaly detection in industrial networks using machine learning: a roadmap. In *Machine learning for cyber physical systems: selected papers from the international conference ML4CPS 2016* (pp. 65–72). Springer Berlin Heidelberg., DOI: 10.1007/978-3-662-53806-7_8

Mishra, A., Alzoubi, Y. I., Gill, A. Q., & Anwar, M. J. (2022). Cybersecurity Enterprises Policies: A Comparative Study. *Sensors (Basel)*, *22*(2), 1–35. DOI: 10.3390/s22020538 PMID: 35062504

Mohamed, N. (2025). Cutting-edge advances in AI and ML for cybersecurity: A comprehensive review of emerging trends and future directions. *Cogent Business & Management*, *12*(1), 2518496. Advance online publication. DOI: 10.1080/23311975.2025.2518496

Mokhtari, S., Abbaspour, A., Yen, K. K., & Sargolzaei, A. (2021). A machine learning approach for anomaly detection in industrial control systems based on measurement data. *Electronics (Basel)*, *10*(4), 1–13. DOI: 10.3390/electronics10040407

Mukesh, V. (2025). A Comprehensive Review of Advanced Machine Learning Techniques for Enhancing Cybersecurity in Blockchain Networks. *Journal ID, 8736*, 2145.

Muneer, S. M., Alvi, M. B., & Farrakh, A. (2023). Cyber Security Event Detection Using Machine Learning Technique. *International Journal of Computational and Innovative Sciences, 2*, 42–46.

Muneer, S., Farooq, U., Athar, A., Raza, M. A., Ghazal, T. M., & Sakib, S. (2024). A Critical Review of Artificial intelligence based Approaches in Intrusion Detection: A Comprehensive analysis. *Journal of Engineering, 2024*(1), 1–16. DOI: 10.1155/2024/3909173

Munir, M., Siddiqui, S. A., Dengel, A., & Ahmed, S. (2019). DeepAnT: A Deep Learning Approach for Unsupervised Anomaly Detection in Time Series. *IEEE Access : Practical Innovations, Open Solutions, 7*, 1991–2005. DOI: 10.1109/ACCESS.2018.2886457

Murugan, T. (Ed.). (2023). *Handbook of Research on Data Science and Cybersecurity Innovations in Industry 4.0 Technologies*. IGI Global. DOI: 10.4018/978-1-6684-8145-5

Musa, T. H. A., & Bouras, A. (2022, January). Anomaly Detection: A Survey. *Lecture Notes in Networks and Systems, 217*, 391–401. DOI: 10.1007/978-981-16-2102-4_36

Nakazato, J., Song, J., Eto, M., Inoue, D., & Nakao, K. (2011). A novel malware clustering method using frequency of function call traces in parallel threads. *IEICE Transactions on Information and Systems, 94*(11), 2150–2158. DOI: 10.1587/transinf.E94.D.2150

Nassif, A. B., Talib, M. A., Nasir, Q., & Dakalbab, F. M. (2021). Machine Learning for Anomaly Detection: A Systematic Review. *IEEE Access : Practical Innovations, Open Solutions, 9*, 78658–78700. DOI: 10.1109/ACCESS.2021.3083060

Naz, H., & Kashif, M. (2024). Artificial intelligence and predictive marketing: An ethical framework from managers' perspective. *Spanish Journal of Marketing - ESIC*. Advance online publication. DOI: 10.1108/SJME-06-2023-0154

Neuman, B., & Ts'o, T. (1994). Kerberos: An authentication service for computer networks. *IEEE Communications Magazine, 32*(9), 33–38. DOI: 10.1109/35.312841

Neupane, K., Haddad, R., & Chen, L. (2018). *Next generation firewall for network Security: a survey*. SoutheastCon., DOI: 10.1109/SECON.2018.8478973

Nguyen, D. C., Pathirana, P. N., Ding, M., & Seneviratne, A. (2020). Blockchain for 5G and beyond networks: A state of the art survey. *Journal of Network and Computer Applications*, *166*, 102693. DOI: 10.1016/j.jnca.2020.102693

Noor, A., Tariq, N., Khan, F. A., & Ashraf, M. (2025). Evolution of Next-Generation firewall system for secure networks. In *CRC Press eBooks* (pp. 263–271). DOI: 10.1201/9781003497851-24

Ofusori, L., Bokaba, T., & Mhlongo, S. (2024). Artificial intelligence in cybersecurity: A comprehensive review and future direction. *Applied Artificial Intelligence*, *38*(1), 2439609. Advance online publication. DOI: 10.1080/08839514.2024.2439609

Ojima John, M., Emmanuel Oche, O., & Blessing Toyin, E. (n.d.). MITIGATING THE IMPACT OF PHISHING ATTACKS ON THE E-LEARNING INFRASTRUCTURE. In Scientific and Practical Cyber Security Journal (SPCSJ) (Vol. 8, Issue 3).

Oloyede, J. (2024). Ethical Reflections on AI for Cybersecurity: Building trust. SSRN *Electronic Journal*. https://doi.org/DOI: 10.2139/ssrn.4733563

Ortiz-Ruiz, E., Bermejo, J. R., Sicilia, J. A., & Bermejo, J. (2024). Machine Learning Techniques for Cyberattack Prevention in IoT Systems: A Comparative Perspective of Cybersecurity and Cyberdefense in Colombia. *Electronics (Basel)*, *13*(5), 824. Advance online publication. DOI: 10.3390/electronics13050824

Oussama, L., Ismail, A., Mohamed, M. E., Fabien, C., & Lahcen, A. I. (2024). Toward a modern secure network based on next-generation firewalls: Recommendations and best practices. *Procedia Computer Science*, *238*, 1029–1035. DOI: 10.1016/j.procs.2024.06.130

Ozohu Musa, M., & Victor-Ime, T. (2023). Improving Internet Firewall Using Machine Learning Techniques. *American Journal of Computer Science and Technology*, *6*(4), 170–179. DOI: 10.11648/j.ajcst.20230604.14

Pang, G., Shen, C., Cao, L., & Van Den Hengel, A. (2021). Deep Learning for Anomaly Detection: A Review. *ACM Computing Surveys*, *54*(2), 1–36. DOI: 10.1145/3439950

Parekh, D., Poddar, N., Rajpurkar, A., Chahal, M., Kumar, N., Joshi, G. P., & Cho, W. (2022). A Review on Autonomous Vehicles: Progress, Methods and Challenges. *Electronics (Basel)*, *11*(14), 1–18. DOI: 10.3390/electronics11142162

Patel, K. N., ... (2024). Cybersecurity risks and countermeasures in the threat landscape of IoT devices. In 2024 4th International Conference on Technological Advancements in Computational Sciences (ICTACS) (pp. 875-883). IEEE. https://doi.org/DOI: 10.1109/ICTACS62700.2024.10841210

Patel, D., Srinivasan, K., Chang, C. Y., Gupta, T., & Kataria, A. (2020). Network anomaly detection inside consumer networks—A hybrid approach. *Electronics (Basel)*, *9*(6), 1–12. DOI: 10.3390/electronics9060923

Patel, M., Amritha, P. P., Sudheer, V. B., & Sethumadhavan, M. (2024). DDoS Attack Detection Model using Machine Learning Algorithm in Next Generation Firewall. *Procedia Computer Science*, *233*, 175–183. DOI: 10.1016/j.procs.2024.03.207

Patil, A., ... (2024a). 5G monetization strategies and business models: An insightful analysis for telecommunications service providers. In 2024 5th International Conference on Data Intelligence and Cognitive Informatics (ICDICI) (pp. 16-23). IEEE. https://doi.org/DOI: 10.1109/ICDICI62993.2024.10810884

Patil, A., ... (2024b). Cyber resilience: Safeguarding India's markets in the post-pandemic cyber landscape. In 2024 4th International Conference on Innovative Practices in Technology and Management (ICIPTM) (pp. 1-5). IEEE. https://doi.org/DOI: 10.1109/ICIPTM59628.2024.10563229

Patil, D. (2024). Artificial Intelligence in Cybersecurity: Enhancing Threat Detection and Prevention Mechanisms through Machine Learning and Data Analytics. Available at *SSRN* 5057410. DOI: 10.2139/ssrn.5057410

Pavithra, J., & Selvakumara Samy, S. (2022). A comparative study on detection of malware and benign on the internet using machine learning classifiers. *Mathematical Problems in Engineering*, *2022*(1), 4893390. DOI: 10.1155/2022/4893390

Pillai, S. E. V. S., ElSaid, A. A., & Hu, W. C. (2022, May). A Self-Reconfigurable System for Mobile Health Text Misinformation Detection. In *2022 IEEE International Conference on Electro Information Technology (eIT)* (pp. 242-247). IEEE. DOI: DOI: 10.1109/eIT53891.2022.9813840

Pineda, V. G., Valencia-Arias, A., Giraldo, F. E. L., & Zapata-Ochoa, E. A. (2025). Integrating artificial intelligence and quantum computing: A systematic literature review of features and applications. *International Journal of Cognitive Computing in Engineering*. https://doi.org/DOI: 10.1016/j.ijcce.2025.08.002

Platt, F. (2015). Physical threats to the information infrastructure. In *Computer Security Handbook* (p. 22.1-22.28). https://doi.org/DOI: 10.1002/9781118851678.ch22

Polese, M., Bonati, L., D'Oro, S., Basagni, S., & Melodia, T. (2023). Understanding O-RAN: Architecture, interfaces, algorithms, security, and research challenges. *IEEE Communications Surveys and Tutorials*, *25*(2), 1376–1411. DOI: 10.1109/COMST.2023.3239220

Pooyandeh, M., Han, K. J., & Sohn, I. (2022). Cybersecurity in the AI-Based metaverse: A survey. *Applied Sciences (Basel, Switzerland)*, *12*(24), 12993. DOI: 10.3390/app122412993

Prabhu, D., & Sudha, L. MR, P. K., Adaikkammai, A., Aparna, P., & Sathya, V. (2025). Machine Learning in Cybersecurity: Challenges, Applications, and Future Directions. *Exploiting Machine Learning for Robust Security*, 25-48.

Prabhu, D., Tejasri, M. V. S. L., Saratha, B., & Anish, T. P. (2025, April). Future Horizons: Key Trends Shaping the Evolution of Machine Learning. In *2025 8th International Conference on Trends in Electronics and Informatics (ICOEI)* (pp. 1091-1099). IEEE.

Preuveneers, D., Rimmer, V., Tsingenopoulos, I., Spooren, J., Joosen, W., & Ilie-Zudor, E. (2018). Chained anomaly detection models for federated learning: An intrusion detection case study. *Applied Sciences (Basel, Switzerland)*, *8*(12), 1–21. DOI: 10.3390/app8122663

Prince, N. U., Faheem, M. A., Khan, O. U., Hossain, K., Alkhayyat, A., Hamdache, A., & Elmouki, I. (2024). AI-powered data-driven cybersecurity techniques: Boosting threat identification and reaction. *Nanotechnology Perceptions*, *20*(S10), 332–353. DOI: 10.62441/nano-ntp.v20iS10.25

Priyadarshini, I. (2017). Cyber security risks in robotics. In *Detecting and mitigating robotic cyber security risks* (pp. 333–348). IGI Global Scientific Publishing. DOI: 10.4018/978-1-5225-2154-9.ch022

Pulyala, S. R. (2024). From detection to prediction: AI-powered SIEM for proactive threat hunting and risk mitigation. *Turkish Journal of Computer and Mathematics Education*, *15*(1), 34–43. DOI: 10.61841/turcomat.v15i1.14393

Putra, F. P. E., Ubaidi, U., Zulfikri, A., Arifin, G., & Ilhamsyah, R. M. (2024). Analysis of Phishing Attack Trends, Impacts and Prevention Methods: Literature Study. *Brilliance: Research of Artificial Intelligence*, *4*(1), 413–421. DOI: 10.47709/brilliance.v4i1.4357

Qiu, W. (2021). Enterprise financial risk management platform based on 5G mobile communication and embedded system. *Microprocessors and Microsystems*, *80*, 103594. DOI: 10.1016/j.micpro.2020.103594

Qurashi, S. N., Sobia, F., Hetany, W. A., & Sultan, H. (2025). *Enhancing cyber-security defenses in healthcare using AI: A pivotal role in fortifying digital health infrastructure*. Deleted Journal., DOI: 10.47852/bonviewMEDIN52024121

Rabiu, S. M., Aminu, B. K., & Zubairu, D. A. (2025). AI-Driven Network Intrusion Detection Systems: A systematic review of hybrid models, Zero-Day attack mitigation, and emerging challenges in cybersecurity. *International Journal of Computer Applications*, *187*(8), 27–33. DOI: 10.5120/ijca2025925016

Radanliev, P. (2025). AI Ethics: Integrating transparency, fairness, and privacy in AI development. *Applied Artificial Intelligence*, *39*(1), 2463722. Advance online publication. DOI: 10.1080/08839514.2025.2463722

Radanliev, P., De Roure, D., Maple, C., Nurse, J. R. C., Nicolescu, R., & Ani, U. (2024). AI security and cyber risk in IoT systems. *Frontiers in Big Data*, *7*, 1402745. Advance online publication. DOI: 10.3389/fdata.2024.1402745 PMID: 39449740

Rahman, M. M., Dhakal, K., Gony, N. M. D., Sd, M. K. S., & Rahman, M. M. D. (2025). AI integration in cybersecurity software: Threat detection and response. *International Journal of Innovative Research and Scientific Studies*, *8*(3), 3907–3921. DOI: 10.53894/ijirss.v8i3.7403

Raina, V., & Krishnamurthy, S. (2022). Anomaly Detection. Building an Effective Data Science Practice, 91–112. DOI: 10.1007/978-1-4842-7419-4_8

Rajawat, A. S., Goyal, S. B., Bedi, P., Kautish, S., & Shrivastava, D. P. (2023). Analysis assaulting pattern for the security problem monitoring in 5G-enabled sensor network systems with big data environment using artificial intelligence/machine learning.

Rajivan, P., & Gonzalez, C. (2018). Creative persuasion: A study on adversarial behaviors and strategies in phishing attacks. *Frontiers in Psychology*, *9*(FEB), 135. Advance online publication. DOI: 10.3389/fpsyg.2018.00135 PMID: 29515478

Ramezanpour, K., & Jagannath, J. (2022). Intelligent zero trust architecture for 5G/6G networks: Principles, challenges, and the role of machine learning in the context of O-RAN.

Rana, M., Mamun, Q., & Islam, R. (2022). Lightweight cryptography in IoT networks: A survey. *Future Generation Computer Systems*, *129*, 77–89. DOI: 10.1016/j.future.2021.11.011

Rashid, A. B., & Kausik, M. K. (2024). AI Revolutionizing Industries Worldwide: A comprehensive overview of its diverse applications. *Hybrid Advances*, *7*, 100277. DOI: 10.1016/j.hybadv.2024.100277

Rastogi, . (2023). Reimagining telecom industry using blockchain technology. In *2023 International Conference on Sustainable Computing and Data Communication Systems (ICSCDS)* (pp. 1261-1265). IEEE. https://doi.org/DOI: 10.1109/ICSCDS56580.2023.10104989

Raut, R., Pathak, P. D., Sakhare, S. R., & Patil, S. (Eds.). (2023). *Generative adversarial networks and deep learning: theory and applications*. CRC Press. DOI: 10.1201/9781003203964

Ravikumar, G., & Govindarasu, M. (2024). Anomaly Detection and Mitigation for Wide-Area Damping Control using Machine Learning. *IEEE Transactions on Smart Grid*, *15*(6), 5939–5951. Advance online publication. DOI: 10.1109/TSG.2020.2995313

Ravi, N., & Shalinie, S. M. (2020). Learning-driven detection and mitigation of DDoS attack in IoT via SDN-cloud architecture. *IEEE Internet of Things Journal*, *7*(4), 3559–3570. DOI: 10.1109/JIOT.2020.2973176

Ravindranathan, P.. (2024). Illuminating the dark: Gaining insights and managing risks with dark analytics. In *2024 International Conference on Intelligent and Innovative Technologies in Computing, Electrical and Electronics (IITCEE)* (pp. 1-6). IEEE. https://doi.org/DOI: 10.1109/IITCEE59897.2024.10467380

Rengarajan, A., & Karpagam, G. R. (2024). Enhancing Cybersecurity Resilience with CYBRANA: A Cyber YARA/YAML-Based Resilience Firewall Solution Applied with Next-Gen AI. *2024 IEEE International Conference on Computer Vision and Machine Intelligence (CVMI)*. 2024, 1-7. DOI:DOI: 10.1109/CVMI61877.2024.10782249

Republic, P. S. (2022). Anomaly Detection. *Survey (London, England)*, *151*, 704062220701–704062220703.

RituRani. (2025). Next-Generation Intrusion Detection Systems with Machine Learning and Deep Learning-Based Firewalls. *2025 International Conference on Intelligent and Innovative Technologies in Computing, Electrical and Electronics (IITCEE)*. 1-4. DOI:DOI: 10.1109/IITCEE64140.2025.10915227

Rosenberg, I., Shabtai, A., Elovici, Y., & Rokach, L. (2021). Adversarial machine learning attacks and defense methods in the cyber security domain. *ACM Computing Surveys*, *54*(5), 1–36. DOI: 10.1145/3453158

Roshanaei, M., Khan, M. R., & Sylvester, N. N. (2024). Navigating AI cybersecurity: Evolving landscape and challenges. *Journal of Intelligent Learning Systems and Applications*, *16*(03), 155–174. DOI: 10.4236/jilsa.2024.163010

Sadik, S., Ahmed, M., Sikos, L. F., & Najmul Islam, A. K. M. (2020). Toward a sustainable cybersecurity ecosystem. *Computers*, *9*(3), 1–17. DOI: 10.3390/computers9030074

Salahdine, F., & Kaabouch, N. (2019). Social engineering attacks: A survey. In Future Internet (Vol. 11, Issue 4). MDPI AG. DOI: 10.3390/fi11040089

Saleh, A. M. S. (2024). Blockchain for secure and decentralized artificial intelligence in cybersecurity: A comprehensive review. *Blockchain Research and Applications*, *5*(3), 100193. DOI: 10.1016/j.bcra.2024.100193

Salem, M. B., Hershkop, S., & Stolfo, S. J. (2008). A survey of insider attack detection research. *Insider Attack and Cyber Security: Beyond the Hacker*, 69-90. DOIhttps://DOI: 10.1007/978-0-387-77322-3_5

Sallai, D., Cardoso-Silva, J., Barreto, M. E., Panero, F., Berrada, G., & Luxmoore, S. (n.d.). *Approach Generative AI Tools Proactively or Risk Bypassing the Learning Process in Higher Education.*

Salloum, S. A., Alshurideh, M., Elnagar, A., & Shaalan, K. (2020, March). Machine learning and deep learning techniques for cybersecurity: a review. In *The International Conference on Artificial Intelligence and Computer Vision* (pp. 50-57). Cham: Springer International Publishing. DOI: 10.1007/978-3-030-44289-7_5

Samuel, A. J. (2024). Advancements in Cybersecurity: Leveraging AI and Machine Learning for Threat Detection and Prevention. Journal of Science. *Technology and Engineering Research*, *2*(3), 64–79. DOI: 10.64206/thwq1548

Sana, L., Nazir, M. M., Yang, J., Hussain, L., Chen, Y. L., Ku, C. S., Alatiyyah, M., Alateyah, S. A., & Por, L. Y. (2024). Securing the IoT Cyber Environment: Enhancing Intrusion Anomaly Detection With Vision Transformers. *IEEE Access : Practical Innovations, Open Solutions*, *12*(May), 82443–82468. DOI: 10.1109/ACCESS.2024.3404778

Sankaramma, T. S. (2025). AI-Driven Phishing Detection: Advanced machine learning strategies for identifying malicious websites. *International Journal of Science Engineering and Technology*, *13*(2), 1–5. DOI: 10.61463/ijset.vol.13.issue2.267

Sarker, I. H. (2024). Introduction to AI-Driven Cybersecurity and Threat Intelligence. In AI-Driven Cybersecurity and Threat Intelligence: Cyber Automation, Intelligent Decision-Making and Explainability (pp. 3-19). Cham: Springer Nature Switzerland. DOI: 10.1007/978-3-031-54497-2_1

Sarker, I. H. (2021). CyberLearning: Effectiveness analysis of machine learning security modeling to detect cyber-anomalies and multi-attacks. *Internet of Things : Engineering Cyber Physical Human Systems*, *14*, 100393. DOI: 10.1016/j.iot.2021.100393

Sarno, D. M., & Black, J. (2024). Who Gets Caught in the Web of Lies?: Understanding Susceptibility to Phishing Emails, Fake News Headlines, and Scam Text Messages. *Human Factors*, *66*(6), 1742–1753. DOI: 10.1177/00187208231173263 PMID: 37127397

Saxena, Y.. (2024). Cloud renaissance: Thriving in the post-pandemic digital landscape. In *2024 Fourth International Conference on Advances in Electrical, Computing, Communication and Sustainable Technologies (ICAECT)* (pp. 1-6). IEEE. https://doi.org/DOI: 10.1109/ICAECT60202.2024.10469149

Sayed, A. K. (2023). Anomaly Detection Using Machine Learning. *International Journal of Advanced Research in Computer and Communication Engineering*, *12*(1), 131–162. DOI: 10.17148/IJARCCE.2023.12103

Schmidl, S., Wenig, P., & Papenbrock, T. (2022). Anomaly Detection in Time Series: A Comprehensive Evaluation. *Proceedings of the VLDB Endowment International Conference on Very Large Data Bases*, *15*(9), 1779–1797. DOI: 10.14778/3538598.3538602

Sekti, B. A. (2025a). Adversarial Machine Learning in Industrial Cybersecurity: Challenges and Solutions. In *AI-Enhanced Cybersecurity for Industrial Automation* (pp. 363–386). IGI Global Scientific Publishing. DOI: 10.4018/979-8-3373-3241-3.ch018

Sekti, B. A. (2025b). Machine learning and artificial intelligence (AI) in manufacturing. In *Integrating Digital Innovation and Integrated Frameworks in Manufacturing* (pp. 255–292). DOI: 10.4018/979-8-3373-1082-4.ch011

Sevilla, J., Heim, L., Ho, A., Besiroglu, T., Hobbhahn, M., & Villalobos, P. (2022). Compute Trends Across Three Eras of Machine Learning. In *Proceedings of the International Joint Conference on Neural Networks* (Vol. 2022-July). DOI: 10.1109/IJCNN55064.2022.9891914

Shafiq, M. Z., Khayam, S. A., & Farooq, M. (2008, July). Improving accuracy of immune-inspired malware detectors by using intelligent features. In *Proceedings of the 10th annual conference on Genetic and evolutionary computation* (pp. 119-126). DOI: 10.1145/1389095.1389112

Shah, N. K. M. D., Ab Aziz, A. A., Juned, A. M., Anuar Yatim, A. I., & Wan Fakhruddin, W. F. W. (2024). Scheming in Syntax: Analysing Scammer-Victim Conversations in Malaysian E-Commerce Scams. *3L: Language, Linguistics. Literature, 30*(4), 47–59. DOI: 10.17576/3L-2024-3004-04

Sharma, R., Sharma, V., Vashishth, T. K., Kumar, B., Sharma, B. K., & Chaudhary, S. (2025, February). Implementation of adaptive cloud security framework for cloud computing monitoring system applications. In AIP Conference Proceedings (Vol. 3224, No. 1). AIP Publishing. DOI: 10.1063/5.0246104

Sharma, H. (2021). Next-Generation Firewall in the Cloud: Advanced Firewall Solutions to the Cloud. *ESP Journal of Engineering & Technology Advancements., 1*(1), 98–111. DOI: 10.56472/25832646/JETA-V1I1P112

Shaukat, K., Alam, T. M., Luo, S., Shabbir, S., Hameed, I. A., Li, J., Abbas, S. K., & Javed, U. (2021). A Review of Time-Series Anomaly Detection Techniques: A Step to Future Perspectives. Advances in Intelligent Systems and Computing, 1363 AISC(April), 865–877. DOI: 10.1007/978-3-030-73100-7_60

Shaukat, K., Luo, S., Varadharajan, V., Hameed, I. A., Chen, S., Liu, D., & Li, J. (2020). Performance comparison and current challenges of using machine learning techniques in cybersecurity. *Energies, 13*(10), 2509. Advance online publication. DOI: 10.3390/en13102509

Shiwangi, K. M., Sandhu, J. K., & Sahu, R. (2023). Effective Heart-Disease Prediction by Using Hybrid Machine Learning Technique. *Proceedings of the International Conference on Circuit Power and Computing Technologies, ICCPCT 2023*, 1670–1675. DOI: 10.1109/ICCPCT58313.2023.10245785

Singh, R., Singh, A., & Bhattacharya, P. (2021). A machine learning approach for anomaly detection to secure smart grid systems. In *Advancements in Security and Privacy Initiatives for Multimedia Images* (pp. 199–213). IGI global. DOI: 10.4018/978-1-7998-2795-5.ch008

Sinha, S. K., Modak, S. K. S., Tyagi, P. K., & Azad, C. (2024). Enhancing Cybersecurity with Blockchain: A Decentralized Approach to Securing Digital Infrastructure. *ACM*, 1–6. https://doi.org/DOI: 10.1145/3745812.3745846

Siniosoglou, I., Radoglou-Grammatikis, P., Efstathopoulos, G., Fouliras, P., & Sarigiannidis, P. (2021). A Unified Deep Learning Anomaly Detection and Classification Approach for Smart Grid Environments. *IEEE Transactions on Network and Service Management, 18*(2), 1137–1151. DOI: 10.1109/TNSM.2021.3078381

Sivakumar, A. A. / P., Fahmi, A., Abdul, M., Ramli, J., Kastriafuddin, T., Yakob, T., Habee, E. A., & Affandy, B. (2023). ANALYSIS THE TYPES AND IMPACTS OF PHISHING ATTACKS ON INTERNET USERS. In Journal of Global Business and Social Entrepreneurship (GBSE) (Vol. 9, Issue 26). Retrieved from www.gbse.my

Sontan, A. D., & Samuel, S. V.Adewale Daniel SontanSegun Victor Samuel. (2024). The intersection of Artificial Intelligence and cybersecurity: Challenges and opportunities. *World Journal of Advanced Research and Reviews*, *21*(2), 1720–1736. DOI: 10.30574/wjarr.2024.21.2.0607

Sowmya, T., & Anita, E. M. (2023). A comprehensive review of AI based intrusion detection system. *Measurement. Sensors*, *28*, 100827. DOI: 10.1016/j.measen.2023.100827

Srivastava, A., ... (2024). 5G network fusion: Exploring the interplay of edge and cloud computing. In 2024 5th International Conference on Image Processing and Capsule Networks (ICIPCN) (pp. 821-825). IEEE. https://doi.org/DOI: 10.1109/ICIPCN63822.2024.00142

Steenwinckel, B., De Paepe, D., Vanden Hautte, S., Heyvaert, P., Bentefrit, M., Moens, P., Dimou, A., Van Den Bossche, B., De Turck, F., Van Hoecke, S., & Ongenae, F. (2021). FLAGS: A methodology for adaptive anomaly detection and root cause analysis on sensor data streams by fusing expert knowledge with machine learning. *Future Generation Computer Systems*, *116*, 30–48. DOI: 10.1016/j.future.2020.10.015

Stoian, N. A. (2020). *Machine Learning for Anomaly Detection in IoT networks: Malware analysis on the IoT-23 Data set*. University of Twente.

Stolfo, S. J., Hershkop, S., Bui, L. H., Ferster, R., & Wang, K. (2005). Anomaly detection in computer security and an application to file system accesses. In *Foundations of Intelligent Systems: 15th International Symposium, ISMIS 2005, Saratoga Springs, NY, USA, May 25-28, 2005. Proceedings 15* (pp. 14-28). Springer Berlin Heidelberg. DOI:_DOI: 10.1007/11425274_2

Sundari, V. M., Rose, R. M., Sassirekha, S. M., Nalini, M., & Girija, P. (2024, November). Deep Learning: Techniques, Taxonomy, Applications, and Future Directions. In *2024 International Conference on Smart Technologies for Sustainable Development Goals (ICSTSDG)* (pp. 1-5). IEEE.

Systems, I. C. (n.d.). Computers in Industry Light-Weight Federated Learning-based Anomaly Detection for Time-Series data in Industrial Control Systems.

Taha, A., & Hadi, A. S. (2019). Anomaly detection methods for categorical data: A review. *ACM Computing Surveys*, *52*(2), 1–35. Advance online publication. DOI: 10.1145/3312739

Tamal, M. A., Islam, M. K., Bhuiyan, T., Sattar, A., & Prince, N. U. (2024). Unveiling suspicious phishing attacks: Enhancing detection with an optimal feature vectorization algorithm and supervised machine learning. *Frontiers of Computer Science*, *6*, 1428013. Advance online publication. DOI: 10.3389/fcomp.2024.1428013

Thiyagarajan, P. (2020). A review on cyber security mechanisms using machine and deep learning algorithms. Handbook of research on machine and deep learning applications for cyber security, 23-41. DOI: 10.4018/978-1-5225-9611-0.ch002

Thuraisingham, B., Khan, L., Masud, M. M., & Hamlen, K. W. (2008, December). Data mining for security applications. In *2008 IEEE/IFIP International Conference on Embedded and Ubiquitous Computing* (Vol. 2, pp. 585-589). IEEE. DOI: DOI: 10.1109/EUC.2008.62

Tian, C., Jensen, M. L., Bott, G., & Luo, X. (2024). The influence of affective processing on phishing susceptibility. *European Journal of Information Systems*. Advance online publication. DOI: 10.1080/0960085X.2024.2351442

Trisolvena, M. N., & Saputra, N. H. (2024). Phishing Cyber Security Threats. *Jurnal Improsci*, *2*(1), 38–48. DOI: 10.62885/improsci.v2i1.440

Understanding and Mitigating Phishing Attacks in the Digital Era. (n.d.). DOI: 10.13140/RG.2.2.19619.98085

Van Eck, N. J., & Waltman, L. (2022). *VOSviewer* manual (Version 1.6.18). Leiden University, CWTS. Retrieved from https://www.vosviewer.com/documentation/Manual_VOSviewer_1.6.18.pdf

Vankadara, Y.. (2024). 6G revolution: Redefining communication systems. In *2024 International Conference on Smart Systems for Applications in Electrical Sciences (ICSSES)* (pp. 1-6). IEEE. https://doi.org/DOI: 10.1109/ICSSES62373.2024.10561292

Vashishth, T. K., Sharma, V., Samania, B., Sharma, R., Singh, S., & Jajoria, P. (2025). Ethical and Legal Implications of AI in Cybersecurity. In Machine Intelligence Applications in Cyber-Risk Management (pp. 387-414). IGI Global Scientific Publishing. DOI: 10.4018/979-8-3693-7540-2.ch017

Vashishth, T. K., Sharma, V., Sharma, K. K., & Kumar, B. (2025). Enhanced Security and Privacy from Industry 4.0 and 5.0 Vision. In Building Embodied AI Systems: The Agents, the Architecture Principles, Challenges, and Application Domains (pp. 133-158). Cham: Springer Nature Switzerland. DOI: 10.1007/978-3-031-68256-8_6

Vashishth, T. K., Sharma, V., Sharma, K. K., Kumar, B., Chaudhary, S., & Panwar, R. (2024). Enhancing Cloud Security: The Role of Artificial Intelligence and Machine Learning. In Improving Security, Privacy, and Trust in Cloud Computing (pp. 85-112). IGI Global. DOI: 10.4018/979-8-3693-1431-9.ch004

Vashishth, T. K., Sharma, V., Sharma, K. K., Kumar, B., Chaudhary, S., & Panwar, R. (2024). Security and Privacy Challenges in Blockchain-Based Supply Chain Management: A Comprehensive Analysis. In Achieving Secure and Transparent Supply Chains with Blockchain Technology (pp. 70-91). IGI Global. DOI: 10.4018/979-8-3693-0482-2.ch005

Vashishth, T. K., Sharma, V., Sharma, K. K., Kumar, B., Chaudhary, S., & Panwar, R. (2024). Security and Privacy Considerations in Cloud-Based Data Processing Solutions for Sensitive Data. In *Developments towards Next Generation Intelligent Systems for Sustainable Development* (pp. 35–61). IGI Global., DOI: 10.4018/979-8-3693-5643-2.ch002

Vempati, N. S. (2024). Securing Smart Cities: A Cybersecurity perspective on integrating IoT, AI, and machine learning for digital twin creation. *Deleted Journal*, *20*(5s), 2817–2827. DOI: 10.52783/jes.3052

Vessels, L., Heffner, K., & Johnson, D. (2019). *Cybersecurity Risk Assessment for Space Systems. In 2019 IEEE Space Computing Conference*. SCC., DOI: 10.1109/SpaceComp.2019.00006

Virk, A., Alasmari, S., Patel, D., & Allison, K. (2025). Digital Health Policy and Cybersecurity Regulations regarding artificial intelligence (AI) implementation in healthcare. *Cureus*. Advance online publication. DOI: 10.7759/cureus.80676 PMID: 40236368

Vulpe, S., Rughini , R., urcanu, D., & Rosner, D. (2024). AI and cybersecurity: A risk society perspective. *Frontiers of Computer Science*, *6*, 1462250. Advance online publication. DOI: 10.3389/fcomp.2024.1462250

Waheed, F., & Ali, M. (2018). Hardening CISCO Devices based on Cryptography and Security Protocols - Part II: Implementation and Evaluation. *Annals of Emerging Technologies in Computing*, *2*(4), 11–27. DOI: 10.33166/AETiC.2018.04.002

Wang, S., Balarezo, J. F., Kandeepan, S., Al-Hourani, A., Chavez, K. G., & Rubinstein, B. (2021). Machine learning in network anomaly detection: A survey. *IEEE Access : Practical Innovations, Open Solutions*, *9*, 152379–152396. DOI: 10.1109/ACCESS.2021.3126834

Wang, Z., & Song, H. (2022). Research on performance test method for the next generation firewall. *2022 IEEE International Conference on Advances in Electrical Engineering and Computer Applications (AEECA)*. 585-589. DOI: 10.1109/AEECA55500.2022.9919085

Watkins, M., & Wallace, K. (2008). *CCNA security official exam certification guide*.

Wazid, M., Das, A. K., Chamola, V., & Park, Y. (2022). Uniting cyber security and machine learning: Advantages, challenges and future research. *ICT Express*, *8*(3), 313–321. DOI: 10.1016/j.icte.2022.04.007

Widjajarto, A., Lubis, M., & Yunan, U. (2019). Architecture Model of Information Technology Infrastructure based on Service Quality at Government Institution. *Procedia Computer Science*, *161*, 841–850. DOI: 10.1016/j.procs.2019.11.191

Xie, M., Hu, J., & Slay, J. (2014, August). Evaluating host-based anomaly detection systems: Application of the one-class SVM algorithm to ADFA-LD. In *2014 11th International conference on fuzzy systems and knowledge discovery (FSKD)* (pp. 978-982). IEEE. DOI: DOI: 10.1109/FSKD.2014.6980972

Xu, H., Sun, Z., Cao, Y., & Bilal, H.XSu. (2023). A data-driven approach for intrusion and anomaly detection using automated machine learning for the Internet of Things. *Soft Computing*, *27*(19), 14469–14481. DOI: 10.1007/s00500-023-09037-4

Xu, J., Wang, Y., Chen, H., & Shen, Z. (2025). Adversarial Machine Learning in Cybersecurity: Attacks and Defenses. *International Journal of Management Science Research*, *8*(2), 26–33. DOI: 10.53469/ijomsr.2025.08(02).04

Yamini, B. MAY, P. M. A., Shobana, R., TP, A., & Nalini, M. (2024, December). Cybersecurity: Strategies, Sector-Specific Challenges, and Future Prospects. In *2024 4th International Conference on Ubiquitous Computing and Intelligent Information Systems (ICUIS)* (pp. 1338-1345). IEEE.

Yan, N., & Au, O. T. S. (2019). Online learning behavior analysis based on machine learning. *Asian association of open universities journal, 14*(2), 97-106. DOI: 10.1108/AAOUJ-08-2019-0029

Yang, Y., Zhang, C., Zhou, T., Wen, Q., & Sun, L. (2023). DCdetector: Dual Attention Contrastive Representation Learning for Time Series Anomaly Detection. *Proceedings of the ACM SIGKDD International Conference on Knowledge Discovery and Data Mining*, 3033–3045. DOI: 10.1145/3580305.3599295

Yaseen, A. (2023). The Role of Machine Learning in Network Anomaly Detection for Cybersecurity. Sage Science Review of Applied Machine Learning, 6(8), 16–34. https://journals.sagescience.org/index.php/ssraml/article/view/126

Yavanoglu, O., & Aydos, M. (2017, December). *A review on cyber security datasets for machine learning algorithms. In 2017 IEEE international conference on big data (big data)*. IEEE., DOI: 10.1109/BigData.2017.8258167

Yeboah-Boateng, E. O., & Amanor, P. M. (2014). *Journal of Emerging Trends in Computing and Information Sciences Phishing, SMiShing & Vishing: An Assessment of Threats against Mobile Devices Campus and a database administrator. 5*(4). Retrieved from http://www.cisjournal.org

Yildirim, M. (2021). *Artificial intelligence-based solutions for cyber security problems. In artificial intelligence paradigms for smart cyber-physical systems*. IGI Global Scientific Publishing.

Yoganandham, G., & Head, P. (n.d.). *THE ECONOMIC IMPACT OF PHISHING, VISHING, ONLINE MARKETPLACES, AND EMERGING CYBERCRIMES: EXPOSING THE CYBERCRIME ECONOMY AND SOCIAL COSTS IN THE MODERN ERA OF DIGITAL FRAUD-AN ASSESSMENT*.

Yoo, J., & Jo, Y. (2023). Formulating Cybersecurity Requirements for Autonomous Ships Using the SQUARE Methodology. *Sensors (Basel)*, *23*(11), 5033. Advance online publication. DOI: 10.3390/s23115033 PMID: 37299766

Yosiandra, S. Y., & Sakariah, D. S. (2024). Unveiling the Romance Scam Scheme: Psychological Manipulation and Its Impact on Victims. *HUMANIKA*, *31*(2), 185–199. DOI: 10.14710/humanika.v31i2.67604

Yusif, S., & Hafeez-Baig, A. (2021). A Conceptual Model for Cybersecurity Governance. *Journal of Applied Security Research*, *16*(4), 490–513. DOI: 10.1080/19361610.2021.1918995

Yusof, A. R. A., Udzir, N. I., & Selamat, A. (2016). An evaluation on KNN-SVM algorithm for detection and prediction of DDoS attack. In *Trends in Applied Knowledge-Based Systems and Data Science: 29th International Conference on Industrial Engineering and Other Applications of Applied Intelligent Systems, IEA/AIE 2016, Morioka, Japan, August 2-4, 2016, Proceedings 29* (pp. 95-102). Springer International Publishing. DOI: 10.1007/978-3-319-42007-3_9

Yusuff, M., Rankine, A., & Wicky, K. (2025). The Impact of Machine Learning on Cybersecurity in Digital Banking.

Zaigham Zaheer, M., Mahmood, A., Haris Khan, M., Segu, M., Yu, F., & Lee, S. I. (2022). Generative Cooperative Learning for Unsupervised Video Anomaly Detection. Proceedings of the IEEE Computer Society Conference on Computer Vision and Pattern Recognition, 2022-June, 14724–14734. DOI: 10.1109/CVPR52688.2022.01433

Zhang, A., Lipton, Z. C., Li, M., & Smola, A. J. (2019). *Dive into deep learning*.

Ziegler, V., Schneider, P., Viswanathan, H., Montag, M., Kanugovi, S., & Rezaki, A. (2021). Security and trust in the 6G era. *IEEE Access : Practical Innovations, Open Solutions*, *9*, 142314–142327. DOI: 10.1109/ACCESS.2021.3120143

About the Contributors

Shahnaz Fatima is working as a Faculty at Amity Institute of Information Technology, Amity University, Uttar Pradesh, Lucknow. Her research interests are Human Computer Interaction, Data Mining, Deep Mining, Semantic Web, Edge and IoT. She is involved in supervising Doctorate Research Scholars and Post graduate Students . Dr. Shahnaz Fatima has published many of the valuable research papers in Scopus and various other national and international conferences and journals. She has also edited a book titled Distributed Computing to Blockchain: Architecture, Technology, and Applications Published by Elsevier and indexed by Scopus She is the member of International Association of Computer Science and Information Technology (IACSIT), IAENG (International Association of Engineers).

Susanta Das is a seasoned educator with a proven record of teaching and mentoring diverse students, working at multiple institutions, and providing service to the various initiatives of organizations. He received his Ph.D. and M.A. degrees from Western Michigan University (WMU), USA, and M.Sc. degree from Banaras Hindu University (BHU), India all in Physics. He continued his research as a Marie-Curie post-doctoral fellow at Stockholm University, Stockholm, Sweden on beam diagnostics for the DESIREE (Double ElectroStatic Ion Ring ExpEriment) in the project DITANET (Diagnostic Techniques for particle Accelerators – a Marie-Curie initial training NETwork), at the Indian Institute of Science Education and Research-Kolkata, India on high-pressure physics as a Project Scientist-B, and at the University of Electro-Communications, Tokyo, Japan on ion-surface interactions as a Post-doctoral fellow. Throughout his career, Dr. Das worked and collaborated with many researchers, Ph.D., master, and visiting students from different countries. He further visited many countries to discuss research and an international conference participant (UK, Italy, Germany, Greece, Belgium, Bulgaria, Romania, Brazil etc.). He co-authored several research articles in WoS/Scopus indexed international journals, conference proceedings, and scholarly book chapters published by renowned international publishing houses. Beyond his research endeavors, Dr. Das has a storied history of service to academic and administrative committees, exhibiting his commitment to the growth and development of educational institutions. His experience includes tenure at Central University South Bihar, Sri Sri University, and P.K. University before assuming his current role at Ajeenkya D Y Patil University. He received the Marie-Curie post-doctoral fellowship in Sweden, Science Academies' Summer Research Fellowship in India, Gwen Frostic Doctoral Fellowship, Department Graduate Research and Creative Scholar Award by WMU, and Leo R. Parpart Doctoral Fellowship by Dept. of Physics, WMU, among many others, throughout his academic journey. At present, Dr. Das continues to delve into cutting-edge fields, with a keen interest in nanotechnology, quantum computing, and data science. His multifaceted contributions, spanning teaching, research, and administrative leadership, showcase a dedicated professional who is instrumental in advancing the vision and mission of the institutions he serves.

Rajiv Pandey is a senior member of the IEEE and currently serves as a faculty member at the Amity Institute of Information Technology, located at the Amity University campus in Lucknow, Uttar Pradesh, India. With a background experience of around 30 years, including 15 years in industry and 13 years in academia, Dr. Pandey has successfully supervised six Ph.D. scholars. He has also edited multiple books that have been published by reputed publishers such as Springer, Elsevier, CRC, and IGI Global. Dr. Pandey's research interests include contemporary technologies such as Semantic Web Provenance, Cloud and Big Data, and Data Analytics. He has published more than 50 research papers in prestigious journals indexed in Scopus and other science indexes. Additionally, he has served as a session chair and technical committee member for various IEEE and Elsevier conferences and has been a member of the technical committees of various government and private universities. Apart from this, Dr. Pandey has been an active contributor to professional bodies like IEEE, IET, and the Lucknow Management Association.

***

Yamini B. is an Associate Professor in the Department of Networking and Communications, School of Computing, at SRM Institute of Science and Technology, Tamil Nadu, India. Her research interests include computer networks, wireless communication, and emerging technologies in computing. She has contributed to several research publications and actively engages in academic and professional development activities.

Sudipta Banerjee is a dedicated educator with 17 years of experience and a UGC NET qualification in Electronics Engineering. He is currently serving as an Assistant Professor in the Department of Computer Science and Engineering at the Symbiosis Institute of Technology, Symbiosis International (Deemed University), Pune, India. Dr. Banerjee holds an M.Tech from IIT Kharagpur and a PhD from IIT (ISM) Dhanbad. He has authored several peer-reviewed journal articles, conference papers, book chapters, books, and patents

Srusthee Bhalerao is PG student of MBA (Digital and Telecom Management) at SIDTM. She belongs to 2022-2024 batch.

Sandeep C. S is an accomplished academician and researcher with over 16 years of experience in teaching, research, and administration in Electronics and Communication Engineering. He serves as Associate Professor and Head of the ECE Department at Jawaharlal College of Engineering and Technology, Kerala. He is also engaged in postdoctoral research at the University of Louisiana, USA, focusing on AI, machine learning, and biomedical signal processing. He holds a Ph.D. from the University of Kerala, with research on advanced biomedical imaging. He earned his M.E. and B.E. from Anna University, Chennai, and an MBA in HRM from IGNOU. A Senior Member of IEEE and a recognized research supervisor under APJ Abdul Kalam Technological University, he has authored over 60 research papers and contributed to books, chapters, and patents. His interdisciplinary projects span healthcare, computing, and intelligent systems. He continues to contribute actively to academic innovation and global research collaborations.

Kashvi Chaturvedi, is studying B.Tech, specialisation in Artificial Intelligence and Data Science at Ajeenkya DY Patil University. She started solidifying her programming skills by completing various certification courses like Data Structures in C, Tableau functions and Operating Systems along with doing few projects using languages like Python, C, C++ and creating Web Page using HTML, CSS and Java Script. She had also attended an Arduino-Based Automation course at Dolphin Labs to enhance her software knowledge. There, she learned how to work with sensors, microcontrollers, and circuit design. She has also written multiple review papers on topics such as Geographic Information Systems, Comparative Analysis of BJT Configurations, Swiss Bank vs. European Central Bank: Data Analysis. She is also researching on and learning many topics such as Small Modular Reactors, Bibliometric Analysis, UNSDGs etc. Because of her interest in latest technologies, she also participated in Global Hyperloop Competition hosted by IIT Madras representing her college as team Vac-Vectoor where she learnt more about various subtopics from the mentors.

Sachin Vasant Chaudhari is a Ph.D. holder in Electronics Engineering. He is an Associate Professor in the Electronics and Telecommunication Engineering Department at Sanjivani College of Engineering, Kopargaon, which is affiliated with Savitribai Phule Pune University, Pune, India. He has worked on a broad range of topics including automated deep learning, UAV route planning, hybrid energy systems, and medical applications. His innovative research also addresses dynamic routing algorithms, channel estimation in OFDM, and advanced materials for medical implants. He has published over 35 papers in reputed International Journals. He is having professional membership of The Institution of Engineers (IEI) & International Association of Engineers (IANG).

Sachin Chaudhary completed his Graduation from MJPRU, and Post Graduation from AKTU, Moradabad, U.P. Currently Pursuing his Ph.D. in Computer Science and Engineering from Govt. Recognized University. Presently, he is working as an Assistant Professor in the Department of Computer Science and Applications, IIMT University, Meerut, U.P, India. He has been awarded as Excellence in teaching award 2019. He is the reviewer member of some reputed journals. He has published several book chapters and research papers of national and international reputed journals.

D. Jayasutha is an Associate Professor in the Department of Computer Science and Engineering at Kathir College of Engineering, Coimbatore, India. Her academic and research interests span artificial intelligence, machine learning, and data analytics. She has actively contributed to research publications, academic development, and guiding students in emerging areas of computer science.

Pooja Dehankar is working in Department of Artificial Intelligence and Data Science, School of Engineering, Ajeenkya DY Patil School of Engineering, Pune. She has completed BE in Computer Engineering from Priyadarshini College of Engineering, Nagpur and ME in Information Technology from Sinhgad College of Engineering, Pune. She has done Post Graduate Diploma in Advance Computing. She is currently pursuing Ph.D. from Symbiosis International Deemed University, Pune. She has 17 years of experience in academics. Her area of interest are Artificial Intelligence, Cyber Security and Data Mining. She has published papers in Scopus Journals. She actively participates in workshops, faculty development programs, short term training programs, conferences and webinars.

Kiranbhai Ramabhai Dodiya is an experienced Cyber Forensic Expert and Assistant Professor specializing in cyber security and digital forensics. He has taught at prestigious institutions and is currently pursuing a PhD in Biochemistry and Forensic Science. With a strong background in ethical hacking and malware analysis, Kiranbhai is passionate about educating students and contributing to the field of cyber forensics. His expertise includes malware forensic, computer forensics, and data recovery software. Kiranbhai's commitment to professional growth is evident through his participation in workshops, seminars, and research publications. He is dedicated to shaping the next generation of professionals in the field and combatting cybercrimes.

Krishanu Kundu received his BTech degree in Electronics & Telecommunication Engineering from Pt. R.S.S. U University, Raipur in 2007 and received his MTech degree in Embedded System Technologies from Anna University, Chennai in 2011. He has completed his PhD degree in Electronics & Communication Engineering from Maulana Abul Kalam Azad University of Technology, West Bengal Formerly known as WBUT in 2021. Presently, he is working as Associate Professor in the department of ECE, G.L. Bajaj Institute of Technology and Management, Greater Noida, India. He has taught subjects like Communication Engineering, Embedded systems in PG level. His main research interest is optimization of different types of antenna arrays using different bio inspired algorithms, IOT, Embedded Systems and Artificial Intelligence. He has published several reputed SCI/Scopus journal and conference papers and attended various National & International Conferences. He has more than 14 years of experience for teaching UG and PG level students.

Fateh Bahadur Kunwar is a distinguished academician and researcher with over 16 years of experience in higher education, currently serving as Assistant Professor (Senior Scale) at Geetanjali Institute of Technical Studies, Udaipur. He holds a Ph.D. in Computer Science & Engineering, an M.Tech. from KNIT Sultanpur (autonomous government institute), and an MCA from Dr. R. M. L. Avadh University, Ayodhya. Kunwar has published extensively in reputed journals and conferences including IEEE and Springer, authored several books and test series, and holds multiple national patents. He has guided numerous B.Tech. and M.Tech. students in research and development projects. His research interests span health informatics, machine learning, deep learning, explainable AI, biometrics, image processing, and soft computing. Actively engaged in the academic community, he frequently delivers expert talks, contributes to conferences, and serves as a reviewer and editorial board member, reflecting his commitment to advancing knowledge, innovation, and interdisciplinary collaboration in computer science.

L. A. Anto Gracious is an accomplished academic professional in Information Technology and Computer Science, known for his dedication to education, technology, and research. He holds a B.Tech in IT from C.S.I Institute of Technology (2006), an MBA in Technology Management, and an M.Tech in IT from Francis

Xavier Engineering College (2011). He began his career as a Programmer at Software Solutions Integrated Limited, later transitioning to academia in 2011 as an Assistant Professor at Marthandam College of Engineering and Technology. Over eight years, he excelled in teaching, led the Software Development Cell, and earned multiple awards for his contributions. He later served at St. Xavier's Catholic College of Engineering and currently holds a position at R.M.K. College of Engineering and Technology. A prolific researcher, Anto focuses on machine learning, wireless sensor networks, and healthcare technologies. His work is widely published, and he has received accolades such as the Best Paper Award and multiple Best Faculty Awards.

M.G.Dinesh is an Associate Professor in department of Artificial intelligence and data science at EASA College of Engineering and Technology, Coimbatore. He has completed his under graduate and Post Graduate in Information Technology. He has completed his Ph.D in Information and communication Engineering from Anna University, Chennai. His research interests include Data mining, Big Data Analytics and Network Security. He has published many papers in International journals and conferences.

P. Ashok is from Chennai, Tamilnadu. He is currently employed as Associate Professor at Symbiosis Institute of Digital and Telecom Management (SIDTM), affiliated to Symbiosis International (Deemed University), Pune from November 2022. His areas of interest include Optical/Wireless Communication, Free Space Optics, Semiconductor Device Modelling, Telecom Regulations and Standards. He does active research in the field of Quantum Cascade Lasers where he has published high quality papers in reputed journals along with this research supervisor Dr. M. Ganesh Madhan from Madras Institute of Technology, Chennai. Other allied fields of interest include AI, ML, DS and modern-day technologies in Telecom networks. His ability to make complex things simple is his way of teaching. He also has 3 patents to his credit in the field of IoT. He has close to 111 high quality research articles indexed in Scopus and Web of Science databases. Dr P Ashok is cited as Top 2% scientist across the world for two consecutive years (2023 & 2024), as rated by Stanford University and Elsevier.

P. Girija is an Assistant Professor in the Department of Information Technology at Panimalar Engineering College, Chennai, India. Her academic interests include artificial intelligence, data analytics, and software engineering. She is actively involved in teaching, research, and guiding students in emerging areas of information technology.

Krutika Patre, is an aspiring programmer and technology enthusiast, currently pursuing Engineering in Artificial Intelligence and Data Science. With a passion for learning, she is building experience in a variety of programming languages and technologies, including C, C++, Python, Data Structures (DS), HTML, CSS, and JavaScript, DBMS (My SQL). After learning this programming language, she has created interest in Full Stack Development. She had also attended an Arduino-Based Automation course at Dolphin Labs to improve my software knowledge. There, she learned how to work with sensors, microcontrollers, and circuit design. She has written review paper on Sustainable engineering on build environment. She is doing researching and learning many topics related to AI, Policy and governance and related to my interest. She has taken part in hackathons, workshops, and tech events to explore many fields. She is also working with a group on Hyperloop. Being part of this project has really helped her grow, especially in areas like teamwork, innovation, and systems thinking.

Prathamesh Prabhu is a student of George Washington University. He is pursuing his MS there.

S. Manikandan graduated from Anna University, Chennai in 2009 with a Bachelor's degree in Computer Science and Engineering. He received his Master's degree in the same subject from Anna University, Coimbatore and is presently enrolled in Anna University, Chennai for a Ph.D. in Wireless Sensor Network. He is currently an Assistant Professor with the department of Computer Science and Engineering at Kongunadu College of Engineering and Technology, Tamilnadu, India with his 14 years of academic experience. His research interests include deep learning machine learning, artificial intelligence, wireless sensor networks, network security, and cryptography. He is having SCI,Scopus indexed publication and participated in several FDPs.

Sunil Sankathala is pursuing B. Tech Computer Science and Engineering at Ajeenkya DY Patil University, with a diverse range of interests that bridge technology, sustainability, and innovation. His academic focus lies in computer science fundamentals like programming, data structures, algorithms, and software development. He actively supplements this with hands-on experience in web development and robotics. Beyond the core curriculum, He has a strong research inclination in emerging and impactful fields. His current research interests include Artificial Intelligence in Healthcare, bioplastics, nano bioplastics, e-waste management, and solid waste management—areas where he believes technology can make a meaningful difference in solving real-world problems. He has been publishing research articles and book chapters in reputed national and international journals and books. He is also part of an ambitious Hyperloop project, which involves interdisciplinary collaboration and cutting-edge engineering aimed at revolutionizing transportation. Working on this project has enhanced his skills in teamwork, innovation, and systems thinking. In the tech domain, he has developed proficiency in web development using technologies such as HTML, CSS, JavaScript, and React. His interests in robotics further reflect building smart, responsive systems that interact with the physical world. Throughout his course, he has helped strengthen problem-solving and collaborative skills. He is proficient in languages such as Python, C, C++, MySQL, Ubuntu, Machine Learning and familiar with frameworks and tools like React, Git. He actively participates in hackathons, coding competitions, and tech events to challenge himself and learn from peers. He is also a quick learner and highly adaptable, with an eagerness to stay updated with the latest trends in the tech world. He aspires to become a skilled software engineer and contribute to building innovative solutions that have a positive impact on society. The long-term goal is to work in a dynamic environment where knowledge, grow professionally, and make meaningful contributions to the field of technology. Driven by a spirit of exploration and sustainability, he aims to contribute to technological solutions that address both human and environmental needs. The long-term goal is to become a versatile engineer and researcher, working at the intersection of computer science, environmental innovation, and human well-being.

Atharva Saraf is currently pursuing a B. Tech degree in Computer Science Engineering at Ajeenkya D Y Patil University. Throughout his academic journey, he has developed a strong foundation in various programming languages, including C, C++, and Python. His interests and focus areas lie in algorithm-based programs, artificial intelligence (with a special emphasis on neural networks), and cybersecurity. His has successfully undertaken several projects that reflect my proficiency and passion in these domains. For instance, he developed a PC-Tuner application aimed at optimizing system performance by employing various methods such as defragmentation. Additionally, he created an automated backup utility capable of securely backing up selected files, folders, and stores them in compressed backup folder in system itself it can also store backups on external hard disk and cloud storages. Beyond project work, he has contributed to the academic community through research articles and book chapters. Notable among these is my co-authored chapter on federated learning techniques, exploring their applications and advancements in the field of machine learning. Moreover, he is currently working on writing a book chapter focusing on federated learning, delving deeper into its methodologies and practical implementations. His academic experiences have honed his skills in problem-solving, critical thinking, and collaborative teamwork. He is eager to further expand His knowledge and expertise in computer science, particularly in areas that intersect with his interests in algorithms, artificial intelligence, and their practical applications.

Binastya Anggara Sekti has been a Lecturer at the faculty of Computer Science, at Esa Unggul University, Jakarta since 2016 and is active in the Artificial Intelligence and Information Security Study Group. He is a graduate of Informatics Engineering from the Bandung Institute of Technology and achieved a Master's Degree from Trisakti University, Jakarta. Before as a Lecture, he was an IT practitioner at several companies in Jakarta for more than 25 years. Some of the projects that have been completed are building Data Centers at Internet Service Providers . He also finished many IT projects.

Mukesh Kumar Sharma is an Professor and Head in the Department of Mathematics, Chaudhary Charan Singh University, Meerut, U.P, India. He has published more than 100 research papers in the reputed journals.

Rajeev Sharma is the Assistant Professor and Head in the Department of Computer Science and Engineering, IIMT Engineering College, Meerut. He has more than 15 years of teaching as well as administrative experience. He has a conference Proceeding on Modified CPU Scheduling Process to his Credit published by Springer Nature. He has published five research papers and reputed journals. He has attended many conferences, workshops, FDP's and symposium and presented research papers. His research area is fuzzy logic, Neural Networks and CPU scheduling.

Sangeeta Sharma is an Assistant Professor in the Department of Computer Applications, IAMR College, Baghpat Road, Meerut, U.P, India

Vikas Sharma completed his Graduation and Post Graduation from Chaudhary Charan Singh University, Meerut, U.P. Currently Pursuing his Ph.D. in Computer Science and Engineering from Govt. Recognized University. Presently, he is working as an Assistant Professor in the Department of Computer Applications, SRM Institute of Science and Technology, NCR Campus Sikri Kalan, Modinagar, U.P, India. He has been awarded as Excellence in teaching award 2019. He is the reviewer member of some reputed journals. He has published several book chapters and research papers of national and international reputed journals.

T.K. Shaik Shavali brings over 24 years of rich academic experience and 7 years in Industry to the field of Computer Science and Engineering. As a dedicated Educator and Researcher, he has been instrumental in guiding students and faculty alike toward academic excellence. As the Head of the Department at Lords Institute of Engineering and Technology, Dr. Shaik Shavali focuses on fostering innovation, encouraging research, and ensuring a holistic learning environment. His commitment to the advancement of technology and education has significantly contributed to the growth and reputation of the institution.

Aditya Shrivastav is an aspiring technologist currently pursuing a Bachelor of Technology (B. Tech.) in Computer Science and Engineering at Ajeenkya D. Y. Patil University. He holds solid programming expertise in C, C++, and Python, alongside strong command over data and business tools such as Microsoft Excel and Tally software. Aditya is a member of Team Vac-Vectoor Hyperloop and participated with the team in the Global Hyperloop Competition organized by IIT Madras, contributing to cutting-edge transportation solutions. He actively engages in hackathons and various technical events to expand his skills and contribute to innovative problem-solving. He has authored and co-authored book chapters in the domains of solid waste management, bioplastics, nanotechnology applications, and artificial intelligence, showcasing his multidisciplinary approach and research acumen. Aditya is also working on an innovative project on predictive e-waste management. The project is targeted toward IT departments, schools, and colleges, aiming to support sustainable practices and resource optimization. In parallel with his academic journey, Aditya is serving as a faculty intern at Disha Computer Institute, where he teaches C, C++, basic Python, basic Java, Excel formulas, and Tally software. His dedication and teaching proficiency earned him a Letter of Appreciation and the opportunity to conduct a workshop on Advanced Excel at G. H. Raisoni College of Arts, Commerce and Science. With a strong foundation in technology, a passion for sustainability, and hands-on experience in both teaching and project development, Aditya Shrivastav is committed to driving impact through research, education, and innovation.

T. Subbulakshmi is currently working as professor at school of computer science and engineering, vellore institute of technology, chennai, tamilnadu, india. she is security specifically cyber security enthusiast. she has published several research articles in reputed journals and conferences.

Brindha Subburaj received the bachelor's and master's degrees in computer science and engineering and the Ph.D. degree in information and communication engineering from Anna University, Chennai, in 2010, 2012, and 2022, respectively. She is currently an Assistant Professor with Vellore Institute of Technology, Chennai. She has proposed several novel multi-objective evolutionary algorithms. She has published several research papers in reputed international journals and conferences. Her research interests include engineering optimization, evolutionary algorithms, and deep learning. She is a Lifetime Member of ISTE.

Varadharajan Bhoopathy is a Professor at Sree Rama Engineering College. He holds a Ph.D. in Information and Communication Engineering from Anna University and has over 16 years of academic experience. Specializing in wireless sensor networks and IoT, he has published numerous research papers and holds several international patents. Dr. Bhoopathy is a recipient of prestigious awards for his contributions to education and research. His commitment to academia continues to drive innovation and excellence in the field of computer science.

Aarushi Vashishth is perusing B.Tech in Computer Science from Ajay Kumar Garg Engineering College, Ghaziabad, U.P, India.

Tarun Kumar Vashishth is an active academician and researcher in the field of computer science with 21 years of experience. He earned Ph.D. Mathematics degree specialized in Operations Research; served several academic positions such as HoD, Dy. Director, Academic Coordinator, Member Secretary of Department Research Committee, Assistant Center superintendent and Head Examiner in university examinations. He is involved in academic development and scholarly activities. He is member of International Association of Engineers, The Society of Digital Information and Wireless Communications, Global Professors Welfare Association, International Association of Academic plus Corporate (IAAC), Computer Science Teachers Association and Internet Society . His research interest includes Cloud Computing, Artificial Intelligence, Machine Learning and Operations Research; published more than 50 research articles with 2 book and 80 book chapters. He is contributing as member of editorial and reviewers boards in conferences and various computer journals published by CRC Press, Taylor and Francis, Springer, IGI global and other universities.

Venkata Ramana Kaneti is an Assistant Professor in the Department of Computer Science and Engineering at VNR Vignana Jyothi Institute of Engineering and Technology, Hyderabad, India. His research interests include artificial intelligence, machine learning, and data-driven systems. He has contributed to publications and academic activities in advancing emerging technologies in computer science.

Index

Symbols

5G 59, 111, 112, 113, 114, 115, 116, 117, 118, 119, 120, 121, 122, 125, 126, 127, 128, 129, 130, 131, 132, 133, 136, 153, 154, 155, 156

A

advanced persistent threats 29, 30, 33, 58, 59, 63, 70, 74, 119, 181, 203
Adversarial Attacks 35, 45, 48, 79, 123, 185, 186, 194, 204
Anomaly Detection 1, 11, 14, 15, 18, 23, 36, 37, 47, 48, 63, 64, 66, 74, 80, 85, 89, 90, 92, 93, 95, 96, 104, 105, 106, 107, 108, 109, 110, 115, 118, 119, 122, 133, 139, 145, 152, 159, 186, 188, 195, 197, 222, 254
Artificial Intelligence (AI) 1, 3, 5, 6, 7, 8, 10, 12, 13, 16, 18, 22, 24, 25, 26, 29, 30, 31, 36, 40, 42, 44, 45, 46, 47, 50, 51, 52, 53, 54, 55, 57, 58, 60, 62, 63, 64, 65, 69, 74, 77, 82, 83, 84, 86, 107, 111, 114, 117, 118, 121, 129, 130, 131, 132, 135, 137, 138, 140, 147, 151, 153, 156, 157, 158, 159, 177, 187, 190, 191, 192, 197, 202, 203, 223, 225, 253, 254, 255
Attack Techniques 183, 186
automated incident response 12, 64, 181
Autonomous Security 144

B

Blockchain 30, 42, 43, 44, 45, 46, 47, 48, 54, 55, 80, 82, 83, 106, 116, 129, 131, 132, 140, 144, 156, 158, 188, 189, 194, 195, 232, 250

C

Cisco Packet Tracer 161, 163, 164, 165, 166, 168, 176
cyber-attacks 36, 60, 63, 66, 69, 132, 152, 153, 155, 175, 176, 181, 182
Cyber security 14, 20, 24, 50, 51, 55, 65, 72, 77, 78, 82, 106, 114, 157, 158, 159, 181, 182, 183, 184, 185, 186, 187, 188, 191, 193, 195, 196, 197, 210, 254, 255
Cybersecurity Awareness 50

D

Deep Learning 7, 8, 9, 10, 11, 12, 18, 19, 20, 24, 26, 30, 31, 32, 34, 37, 42, 44, 58, 60, 61, 62, 63, 65, 66, 67, 68, 72, 78, 79, 82, 90, 97, 102, 105, 107, 108, 109, 129, 131, 135, 137, 138, 140, 141, 143, 145, 146, 150, 151, 152, 153, 156, 157, 158, 159, 185, 187, 188, 189, 193, 194, 195, 202, 223, 225, 226, 232
deep packet inspection 201, 203, 206, 208, 209, 214, 223, 227
Domain Name System (DNS) 215
Dynamic Host Configuration Protocol (DHCP) 166

E

Ethical AI 35, 48, 153
Explainable AI (XAI) 21, 23, 26, 30, 34, 37, 44, 47, 48, 79, 124, 155, 156

F

firewall 14, 59, 65, 69, 91, 142, 201, 202, 203, 204, 205, 206, 207, 208, 209, 210, 211, 215, 216, 217, 218, 219, 220, 222, 223, 225, 226, 227, 245, 256

I

Internet of Things (IoT) 3, 25, 27, 30, 34, 55, 60, 63, 77, 84, 105, 109, 116, 183,

184, 193, 194, 195, 196
Intrusion Detection 6, 16, 18, 30, 34, 35, 37, 38, 42, 43, 44, 46, 48, 51, 53, 54, 56, 58, 59, 63, 66, 67, 82, 91, 93, 94, 97, 107, 108, 121, 124, 125, 163, 177, 182, 183, 185, 186, 193, 194, 195, 199, 202, 203, 204, 207, 208, 209, 219, 220, 225, 226, 232
Intrusion Detection Systems (IDS) 6, 34, 53, 59, 63, 66, 67, 93, 107, 163, 177, 186, 199, 219, 226, 232
intrusion prevention system 201, 209, 213

M

Machine Learning (ML) 1, 2, 3, 6, 7, 8, 10, 12, 13, 14, 15, 16, 18, 19, 20, 22, 23, 24, 25, 26, 27, 30, 31, 33, 34, 35, 36, 37, 40, 42, 44, 45, 46, 47, 50, 51, 54, 56, 57, 58, 60, 61, 62, 63, 64, 65, 66, 67, 68, 69, 70, 71, 72, 74, 76, 77, 79, 82, 83, 84, 85, 90, 106, 107, 108, 109, 110, 113, 115, 116, 118, 124, 129, 130, 131, 132, 133, 135, 137, 139, 140, 141, 143, 144, 145, 146, 147, 151, 152, 156, 157, 158, 159, 181, 182, 183, 184, 185, 186, 187, 188, 189, 190, 191, 192, 193, 194, 195, 196, 197, 198, 201, 202, 204, 207, 217, 218, 219, 223, 225, 226, 227, 232, 255

N

Natural Language 2, 5, 7, 9, 19, 27, 32, 34, 36, 43, 62, 68, 71, 84, 135, 137, 138, 142, 144, 156, 157, 185
Next generation firewall 201, 208, 209, 210, 211, 215, 223, 225, 226

P

Phishing Scams 112, 156, 229, 230, 232, 242, 243, 246, 247, 250, 251, 252, 253
Predictive Analytics 7, 8, 14, 19, 30, 36, 68, 71, 76, 77, 139, 141, 143, 149
Psychological Manipulation 256

S

security challenges 112, 113, 114, 115, 119, 128, 190
Social Engineering 33, 34, 68, 137, 139, 140, 231, 233, 234, 235, 246, 247, 255
Support Vector Machines (SVM) 34, 46, 141, 147, 187, 199, 204, 232

T

Threat Detection 2, 7, 12, 16, 17, 18, 21, 29, 30, 34, 35, 50, 52, 54, 56, 57, 58, 61, 63, 65, 74, 75, 78, 79, 80, 81, 82, 83, 84, 125, 135, 139, 141, 149, 151, 184, 188, 190, 201, 203, 205, 206, 218, 223, 224

U

UTM 206, 207, 208

X

XGBoost 177, 201, 204, 217, 218, 219, 220, 222, 223, 225

Z

Zero-Day Attacks 15, 30, 58, 59, 61, 65, 66, 119

www.ingramcontent.com/pod-product-compliance
Lightning Source LLC
LaVergne TN
LVHW081525300926
849161LV00006B/1304